CW00448104

Mrs Bentham's Tour to Italy

(PRO 30/9/43–44)

transcribed and edited by

ROBERT SÉNÉCAL

Best wishes

Robert Sénécal

GATEHOUSE EDITIONS

EYTHORN

Gatehouse Editions
17 Waldershare House
Eythorne
Kent
CT15 5LS

info@gatehouseeditions.co.uk

First published in the United Kingdom by Gatehouse Editions 2019
Copyright © this edition Robert Sénécal 2019

A catalogue record for this book is available from the British Library

ISBN 978–0–9927342–5–1

Typeset in Monotype Ehrhardt by Discript Limited, Chichester
Printed on woodfree paper by Grosvenor Group (Print Services) Limited

Dedicated to Chris Michaelides (1949–2017),
librarian, scholar and friend.

A great traveller on the Continent.

Acknowledgements

As per usual, most of the research for the footnotes provided in the text was undertaken at the Warburg Institute and the British Library. Creative interrogation of "Google" has also happily produced good results where Mrs Bentham has been similarly creative with her spelling. Judith Russell kindly assisted with a number of German queries; and Christiane Ten-Hoopen again happily quizzed "Google" in Dutch. I would also like to thank the following for assistance with individual problems – Clare Boulton of the Royal Royal College of Veterinary Surgeons; Dr Rüdiger Kröger of the Landeskirchliches Archiv, Hannover; Ilse Moshagen-Siegl of the Stadtarchiv, Helmstedt; Dr. Paul Taylor of the Photographic Collection, Warburg Institute; Dr Johannes Röll of the Bibliotheca Hertziana, Rome; and Westminster Abbey Archives for assistance with two enquiries concerning the funeral and burial of Mrs John Abbot in the abbey. Valerie Scott kindly provided the cover image by James Hakewill from the collection of the British School at Rome, and finally, I would like to thank my designer and copy-editor, Richard Bates of Discript Ltd for his continuing patience with the habitual idiosyncrasies of the editor.

INTRODUCTION

Sarah Bentham (née Farr) (1733–1809) first married John Abbot (1717–1760), and had two sons, John Farr Abbot (1756–94), and Charles Abbot (1757–1829), the latter later becoming first Baron Colchester. Subsequently she married Jeremiah Bentham (1712–92), an attorney, and was thus stepmother to Jeremy Bentham, the philosopher (1748–1832). The reader will discover that Mrs Bentham's travelling party included both her sons and her daughter-in-law, Mary, Mrs John Abbot, and that the ostensible reason for undertaking the trip was, of course, that she was then recently widowed but also because "Mrs. A.", her son's wife, did not enjoy good health. Mrs Abbot subsequently died in Naples in December 1793, her body was shipped back to England, and buried in Westminster Abbey.

Mrs Bentham's journal is now in the Colchester Papers presumably due to the fact that her second husband predeceased her, and she had no children by her second marriage. Her second and surviving son, Baron Colchester was also known to have had a passion for the preservation of historical records hence the happy but not unexpected, survival of this journal. Subsequently, the 3rd Lord Colchester died without issue and the Colchester Papers passed into the possession of the Public Record Office and are kept in the National Archive at Kew.

The journal is now in the guise of two volumes of some 300 numbered pages in each. The pages are ruled with margins at top and bottom and both sides. These volumes are bound in red leather with gold tooling, and have marbled endpapers. It seemed unlikely that these were the original journals – the handwriting appears very even throughout and quite unlike a journal that would have been written almost every night, perhaps sometimes in difficult or uncomfortable circumstances. I presumed that Mrs Bentham took the trouble to make a fair copy at some later date and this assumption is proved correct by her noting on page 157 (writing in December, 1793) that she received letters from her son Charles, dated March 1794, referring to the arrival of her daughter-in-law's corpse in London and its subsequent burial in Westminster Abbey.

The reader will immediately note that because of the outbreak of war with France, Mrs Bentham did not take the usual route of such a journey, that is by crossing the Channel to Calais and then going on to Paris, but sailed from Harwich to Holland instead. Also, though the major part of the journal is concerned with travel in Italy, quite a large proportion is given over to the outward journey through Holland, Belgium, Germany and Switzerland, and an even greater proportion to the return journey through Switzerland, Austria, what is now the Czech Republic, and Germany and Holland again. As is the case with such journals, much is said about the usual sights and sites in these countries but Mrs Bentham also tells us a good deal about agriculture, social conditions, clothing and what we would now call industry. The party travelled in Charles Abbot's own coach. This was not unusual and we learn a good deal about changing horses and the state of "posthouses".

Though one might say that the *ancien régime* (using this term in its widest sense) was in its death throes, and that the war and the activities of the French revolutionaries are mentioned on several occasions by Mrs Bentham, she was nevertheless accepting of the then present status quo. Royal personages are generally described reverentially and their palaces, though frequently aping Versailles in scale, are not criticized for such *folie de grandeur*. However, this is not to say that Mrs Bentham was not forward looking. She frequently expresses an interest in scientific concerns and thus demonstrates a progressive turn of mind for a woman of her age and time.

The only "mistakes" to be found in the journal are a handful of insertions in superscript. As with other such journals of this date, Mrs Bentham's spelling and punctuation is erratic. Her use of capital letters is also haphazard and it is not always certain as to whether a capital letter is necessarily intended. I have followed her usage meticulously, referring to Murray's dictionary in the case of alternative spellings. Because Mrs Bentham's pages are also rather short, more than one page of her text may appear on a page of this edition and therefore the index entries refer to her individual pages.

As is usual with a publication of this kind, footnotes have been added for persons, places and unusual topics; and an index of the same has been provided to assist the interested scholar. I have found Mrs Bentham to be extremely accurate in her remarks but a small number of items have proved to be extremely diffi-cult to track down. I have therefore noted these as "not traced". References have also generally been eschewed unless the items are particularly pertinent or esoteric.

Robert Sénécal
June, 2019

My Mother's own Journey to

Naples and home through Germany – 1793–1794[1]

---

1. This title is written in pencil on the first leaf of the volume presumably by Charles Abbot.

Tour to Italy in 1793[1]

Volume 1

11[1]

Wednesday August 14th
Left Harwich[2] at 3 o Clock in the Afternoon, Accompanied by my dear Farr, and Char – and no less dear Mrs A for whose Health we left England.[3] We went on Board the Prince of Wales Packet Boat[4] Capt. Deane[5] & Sailed out of the Harbour at Six o Clock. Passed the Point of Land Called Orford ness[6] at Eight o Clock & went into the Cabbin[7] Sick.

Thursday August 15th
Having passed a most wretched Night I was carried upon Deck at Nine o Clock, where I continued very Sick the whole Day till we Landed at Helvoet[8] At Eight in the Evening –

during the Day the Packet was Chased by a French Privateer[9] for Seven Hours, and it being Calm we found she gained upon us, and that she was hastening her speed by her men Rowing a Boat at

---

1. The journal begins on the 8th leaf of the volume which is numbered as page 1.
2. Harwich – port in north Essex. Its position on the North Sea coast and the only safe anchorage between the Thames and the Humber has led to its continuous importance as a route to ports in Holland and Belgium.
3. Char and Farr – Charles Abbot (1757–1829) and John Farr Abbot (1756–94), the sons of Mrs Bentham by her first marriage. John Farr Abbot's wife Mary Pearce (Mrs A.) was of the party. She died in Naples later that year.
4. Prince of Wales Packet – ship operating on the popular route between Harwich and Holland.
5. Possibly Joseph Deane of Harwich (b.1762), the son of Joseph Deane (1726–1800), the owner of a cod smack fishing vessel and a burgess of the town.
6. Orford Ness – a spit of shingle stretching down the Suffolk coast.
7. Murray gives this spelling, i.e. – Murray, James A.H. – *A new dictionary on historical principles*. Oxford, 1888-
8. Presumably Hellevoetsluis in the southern Netherlands close to Rotterdam. It was formerly a naval base but in more recent times the port has been overtaken by the larger size of modern shipping.
9. France declared war on Britain on 1st February 1793, hence the crossing to Holland rather than the more usual route to one of the French channel ports.

2

the Head of her Vessel; Our Captain now Ordered the Deck to be Cleared And the Guns to be prepared for an Engagement, The Box of Small Arms was Opened, and the mail brought to be thrown Over Board if necessary. The Captain then told Mr Abbot that a very little Time would determine whether his Travelling Coach[1] (which was upon Deck) must not be thrown Over Board as it certainly stood in the way of the Guns, which must be made use of to Save us from a French Prison – mean times the Ships Boat was let down & our Sailors fast'ning it to the Head of the Ship Rowed with all their Strength; yet all they beleived[2] would have been useless had not a Breeze Sprung up and helped us forward; Soon after we met the Packet Coming from Helvoet, to whom Our Captain gave notice that the Privateer had tacked about & was lying in wait for her, upon which She Returned & we proceeded – Our Captain appeared very much agitated for he had once Experienced the horrors

3

horrors of a French Prison having been Captured in the American War,[3] by being Surprised One morning in a Calm to find a French Cutter on Each Side of his Ship with One Hundred & Twenty men on Board of Each, who Instantly Attacked him, And, Carried him into a French Port where he was put into prison for Four months – and besides Losing many Thousand Pounds belonging to Government, He Lost Four Thousand Pounds himself –

Friday August 16
After Breakfasting at Helvoet, went through Several Small Dutch Towns And passed over Three Considerable Ferries in Our way to Rotterdam[4] which we reached at Six o Clock in the Evening And

---

1. It was not unusual for travellers to take their own means of conveyance when undertaking such a journey.
2. Murray gives this spelling.
3. Presumably the American War of Independence fought against Britain from 1775–83.
4. Rotterdam – major Dutch port at the mouth of the Meuse.

took Lodgings at Klein Schippershuis[1] Near the Entrance of the Harbour –

At Helvoet we observed heaps of Dirt & Filth lying in the Street – The women wore close round Caps,

4

no Hair to be Seen, a Black Patch on each Side of the Temple, & even the Poorest had Earrings in their Ears. Yet the Women appeared to do more work than the men, as we Saw them Wheeling Barrows, Drawing & Steering of Vessels upon the Canals –

No Dogs Suffer'd to run about the Streets, but all had a String tyed[2] round their Necks by which they were Led –

Saturday August 17th.
At Noon Mr. A & his Brother left us to Amuse Ourselves while they went to Dort[3] & Williamstadt[4] – I Rode with Mrs. A in a Hired Glass Coach about Rotterdam, went to the Bomb Quay where the principal merchants Reside.[5] The Houses are Large & Handsome with Trees planted in Front & behind they have Warehouses Close to the Canal where the Ships load & unload – We likewise went to the Exchange[6] & to the Publick[7] Walks on the Banks of ye Maese.[8]

Sunday August 18th.
Mrs. A very Ill & her Spirits Low all the morning, but at Noon took a Ride. And in the Afternoon went to the principal Church[9] where we saw a

---

1. Klein Schippershuis – formerly a well-known inn.
2. Murray gives this spelling.
3. Dort – the English name for Dordrecht.
4. Willemstad in north Brabant province.
5. The Bomb Quay – parallel to the Meuse and one of Rotterdam's principal through-fares at the time.
6. The then extant building was erected in 1736.
7. Murray gives this spelling.
8. The river Meuse.
9. Presumably the Groote Kerk, or St. Laurentiuskirche

5

a large Assembly of Persons; but the men Sat with their Hats upon their Heads, and the Preacher had an Orange Ribband[1] in the Buttonhole of his Coat – He Seemed to have a good manner & to be well attended to, from thence we went to the Roman Catholic Church[2] & Staid[3] till Vespers was Over, took a Ride round the Plantation, which is on the Outside of the Town, and formed into Walks by Trees planted so close as to unite at Top & the whole forms a Circular Drive part of which is close to the River & turns round by the Dock yard. In the Evening M[es]. A & Chas[l]. Returned –

Monday August 19th.
I took a Walk before Breakfast to the Extent of the principal Canal from the Entrance of the Harbour – Observed that the Marechal de Turene appeared as very good Hôtel,[4] but the Canal before it was not so busy a Scene as that before the Hotel we were at –

The Rooms at the Inns here have not any Ceilings, but are Separated only by Floors & Joists, Consequently the

6

The Noise of Walking with Wooden Slippers which are worn generally by Servants is very disagreeable

In many of the Streets Heaps of Dirt lay like so many Dunghills. The Dutch Families never Wash their Linnen[5] at Home, It is carried to Houses Erected for the purpose on the Outside of the Town, where it is always Washed & Bleached upon adjoining Grass & then Carried home Wet to be dried & Ironed.

We Observed that the Trees at Rotterdam grew to a great Heighth[6] & the Foliage very thick And being Planted in Rows on the Sides

---

1. Murray gives variants of this spelling.
2. Possibly the Paradijskerk, the Old Catholic Church dating from 1718. It survived the bombing of WWII.
3. Murray allows this form for the verb as well as noun and adjective.
4. Auberge du Maréchal de Turenne.
5. Murray gives this spelling.
6. Murray gives this spelling.

of the Canals opposite to the Houses & the Masts of Ships mixing with them formed a Singular And very Picturesque Appearance; The whole Town Exhibits a very busy and Romantic Scene The Masts of the Ships are all of a light yellow & highly Varnished And it certainly is the most pleasing Commercial Town that can be imagined –

Tuesday August 20th.
Left Rotterdam After Breakfast & went to Delft[1] – on our Road observed the Turf Pits for Fuel – The Turf is Cut into the Shape of Bricks and in Stacks covered with Reeds

7

Reeds is left in the Fields to Dry –

At Delft we Saw the Churches & the Monuments of William the First Prince of Orange[2] – Here we met a Boy who had the Impudence to refuse taking a Piece of Money Value 4[d3]. for having walkd with us the length of a Street; and because we would not give him more he Snatched a Stick from M[r]. A.[s] Hand & it was with great difficulty our Servants got it again –

From Delft we went to the Hague,[4] great part of the Road was by the Sides of the Canal, we observed Sever' Carriages with 4 wheels & only one Horse in one of these were Two Ladies with Two Gentlemen Sitting before Them and Another Gentleman Sitting still more forward to drive the Horse & a Footman Standing behind the Carriage viz Six Persons.

A Glass Coach Lined with Cut Velvet may be Hired at a Florin p Hour Viz One Shilling & Ninepence English money.[5]

---

1. The city is in South Holland between Rotterdam and the Hague.
2. Mrs Bentham is referring to the Nieuwe Kerk. It contains the mausoleum of the Dutch royal house including the tomb of William the Silent (d.1584) by Hendrik de Keyser, 1623.
3. Four pence in pre-decimal currency.
4. Den Haag – capital of the province of South Holland and the seat of the Dutch government.
5. One shilling and nine pence – untranslatable into decimal currency, one shilling being five new pence and nine old pence being three-quarters of a shilling.

We observed at the most Considerable Merchants Houses in Rotterdam, the maid Servant leaning half way out of the window on ye first Floor & throwing up Water above

8

Above their Heads to Wash the Windows which they Clean with long Brushes –

At the Hague we went to the Hôtel Marechal de Turrene where we Dined & Engaged Rooms for ourselves and Servants – The Sitting Room 32 by 16 –[1]

Wed August 21st
After M[es] A & Chas'. had made their Visit to M[r]. Elliot[2] the English Minister here And Called on Moline the Banker,[3] we Rode with them to the Parade & Saw the Guard Changed – from thence we went to the Picture Gallery belonging to the Prince of Orange in which were Several Specimens of the Princess of Oranges' Ingenuity both in Painting & Needle Work[4] Afterwards we went to the Museum belongg to the Prince Consisting of Birds, Corals, Animals, Butterflies & Minerals – there was a very large Piece of Topaz & two pieces from it Polished for Rings. Some very Curious Chinese Models of Palaces, Cut in Ivory &c – the whole was arranged in Ten Rooms, 7 in the First Floor and Three over – but the whole is a House at Some distance from the Palace where the Family Reside: Went from here to the Village of Scheveling[5] Chiefly Inhabited by

1. The Hôtel du Maréchal de Turenne – a French institution and notable stop for tourists at the time. Mrs Bentham is presumably using "feet" for the size of the room and it was thus quite large.
2. William Eliot (1767–1845), later Earl of St. Germans. He was a diplomat and politician.
3. Moline – not traced.
4. Most of the collections of the Princes of Orange are now in the Mauritshuis, opened as a gallery in 1821. Before this time the collection of William V (1748–1806) was kept at the Buitenhof. The prince married Princess Wilhelmina of Prussia (1751–1820) in 1767.
5. Scheveningen – the port of The Hague.

9

by Fishermen as it lies open to the Sea. And upon Our Return stopt[1] at the Garden belonging to Count Bendinck, which is more like a wood with walks Cut through it.[2]

We then went to See the Garden belonging to Greffier Fagel, half a mile On the Other Side of the Hague; [3] It consisted Chiefly of a wood walk round meadows & generally a green Ditch on the Side which was probably made to Drain the Land, from a Small Building Called The Tower upon the Sand Hills which lie behind this Garden we had a very Extensive View of the Sea & a Long Tract of Sand Hills, with Harlem & Delft and a fine View of the Hague –

Thursday Aug^st. 22^d.

We Walked & Rode about the Hague, the Vyverberg[4] appeared to me the most desirable Situation as a Town Residence and my Favourite House was Baron Opdams[5] at the End of the Voorhout,[6] It consists of Nine Windows, The 3 Center[7] is in the Angle with a Cupola over, – We went to See the Palace of the Stadholder,[8] The Apartm^ts. Belonging to Him were but Indifferently Furnished, but those belonging to the Princess of

10

Of Orange[9] which was the Floor Over, was Furnished very Handsome & filled with Family Pictures – her Suite of Rooms Occupy the whole Front of the Court. On One Side were the

1. Murray gives this spelling.
2. Probably Willem Gustaaf Bentinck (1762–1835). The garden originally stretched from the outskirts of The Hague to the port of Scheveningen.
3. Gaspar Fagel (1634–88) – greffier (secretary) to the States-General.
4. The Vyver (meaning fish-pond) was a sheet of water with an island in the middle of the town. It was surrounded by avenues making it the most fashionable quarter in which to live.
5. Jacob van Wassenaer, Lord Obdam (or Opdam) (1610–65), Dutch admiral.
6. Lange Voorhout – a wide street in the centre of The Hague.
7. Murray gives this as the prevalent spelling at the time.
8. The Noordeinde Palace – that of the Stadholder William V. It remains the official residence of the Dutch monarchy but not the family home.
9. Presumably Princess Wilhelmina of Prussia. She married William V in 1767.

State Apartments consisting of Two Anti [*sic*] Rooms with Two Windows in Each furnished with Rich Lyons Silk Crimson & White – A Musik[1] Room of Three Windows and a Dining Room of Seven Windows Painted White & Ornamented with Gilding but very injudiciously had yellow Silk furniture, & at the End was a Boudoir or Small Room with Green Silk furniture – all the Chairs were Painted white with Cane Backs and Seats painted the Same. The whole lately New, and Over these Apartments were those belonging to Prince Henry likewise New furnished & very much in the English manner.[2]

We went afterwards to the Old Court Inhabited by the Hereditary Prince & Princess[3] the Apartments but Indifferently furnished and the Situation very much Confined being in the middle of a Street.[4]

Went to the New Church Built in the Form of an Octagon,[5] In this the Stadholder has a Closet opposite to the Pulpit with a Fire Place & private Staircase from hence we went to the

11

The Chamber of the States, who meet Every Day to do Business Except Saturdays & Sundays: There are Two Rooms, One the Winter Chamber, the Other much Larger for Summer & fronts the Vyverberg –[6]

After driving through Streets and Examining the Houses & Every thing worth notice we went to the House in the Wood.[7] The Road

---

1. Murray gives this spelling.
2. Prince Henry – not traced.
3. Karl Georg August, Hereditary Prince of Brunswick-Wolfenbüttel (1766–1806) who had been married to Princess Louise of Orange-Nassau in 1790.
4. Old Court – probably meaning the Binnenhof – now used as part of the government buildings.
5. The Nieuwe Kerk designed by Peter Noorwits on a centralized plan and erected 1649–56.
6. The Chambers of the States General – part of the Binnenhof, an irregular group of buildings once surrounded by a moat.
7. The Huis ten Bosch erected about 1645 for the Princess Amalia. The Orange Saloon – an octagonal hall with a cupola – is adorned with scenes from the life of Prince Henry Frederick.

to it a deep Sand but the Closeness of the Trees makes it a pleasant Ride – The House consists of a Center in which is the Door & a Window on Each Side, the whole forming the Hall of Entrance to which you Ascend by a Large flight of Steps, and the Room behind the Hall is of an Octagon Form 50 feet Diameter and 60 feet High with a Cupola on the Top – On Each Side the Center are Three more Windows being the whole of the House & containing Three Rooms on Each Side with Views to the Garden Front – those that we saw were fitted up in the Indian Style with Black Japan Chairs & Cushions and Window Curtains of Rich Embroidered Silk. From the above Center Building are Two Extended Wings, in One is a Spacious Dining Room & Rooms for Attendants, the

12

The Other is Entirely for the Family And never Shewn – The Garden behind the House is a Small Lawn with Shrubs & Serpentine Walks, but the Want of Gravel renders walking very unpleasant.

NB. The Side Wings of the House Consisted of a Center of Five Windows and Two on Each Side making Nine Windows in Each Wing, & Nine in the Principal Center Building all United to Each Other formed one Extended Front towards the Wood & the Approach was Handsome –

During Our residence at the Hague we went Every morning at Eleven o Clock to the Parade, but the Dutch Soldiers neither Walk nor do their Exercise well. Mon[r]. Bootezlar governor of Williamstadt was the Commanding Officer each morning[1]

The Women wear Black Callimancoe[2] Aprons, & a Sort of Shawl made of the Same with which they Cover their Heads when it rains as none but the Peasants wear hats & those are large made of Straw & as large as an Umbrella – The

---

1. Bootezlar – not traced. Possibility that the surname is Butzelaar.
2. A woollen stuff of Flanders, glossy on the surface, and woven with a satin twill and checkered in the warp, so that the checks are seen on one side only; much used in the eighteenth Century.

13

The Principal Families Burn Coals which are brought from England –

In Every Town in Holland are a great Number of Apothecaries Shops & the Ladies in general are Said to be Valetudinarians –

Friday August 24th.
Left the Hague after breakfast and went 9 miles to Leyden,[1] the Road a Deep sand all the way – passed the Prince of Oranges House in the Wood[2] & afterwards went through Several Plantations in which were Large Houses belonging to Gentlemen.

At Leyden we visited the Stadthouse[3] were [sic] was two very Large Plans of the Town & part of Holland – Went to see the Celebrated Boerhave' Monument in the Church[4] – & the Botanic Garden in which is a large Palm Tree[5] Went to the University which appeared more like a Large School.[6] But the School for Anatomy was admirably constructed for the purposes having Several Rows of Benches Elevated one above Another in the form of a Circle & in the Center is a Table where the lectures are Read –[7]

14

The Berg is a Round Hill like a Tumulus, & almost Perpendicular, It is Walled round the Top with Battlements & a Steep flight of Steps leads to them[8] – but the View is not very Extensive – We

---

1. Leiden – city in south Holland with a notable university.
2. The Huis ten Bosch already mentioned above.
3. The Stadhuis – begun in the late sixteenth but enlarged in the following century.
4. The monument of the Dutch botanist & physician Herman Boerhaave (1668–1738) in the church of St. Peter. He was a scientist of European renown and was tutor to Peter the Great, amongst others, when the latter visited Holland.
5. The Botanic Garden – one of the earliest to be established in Europe.
6. It was founded in 1575 and is the oldest university in The Netherlands. The old University building was originally a nunnery.
7. The anatomical theatre of the university was built in 1596 and was a notable early example of the genre.
8. The castle or De Burcht – a circular structure at the centre of the town. It has its origins in the tenth century or earlier.

Staid the Night at the Golden Lyon, the Accomodations [*sic*] very Indifferent And the Charge Extravagant[1]

Saturday August 25th
Walked about the Streets of Leyden which are in general good; the Principal One is Spacious & extends by a gentle Curve, the middle part Paved with Small Stones for Carriages & on Each Side are Clinkers for foot Passengers.[2] & Close to the Houses is broad marble pavement which is Crossed at Every Door by Benches On which the Inhabitants frequently Sit. The market for meat is under the Stadthouse,[3] & I observed the Butchers were much Employed in Chopping Beef & Veal very Small like forced meat for Sausages.

We left Leyden after breakfast and with Four Horses were Six Hours in going fifteen miles to Harlem,[4] the Road all the

15

The Way being a Deep sand, yet a great number of Gentlemens Houses & large Plantations on Each Side of the Road, with Summer Houses Close to a Stagnated Ditch Covered with Green Weeds

In the Center of a Beautiful wood near the Entrance of the Town of Harlem M[r] Hope[5] has Built a very Handsome House where we Stopt and desired permission to See his Gallery of Pictures which fitted Three Rooms Uniting & forming a noble Exhibition. The Entrance is a Large Circular Room designed for Musick[6] & has a fine Echo, which the Servant who attended us, proved by Clapping his Hands & the Sound Reverberated – The Center Room of the Picture Gallery is Oval & a Long One at Each End – The Fire Places are Inclosed[7] during Summer with Painting on Canvass

---

1. Hôtel du Lion d'Or.
2. Breestraat.
3. The Stadhuis – begun in the late sixteenth century but enlarged in the seventeenth.
4. Haarlem – capital of the province of North Holland.
5. This was Jan Hope (1737–84) of the famous Anglo/Dutch merchant banking family – see below. After his death his eldest son Thomas (1769–1831) added to the collections and they were later moved to London in the face of the invading French. Subsequently, Thomas became a notable connoisseur, later moving a large part of the collection to Deepdene at Dorking in Surrey. The collection was dispersed in 1917.
6. Murray gives this spelling.
7. Murray gives this as a variant spelling.

resembling the marble that Surrounds – The Floor mosaic and very highly Varnished –[1]

When M^as Hope Purchased the 40 Acres of Ground on part of which He Built this House, he obtained Leave of the City of Harlem to Cut the Wood into

16

Into Walks which gives it the appearance of being his own Park, and is likewise a delightful Promenade for the Inhabit^s. of Harlem – We Dined & Staid the Night at the Golden Fleece at Harlem which we found a very Comfortable Inn.[2]

Sunday August 25th.
Chas' Left us after Breakfast & taking his Own Servant Prisoner in a Cabriolet went to make the Tour of North Holland.

I went with Farr and M^rs. A to Church[3] And Staid the whole Service – We Observed that the men (women? – ed.) in general kept their Hats upon their Heads during the Sermon & only held their Hats in their hands during the time of Prayers – but the Gentlemen never put their Hats ^on in the Church – The Organ which is Esteemed the finest in Europe was played after Service was over.[4]

We left Harlem at Noon & went by the Side of a Canal to Amsterdam In the mid-way we passed over a Lock or Flood Gates which Separated Harlem Meer from the Sea –[5] On Each Side of the Canal were many Country Houses Each having a Summer House at the End of a garden hanging over a Ditch of

---

1. The Paviljoen Welgelen erected 1785–9 by Henry Hope. It replaced an earlier structure and is now used as government offices.
2. The Golden Fleece – it seems to have been called a tavern and was therefore presumably modest. It no longer exists.
3. Presumably the Groote Kerk (St. Bavo) dating to the late fifteenth century.
4. The notable organ built by Christiaan Müller, 1735–8. It was restored in 1868 and 1959–60, and was long considered the largest and most powerful instrument in the world. The pipe-case is something of an eye-catcher.
5. The Haarlemmer Meer – a shallow lake which was drained between 1840 and 1853.

17

Green Stagnated Water Covered with filth – The Window Frames are in general Painted Green & likewise the Shutters, which tend to give a Green Colour to the Glass – Most of the Inns have the Place Secrete upon Each Floor as well as upon the Ground & in general they are kept very Neat. tho' certainly the Dutch are not very Cleanly either in their Houses or Streets

We arrived at Amsterdam[1] at Three o Clock & went to the Arms of Amsterdam which we found a very good Inn, much Superior to any we had Seen in Holland –[2] The mistress spoke French was very Attentive and pleasing in her Manners – The Apartm[s]. were good & for our Sitting Room upon the First Floor we were Charged Two Florins each day, and One Florin for each bed upon the Second Floor. And always found Two Beds in One Room for which we were Charged used or not.[3]

We immediately Hired a Valet de Place and went to See Several of the Churches &c – – – – –

18

Monday August 26th.
I walked with Farr before Breakfast to M[r]. Hope' the Bankers,[4] and while He was Receiving money I walked by the Side of the Canal, but in a little time a Croud[5] of People collected to Stare at me, when a Gentleman passing came to me & in the French Language desired to know why I walked there; I told him that I only Waited for a Gentleman who was at M[r]. Hope' House upon Business upon which He Bowed & we Parted; But I had reason to beleive that he immediately went to M[r]. Hope' for Soon after a Clerk belonging

---

1. Amsterdam – the capital of The Netherlands though the seat of government is at The Hague.
2. Het Wapen van Amsterdam on the Kloverniersburgwal. The building still exists.
3. Possibly the Handboogdoelen on the Singel Canal. It originally served as the HQ and shooting range of the civic guard. Florin – two shillings in pre-decimal currency.
4. Mr Abbot probably met Henry Hope (1735–1811) who was actually born in Boston Massachusetts and ran the business at this time.
5. Murray gives this spelling.

to that House Came to me and in the most polite manner desired me to go with him as the Dutch people he said, were often Insolent to Strangers – however while we were Talking Farr Came & we Returned to the Inn together –

After breakfast Farr took his Valet de Place & went to Broek a Small Town in North Holland,[1] & I went in a Coach with Mrs A. through the principal Streets and into the Jew Quarter[2] & from thence to their

19

Burying Ground, which is out of the Town[3] And afterwards we drove upon the Bank on the Shore in full View of the Zuder Zee[4] with the Opposite Shore of North Holland & the Towns of Eidam and Moneikdam[5] And then Rode the Circle of the Environs & Returned to Amsterdam by the Side of the River Amstel, on which the Treckschuytes go to Utrecht –[6]

After Dinner I walked with M^rs A to the Stadthouse[7] & in the Evening Farr Returned –

The Canals thoughout the City are very offensive both to the Sight and Smell; Filthy to Look upon and the Stench Intolerable – The only Situation to be Comfortable is on the Side of the River Amstel without the Gates of the City on the Road towards Utrecht –

Every House has a Crane fixed at the Top, by which the Peat for Firing, and the Wet Linnen to be Ironed, and Every thing wanted

---

1. Broek in Waterland, eight kilometres north-east of Amsterdam.
2. The Jodenbuurt on the east side of the town. Not a great deal survived the Nazi occupation of Holland in WWII.
3. The Jewish Cemetery of Amsterdam, or Beth Haim of Ouderkerk aan de Amstel. It was purchased by the Jewish community in 1614, surviving WWII, it has recently been restored by a group of volunteers.
4. The Zuiderzee (southern sea) – a shallow and extensive bay in the north-west of the Netherlands. A dam was built in the twentieth century to prevent the frequent flooding and much of the area reclaimed as farmland.
5. Eidam (or Edam) and Monnickendam.
6. Trekschuit – a sort of tugboat used on the canals.
7. The building was erected as the town hall in 1655 but was converted into a royal residence by Louis Napoleon, King of Holland. After the restoration of the House of Orange it remained the official residence of the Dutch monarchy.

in the Upper Rooms are carried up by Baskets, instead of the Stairs –

20

Tuesday August 27th

Early this morning Farr went to Sardam[1] in North Holland, and about Ten o Clock Chas. Arrived from his Tour; & after taking his Breakfast with me & M^{rs}. A. He took us to See the Stadthouse from the Tower of which, we saw the whole City,[2] with the Port full of Shipping, & many of the Towns in North Holland, Viz Sardam, Buyhsloot, Moneiksdam &c. [3] After Seeing Several Rooms in the Stadthouse where the Courts of Justice Are held & admiring the Large Hall, which is Lined with Marble on the Sides from the Top to the Bottom & Ornamented with Figures of the same larger than Life [4] We went to the Port from whence the Boats go to Sardam and Broek[5] We there took a Boat & went round the Ships & to the Point of View from whence Sardam & the Villages in North Holland appear to the greatest advantage.

We then landed & Rode through the Principal Streets & at our Return to the Hotel found Farr just Come from Sardam – In the Eveng the Two Brothers went to the Play & I Staid at Home with M^{rs}. A

21

Wednesday August 28th.

Walked before Breakfast to the Port And Observed in many of the Streets Coffee Roasting, for as the Houses are very Close to Each other without yard or Gardens behind many things are done in the Streets before the Front of the House.

---

1. Saenredam or Zaandam.
2. Baedeker for 1885 still gives the tower as commanding an extensive view.
3. Zaandam, Buiksloot, and Monnickendam. Traditionally one could see the ships arriving and leaving the harbour from the old Stadhuis cupola.
4. The hall is lined with a white Italian marble according to Baedeker.
5. Presumably again Zaarndam and Broek in Waterland.

At Noon we left Amsterdam & Went 24 miles to Utrecht,[1] within a few miles of which the Road continued between Plantations belonging to Country Houses which had likewise very Extensive Gardens – One in particular Named <u>Over Holland</u> was in the Style of English Gardening[2] & had near it a Larger Handsome House not quite finished belonging to the De Witts, who was a Leader in the Patriotic Party against the Prince of Orange –[3] We Dined and Staid the Night at the Castle of Antwerp a Comfortable good Inn –[4]

Friday Aug[st] 29th
Walked before Breakfast and observed the market which was well Supplied with Fish, Salmon Caught in the adjacent River Vetcht,[5] Turbot Caught from the

22

Zuyder Zee, Soals[6] and many Sorts of Flat Fish The Poultry very Large and fine & the Chickens delicately while mutton so Small that part of the Loyn[7] was always cut with the Leg And both together only used as a Side Dish at Table. Fruit & all sorts of Vegetables remarkably Fine – and the Water and Air of Utrecht so Pure that it is certainly the most Healthy part of Holland

The Mall with the adjoining Cradle Walks are very Shady and pleasant to Walk in Even at Mid:Day –[8] We Visited a garden belonging to a Widow lady who had a Considerable manufactory adjoining to her House. The Garden was about Two Acres, Ornamented in the Dutch taste with a great Variety of Statues & Busts a beautiful Grotto formed with Shells & a profusion of Jet d'eau & as many of the Statues & Vases were of Exceeding Fine Marble it must have been very Expensive, but many of the Small

---

1. Utrecht – city with a notable university and capital of the eponymous province.
2. Over-Holland – estate on the river Vecht close to the village of Nieuwersluis, NW of Utrecht. The house is largely built of brick and the garden was laid out in an English manner in the mid–eighteenth century.
3. Johan de Witt (1625–72), Dutch politician.
4. Vieux Château d'Anvers – still listed in Baedeker for 1885.
5. The river Vecht – it empties into the Zuiderzee.
6. Murray gives this spelling.
7. Murray gives this spelling.
8. The Mall – the Maliebaan, originally laid out for the playing of games.

Box Parterres were filled with pieces of Coal by way of Ornament & others with little bits of Tiles & Red Brick – – –

23

Within Six miles of Utrecht the Moravians are Settled, and Supposed to be in Number more than Six Hundred – The Unmarried men in One House, and the Women in Another, but when they Marry They Live in a Small House to themselves & compose A Village, where all Sorts of Trade is Carried on, and People from Utrecht & Other Places go there & Buy & Sell –[1]

At Noon We Left Utrecht And went 24 miles to Gorcum[2] Crossing a Ferry which took us 40 minutes to get Over – and going through several small Villages; The Country a Level Flat & the Cheif[3] produce Hemp & the Meadows very Extensive – We found Gorcum a Small Neat Town Surrounded with Ramparts[4] – And One good Inn the Dole where we Dined & Staid the Night –[5]

Saturday August 31ˢᵗ
From Gorcum we went Early & at the End of the Town Crossed a large River Called the Waal[6] which took us 30 minutes to get over, & upon the Edge of this River is a Large House in which Mʳ. Byland

24

The late Governor of Breda is now Confined and of which we had a good View[7] – from hence the Country was an Extensive Marsh, drained by Ditches & those Ditches draining into still Larger Ditches on Each side of the Road which was continued deep Sand till within Three miles of Breda, where the Road was Paved and Trees Planted on Each side –

---

1. This was the small town of Zeist close to Utrecht. The Moravians or Evangelische Broedergemeente settled there in 1746.
2. Gorinchem or Gorcum – town on the river Linge.
3. Murray gives this spelling.
4. Some of the fortifications still remain.
5. Dole Inn – not traced.
6. River Waal – a tributary of the Rhine.
7. This was Alexander, count of Byland who was confined due to his less-than-vigorous defence of the town earlier that year against the French.

Upon Passing the first Bridge a Soldier left his Centry[1] Box & walked before Our Carriage to the Gate of the Town where we were stopt to give Our Names, and where we Came from And whither going; after which we went to the Prince Cardinals' a very Clean good Inn, with Excellent Beds but Extravagantly Dear both for Diet & Lodging[2]

The Town is large and many Streets of great Length kept very Clean. The Ramparts Planted with double Rows of Trees forming pleasant Walks[3]

One Circumstance that makes Every Dutch Town appear Neat is that all the Houses are Sashed[4] and

25

Inclosed upon the Ground Floor & Appear like Private Houses, tho' upon Examination you find these Lower Rooms occupied with meat – Bread & Every Article of Sale – – – –

Sunday Sep[ter]. 1st.

Before breakfast we went up the Tower of the Great Church & Observed that the Country appeared to be Planted for about Two miles in Every direction round the Town & from that distance nothing but a dreary Heath or Marsh land, but all a deep Sand for an Extent of Twenty miles.[5]

We went into the principal Church at Seven o Clock, and found a very respectable Congregation Assembled – And at Ten we saw a still larger Congregation together. In this Church, like all other Dutch Churches, were a great number of Atcheivements[6] with the Arms on Black Velvet, the Dates & Age put on but no Name –

---

1. Murray gives this spelling.
2. The Prince Cardinal – the inn no longer exists but Elizabeth Percy, Duchess of Northumberland also found it expensive some 20 years earlier.
3. Breda – fortified town in the southern Netherlands on the rivers Mark and Aa. It has always been strategically important.
4. Sashed – furnished with sash windows rather than casements.
5. The Grote Kerk – a late Gothic building. It was originally Roman Catholic. The tower is 97 metres high.
6. Murray gives this spelling, here meaning, of course, escutcheons.

26

After Breakfast went to the Chateau belonging to the Prince of Orange. It is Surrounded by a Moat, the Building is Gothic and the Apartments form Three Sides of an Inner Court, the Fourth is a Ball Room 150 feet in Length & 36 ft wide – Five large Chandeliers Hang in the middle of the Ceiling down the Length of the Room the Sides of which were wainscot – The other Suites of Rooms were Five on One Side & Three on the Other, but all the Chairs were Brown Oak with Cane Backs & Seats & the Sides of the Rooms were Hung with Tapestry but all very ancient –[1]

The Town of Breda has Several Streets of considerable Length The Houses not Large but Neat and as Every Dutch Town conceal their Shops by having all the Houses sashed and the Door like that of a Private House, the difference is not perceived by a Passenger between a Butchers Shop and the Parlour belonging to a Genteel Family –

The great number of Windmills

27

that are generally Close to a Dutch Town give the appearance of Consequence at a distance

We left Breda at Noon and going through Plantations for Two miles, came to a dreary heath which continued for Twenty, & Ended Only One mile distant from Bergen op Zoom,[2] the whole way a deep Sand which took us Eight Hours in getting over it –

At the Entrance to the Fortifications, viz the first Draw-Bridge, the Centinel[3] left his Box & Walked before our Carriage to the Gate of the Town, where the Officer upon Duty Enquired Our Names, & where we Were going, & from whence we Came, after

---

1. The Castle of Breda – originally a fortress it was turned into a palace in the sixteenth century but remained a moated structure.
2. Bergen op Zoom in the southern Netherlands. It was originally strongly fortified but these were demolished in 1867. One of the gateways – the Gevangenpoort still exists.
3. Murray gives this spelling.

which we proceeded to the Golden Lyon, and found Good Beds & Civil Treatment but the House Old , & Situated in a Narrow Street; However at a Dutch Inn the Plenty of Clean Linnen is a most Comfortable Circumstance –[1]

28

Monday Sep[r]. 2[d].
After having walked upon the Ramparts which are Planted with Trees and through the principal parts of the Town, in which the Parade and the Market Place[2] are the only Situations tolerable, we left Bergen op Zoom, The Streets of which were Narrow & the Houses very Old: We Rode within Sight of the Scheld[3] for more than one Hour after leaving the Town, afterwards it took us Three Hours to get over a deep Sand, before we Entered the Netherlands; where the Road was Paved and Trees & Hedges On Each Side, with Small Inclosures[4] of Meadows & Land Cultivated with Corn and Rape Seed – continued to Antwerp[5] where we found an Excellent Hotel called Les Grand Laboureur,[6] & had the pleasure of Seeing Charles Arrive from Williamstadt just as we were going to Dinner

Tuesday Sep[r]. 3[d].
M[rs]. A having hired a Lacquais,[7] or Valet des Places, and a Remise,[8] we all of us went after breakfast to see the Churches And first to Nôtre Dame[9] which exceeds in magnificence most other Catholic

1. Unusually this inn – De Gouden Leeuw – still partly exists and is now a section of the Grand Hôtel de Draak.
2. The Grote Markt – still a charming location.
3. The river Scheldt – it rises in the Aisne Department of northern France and flows through Belgium before entering the sea in the southern Netherlands.
4. Murray gives this spelling.
5. Antwerp – historic port city on the river Scheldt.
6. Hôtel du Grand Laboureur – it was still listed in Baedeker for 1885.
7. Laquais – footman or lackey.
8. Remise – a hired carriage.
9. The cathedral of Notre Dame. It was begun in the fourteenth century but never completed and suffered depredations due to both Protestant iconoclasm and the Napoleonic invasion of the 1790s.

29

Churches, from thence to the Dominicans to See mont Calvert,[1] afterw^d to the Carmes des Chausées,[2] and the Carmes Chanpées, where we saw the Monks in their Chapel Singing their Evening prayers –[3] We likewise saw the Apartms in the Abbaye S^t. Michel of the Order Premontre – The Apartments of the Abbot are delightful, commanding a beautiful View of the River Scheld And Enriched with many fine Pictures –[4]

We went to the Citadel & Saw the Barracks demolished lately by the French when they Beseiged[5] it,[6] & from thence we went to the Quay[7] And to the Ramparts, upon which is a pleasant Walk between a double Row of Trees – Went to the Hôtel de Villes[8] & to the Exchange where we saw Several Shops with Toys, Trinkets and Millinery placed under the Arcades it being the time of the Fair –[9]

At our Hôtel we Saw a List of the Company who had lately been at the House, & amongst many English Names was his Royal Highness the Duke of York[10] who Lodged here Several Nights

The Houses in this Town are in general large & Handsome & the Streets

---

1. This is the Sint-Pauluskerk. The Calvary, a group of statues, still exists in a court-yard adjoining the church. It was begun in 1697 but figures continued to be added into the following century.
2. Couvent des Carmes Chaussés – the monastery began life in 1486 but was suppressed in 1796 shortly after Mrs Bentham's visit and the church was demolished.
3. Eglise des Carmes déchaussés?
4. A Premonstratensian institution, as Mrs Bentham notes. It was founded in 1124 but was laid waste by the French in 1796.
5. Murray gives this alternative spelling.
6. The Citadel or Castle was erected by order of the Duke of Alba from 1567 to 72. It was finally demolished after the Belgian Revolution of 1830.
7. The quays or wharfs of Antwerp along the river Scheldt. The town was a notable mercantile port.
8. Hôtel de Ville – the building was erected 1561–5.
9. The Bourse or Exchange – the late Gothic structure of 1531 seen by Mrs Bentham was burnt down in 1858 and replaced.
10. Frederick Augustus, Duke of York & Albany (1763–1827), second son of George III.

30

Spacious, particularly La Rue de Mer in which our Hôtel was Situated –[1]

Here we began to Eat good Fruit, the Peaches & Green Gages were well flavoured, whereas all the Fruit in Holland was tasteless & Insipid. Yet the Trees at Rotterdam were more Luxuriant & of a greater height than any I recollect having Seen in England

Wednesday Sepr. 4th.
We left Antwerp after walking once more upon the Ramparts – & went upon a Road Paved in the middle with Trees on Each Side, Inclosing Cultivated Grounds Separated by Hedges like those we have in England –

At the distance of Twelve miles we came to Mecklin, the first Town that had Post Horses, we went to the Great Church which is handsome tho' the Town is Ancient & Ill Built –[2]

From Mecklin it is Twelve Miles to Brussells [sic] – a most delight-ful Road, Planted on One Side with fine Trees and on the other Side a fine Clear Navigable River Continued for Six Miles before we Entered Brussells, at the

31

Entrance of which the Road went through the Allée Verd, which is the Publick Ride for the Inhabit[ts] to Shew themselves on Gala days –[3]

The Country around Rises gently, and many fine Houses are in

1. The hotel was actually in the Place de Mer. The square was painted by Thomas Rowlandson.
2. Mechelen or Malines – town between Antwerp and Brussels. The Cathedral of St Rumbold was begun at the end of the twelfth century but much rebuilding took place later.
3. Allée Verte – a double row of lime trees extending along the bank of the Willebroeck Canal. It was originally planted in 1707 and became a fashionable promenade.

View of the River, amongst Others the Noble Chateau du Lac
belonging to prince Charles the Governor of Brussels[1]

Our Inn was the L'Hôtel D'Angleterre[2] where we had a very
Excellent Apartment, but was Charged the Extravagant Price of
One Guinea [3]and Half Each Night; tho' the House was in a very
bad Situation, being in the middle of the Town, & in a Street; but
we could not get any Apartment at Belle Vue,[4] nor at the Prince of
Wales both of which are delightfully Situated near the Park[5]

Thursday Sep[r]. 5th
M[r] A having Hired a Glass Coach & a Valet de Place we Rode
before Breakfast to the Park for the Sake of taking a walk there; It
is a Large[6]

32

Space of Ground of a Triangular form Inclosed with Sticks three
foot High which forms a Hedge like Boundary; a wide Walk goes
through the Center, with Three Others on Each Side, & those
Crossed again by Two more, thus forming Eight distinct Plots of
Ground, which Are thickly Planted, & have high mounds of Earth
round Each; & within formed into Serpentine walks; The Center
of Two of these Plots of Ground appears to have had the Earth
dug up to form artificial Hills, leaving the bottom very deep, with
walks running down from the Top, leading to Grotto[s] and Woody
Retreats; The walks are of Sand & kept very nicely Swept, & in
many places are Ornamented with Statues –

The Houses that are Built round this Square are in general very
Large & Handsome & as the Place Royale which adjoins this Square
is likewise well Built, It is certainly the most desirable Situation to

1. Prince Charles Alexander of Lorraine (1712–80) joint governor of the Austrian
   Netherlands with his wife, Archduchess Maria Anna of Austria.
2. Presumably notable at the time because Napoleon Bonaparte stayed there in 1798!
3. Guinea – one pound one shilling in pre-decimal coinage although after WWII it
   became old-fashioned and was only used for items of luxury or high value.
4. The Bellevue was still listed in Baedeker for 1885.
5. A "Prince of Wales" hotel is still mentioned in Baedeker's Belgium & Holland for
   1875.
6. The Park was originally the garden of the Dukes of Brabant and was laid out in the
   form seen by Mrs Bentham in 1774.

Reside in & commands some fine Views of the Country which is Varied & very Picturesque[1]

After Breakfast we went to see the Palace[2] belonging to the Arch Duke[3]

33

Who is Governor of Brussels – This Palace was Pillaged by the French in 179[4] and the Apartments almost destroyed; tho' Dumourier[5] who Commndd Gave Orders that the Soldiers sh^d not touch the Palace; but the Commissioners from the Convention who arrived afterwards produced Orders for the Palace to be Plundered –

And the Soldiers did it Effectually; for they took the Furniture into the Park & Sold it to the Citizens and Shop-keepers – many Articles were Bought by Persons attached to the Duke and carried back to the Palace where we now saw them lying in some of the Rooms, Such as Rich Silk Hangings with Correspondent Chairs – but such Articles as were not Portable, the French Soldiers wantonly Broke, & tore down even the Gilt Mouldings & Carvings round the wainscot & Glasses –

Many of the Rooms are Large & well Proportioned, but the View from Every Window disagreeable & from many disgusting, looking upon wretched Shabby Buildings – We saw the Public Ball

34

And Concert Rooms – The manufactory of Tapestry,[6] & walked

---

1. Many of the houses were designed by Gilles-Barnabé Guimard (1734–1805), a French architect who spent his career in the Habsburg Netherlands.
2. The Palais Royal – the building seen by Mrs Bentham has been much altered.
3. Prince Albert of Saxony, Duke of Teschen (1738–1822). He married the Archduchess Maria Cristina of Austria and was given the courtesy title of archduke. The couple were given the governorship of the Austrian Netherlands.
4. A space has been left for a further number here.
5. Charles François Dumouriez (1739–1820), French general.
6. Brussels was of course noted for the production of tapestries though by the time of Mrs Bentham's visit the demand for the product was declining. The upheavals of the French Revolution in the years following also dealt a death blow to the industry.

upon the Ramparts –[1] Farr & Chas. Dined with M[r]. Bruce Brother to Lord Elgin & went with him to ye Play[2]

Friday Sepr 6th

Walked before breakfast in the Park Afterw[ds] Rode through the Allée Verd to the Chateau du Lac,[3] or Palace of Schoonenberg belonging to the Arch Duke – It is about (-)[4] miles from Brussels; a very Handsome Stone Building consisting of a projecting Center of Three Windows to which you Ascend by a Spacious flight of Steps and Enter the Hall under a Colonade [sic]; On Each Side the Center is a Range of Five Windows, with Small Attic[s] Over – The Hall is paved with marble and Opens to a Large Circular Room which forms the Center of the Back Front – this Circular Room is Paved with marble of various Colours in forms correspondent to the Circular Shape of the Room which has a Dome Ceiling – On Each Side are Four

35

Rooms, the Floors of which are Parqué [sic] in different Forms of mosaic The Furniture Chiefly India Tastely[5] Painted, and Beautiful Chintz – the Hangings the Same as the window Curtains & likewise the Cushions to the Sofas and Chairs – All the Chimney Pieces were of Marble very neatly Carved and all very Low; The Inside of the Chimneys were Lined with Copper and kept very Bright, and not like those in England which are usually with Black marble –

From hence we passed the Kitchen Garden, The Orangerie, and

---

1. At the time of Mrs Bentham's visit the fortifications of Brussels were already being demolished by order of the Emperor Joseph II. The ramparts finally disappeared in the early nineteenth century, replaced as elsewhere by the usual boulevards.
2. This could be either of the two younger brothers of the 7th Earl of Elgin, Thomas Bruce (1766–1841), a diplomat and most famous for purloining the "Elgin marbles". The Earl was British envoy in Brussels at the time and had already succeeded his elder brother to the title.
3. The Royal Palace of Laeken. It was originally built for the Archduke and duchess in 1782 and is now the residence of the Belgian royal family.
4. A space has been left here for the number – ed.
5. Murray gives "tastily".

a Pagoda like that at Kew Gardens[1] & went to a Villa belonging to Mons[r] Walcheir which was in the English Style and Extremely Elegant, the View from it most beautifully Picturesque Commanding the City of Brussells[2] – many of the Rooms were hung with Plain Paper, formed into Compartments by Borders, in which were Painted Small Animals & Birds with Fruits & Flowers – The Center of this Villa consisted of a Hall of Entrance in the Back Front with a

36

Dome Ceiling & communicating by folding Doors to a Circular Saloon which forms the Center in the Front of the House Opening under a Colonade by Two Large Windows like folding Doors The Glass Panes being so Large, that Three in Each Door went from the Cornice of the Room to the Base And Cost Ten Pound Each Pane – the Glass came from Tournay –[3]

The depth of the House allowed Only Two Rooms on each Side the Center Viz One to Each Front –

On the Left Side of the Hall, the Stairs appeared under an Arch, they Ascended in a Semi Circle, in the Center of which was a fine Perspective View of Tivoli, to which the painter had added L'Arc en Ciel over the Landscape[4]

The Fuel of this Country for Gentleman' Families is Wood; but the Common People get Coals from Charleroi,[5] which is a Cheaper Firing – as the Dutch Burn Turf or Peat but Families at the Hague get Coals from England

---

1. The Chinese pagoda was indeed inspired by that at Kew by Sir William Chambers. It was a structure of some 9 storeys attached to an oriental style orangery but was destroyed by the French during the revolutionary wars.
2. The Chateau du Belvédère designed in 1788 by Antoine Payen for Edouard de Walckiers (1758–1837), banker and politician. The Belgian *Biographie Nationale* gives it as in the Italian style and based on the Villa Capra at Vicenza by Palladio. It does however resemble Lord Burlington's Chiswick Villa which perhaps Mrs Bentham thought of as being in the English style.
3. Tournai – town in southern Belgium close to the border with France. It was noted for its glass making.
4. Arc-en-ciel – a rainbow.
5. Charleroi – town in southern Belgium once noted for coal mining.

37

Upon Our Return from Our morng Ride we went to See the Hotel de Ville,[1] The Quay, & the New Church at the Place Royale which is very Neat & Handsome but its Extreme Plainess[2] makes it resemble more a Protestant than a Catholic Church[3]

M$\underline{r}$ Bruce, Brother to Lord Elgin, who is at this time Resident Minister Dined with us, & likewise M^r. Woodcock,[4] who was going to Holland While these Gentlemen took their Coffee I rode with my dear M^{rs}. A. round the Park but Returned to make Tea.

Saturday Sepr. 7th.
Left Brussels at Noon & went for Twelve miles through a very pleasant Country to Louvain[5] = the first Six mile was well Planted & the Inclosures Small; afterwards the Country was open and Chiefly Arable

Our Inn at Louvain was Le Ville de Cologne,[6] a very Indiff^t House but the best the Town afforded – no Room to be in without a Bed and these very Shabby = we went to See Several of the Colleges, which are upon

38

The Plan of Large Schools[7] – The Town is Old and the Houses Ill Built – and The Streets Narrow = Brewery is the Chief trade carried on –[8]

---

1. The Hôtel de Ville was begun in 1402 but parts were only completed in the eighteenth century. In the mid nineteenth century the interior was remodelled by Victor Jamar in the manner of his mentor Viollet-le-Duc.
2. Murray allows "plainesse".
3. St. Jacques sur Caudenberg begun by Guimard in 1776. Baedeker (1885) describes it as a "handsome and chaste edifice".
4. Mr. Woodcock – not traced.
5. Louvain or Leuven – a Flemish-speaking town 16 miles east of Brussels. It has an ancient university.
6. Hôtel de Cologne – a notable inn at the time. It survived into the early nineteenth century.
7. The university was badly damaged in WWII.
8. Brewing is still carried on, famously Stella Artois is brewed here.

At this Time was an Annual Fair of a fortnights Continuance and Every Publick Hall in the different Colleges and likewise the Hôtel de Ville[1] was fitted with little Shops of all kind of Articles that could be Sold by Retail.

Sunday Sepr. 8th

Went before Breakfast to the Great Church,[2] where a Monk was Preaching with a great deal of Action; The Church was Crouded with People, who we Saw immediately after the Sermon Running into the Fair – at the Entrance of which Puppet Shows were Acting.

After Breakfast we left Louvain, and went through Tirlmont a handsome Country Town,[3] & from thence to S[t] Tron[4], a poor Town to Liege,[5] where we staid the Night at a very good Inn, the Cour de Londres the Landlord of which was a Sensible well behaved man[6] – From Louvain

39

The Country was Open Common Field Land like Northamptonshire – till the Hill descended to Liege – which Town is most beautifully Situated in a Semi Circular Valley = The Hills Rising directly from the Streets And are well Cultivated to the Top In this Country are many Hop Grounds And On One Side towards the South I Saw Vineyards –

The Citadel[7] is upon the Summit of One of the Hills above the Town, the Ascent to which is very Steep, and much resembles the Hills in the Environs of Bath[8] or those in y[e] Neighborhood[9] of

1. The Town Hall dates to the fifteenth century and is in the late Gothic style.
2. Presumably St Peter's Church erected in the fifteenth century.
3. Tirlemont, or more properly Tienen, as the town is Flemish-speaking.
4. Saint-Trond, or again more properly Sint Truiden, as the town is Flemish-speaking.
5. Liège – city in French-speaking Wallonia.
6. L'Hôtel de la Cour de Londres – a notable hotel at the time. The building still exists.
7. The Citadel of Liège was an important fortification, originally dating to 1255 but rebuilt several times later. It was largely razed in the 1970s and a hospital built on the site.
8. Bath – the spa town in the west of England. It is indeed very hilly.
9. Murray gives neighbor as an alternative to neighbour.

Rodborough in Gloucestershire;[1] but the Town is one of the most dirty, & Ill Built, that I ever Saw, for the Cheif Trade being the manufactory of Guns Every House Appears like a Black Smiths Shop –

Some of the Churches were adorned With Orange Trees and Olianders, put into Tubs which had a pleasing Effect

Monday Sep[r]. 9th.
From Liege we went Five miles to Chaud =fontaine, the Road all the Way

40

Winding between Hills which were Covered to the Top with Wood and formed a Narrow Valley, with [a] Shallow Rapid Rivulet running Over a bed of Stones like the most romantic parts of Derbyshire

The Baths at Chaudfontaine[2] are of a pleasant Warmth; <u>not</u> so Hot as the Bath Water in England but much warmer than the Bath at Buxton in Derbyshire[3] = The Accomodations are very Indifferent, there is One Large House, upon the Plan of that at Malvern in Worcestershire[4] but much worse –

From the Entrance of this Valley to the Road leading to Spa, the Ascent is very Steep; afterwards the Country is Open partly Cultivated And partly Wild Heath till within Five Miles of Spa when we descended from the Open Hilly Country & again Entered a Narrow Valley; winding like the former, & the Hills on each Side Covered to the Top with Woods –

At Spa[5] the Valley becomes rather more Extended and the Town consists of One Street, in which Every House has a

1. Rodborough – town close to Stroud in Gloucestershire.
2. Chaudfontaine – spa town in Wallonia with hot springs as its name indicates.
3. Buxton – spa town in Derbyshire which, like Bath, became a popular cultural centre in the eighteenth and nineteenth centuries due to its hot natural spring.
4. Malvern – town like Bath and Buxton known and visited for its hot springs.
5. Spa – town in the Ardennes Mountains of eastern Belgium. It is of course famous for its mineral springs, giving its name to every other such feature in the world.

41

Nominal Sign Over the Door as if it were an Inn; for Instance,
the House We Lodged in was Called Le Lion Noir, tho' a private
House; And the best in the Town; We paid Seven Louis d'ors[1] a
Week for Our Apartment, which upon the first Floor had a Sitting
Room, & one Dressing Room, all adjoining Each other, with upper
Rooms for our Servants. this House was Situated upon the Grand
Place and had been Inhabited by the King of Sweden, and the
Duke of Cumberland when he was last at Spa.[2]

Tuesday Sepr. 10th

Upon Our Arrival at Spa last Night We stopt at the Hotel du
Loup, the best Inn in the Town;[3] but found Every Apartment
Engaged; and therefore went to a Private House belonging to the
Inn Called the Hôtel de York – but finding the first Floor Engaged
we Only Staid the Night, Paying Half a Guinea for our Lodging &
being Supplied with Food from the Inn – and this morning M^r A
Engaged a most Excellent Apartment[4]

42

At the Lion Noir,[5] and Our Dinners was Served from the Inn at a
Crown Each Person, Including Suffici^t to Serve the Servants; but
the Desert, and the Bread was to be a Separate Expence –[6]

The Morning was passed in removing Our Baggage – at Noon
We Rode to See the different Springs And the Assembly Rooms –
these Rooms Were truly magnificent; consisting of Three adjoining
Rooms with a Door at the bottom of the Largest Room Opening
into an Elegant Theatre[7]

1. Louis d'or – French coin first issued by Louis XIII of France in 1640. That issued by
   Louis XVI between 1785 and '92 was replaced by the French franc during the suc-
   ceeding revolutionary period.
2. The former was Gustav III (reigned 1771–92) and the latter was probably William
   Augustus (1721–65), third son of George II. He was a general and took part in the
   Continental wars against the French.
3. Hôtel du Loup – not traced.
4. The Hôtel d'York was still mentioned in Baedeker of 1885.
5. Hôtel du Lion Noir in the Grand Place. It was a notable inn at the time.
6. Murray gives this spelling.
7. Assembly rooms – not traced.

Wednesday Sepr. 11<u>th</u>
M^r. A^s. Carriage being a Travelling Coach, He hired Horses and Postillion[1] for Chas Carriage which M^{rs}. A & myself Rode in, while himself and Brother Rode on Horseback = And this morning We all Went to the Spring out of the Town, and adjoining to which is a Wood Cut into Several Walks & very pleasantly Situated. from hence Crossed over the Hill about 20 minutes Ride to another Spring Called the Gironssere;[2] and from thence to the

43

Wauxhall, which is a Large Handsome Building contai[n]ing Two large Rooms, to which you Ascend by a Spacious Stair Case, at the Top are Soldiers Standing as upon Duty –[3]

At the First Room the Company Assemble about Twelve at Noon, to Play Biribbi,[4] which is a kind of Lottery. And before Two, they go into the Room adjoining to Play Faro;[5] & afterw^{ds} Cribbage;[6] these Games are generally Continued till Three, & Sometimes Even till Six in the Evening –

At Eight o Clock, the Company meet again in the Assembly Rooms, to Play as before, begining[7] in the Small Room, Room [sic] & going afterwards to the Larger; Play being the whole Business of this Place –

In the morning about Seven o Clock, the Peasants of the Country bring Horses Saddled & Bridled to the Pohoun Spring,[8] which is in the Center of the Town, & there they Stand for Gentlemen to Hire, to Carry them to the Other Springs, which are about a mile, or Two distant, and where they drink the water, & wash or Ride till

---

1. Murray gives both postilion and postillion.
2. The Géronstère Spring – known to have been patronised by Peter the Great.
3. The Waux-hall, named after London's Vauxhall Gardens – one of the casinos originating in the eighteenth century catering especially for English visitors.
4. Biribi – a betting game played on a board. It originated in France.
5. Faro – a French gambling card game.
6. Cribbage – a card game involving the use of a "cribbage" board for score-keeping.
7. Murray does not give this spelling as an alternative.
8. The Pohoun Spring – the mineral water was exported as a tonic.

44

The Hour of breakfast = In the Town are Two Publick Walks, One very Small opposite the Pohoun Spring And Used in a morning by those who drink from that Spring = The Other is Called Le Promenade de Sept heures And is the Evening Walk before the Company meet at the Rooms; It is Situated near the Entrance of the Town is formed into many walks and is upon a more Extensive & Varied plan than the other –[1]

The Houses at Spa are Chiefly Built of Stone, tho' there are Some of Brick but all are Slated Roofs.

From Thursday Sepr. 12th. to ye 18th –
We Continued at Spa; Riding Every Day at Noon and Walking in the Evening, Sometimes we Rode to the Springs & there Walked in the Wood-Walks which are delightfully pleasant – Some Days We Rode to Theux the Road to which was winding between Hills that formed a Narrow Valley, often appearing Closed at the End, & there opening again to another –[2]

45

Some Days We Walked Sur le Haut Montagne,[3] which is formed by Two Hills joining each other under, which, lies the Town of Spa; The Walks upon these Hills are Continued in a Zig Zag manner from the beginning of the first to the bottom of the Last, making an Extent of Two Miles; Some past open, and Some through Wood, with Paths Intervening to Ascend or descend in many Places; the whole commanding a good View of the Town & the Roads & Country about it –

Much Mischeif[4] was done to this Town by the French in the year 1792. At the House we now Lodged in, the Doors of the Rooms

---

1. The Promenade de Sept Heures was an avenue of elms at the time.
2. Theux – town between Pepinster and Spa surrounded by wooded hills.
3. Haut montagne – not traced.
4. Murray gives this spelling.

had a Seal put upon them; but They broke through the Pannels[1] of the Doors & demolished the Rooms & every thing in them[2]

Wednesday Sep[r]. 18th.
Left Spa this morning & going through Verviers[3] a Large manufacturing Town for Coarse Woolen[4] Cloth[5] we went on to Aix Le Chapelle –[6]

46

The Country Surrounding Verviers is Rich in Cultivation; The Town is in a Bottom, with Hills rising immediately from it, and for many Miles after leaving the Town, the Road is upon the Top of a high Hill resembling that which is Called the Hogs Back between Guildford and Farnham in Surry[7]

Within a few miles of Aix Le Chapelle the Country is more Inclosed and Woody; We met many Waggons Loaded with Coalls[8] of a Size like those we Call Scotch Coal, and it Comes from Mines within Two Leagues of Aix – at a Place Called Robuc –[9]

We found Several of the Inns So full of Company that we could not be admitted; However we got Excellent Apartments at the Cour de Londres which we found to be in Every respect a very good House[10]

---

1. Murray gives this spelling.
2. During the invasion by French Republican troops. Being under the control of the Austrian Habsburg monarchy at this time, the local population found itself in a difficult situation.
3. Verviers – French-speaking town in the province of Liège.
4. Murray gives this spelling.
5. As Mrs Bentham relates, Verviers was known for the manufacture of cloth.
6. Aix-la-Chapelle – town in north-western Germany now more properly known as Aachen and the preferred seat of the Emperor Charlemagne.
7. The Hog's Back – an elongated ridge, part of the North Downs.
8. Murray does not give this spelling.
9. Robuc – not traced.
10. Cour de Londres – not traced.

Thursday Sep[r]. 19th.

We went this morning to See the Hot Baths which are full as warm as the Hottest Bath Water in England.[1] And the Apparatus for Pumping on Any particular part is in the Same manner

47

But the Baths are not so Neat nor so Well fitted up. All looks Dirty: The Spring is under an Arcade And Pumped Every morning from Six o Clock till Nine – The Arcade continues a great Length, and forms a very good Covered Walk for the Company in bad Weather; And likewise leads to an Opening into a Square Piece of Ground which is Planted with Trees and formed into Three Open Walks.

On One Side the Arcade is a Publick Book Room, and on the Other a Stair Case leading to a Large Ball Room, which is daily used as a Card Room where the Company meet at Noon & again in the Evening as they do at Spa to Play in the Same manner a Variety of Games – but all is Extremely Dirty –[2]

We went a mile out of the Town to Bourcat,[3] where we saw the Boiling Fountain in the middle of the Open Street, where the water, tho uncovered And in the Open Air really Boils & is continually Sparkling up in Bubbles[4] – we Entered a House nearby adjoining where we saw Several Neat Warm Baths –

48

And Some very Curious Vapor[5] Baths –

The Price paid by an Invalid for Lodging and Boarding and Using the Bath is Five Shilling Each Day;[6] but they must find their own Wine and Breakfast = Tho' this is a poor Village yet the Houses

---

1. The tradition is still carried on at what are now known as the Carolus Thermen and in rather more salubrious circumstances.
2. There were considerable improvements in the nineteenth century.
3. Now Burtscheid – the town remains a health centre.
4. The water was once used to boil eggs as a tourist attraction but the spring has now been contained. It is the hottest hot water spring in Germany.
5. Murray gives this spelling.
6. Five shillings – that is 25 pence in decimal currency.

and Baths appeared So much Neater than those at Aix as to make them far preferable for An Invalid who did not wish for Publick Amusements –

Upon our Return to Aix we went to the Great Church[1] and were Shewn Les Tresors – Amongst which is a Bust of Charlemagne, cased in Gold & Silver washed with Gold and richly Ornamented with Pearls & Diamonds And other precious Stones – Upon this Bust the Emperor Lays his hand, when He takes his first Oath at the Coronation = We likewise Saw the Bible belonging to Charlemagne richly Gilt and Ornamented with Precious Stones. The Leaves were of papyrus; the Letters in Gold; and upon this Bible the Emperor Lays his Hand when He takes his Second Oath –

We also Saw the Sword of Charlemagne which the Emperor Wears[2]

49

For the first Three days after he is Crowned – many Other rich Relics & Dresses with which they Cloath[3] the Image of the Virgin were shewn us, And likewise Two Elegant wrought Crowns for her and Le Bon Dieu –

On Each Side the Altar of the Great Church were Semi circular Recesses with a Gothic Front, more resembling Boxes at a Theatre than a Place of Worship –

The Town of Aix is Old, Ill Built and very Dirty = The Hotel de Ville is the Only handsome Building And that is Situated in a Large Square, but in general the Streets are narrow.[4]

The Country near Aix is Woody And the Hills above the Town

---

1. The Cathedral or Dom – its construction was ordered by Charlemagne some time before AD800 but there are many later additions.
2. Most of these treasures are still kept in the Domschatzkammer.
3. Murray gives this spelling.
4. The Town Hall or Rathaus was built on the site of Charlemagne's palace and dates to the fourteenth century. It faces the Market Square (Markt).

resemble Malvern in Worcestershire;[1] but within Three miles the Country becomes Open & Arable resembling Leicestershire till the Entrance to Juliers[2] a Small Country Town but Fortified by Ramparts and a Citadel

Here we staid the Night at the Inn called Deux Ponts a Small House with Clean Beds but Extravagant in Charges.[3]

50

Friday Sep[r]. 20th.
Left Iuliers after breakfast & went through Open Country with Sandy Roads to Dusseldorf[4] = a mile before We Came to this Town We Crossed the Rhine a passage of fifteen Minutes, and went to the Inn Called Deux Ponts[5] – an excellent House with good & Clean Beds And more reasonable Bills than we had yet found; Our Dinners being Half a Crown Each (English Money) & Beds at Two Shillings each –[6]

Saturday Sep[r]. 21st
Went before Breakfast to the Cathedral,[7] the Quay and the Ramparts Afterwards went to the Gallery of Pictures belonging to the Elector Palatine,[8] The Gallery is divided into Five Rooms & is in the Palace which is an Old Building having a Guard Room in the Front with a Small Court yard before it and adjoins to a Square Piece of Ground which is the market Place for Vegetables – In the Middle of the Square is an Equestrian Statue of [. . .][9]

---

1. The Malvern Hills.
2. Jülich, or Juliers in French. The town is now part of Germany but was occupied by the French in the Napoleonic period. Much of the town was destroyed during WWII.
3. Deux Ponts – not traced.
4. Düsseldorf – town on the right bank of the Rhine where the Düssel joins the main river.
5. The Zweibrücker is listed in Baedeker's *Die Rheinlande* for 1888.
6. Being twelve and a half pence and ten pence accordingly in decimal currency.
7. Presumably St Lambert's Basilica
8. The Electoral Palace was destroyed by the French in the following year and in 1805 during further troubled times, most of the paintings were transferred to the Alte Pinakothek in Munich.
9. The space is left blank – ed. The statue to the Elector Jan Wellem in the Marktplatz still exists and dates to the early eighteenth century.

The Town is Old & very Ill Built but there is now Some New Buildings

51

begun which is to form a New Square with Several Large Houses in it, tho' the generality will be but of a moderate Size and there are Several Streets laid out to lead to the Square.[1]

The Women of this Place and likewise at Juliers wear Small Caps made of Coloured Linnen without any Border but in Shape like a Childs Scull[2] Cap – and are Extremely Ugly

Upon quitting Dusseldorf we went about a mile to the Banks of the Rhine which we Crossed by a Flying Bridge; This consists of a Large Square Platform, Railed round the Top & is capable of holding Three Carriages with Horses & People, The Platform is fixed upon Two barges, with a machine in the Form of a Gallows having Cordages tyed[3] to it; It is connected with Eight Small Boats which are Linked together at considerable distances And by this method the Passage is perfectly Safe and Easy[4] –

From hence we went through a Sandy Country to Cologne[5]

52

having frequently a View of the Rhine which appears here like the Thames at Chelsea Reach[6]

At Cologne we went to the Saint Esprit a very good Inn & very

---

1. The Carlsplatz – it was laid out in the late eighteenth century.
2. Murray gives this spelling.
3. Murray gives this spelling.
4. The bridge once existed at Mülheim.
5. Cologne – now one of Germany's largest cities lies largely on the left bank of the Rhine south of Düsseldorf.
6. Chelsea Reach – the section of the foreshore of the Thames existing at the western end of Chelsea before the river was embanked, and that connection of the village of Chelsea with it lost.

pleasantly Situated upon the Banks of the Rhine with very good Accomodat[n] both for Eating and Sleeping –[1]

Sunday Sep[r]. 22[d].

The morning being Rainy we could not get Post Horses till Noon, but as many of the Rhine Boats were lying almost directly under the Windows of Our Inn We Went on Board them And Amongst others we saw that which brought the Dutchess[2] of Devonshire[3] Down the Rhine within the last fortnight; It contained only one Cabbin being formed like what we Call in England a House Boat; It was very Dirty and in Every respect must have been very Inconvenient as the only Place to Retire to was literally a Closet, yet they Asked Sixteen Guineas to take us to Mayence[4] And our Two Carriages with Eight Post Horses amounted only

53(a)[5]

to Ten Guineas = This being Considered with the Shortness of Day light and the Change of Weather to be Expected at this Season we determined to Continue Our Journey by Land; and we reached Bonn[6] before Six in the Evening and went to L'Hotel D'Angleterre[7] a very Neat Clean Inn opposite the Palace belonging to the Elector of Cologne[8]

Between Cologne & Bonn We saw Vineyards on Each Side of the Road, and the Country became very Picturesque = The Hills Rising beautifully & Cloathed with Vines & Trees. And the Road Planted on Each Side with Elms = We passed through a Village

---

1. The Hôtel du Saint Esprit changed its name to Hotel Royal in the mid nineteenth century.
2. Murray gives this spelling.
3. This was the famous Georgiana Spencer (1757–1806), Duchess of Devonshire. Her every move was "noted" by society something in the manner of that later relative, Diana Spencer, Princess of Wales.
4. Mayence – Mainz, the capital of the Rhineland Palatinate. The French name was more usual at the time for English-speaking visitors.
5. There are two pages numbered 53 – ed.
6. Bonn – city on the Rhine, now probably most notable for having been the capital of "West" Germany in the previous century.
7. Given elsewhere as La Cour d'Angleterre but it no longer exists.
8. The Elector of Cologne was also the archbishop – at the time Maximilian Franz of Austria (1756–1801). The Electoral Palace (Kurfürstliche Residenz) was later occupied by the university.

about Three miles before we came to Bonn that had lately been destroyed by Fire owing to Charcoal having been put into a Stable where a Horse Kicked it down and it fired the Building

Monday Sep$^{r.}$ 23^{d}.
Went before Breakfast to See the palace belonging to the Elector of Cologne a very Extensive Range of Building, The principal Apartments looking upon the

53(b)

Garden at the bottom of which flows the Rhine; Some few years ago many Rooms in the Palace were destroyed by Fire, and at present the Apartm^t Inhabited by the Elector is very Indifferently Furnished; but the State Apartments are most Superb and are in the Opposite Wing – consisting of Anti Room, Saloon of Audience, & a most magnificent State Bed-Chamber of Crimson Velvet Embossed with Gold. The Bed Standing in a deep Recess forming One Large Arch with Two Smaller Ones on Each Side; the whole of Lattice Work in Gold & mixed with wreaths of Flowers – there is likewise A Suite of very Handsome Apartments with an Elegant Chapel adjoining for the Accomodation of Visitors –[1]

The gardens[2] are Extensive and Always Open for Strangers to Walk in, and the View very Picturesque, for the Seven Hills[3] which begins the Chain of mountains along the Rhine are Opposite the Palace – From hence we Rode Forty Two miles

54

On the Banks of the Rhine, at the foot of High Rocks Covered to the Top with Wood, or Vineyards rising gradually from the Bottom, & Sometimes intermixed with Orchards & Villages; The Rocks are often of an Astonishing Height & many of them Crowned with Ruins of Old Castles and Convents and frequently these Hills Seem to unite at the Top, tho the Rhine actually Seperates[4] them at

1. The chapel later became a Protestant place of worship.
2. The Hofgarten – it still exists.
3. Seven hills – Siebengebirge.
4. Murray gives this spelling.

the Bottom – And this Effect is particularly at Andernach a Small Town from whence the Dutch get the Seriff = Stein which Stone They use for the Dykes in Holland.[1]

From Andernach we Soon Came in View of the Pretty & remarkable neat Town of Neuvied; where the Prince of the Place is said to be more like the father of his Subjects than their Governor –[2]

On Leaving Bonn we had Observed a Round Hill on the Right hand of the Road with the Ruin of a castle

55

On the Top, and Several little Hermits Cells on the Side, all together forming A Very Picturesque Scene – near this Hill is Cottesberg,[3] where Several Houses Are Built at the End of a Cultivated Field, for the Accomodation of those who may be desirous of drinking the Mineral water which is here; and at this Time, the Elector himself was there.

Having Travelled through a most Beautiful Country from Bonn to Coblentz;[4] we there Rested, & went to the Hotel des Treves an Exceeding good Inn.[5]

Tuesday Sepr. 24th

Went in the morning to see the Palace belonging to the Elector of Treves –[6] It is a Handsome Stucco Building Situated On the Banks of the Rhine And Opposite to the Fortress of Ehrenbrestein which is upon an Exceeding High Hill –[7]

1. Andernach – town on the Rhine of Roman origins. Its local stone was used for mill-stones in particular.
2. Neuwied on the east bank of the Rhine. Mrs Bentham is probably referring to the fact that Count Frederick had invited settlers of whatever religion to settle there in the previous century.
3. Bad Godesberg – now a suburb of Bonn.
4. Koblenz – town at the confluence of the Rhine and Mosel.
5. The Hôtel de Trèves – it still existed in Baedeker's guide to the Rhine for 1911.
6. The palace was built between 1778–86 for the Elector Clemens Wenceslaus (1739–1812), the last elector, but it suffered during the French invasion of 1794 and later.
7. The Ehrenbreitstein Citadel – the location of strategic importance was occupied by a citadel from the tenth century onwards. That seen by Mrs Bentham was destroyed by the French in 1799 but later rebuilt by the Prussians.

The Palace consists of a Center with Five Windows and a Colonade in Front, Eleven windows on Each Side of the Center, Ending with Five more Corresponding to the Center –

The Furniture rich Lyons Silk = The Chapel Lined with a Composition

56

Resembling Marble, & is truly Elegant; a beautiful Simplicity running through the whole –

The Situation of Coblentz being upon the Banks of the Rhine is very Picturesque, and the Fortress of Ehrenbrastein is a very fine Object, being Situated upon the Hill Exactly Opposite the Quay, and at present, Contains a Thousand Troops; but when the French General Custine[1] was within Five Leagues of this Place, there was not a Single Soldier in the Garrison, And So much reason had the Elector to fear being Plundered, that he left his Palace, And So many of the Inhabitants quitted their Houses, that the Rhine was Covered with Boats filled with People –

At the Bottom of the Hill, or more truly the Rock, is the Old Palace, immediately under the Fortress, and now Converted into an Hospital –[2]

Upon quitting Coblentz, we Crossed the Rhine by a Flying bridge,[3] Similar to that at Dusseldorf – and

57

Ascended the Hill upon which is the Strong Fortress of Ehrenbrastein, from thence we Soon descended into a most Romantic Valley Extremely Narrow with a Small Stream running

1. Adam Philippe, comte de Custine (1740–93), French general. He had previously fought in the American war against the British, but serving the Republicans, he eventually falling victim to the Terror. He was guillotined the month previous to Mrs Bentham's comment.
2. The Burg – it was originally built in the 1280's but partly reconstructed later.
3. The bridge survived into the nineteenth century and was sketched by J.M.W. Turner

through it and mountains on Each Side Rising Perpendicular, those to the North Cover'd with wood & those to the South had Vines; The Turning & Windings in this Valley were so frequent, that Hill often appeared to touch the opposite for many miles till we Came to Nassau which was Twelve miles from Coblentz –[1]

This Village gives to the Prince of Orange his Family Name, and in Our way to it we had passed through Ems, Celebrated for its mineral Spring of Warm Water[2]

From Nassau we again Ascended a very high mountain And then went Ten miles over Open Country well Cultivated with Inequalities of Ground and Small woods Intermixed – And then descended to the Poor Village of Nastatten where we thought it prudent to Stop, as night was Advancing tho' the Inn was much worse than any we had yet been at & the Accomodations very bad –[3]

58

Wednesday Sep[r] 25th
Left Nastatton in the morning and Ascended a Steep Hill, then went Twelve miles Over an Extensive Open Country Cultivated with Corn, & upon the Rising Ground Small Open Woods resembling the best parts of Oxfordshire

We then descended again to Schalbac a Small Town between the Hills, where there is a mineral water which appears to be frequented, as we observed there was publick walks made near the Spring[4] – from hence we again Ascended a Steep Hill And went through a Woody Country for Nine miles & then descended and Came in View of the Rhine & Mayence[5] Three miles before we reached the City the Road had Orchards on Each Side where

---

1. Nassau – small town on the river Lahn. It was badly bombed during WWII.
2. Bad Ems on the river Lahn.
3. Nastätten – town in the Rhineland Palatinate.
4. Bad Schwalbach – spa town close to Mainz. It came to prominence in the nineteenth century as a place to take the waters.
5. Mainz – town on the Rhine where the river turns to the west towards the Netherlands.

People were gathering Apples & Walnuts – and upon the Banks of the Rhine we Saw the Fortifications left by the Prussians – we Crossed the River by a Bridge of Boats which Lay across the Rhine opposite to Mayence –

In ye Eveng wrote Letters to M^r. Palmer, M^rs. Bankes, M^rs. Mainwaring & Miss Dyer, which Chas. was to take with him to England –

59

On the Road I saw a Specimen of the Laborious Work which the Female peasants of this Country are Obliged to do – A woman was Employed in knocking on the Iron that went round the Axle-tree of a Cart wheel while a man with a Pipe in his mouth held the wheel

Thursday Sepr. 26th.

We found Our Inn which was the Hotel de Mayence[1] a very good One, having been very lately Repaired; but the Landlord ^was confined to his Bed from an Illness contracted during the Siege, And we found at this time very bad Smells in the Streets as we passed through, owing to the number of Dead Persons who had lain above Ground a considerable time before they were Buried; on which account we kept Camphire[2] continually in our hands, and made use of our own Bed Linnen and Blankets' it being here that we found for the first time a double Feather bed instead of Blankets

We walked about the Town and Observed the dreadful havock[3] of war.[4]

60

The Cathedral was one heap of Ruins nothing remaining but part of

---

1. Hotel de Mayence – not traced.
2. Murray gives this spelling.
3. Murray gives this spelling.
4. The town had been besieged by the French in October 1792 and a republic formed, only to be retaken by Coalition forces in July of the following year shortly before Mrs Bentham's arrival.

the Outward Walls[1] = many magnificent Houses likewise Burnt &
only the Walls remaining, and in One House that was left Standing
we Counted Nine Canon Balls Sticking in the walls – The palace
of the Arch- Bishop was now converted into a Lazaretto – upon
the Road to this Town, we had met great Numbers of Wounded
Soldiers, & some Hundreds of Prisoners, with Parties carrying the
Stores & Artillery from different Towns. The whole Country one
melancholy Scene, And we Ourselves a Group in it for here we
Separated with Tears on all Sides, Sad Presage of Last Farewell –
Each most Sensibly feeling the Separation; Chas Hired a Rhine
Boat to take himself his carriage & Friponé his Servant down the
Rhine to Cologne for Six Guineas & Half, He proposing to go this
Night to Bingen[2] – And we to Frankfort –

upon Leaving Mayence we Observed the Mouth of the Mayne[3]
which here flows into the Rhine; and likewise the

61

the Nine Mills Opposite Mayence which are fixed for Grinding
flour to Supply the City

We Crossed again the Bridge of Boats, and going to Frankfort[4]
went through a Country famous for the wine we call Hock[5] a Ton
of which containing Twelve Aume' has been Sold here for one
Thousand Louis d'ors –[6]

The Road very good & Paved in the middle, with walnut Trees –
Apple Trees, & Pear Trees, Planted on Each Side The Country
Flat, open, & full of Vineyards intermixed with Corn, we Went
to the Maison Rouge a most magnificent Inn – where we had an
Apartment consisting of a Dining Room with a good Bed Chamber

---

1. The cathedral suffered much damage during the siege of the town and was for some
   time used for the quartering of troops.
2. Bingen am Rhein – town on the eponymous river chiefly known today for its celebrated mediaeval composer Hildegard von Bingen.
3. The river Main joins the Rhine close to the city centre.
4. Frankfurt am Main.
5. Hock- an English term used generally for white wine from the Rhine region but
   which should properly apply to that from the town of Hockheim am Main.
6. Aume – an ancient German measure for Rhenish wine equalling forty gallons.

on Each side And Two for servants adjoining for which we were Charged at the Rate of one Guinea & Half each Night tho' it was upon the Second Floor[1]

We Walked about the Town and went through the principal Streets & to the Quay[2] which was Lined with Boats Receiving and unloading all kind of Goods it being the last week of the Fair –

62

Five miles before we Arrived at Frankfort[3] we passed an Exceeding Large white House resembling a Palace; the Center consisted of Seven windows; then a break & Three windows on Each Side with another projection of Three windows then Three more windows & Ending with a wing of Five windows making in all a Range of Thirty Five windows & Built for a Person who had gained a Fortune by Trade at Frankfort, & who proposed Living here; but had not the least piece of Land nor Garden adjoin y^e House.[4]

Friday Sepr. 27

Went to the Cathedral;[5] the Tower of which is Inhabited by a man & his wife, who Come out upon the Leads Every morning at Ten o Clock & Blow a Trumpet, which we saw him do this morning, but could not learn for what purpose = If during the Night any Fire, or any Riot happens in the City their business is to give Notice by Blowing this Trumpet –[6]

The Houses are in general Built of Stone, plaistered[7] over & Coloured with Red, the Inn we occupied was done in this manner

---

1. Maison Rouge – a notable inn at this time. It survived into the nineteenth century.
2. The quays on the river Main.
3. Frankfurt am Main – as its name suggests the city is on the Main, a tributary of the Rhine and east of Mainz. The party left the Rhine at the latter town and were making a diversion to Frankfurt and Darmstadt.
4. Not traced.
5. The Kaiserdom – not actually the seat of a bishop but an important election church of the Holy Roman Empire. The building seen by Mrs Bentham was destroyed by fire in 1867 and rebuilt but again largely destroyed in WWII and reconstructed in the 1950s.
6. The fifteenth-century tower is one of the chief features of the cathedral.
7. Murray gives this spelling.

& the Apartment under that we Inhabited is always kept for the King of

the following two leaves are blank – ed.

63

of Prussia, who generally Comes here in Winter.[1]

We left Frankfort at Noon, & went 16 miles to Darmstadt; the Road for a few miles was through a very fine Plantation of Various kinds of Trees, but afterwards a deep Sand, and Some part Paved in the middle; there were foot Paths on Each Side, and the Country Women who passed us on the Road were without Shoe or Stocking many of them Carrying Baskets of consider[able] Size on their Heads, whereas the men had both Shoe & Stocking & generally were Smoaking[2] a Pipe as they walked

The Country flat open and well Cultivated with a mixture of Corn & Vegetables – The town of Darmstadt is Small, very old & Ill Built,[3] but the Palace appeared to be in a good Style of Building tho not Inhabited; for all the windows were Closed with rough Boards on the Outside as if unfinished within = tho' at the same time Centinels[4] were at the Outer Gates & a great number of Soldiers about the Outer Courts –[5]

64

Near the Palace is a Small Garden Open to the Publick;[6] It is formed by thick Plantations with winding walks, and at the Entrance is a Large Room capable of Exercising fifteen Hundred Soldiers in the Winter Season –

---

1. Friedrich Wilhelm II (1744–97). He reigned from 1786 and his second wife was Frederika Louisa of Hesse-Darmstadt.
2. Murray gives this spelling.
3. Darmstadt – at the time the capital of the Grand Duchy of Hesse. Much of the old city centre as seen by Mrs Bentham was destroyed by a fire-storm raid in WWII.
4. Centinel – Murray gives this spelling.
5. Presumably the Schloss, formerly the residence of the Landgraves of Hesse.
6. Presumably the Herrn-Garten.

Our Inn Le Poste,[1] the best in the Place was very Indiff[t] only white washed walls; poor Beds, Food badly Cooked, but the Bread & Tea was good = The Beds had neither Tester, nor Head Cloth only Old green Stuff Curtains, no Blankets only a Small feather Bed for covering but Charged Equal to Two shillings Each – And we all passed a most uncomfortable Night –

Saturday Sep[r]. 28th
Left Darmstadt after Breakfast And proceeded towards Manheim [sic] – the Country Cheifly[2] Sand & the Road Paved, the first Two miles was through a fine wood of Firs afterw[ds] Vineyards on One Side, & on the other Corn mixed with vegetables and Planted with Walnut and Apple Trees; The whole

65

Length of the Way is bounded on One Side by a Beautiful Chain of circular Hills, covered to the Top with Trees, and frequently a Ruin Standing at the Edge

At the distance of Twelve mile we Stopt, and while the Horses Baited[3] we walked to See the Landgraves Summer Residence about a mile distant. It was a Small white House, the Ground Floor had Nine Windows & Three Doors, there was only One Floor Over, The House Standing upon a Rising Ground, in a very narrow Valley winding between Hills, had a very Romantic Appearance, & the Approach to it was guarded by Several Scatter'd Apartments for Officers belonging to the Prince and Servants –[4]

Six miles further we Stopt at the Post to Change Horses & during Our Stay, the baron Groslear with his Family in a Coach & Six arrived for the Same purpose, but as we had Come first they were Oblig'd to wait till

1. Hôtel de la Poste – it was still listed in Baedeker's "Rhine" for 1873.
2. Murray gives this spelling.
3. To bait – feed a horse, especially on a journey (archaic).
4. Probably Schloss Wolfsgarten, it was built as a hunting lodge by Landgrave Ernst Ludwig in the 1720s and is still the home of the Landgraves of Hesse.

66

We went On;[1] And this Etiquette is attended to so strictly that when M[r]. A was afterwards Oblig'd from Necessity to Stop at a Village & go into a poor Cottage where he was detained near a Quarter of an Hour both the Carriages belonging to the Baron were Obliged to wait, till He Returned and we went on –

We reached Manheim[2] at Three o Clock & went to le Cour palatin,[3] a most Excellent Inn, with Elegant Apartments & Neat Beds – before Dinner we walked to the Observatory & went to the Top,[4] from whence we Observed the Rhine & the Necker[5] Close to the Town & both Navigable – The Churches at Spires & Worms[6] were clearly Seen as well as many other Towns – Sir John Davy a young Gentleman just Come of Age,[7] was in the Observatory with M[rs] Newnham an English lady with whom he had unfortunately become Acquainted at Frankfort, and who was now going with him to Italy –[8]

We made a late Dinner at Our Inn & in the Evening walked in the different Parts of the Town –

67

Manheim Sepr. 29th.
Went before Breakfast to the Cathedral[9] where all the Soldiers were Assembled to hear mass – afterw[ds] went to the Jesuit Church

---

1. Baron Groslear – not traced.
2. Properly Mannheim – town at the confluence of the Rhine with the river Neckar in the state of Baden-Württemberg.
3. La Cour Palatine – a notable hotel. Mozart stayed there in 1778 and the business survived into the nineteenth century.
4. The Observatory was built between 1772–4 and remained in use until 1880 when the function was transferred to Karlsruhe. After WWII the tower was converted into apartments.
5. The River Neckar – it rises in the Black Forest and is a tributary of the Rhine.
6. The cathedrals at Speyer and Worms.
7. A Davy is listed in Ingamells' Dictionary, possibly Sir John.
8. A Mrs Newnham is listed in Ingamells' Dictionary as being referred to by travellers on several occasions but nothing else is known about her.
9. The town does not appear to have had a cathedral – ed.

which was more magnificent[1] – near it is the Electors Palace which
is a handsome Building forming a Large Semi Circular Court. The
Center is the Apartments belonging to the Elector & the Electress
& Visitors for the Rooms are en Suite 565 feet.[2] The Floors in
general Parqué. The Furniture Velvet but much of it is Old. The
Semi Circular Sides of this Palace are long Galleries in which are
a great number of Doors leading to the different Apartments of
those belonging to the Household; the Galleries are terminated by
an Elegant Chapel and Library.[3] The Room of the latter not unlike
the Library of All Souls in Oxford,[4] and here was an Orrery by
Adams of London,[5] and Permission for any Person to read & make
Extracts during Six Hours Every Day & an adjoining Room with
Pen Ink &c.

68

Adjoining the Center of the Palace on each Side is a long Range
of Building containing on the One Side a Suite of ten Rooms, in
which is a fine Collection of Pictures,[6] those that pleas'd me best,
were Teniers, Meiris, & Gerard Douw[s] –[7] The other Range of
Building contained a Collection of Natural History –

At Noon we saw all the Troops Reveiwed[8] on the Parade. The
Uniform white, turned up with different Colours; The leather
caps & the Brass Plate on the Front of the Cap had a good Effect

---

1. Jesuitenkirke – designed by Alessandro Galli da Bibiena and completed in 1760. The
   Baroque interior owes a good deal to the Rococo style of southern Germany.
2. Charles Theodore (1724–99). He also became Duke of Bavaria in 1777, then spending most of his time in Munich. He married Elizabeth Auguste of Sulzbach in 1742.
3. The Mannheim Palace is a grandiloquent Baroque structure second only to Versailles
   in size. It was completed in 1760 and almost bankrupted the state. Damaged in
   WWII, the building was repaired and now houses the University of Mannheim.
4. The Library of All Souls College, Oxford – a sixteenth-century interior, late Gothic
   in style with a plastered barrel vault.
5. George Adams (1750–95), the notable instrument maker.
6. On the death of Charles Theodore the electorship passed to the Bavarian monarchy
   and the paintings to Munich, though a painting by Teniers the Younger is still listed
   as shown in the gallery in Baedeker's Rhine guide for 1911.
7. There were "elder" and "younger" David Teniers and Frans van Mieris. The Old
   woman cutting bread by Gerrit Dou (1613/9–75) formerly at Mannheim is now in
   the Museum of Fine Arts, Boston.
8. Murray does not give this alternative.

From Manheim we Went to the Electors Country palace at Schwetzingen[1] – The House very Old And Shabby, but the Gardens laid out in the French Style of Cradle Walks & Jet d'eaus were very Extensive And a Semi Circular Orangerie on Each Side very handsome –[2]

69

Schwetzingen was Nine miles from Manheim, & Six miles from Heidelberg[3] where we went and Staid the Night at the 3 Kings;[4] a dirty Inn & very bad Accomodations; We walked before Dinner to the Castle, which is a very fine Ruin,[5] & there we Saw the famous Tun;[6] but the Echo is most Extraordinary, as it repeats distinctly the Words Spoke – The Coup d'oeil from this Spot is truly delightful, Commanding the Hills beyond Landau,[7] & the River Neckar which runs at the foot of the Castle, with the Town and the beautiful Circular Hills which Surround it, that are Covered to the Top with Wood, & Vineyards as High as the Industry of Man can Carry them; altogether forming the most Romantic Scene imaginable –

Heidelberg Monday Sep[r]. 30th –
We Walked before Breakfast upon the Bridge. It was Rebuilt in 1786, It is of Stone & very Neat. It Crosses the River Neckar at the Entrance of the Town leading to Franckfort –[8]

70

Heidelberg is Situated between Two Circular Hills forming part of the Chain of Hills from Darmstadt – It is a most beautiful

---

1. Schwetzingen is south of Mannheim and closer to Heidelberg.
2. The park was laid out in the late eighteenth century by Nicolas de Picage (1723–96), an architect from Lorraine and largely survives intact to this day.
3. Heidelberg – university town on the river Neckar.
4. Drei Könige – Mozart, Schumann, Goethe and others stayed at this hostelry. The building still exists.
5. The castle is of mediaeval origin but was struck by lightning on more than one occasion. It was left as a partial ruin when seen by Mrs Bentham but some restoration work was carried out in the nineteenth century.
6. The Heidelberg Tun – a very large wine vat in the cellar of the castle. It has seen many famous visitors.
7. Landau – town in the Rhineland Palatinate south-west of Heidelberg.
8. The Alte or Karl-Theodor Brücke was built in 1788 for the eponymous Elector.

Situation; but the Town is Old. The Houses Ill Built & the Streets Narrow –

From Heidelberg we went Thirty Six miles to Heilbrun[1] through an Open Cultivated Country = In the Feilds[2] we Saw many Women Digging Potatoes, others Driving the Horses while the men held the Plough. At the Entrance of Heilbrun we Crossed the Neckar Over a Long Covered Bridge resembling a Barn; the reason given for Covered Bridges is that they being made only of Planks of wood, would Soon Decay if Exposed to the Weather – the Bridge Opened in the middle for Boats with masts to Pass through –[3] The Town is Old, & Ill Built & Situated between a Range of Hills that have a Barren Appearance, we took this Route to Avoid the City of Spires –[4]

71

The French & Prussian Armies being near that City, and Landau at this time actually Beseiged by the King of Prussia, for the Day we Entered Heidelberg Three Thousand Soldiers had marched through to join the Prussian Army –[5]

Tuesday Oct[r] 1st
Left Heilbrun in the morning and Went through an Open Country full of Vineyards, & Vegetables Viz Potatoes, Beet-Root, Gourds &c for Two Hours, Afterwards Cheifly Vineyards & the Road frequently went between Hills Covered with Vines as high as the Eye could reach – They were planted in Rows of 16 or 18 Vines in Length Six Rows deep Supported by a Low Wall, & Steps made on Each Side leading to the very tops of the mountains as the different Plantations Ascended

---

1. Heilbronn – town on the river Neckar.
2. Murray gives this spelling.
3. According to the town archives the first wooden bridge was built some time after 1691 and rebuilt in 1807 only to be replaced by a stone bridge in 1867. That the wooden bridge was rebuilt suggests that the original may have been destroyed during the Napoleonic Wars.
4. Speyer – town notable for its Romanesque cathedral. It was at the time under French control.
5. Frederick William II (1744–97) took part in the coalition against the French revolutionary forces but was hampered through lack of funds. The war was subsidized by the British in 1794.

Here we gathered from the Road Side, the Largest Grapes <u>I ever</u> Saw. The Road continued winding round Hills with frequently a River running Close on the other Side for many miles.

72

With a Continuance of Vineyards, tho' in a more Open Country we Came to Lenisberg[1] a Small neat Town with Broad Streets & good Houses; Here we Saw a large Handsome Stone Palace belonging to the Duke of Wirtemberg;[2] the Grounds about it were Planted and looked Chearful[3] – from hence we went to Stutgard[4] the Capital of the Duchy of Wirtemberg where the Duke has a Noble Palace,[5] but no Ground adjoining it Except a Small Plantation in Front formed into three or four Parralel[6] Walks for the Publick, And the Back of the Palace is Close blockaded with different Buildings. The Duke uses this Palace only for State as the King of England does S[t] James[7] for both himself and the Dutchess[8] Reside constantly at Hoeing Six miles distant from Stutgard – In the Evening we Saw both the Duke & Dutchess go from this Palace in a Landelet[9] with Eight fine Cream Colour'd

73

Horses, One Postillion Rode the Leaders and the Duke held the Reins of the Other Six; His Officers of State Attended him in full Dress at the Door of the Palace; but the Duke himself was in Undress with a Brown Great Coat, And the Dutchess with a Black Bonnet; He appeared more than Sixty, his Hair Grey and had an

---

1. Probably Leonberg, west of Stuttgart.
2. At the time Karl Eugen (1737–93) who died later that month and was succeeded by his brother.
3. Murray gives this spelling.
4. Stuttgart – now the capital of Baden-Württemberg.
5. The Neues Schloss – the construction of the palace continued for most of the duke's reign. It is now mainly used for government offices.
6. Murray gives numerous alternative spellings.
7. St James's Palace in London – the official residence of the British monarch though not used as such. Foreign ambassadors to Great Britain are still accredited to the court of St James.
8. Franziska von Hohenheim (1748–1811). She married the duke in 1780 having already been his mistress for a number of years. The marriage was at first morganatic as she had a first husband still living.
9. Landelet – a reduced version of a landau, a horse-drawn carriage.

Officer like appearance, The Dutchess had a pleasing Cheerfull Countenance And appeared to be about Ten Years Younger than the Duke They both Noticed us & Bowed as They passed –

We Returned to Our Inn L'Empereur where we had the most Comfortable Apartment that we had Seen Since Leaving England. It consisted of a very good Sitting Room fronting the principal Street, and an Excellent Bed Room at Each End, all Communica^g with Each Other, and all likewise had Separate Entrances – The Charge per Night Six Florins about 12^{s1} English, the Furniture was Lutestring,^{2} perfectly Clean the Dinner, well Served & we almost Regretted that our Stay must be Short.^{3}

74

Wed Octr 2^d Stutgart –
Went to See the Palace of the Duke of Wirtemberg = The Apartments Were Separated by Anti [sic] Rooms for Servants to wait in, and Each Apartm^t Consisted of Five Rooms well furnished but without Ornaments; The Rooms were Hung with Silk & the Chairs Covered with the same. One very Large Concert Room with 27 Lustres hanging from the Ceiling, which was Used when the Grand Duke of Russia was lately here upon a Visit.^{4}

Each Suite of Apartments have Halls of Entrance as well as Anti Rooms for Servants to wait in, and as all are upon the Principal Floor they Seem Intended for different Branches of the Family, tho' not at present made use of for that purpose^5

The Town of Stutgart, tho' not Large has One Spacious hand-some Street, & many Smaller, at the upper End of the principal

---

1. Twelve shillings in pre-decimal currency, i.e. 60 pence.
2. Lutestring – a strong plain silk cloth usually used for women's dresses, etc.
3. Hôtel de L'Empereur – not traced.
4. Possibly referring to the Grand-duke Paul (1754–1801), son of Catherine the Great, who reigned as Paul I from 1796. His second wife was Sophie Dorothea of Württemberg.
5. The Neues Schloss – it was begun in 1746 for Duke Karl Eugen and a number of architects had a hand in the design. It was badly damaged in WWII leaving only a shell, but was rebuilt and now houses several government departments.

Street & looking down it, are Barracks for Soldiers, the Building is
Neat & the Town has a Chearful

75

Appearance. The Situation of it is Extremely pleasant, between
Hills which are Covered with Vineyards –

From Stutgard the Road was for many miles Level, & winding
at the bottom of beautiful Hills Cover'd at the Top with Wood,
and Vineyards running upwards from the Road to a great Height,
with a Shallow Clear running Stream on the other Side; In about
Two Hours We Crossed the River & the Valley became Wider
with Corn Fields & meadows intermixed with Vegetables – but
Soon again we had Hills, the South Sides of which were Covered
With Vineyards producing very fine Grapes. Till we Came to
Blockingen[1] Where we passed a very neat Cover'd Bridge of One
Arch with Five Windows in Length Shut with Venitian[2] Blinds,
like Shutters, and had very much the appearance of an Assembly
Room –[3]

Twenty Four Miles distance from Stutgard we Came to
Goeppingen,[4] where

76

We found a tolerable Inn & Staid the Night;

The Female Peasantry in this Country wear a Small Scull Cap
made of Coloured Linnen generally a black ground with Red flowers & a Black Gause[5] Border. Some have the Cap Black as well as
the Border – They work in the Fields at Dung Carts, and Dig the
Ground – The Cows have Bells put round their necks & are frequently Used to Plough the Ground –

---

1. Town at the confluence of the rivers Neckar and Fils now usually known as
   Plochingen
2. Murray gives this spelling.
3. The bridge is mentioned in Murray's guide for 1837 but not in Baedeker's *Southern
   Germany and Austria*, 1873.
4. Göppingen.
5. Murray gives this spelling.

Thursday Octr. 3^d.

Left Goeppingen in the morning, the Town little better than a Village, the Road had Cultivated Land on Each Side but not any Vineyards; at a little distance were Hills of a Pyramidical Form with Fortresses on the Top & all Covered with Wood. In about Eight miles the Hills began to meet and at the first Post which was a little dirty Town where we Changed Horses we found it Compleatly[1] Encircled with Lofty mountains at the feet of which the Road had been

77

Winding about for Some miles, and within these Mountains we now appeared to be Entirely Shut up – And the Only Opening was by Ascending A Steep Mountain the Sides of which were Craggy Rocks almost joining Each Other a Cross the Road.

As soon as we gained the Top of this mountain we at Once Entered upon an Open Country with Small Woods upon distant Eminences very much resembling an English Park. And this Sort of Country continued to Ulm[2] – a Small Antient[3] Town Situated upon the Danube where it first becomes Navigable and from this Town a Boat goes Every Week to Vienna –

We Dined & Staid the Night at L'Arbre Forte[4] a Comfortable Clean House, & before Dinner we walked upon the Ramparts, for like most other German Towns this is Fortified & at the Entrance we were, as usual, Stopt[5]

78

to give Our Names, and where we were going –

The Female Peasants in this Country had their Hair hanging down their Back, Plaited in Two Small Braids. The men wore

---

1. Murray gives this spelling.
2. Town in Baden-Württenberg famous for its cathedral.
3. Murray gives this spelling.
4. The inn is mentioned in other traveller's guides but no longer exists.
5. The town's fortifications were greatly developed in the nineteenth century and eventually largely demolished.

Caps which they took off as we passed as an Englishman would his Hat –

The Womens Caps were still in the form of a Scull Cap, only instead of Black Gawse[1] Borders they had prodigious deep Lawn or Coarse Muslin Borders –

Friday Oct[r]. 4th. Ulm –
Upon quitting Ulm this morning we Could perceive the Alps which we Saw again more Clear in the Eveng at Augsbourg[2]

From the Hills above Ulm which we descended last Night we Counted at One View Fourteen Villages or Small Towns many of which we passed this Day – The Road from Ulm for a little way was upon the

79

Banks of the Danube & then Crossed the Extensive Valley at the Entrance of which Ulm was Situated – The Road quite to Augsbourg had Corn & Vegetables on Each Side with Woods at a very little distance, and Sometimes the Road went through the Woods, which consisted of a great variety of Fir Trees mixed with Elm Oak & Poplar – making a most picturesque Appearance –

The first Post from Ulm was Guntsbourg,[3] the Town Ill Built but the Post House appeared tolerable much better than the next which was Summerhausen[4]

The Houses throughout Germany on this Side of Franckfort continue to be Painted upon Plaister And when done Stone Colour border'd with Grey look Neat

We passed through many wretched looking Towns where the Houses had only One Small Square of Glass for a Window, & to

1. Murray gives this spelling.
2. Augsburg – one of the most ancient of German towns, founded by the Romans in 15 BC.
3. Günzburg – town in Swabia at the confluence of the river Günz with the Danube. It was founded by the Romans as Castellum Guntia.
4. Presumably Zusmarshausen on the river Zusam between Günzburg and Augsburg.

See the number of Heads and Only Heads peeping through these Holes had a very Singular Effect –

80

The Cows are Drove Every morning into the Towns & Villages to be Milked, and I have Counted more than a Hundred Coming together with Each a Bell hung round its Neck –

Great numbers of Geese are kept for the Sake of the Down from their Feathers, which is Used for the Beds that Cover instead of Blankets as the Lodging in this Country consists of Two Straw Mattrasses, [1]& Two Cotton Over these are put Sheets & a Down Bed with a Counterpane is the Covering – The Bedsteads are Seldom more than Three feet & Half wide – often not more than Two feet & Half without any Top, having only an Iron Rod to hold a Curtain which is always Scanty never going half way round –

The Postillions throughout Germany always wear a Yellow Coat Lined with Black, The Cuffs & Collar Black, with the Eagle worked in Black upon the Left Arm & a Cord of Yellow mixed with Black is Slung over the Shoulder & Crosses the back with a Horn to be Blown as They

81

Approach the Post House, or to give Notice upon the Road for Carts to give Way. The Postilion likewise Wears a Large Hat with a Broad Gold Lace –

Augsbourg Oct[br]. 5th.[2]

Left this Town after having Seen the Aqueduct which Supplies the Inhabitants with Water –[3] The principal Street is very Wide & Spacious with Handsome Houses on Each Side, and the Senate House[4] a fine Building And One Fountain in the Center of the market Place had Twenty Four Jet d'eau[s] with a great number of

---

1. Murray gives this spelling.
2. Augsburg.
3. The water supply system was begun in 1416 and has recently been restored.
4. Presumably the notable town hall or Rathaus.

Figures;[1] Our Inn the Three Moors was in the principal Street & a very Excellent House;[2] the Apartments Good And what to us was Still more pleasing An Open Fire Place with Wood to Burn instead of a disagreable[3] German Stove –

Augusbourg tho' the Capital of Swabia is Ill Built, & Except the one principal Street, the Others are very narrow & the Houses very Old, The

82

Town is Situated in a Valley, but the Hills are not far distant – & we Soon Ascended & went through a Country for the Two next posts much resembling a Ferme Ornée.[4] The Small Clumps of Trees which were frequently near the Road & Sometimes On each Side were mixed with Various Sorts of Firs – and Other Trees.

The first Post from Augsbourg was Eversberg, The Second Schwabhausen[5] from this last we began to lose Our Picturesque Woods & descending from High Ground we Saw Munich at a distance Situated in a Vast Plain resembling Romney Marsh in England,[6]

The Female Peasantry throughout this Country work in the Fields, I often Saw women holding the Plough while a Man with a Pipe in his mouth Drove the Horses – & in many Places I Saw the women Threshing Corn in the Barn –

1. The Augustus Fountain – a late Renaissance confection with bronze figures by Hubert Gerhard dating to 1589–94.
2. The Drei Mohren – a notable hotel which survived until WWII but was rebuilt after being bombed.
3. Murray gives this spelling but it is not usual and is probably therefore an error.
4. Ferme ornée – term coined by Stephen Switzer to describe a gentleman's estate laid out on aesthetic principles yet mixed with agriculture.
5. Eurasburg, south-east of Augsburg and Schwabhausen, north-west of Dachau.
6. Romney Marsh – low-lying flat coastal area between Rye in East Sussex and Hythe in Kent.

We arrived at Munich[1] the Capital of Bavaria in the Evening & went to the Golden Hart Viz Le Cerf D'or –[2]

83

Munich Sunday Oct[br]. 6

We walked in the morning about the Town, and Visited the Churches which are in general very Handsome, but the Streets rather Narrow Except the Square Place for the Market –

M[r]. Walpole[3] Called & offered Every Assistance, & if we Staid, Should hope to have Our Company to Dinner w' Him At Noon we Rode to See Some Ground laid out in the English Style by a M[r]. Thompson, but done at the Expence of the Elector, It is Called the English Garden and adjoins to the Palace and is a very pleasant drive as well as walk.[4]

At One o Clock we went to See the Palace where the Elector has Every Day a Drawing Room from Twelve o Clock to One – after which he Retires to Dinner & Sits at Table till Three during these Hours Two Hours [sic] the Palace is to be Seen, & tho' the Building is Old and Irregular, yet the Apartments are most magnificently Furnished with Every thing that is Costly and Rare –[5]

84

A very Small Chapel, used only by the Elector and Electress when They Receive the Sacrament is Le Cabinet des Tresors – The

---

1. Munich – now a large city and as Mrs Bentham points out, the capital of the state of Bavaria.
2. Le Cerf d'Or – hotel popular with early tourists but no longer existing in the era of the Baedeker guides.
3. Thomas Walpole (1755–1840), politician and diplomat.
4. Sir Benjamin Thompson, Count Rumford (1753–1814). Thompson was an American by birth but a loyalist and came to England in 1776. He had an interesting and very varied career. Being introduced to Karl Theodor, Elector of Bavaria, he assisted the monarch in modernizing his domain. This work included the creation of the Englischer Garten from the Elector's former deer park. The work was begun in 1789 and the park still exists.
5. The Residenz – originally a castle but much expanded during the Renaissance and later.

Crucifixes are formed in Every thing that is most Expensive, The Nails in the Feet are Large Brilliants, & the Crown of Thorns is composed of Diamonds & Pearls, Rubies, Emeralds and all kind of precious Stones are crouded together in Every Shape that Fancy can devise[1]

Adjoining to this Chapel is Another where the Elector and Electress go Daily with the Gentlemen and Ladies belonging to the Court –

The Apartments in the Place are full of Gilding and large Glasses the latter So judiciously Placed as to Extend and double the View; but the Rooms that pleased me most were Lined with a Composition resembling Marble but Expressive of perspective Views – There was likewise a Noble Concert Room –[2] And an Elegant Apartm[t] detached, & yet Communicating with the Palace designed for Visitors and

85

The Pope had lately Occupied it.[3] The Suite was an Anti Chamber [sic], A Saloon, A Room of Audience A Dining Room, A Bed Room & Dressing Room –

We likewise Saw the Gallery for Antiques and the Suite of Seven Rooms for Pictures –[4]

The Riding House[5] is a fine Building and adjoins to the Publick Gardens, which have a Spacious Colonnade on Two Sides, by which Exercise may be taken with Pleasure Even during the Winter months Either on Foot or Horse; when in the Open Air the Snow lies in this Country many feet thick upon the Ground; And therefore Every Amusement is provided pour passer les Tems [sic]

---

1. The Reiche Kapelle – it was consecrated in 1607. The treasures are now shown in the Schatzkammer.
2. Presumably Mrs Bentham is referring to the Altes Residenztheater erected by Cuvilliés in the early 1750s.
3. The Elector Karl Theodor met Pope Pius VI (Braschi) in Munich in 1782.
4. Presumably shown in the Antiquarium, a hall erected in the sixteenth century and which still exists.
5. The Marstall, the current riding school was erected by Klenze in the early nineteenth century.

The Female Servants, and Daughters of Tradesman wear a Gold band or Belt upon their Caps worth 14ˢ. English[1]

86

Munich Oct^{br}. 7th –
About Ten o Clock left Munich The Country for many Miles very flat but the Road often went through a Forest of Small underwood = at Wolferthausen[2] the first Post, we Entered a more pleasant Country, the Road continually winding round Small meadows Surrounded by Fir Trees of Every Species, resembling the Approach to a Gentlemans House more than a High Road – The Houses in the different Villages were Built Entirely of Sticks of Fir Trees, Standing upright resembling a Barn; The Ground Floor had One or Two little Holes for Windows with a Small Door of Entrance – & the Floor Over had a projecting Gallery that went round this Barn like House; So that the Inhabitants could Walk & get fresh Air there when the Lower Floor happens to be blocked up with Snow = The Roofs were of Wood Cut

87

Cut into the Shape of Tiles and many Large Stones placed Singly upon the Roof to keep these Tiles of Wood Close in Windy Weather –

The Road soon came very near to the foot of the Mountains, which were Covered with Wood & the Alps appeared Close behind them & were in full View from our first Post Wolfirthausen to Benedict-Bairn Where we were Obliged to remain for the Night at a most Miserable Wretched Post House[3]

---

1. Fourteen shillings – 70 pence in decimal currency.
2. Wolfratshausen.
3. Benediktbeuern – town in Bavaria originally named after its large Benedictine monastery. The latter still exists and is now given to the Salesian order. The library of the monastery originally housed the Codex Burana, now in the State Library, the source of Carmina Burana.

Tuesday Octr. 8th.

We Were to pursue Our Journey Early this morning & therefore began Dressing by Candle Light – & the Scene of Our Chamber was Sufficiently Ludicrous for the Pencil of a Hogarth[1] Three beds without a Curtain for Mrs A. Myself & our Servant Maid – Pewter Plates upon a Shelf on One Side, and on the Other Crucifixes with Le Bon Dieu, & through this Room M^r. A was obliged to Pass to

88

get to his Bed which was in a Small Closet adjoining –

Soon after Day Light, We left this Place having had Our Own Tea & got Some Boiled milk for Breakfast with Bread we had brought from Munich

In a Short time we begun to Ascend a Very High mountain with a great number of Cataracts falling down astonishing Precipices On Each Side, The Noise of which was both Awful & pleasing –

The Ascent was very Long, The level at the Top very Short, for We almost immediately began to Descend again & at the Bottom Came to a most Beautiful and Extensive Lake called Water Sea[2] It was Surrounded on Every Side with Lofty Mountains Covered with Trees from the Top to the very Edge of the water Except the narrow winding Path which was Our Road And upon which we went nearly Three parts round the lake; & at One Side Stood the Post House –

89

Called after the Lake Water Sea. Opposite was a Boat House in which were Several Small Canoes to go upon the Lake, they were made very Long & very Narrow with One Bench at the End to Sit upon, near this Boat House was Another Wooden Building for a Cold Bath – The Post House appeared Clean & the Beds tolerable Neat & we much regretted that we had not been able to reach it the Even'g before –

1. Referring to William Hogarth (1677–1764), the pictorial satirist.
2. Presumably the Walchensee.

From this Beautiful Lake upon which are Several Islands, We Went to Mittenwald[1] a Small Town Situated in the midst of the most Sharp Pointed Alps, very High and bare Rocks without any wood to Soften the Scene – The Post House appeared to be a Clean Inn, And the Women belonging to it more Feminine & Decent than any we had Seen in this Region, for in general They have Sun burnt Countenances, with woollen Caps, borderd with Furr,[2] Coloured Stiff Stays and

90

a Coarse Cloth Hankercheif[3] twisted round their Neck; Not any Gown but Coarse Shift Sleeves a dark Blue woollen Petticoat & Sometimes Stocking but not always.

From Mittenwald these vast Mountainous Bare Rocks Soon Closed So near together as to leave Only the breadth of the Road, which went through a gate Way like a Fortification and is Capable of being Defended by a Few against Numbers. Here we were Stopt to give our Names, & where we were Going –

From hence the Valley began to Expand a little, & passing through a Small Dirty Town the Road Continued winding at the feet of mountains of bare Rock till we descended a Steep Hill & Came to the Side of [ye] River Inn by which we went to Innspruck,[4] – Crossing over a Bridge at the Entrance to the Town & Staid the Night at the Golden Eagle a large Dirty Inn with wretched accomodations [sic] and not a Curtain to any Bed in the House[5]

91

Inspruck Oct[r]. 9th.

In the morning we Walked about the Town, which consists Cheifly in One Broad Street in which are Several Large Houses Built in a

---

1. Mittenwald – a frontier town on the pass into Italy.
2. Murray gives this spelling.
3. Murray gives *hankerchief.*
4. Innsbruck, capital of the Austrian Tyrol.
5. The Goldener Adler – the ancient inn still exists.

magnificent Style – Near the River is the Governors Palace[1] which is a handsome Range of Building and near it is the Barracks & Guard House

The River near the Town is Wide And the High Rocky mountains which come close to the Side of the River leaving Only the Breadth of the Road in the Front of a Range of Houses gives the Town a Romantic And very Singular Appearance –

We left it at Noon & went Out of the Town through a Triumphal Arch, on One Pillar of which was a Latin Inscription relative to Joseph 2[d]. & upon the Other an Inscription relative to Maria Theresia[2]

92

On Leaving Inspruck we Ascended a most Stupendous mountain before we Came to the first Post called Shoenberg;[3] but the Hills on Each Side were here Covered with Wood, And the Narrow Valley Rising gradually from the bed of a Rocky River which ran in a Clear Stream at the Bottom, was Cultivated a great way up, and many white Houses were Scattered upon the Eminences, with Wood Fences in the form of Chevaux de Frise[4] dividing the Grounds, making the whole Scenery most beautifully Picturesque

At the Second Post Called Steinach[5] the houses appeared very Clean and Neat, the landlady Good Humoured & uncommonly Civil & Attentive; She brought us a Small Tub filled with Live Trout, hoping to Engage us to Stay [to] Dinner, but Our motive for this Journey forbid delay, & we proceeded as Soon as possible to the next Post Called Brenner, which we found Equally Neat[6]

---

1. Presumably the Hofburg.
2. The Triumphal Arch built in 1765 to celebrate the marriage of the Grand-duke Leopold of Tuscany (later Emperor Leopold II) and the Infanta Maria Ludovica of Spain.
3. Schönberg im Stubaital in the Austrian Tyrol.
4. Cheval de fries – a type of fence originally designed as a defence against cavalry.
5. Steinach am Brenner on the river Sill in the Austrian Tyrol.
6. Brenner, or Brennero since it was assigned to Italy after WWI, town on the eponymous pass, north of Bolzano.

93

And upon the Door of a Small Room, in which were Two Beds, without any Curtain to Either, was this Remarkable Inscription

"Madama Belle Sœur du Roi de France, Coucher Ici, 21 April 1792[1]

Near this Post House was a Small but most Beautiful Lake. The water of which was so Clear that it reflected in it the Adjacent mountain, which at this Time was Covered with Snow – And Our Road from Hence continued winding and Descending round the Base of High Mountains, in a Valley So Narrow as to admit only the Road & the River, or rather the Torrent, which Runs Close to the Road = upon this Torrent are many Mills for Sawing the Fir Trees. And these Mills, with the numerous Cataracts of Water, which falls down from these High Mountains like So many Cascades, give a most Extraordinary Velocity to the Water, which running Over many Large Rocks, that are in the Bed of these Streams, Creates

94

A Noise like the Roaring of the Sea, and continues to Sterginzen[2] where we Staid the Night

Thursday Oct[r]. 10th
The Post House at Sterginzen produced but very indifferent Fare, tho' the Door of the Room we Sat in, & the Cornice to the Windows had a little Gold round the Pannels. The Walls were merely white washed And not any Curtain to Our Beds. The Women Servants who waited upon us, more like Savages than it is possible to Conceive, and Extremely Dirty No Cap upon their Heads, but their Hair Combed Strait back, & Plaited behind, & then turned up and fastened with a Bodkin, & a large Piece of Black Crape tyed round their Throat, Stiff Stays or Boddice,[3] & no Covering upon their

1. Presumably one of the many daughters of the Empress Maria Theresia and sisters of Marie-Antoinette.
2. Sterzing or Vipiteno in the Italian Tyrol close to the border with Austria.
3. Murray gives this spelling.

Arms, but Coarse Shift Sleeves, with Long Ruffles of very Coarse
Lace dangling from the Elbow, the Petticoat of Coarse Woolen and
an Apron of the Same Sort – And Earings[1] in their Ears –

95

From Sterginzen, we Entered a narrow Valley, yet much wider
than those we had passed through Since leaving Inspruck, on Each
Side the Road was Indian or Turky[2] Corn, with meadows & Vines
intermixed till we Arrived at Brixen,[3] a Town that appeared very
considerable at a Distance, having a Cathedral with Two Towers;[4]
but the Streets were Narrow, with an Arcade on Each Side, and
Extremely filthy; for the Ground floor level with this Arcade is
used as Stables, & the first Floor as Kitchens &c; the Lodging
Rooms upon the Second, and those very dirty & Ill Furnished –

From Brixen the Road went close to a River which soon became
a Torrent, and the Valley again So Narrow, as to Admit only the
Road, which continued winding round the Bottom of Stupendous
Rocks, covered Higher than the Eye could reach with wood, &
upon the Summit of many, were Ruins of Castles. The Torrent
often appeared to be Inclosed by these Lofty mountains, & this

96

Romantic and Beautiful Scenery Continued to the Ascent above
Bolzano,[5] where we Arrived this Eveng And Staid the Night at
the Sun, a very Clean House, and for this Country a Comfortable
One, where the Inns have Only Plaister'd Walls, And never Any
Curtains to the Beds[6]

---

1. Murray gives this spelling.
2. Murray gives this spelling.
3. Brixen – now Bressanone in Italy.
4. The cathedral originally dated from the fifteenth but was rebuilt in the mid–
   eighteenth century.
5. Bolzano – the capital of Alto Adige, the town now has an industrial base and is also
   known as a tourist centre due to its proximity to the Dolomites. The residents are still
   likely to speak German though the region is now firmly part of Italy.
6. The Gastof zur Zonne. Mozart also stayed here in 1769 but the building no longer
   exists.

Friday Oct^{br}. 11th.

As we could not be Supplied with Horses till the middle of the
Day we Amused Ourselves with Seeing the Market, in which were
many People Selling Frogs, Snails, Sour Crout,[1] &c The Frogs
were skinned & looked very white, it being only the Legs united by
a very Small piece of the Back that is used for food –

The principal Females of this Town, Tradesmens Wives &c wear
a Head Dress made of Black Gawse, Crimped & Plaited in the
Form of a Man'[s] Hat; & with an addition of this Same Gawse
Plaited at the back of this Hat Stuck upon the Head having the
Hair Combed Strait back.

97

From the Bridge at Bolzano is a fine Point of View; On One Side
a Torrent running between mountains which we had Passed yesterday, and On the Other Side, a Valley more Wide, with the
River Adige flowing to Trent, and both at this Bridge forming a
Triangle[2]

Our Road towards Trent not so Interesting as that of yesterday,
but on Each Side we had frequently Vineyards, where the Vines
were trained over Wood formed in long Arches like Cradle Walks:
In other places Turky Corn, & Grass.

At Trent[3] we found Our Inn, the Europa,[4] So full of Company that
we were obliged to Submit to Stay the Night in a most miserable
Apartment, The windows Broken, the Beds & Rooms So Dirty
that I could not Venture to Undress, but Stretched myself on the
Outside [of] the Bed with my Cloathes on –

Trent Oct^{br}. 12th.

Left this Old Dirty Town with narrow Streets, and wretched looking Houses, very

1. Sauerkraut – Murray gives Mrs Bentham's spelling but as one word.
2. The town is at the confluence of the rivers Talvera and Isarco which join the Adige to the south.
3. Trento – town on the river Adige, famous as the seat of the eponymous church council in the mid sixteenth century.
4. The Hof von Europa.

98

Early, and tho' Craggy rocks still Continued, yet the Valley became Wider, with Vines trained between Pollard Trees hanging in Festoons – Intermixed with Turky Corn, & Grass – We went through Roveredo,[1] an Old Busy Town, but appeared to be at the Entrance in an improving State, as Several Large Houses were Buildg. We afterwards Passed through Ala,[2] and Stopt a little time at the Post House, but it was too Bad for us [not] to Continue; and we went on to Volarni,[3] but before we reached it, the Valley appeared to Open wide in Front, and the mountains on One Side disappeared, and all was Level; when Turning Short upon the Left, A very High Rock appeared, & the Road ascended it to a Considerable Height, but So narrow, as barely to Admit the Carriage, with a Low Wall on the Side next the River, which ran Close to the foot of the Rock; And the Ascent was So Steep, with an immediate Descent So Sudden,

99

that near Twenty Men were Employed to Steady the Coach and prevent it falling over the wall down the Precipice; or afterw[ds] going too Quickly forward, for at the Bottom of this Steep Descent, Stood a High Rock Inclosing within it the Town Gate of Volarni, And Separated Only by the River Adige, from Other Rocks of Equal Height –[4]

The Rapidity with which the Coach was carried thro' the Gate of the Town, and the Awful Scenery of High Rocks with the River flowing close to them, was Such, as I well remember but cannot describe; we Seemed to be Inclosed in a Cavern Surrounded by Water, and the Close of the day added to the Solemnity of the Scene –

We doubted whether it would not be advisable to Stay the Night at Volarni, but the Post House Accomodations appeared So much

1. Rovereto
2. Ala – town on the eponymous river close to Rovereto.
3. Volargne – town on the river Adige.
4. Mrs Bentham is presumably referring to the Chiusa di Rivoli.

like those we had had at Trent, that we determined to go on to
Verona where we Arrived at Eleven O Clock,

100

but were kept So long at the Gates of Verona,[1] before we could pro-
cure Admittance, that it was Two o Clock in the morning before
we got to Bed at Our Inn, Le Due Torri, which we found a good
House, tho the Floors were Brick And Beds without Curtains, and
no Room to sit in without a Bed in it, and Charges Extravagant[2]

Verona Sunday Oct[br]. 13th-
In the morning went to see the Amphitheatre, more Compleat[3]
than Any Other in Europe; It is Said to Contain above Twenty
Thousand Persons And may be full, & yet Cleared, in One Quarter
of an Hour; there being So many Avenues leading to the different
Seats for the Spectators –[4]

Went to the Philharmonica,[5] The Theatre,[6] The Churches &
Convents, Observed the Arch of the Bridge[7] Over the Adige,
which River Runs Close to the Town; The Houses in general are
Old & Ill Built; tho'

101

Tho' there are a few Houses Handsome and the Architecture fine;
in One we Counted 17 windows in Length: The Streets are narrow, but the Situation of the Town is Pleasant And the Small Hills
near give much Beauty to the Prospect –

The Ladies at Verona wear a Black Silk Petticoat Over their other
Dress when they walk in the Town, with a larger Black Silk Hood

---

1. Verona – town on the river Adige in the Veneto and directly west of Venice itself.
2. A hotel of the same name still exists.
3. Murray gives this spelling.
4. The Arena – it probably dates to the first century AD. Operatic performances are
   famously given in the summer months.
5. Bibbiena's Teatro Filarmonico was destroyed in WWII.
6. Presumably the Roman theatre close to the Ponte Pietra.
7. It is not clear to which bridge Mrs Bentham is referring since the Scaliger Bridge has
   three arches and the Pietra Bridge five arches.

like veil, The Hair Dressed and Powdered with a Small Cap. The Lower Rank of women are Cheifly Employed in Spinning Silk.

We Visited the Convent of Santa Lucia, where Three Nuns came to the Grate & Chatted with us – & with them Came a very Pretty Young lady who was in her year of Probation[1]

This being the first Town in Italy, we found upon our Beds Cotton Coverlets, instead of Feather or Down Beds, which we had throughout Germany

The Town of Verona is Sometimes Overflowed, and in the year 1776 the

102

Water was many Feet high in the Streets, and consequently the Lower Apartments of the Houses were under water;[2] The want of Sewers make the Streets often very Offensive from the Stench of the Filth

Verona Monday Oct^{br}. 14th.

Left our Inn the Due Torri or in English the Two Towers,[3] and Lord & Lady Palmerston, who with Three Children & Three maid Servants, and Six men Servants, had been there a considerable Time;[4] And tho' the House may be good for Italy as the Rooms were Large & Lofty; yet the Brick Floors & Dirty Furniture made me wonder that an English Family could like such a Residence

Upon Leaving Verona Observe the Situation of it when you are about a mile distant; Turn, & Look at the City, The Battlements & Towers – all Appear Handsome, & the Small Hills adjoining,

---

1. The convent was suppressed during the Napoleonic period.
2. The river Adige frequently flooded. Finally, after a severe flood in 1882, the river was embanked.
3. The Due Torri still exists.
4. This was Henry Temple, 2nd Viscount Palmerston (1739–1802), politician. The Palmerstons made a lengthy Continental tour from 1792–4. Palmerston's more famous son, later prime minister, had an Italian tutor on their trip and leant to speak the language fluently.

add much to the Beauty, with the River Adige which Runs from thence to Vicenza – and at this Time[1]

103

The Road was Lined on Each Side with Vines hanging in festoon like Arches from Tree to Tree Loaded with Grapes; the Quantity incredible, And the Scenery Picturesque, for between the Pollards which Supported the Vines, the Land was Cultivated with wheat – maiz or Turky Corn, and upon the Road were many Large Casks Drawn by Oxen full of the present Vintage

Our Postillions now began to wear Earings, a Custom throughout Italy = we passed through Monte Bello,[2] and Arrived before the Hour of Dinner at Vicenza,[3] & went to L'Ecu de France –[4]

Walked to the Church of Santa Maria del Monte, through a Beautiful Arcade, near a Mile in Length; the Situation delightful, Commanding Four different Views of the adjacent Country and the City of Vicenza Lying beneath: The Mountains of the Tyrol, & the Flat Country leading to Padua, & likewise that to Verona in full View.[5]

104

The Number of white Houses which are intermixed with the Trees had a most pleasing Effect – after going into the Church[6] (which is Resorted to by many Pilgrims) we Visited the Refectory (where the Cloth was laid for Supper) to See a fine Picture by Paul Veronese, The Floor of the Room was a Composition & very nicely Polished[7]

1. The town was fortified and still has a castle which guarded the crossing of the river, the latter now a museum.
2. Montebello Vicentino.
3. Vicenza – town in the Veneto important for its numerous buildings by Andrea Palladio.
4. L'Ecu de France – a well-known inn at the time.
5. The Basilica di Monte Bérico – the site commands an extensive view.
6. Santa Maria di Monte Bérico.
7. Veronese's Cena di San Gregorio Magno dating to 1572. It was badly damaged by Austrian troops in 1848 but later restored.

Tho' I thought Our Inn but very I[n]different, yet the Comte D'Artois Brother to the King of France, had Lived here Thirty four Days.[1]

Vicenza Oct[br]. 15th.
Went before Breakfast to the Campus Martius,[2] & adterw[ds] to the Olympia Theatre,[3] and to the Rotunde del[4] Monte Built by Palladio;[5] and from which Lord Burlington Built the House at Chiswick, now Inhabited by the Duke of Devonshire[6]

Near the Campus Martius Mons' Calonne has lately Purchased a House where he now Resides with his Family[7] It appeared a very Eligible Habitation

105

And the Situation very pleasant.

At Noon we left Vicenza and went to Padua[8] where we found L'Aigle D'or a very comfortable Inn And the Town much Cleaner than Either Vicenza or Verona –[9]

The Country about Padua is Flat, but well Cultivated. Corn & maize between Rows of mulberry Trees with Vines Hanging in Festoons

We Visited Several of the Churches which were Large & magnifi-

---

1. Charles de Bourbon, Comte d'Artois (1757–1836), brother of Louis XVI. He later reigned as Charles X (1824–30).
2. Campo Marzio – park to the south of the town.
3. The Teatro Olimpico designed by Andrea Palladio and erected between 1580 and '84.
4. Mrs Bentham has added "vide Cha' Journal" in the margin here.
5. The Villa Rotonda by Andrea Palladio begun in 1550.
6. Chiswick Villa designed by Lord Burlington but inspired by Palladio's Villa Rotonda was completed in 1729. The house was inherited by Burlington's son-in-law, William Cavendish, 4th Duke of Devonshire.
7. Charles Alexandre, vicomte de Calonne (1734–1802), French statesman. He was known as "Monsieur Déficit" due to his tax raising measures and was dismissed by Louis XVI.
8. Padua – town in the Veneto close to Venice itself. It is now an important commercial and industrial centre but has also always been known for its renowned university.
9. L'Aigle d'Or – a well-known inn at the time.

cent[1] And Abounded in Ornaments, Saint Antoine has Four organs and Forty Performers of Church Musick,[2] and Saint Giustian is said to have within it the finest work in Italy –[3]

We found here some Excellent Small Birds Roasted for Dinner, which they called Thrushes – And Sheeps Brains fryed in Small Pieces & put upon Stew'd Sorrel generally made a Side Dish And meat Pounded in a morter[4] & Baked in a mold[5] often appeared like a Pudding And macaroni in a Variety of Forms –

106

The men at Padua wore Large Cloaks of Scarlet Cloth, Such as in England many years past were Called Roquelear –[6]

Padua Oct[br]. 16th.
We left this City at Noon, The Country continuing Flat, And the Road often going by the Side of the River[7] adorned with Villa[s] belonging to the Venetians, till we came to the very Small Village of Fusina, [8]where we Embarked for Venice; leaving our Coach in one of the Houses there Built on purpose to receive those belonging to Passengers; & where they remain perfectly safe till their Return Paying Two Pauls Each Night for its Standing. There is a long Range of Coach Houses but no Stables for the Horses Return, & when wanted are Sent for again from Padua – And many prefer Leaving their Carriages likewise at Padua, & from thence coming in the Passage Boat, which goes Daily down the River Brenta to Venice – but as that was not our Plan, Here we got into a Boat

107

With our Trunks to go to Venice And during the Short Passage we

1. Mrs Bentham has added "vide Cha' Journal" in the margin here.
2. The Basilica of Sant'Antonio of Padua.
3. The Basilica of Santa Giustina of Padua.
4. Murray gives this spelling.
5. Murray gives this spelling.
6. Roquelaure cloak – a knee-length cloak often lined in a bright colour and trimmed with fur popular for men in the eighteenth century.
7. The Naviglio del Brenta.
8. Fusina on the Venetian Lagoon. Boats still ply to and thro to Venice itself.

were Stopt Three times by Custom House Officers, who Came in
a Boat along Side of us and with Long Hooks Grappled Our Boat
and Demanded money; after the first Boat had Stopt us & received
the usual Fees, we Offered the Keys of our Trunks; but They were
not Inclined to Search, nor Easily Satisfied with the money we
gave However upon being Stopt by a Third we would no longer
be Duped; but absolutely Refused giving more & threatened them
with Our making a Complaint when we landed which we Soon did
at Petrillo's near the Rialto,[1] upon the Grand Canal, & found a Very
Comfortable Apartm[t] consisting of a Sitting Room and Two Good
Bed Rooms & Serv[ts] Room adjoining all looking upon the Canal

Venice Oct[br]. 17th.

After Breakfast went into a Gondola And was carried to Place de
S[t]. Marc –[2]

108

Visited the Church,[3] The Doors of which are of Corinthian Brass
and were brought from Constantinople.[4] The Floor of Beautiful
marble laid in mosaic[5] – went after[wds] to the Library,[6] the first Room
of which was filled with Antique Sculpture[7]

We likewise Visited the Doge' Palace[8] described fully by C. A---
And we Saw the Dress worn by the Doge when Acting officially –

Went to Some of the principal Casinoe[s9] And afterw[ds]. Ascended
the Tower which Stands in the Place de Saint Marc,[10] and the Tide

---

1. Petrillo – a well-known inn at the time close to the Rialto Bridge.
2. Piazza San Marco.
3. Of course, the eponymous basilica.
4. The bronze doors of the central arch date from the sixth century and probably came
   from Byzantium.
5. The marble floors date to the twelfth century.
6. The Biblioteca Sansoviniana or di San Marco designed by Jacopo Sansovino and
   begun in 1536. It faces the Doge's palace.
7. Mrs Bentham has added "vide C. A'[s] Journal" in the margin here.
8. Palazzo Ducale.
9. Murray does not give this form of the plural.
10. The Campanile of the basilica. The original dated to the tenth century but this collapsed in 1902 and was faithfully rebuilt.

being Out we had a compleat View of all the Sands and Shallows which render Venice so Secure from the Attempt of an Enemy –

In the Doges Palace we attended to a large Picture by <u>Palma</u> of the Last day, in which he had placed a Portrait of his favorite[1] mistress in Paradise; but She having proved False to him before he had finished this Picture, he repented the Likeness And Placed her in Hell – – – –[2]

109

Venice Oct[br]. 18th.
Went in a Gondola to the Arsenal where 2500 Men are constantly Employed; In the Armory they can equip 20:000 men upon any Emergency in a Week, as Every thing is kept in perfect Order –[3]

The Ships are all Built under Cover'd Roofs Sixty upon the Stocks at One time Including Frigates – The King of Naples Visited this Dock yard Three years ago & was most magnificently Entertained in the Great Room where the Arms are placed.[4]

We went on Board the Bucentaur or State Barge,[5] which is very Splendid being most highly Ornamented with Gilding in Every part; In this Barge The Doge goes Annually upon Ascension Day, and drops a Ring into the Adriatic Sea, Attended by all the Nobility of Venice, This is thought a most Superb Sight, and generally brings a Number of Strangers who continue to be at Venice at this Season –[6]

After quitting the Arsenal

---

1. Murray gives this spelling.
2. Mrs Bentham is almost certainly referring to the huge *Paradiso* by Jacopo Tintoretto in the Sala del Maggior Consiglio dating to 1588.
3. The Arsenale, Venice's famous ship-building yard.
4. Ferdinand IV, reigned 1759–99.
5. The Bucintoro – the last version was built in 1729 and was destroyed on the orders of Napoleon in 1798.
6. The ceremony called the *Sposalizio del mare*, it was begun about 1000 AD.

110

We went on Board a Galley, where a great number of Slaves were Chained to the Oar. Three together – And from their Behaviour Seemed a desperate Sett of Wretches –[1]

We went from hence to the Isle of Zecca[2] and Visited the Church of Saint Georgio [*sic*] Maggiore and likewise Il Redempta Le Carita, both Paved with beautiful marble – afterwards went to See the Palaces of Pisani, Barberigo &c &c – containing Large & Spacious Rooms, fine Paintings &c but being Situated at the very edge of the Canals, can have no other Conveyance to or from them but Gondola[s].[3]

Saturday Oct[br]. 19th.
Went in a Gondola to the Place de S[t]. Marc which to Day was crouded like a Fair – a great number of Booths being upon the Pavement, in which were all kind of things. Some had Old Cloaths,[4] others Pewter Plates &c. in Another Fruit & Vegetables – Some with Wooden Bowls – & Some with Shoes –

111

And many Coops with Live Fowls, And in this manner S[t]. Marc' Place is Covered Every Saturday; from hence we walked through the Streets which are truly no wider than Alleys with Small Shops on Each Side –

We went to the Opera House which was lately Built and very Elegantly fitted up – The Logements are Rented for the Season at 40 Sequins ab[t] £20 English and contain Six Chairs Or Two Chairs & Two Sofas – with a Looking Glass in each Side Pannel and a Glass in the Door to let up & down like a Coach Window And

---

1. The practice of using convicts as galley slaves was widespread in Europe but surely frowned upon by this date in more advanced states.
2. La Giudecca. San Giorgio Maggiore is actually on its own eponymous island adjoining. Il Redentore is on the Giudecca facing the main island of Venice. San Giorgio was begun by Andrea Palladio in 1565, who likewise designed Il Redentore in 1577.
3. There are several palaces belonging to each family.
4. Murray gives this spelling.

Spring Blinds to admit Air when the Glass is not used & in Each Corner a Commode[1]

The Noble Venetian generally wears at this Season of the year a white Lutestring Silk Cloak over his Dress & Every other Person wears a Cloak of Scarlet or Brown Camblet[2] or thin Cloth –

112

After walking Some Hours we Returned to the Gondola & took a Circuit round by the Arsenal from whence Seven different Islands appear at One View Rising from the Sea –

In the Evening M[r]. Martin the Banker[3] Called & Endeavoured to persuade us to take Horses from hence to go to Naples the price Fifty Louis, but we reckoned the Post Horses would not amount to more than 28 Louis & with Fees to Postillions would not Exceed 43 Louis & therefore declined Obliging our Banker at both Our own Expence as well as Inconvenience in respect to Slowness of Travelling

Sunday Oct[br]. 20th.
Left Venice at Noon & went in a Gondola in One Hour to Fusina where we found Our Coach as we had left it, Locked up in One of the Coach Houses which are Built upon the Shore. The Doors of which are Locked without Side but no other Security

113

The Day was Calm & Serene and the City of Venice looked Beautiful Rising from the Sea – but there Appears a great mixture of meaness[4] with magnificence in the Buildings The Window Shutters being generally a white Board Hanging on the Outside of the House against the Stone or Plaister'd House without being Painted, & this is Customary throughout the Route to Padua in

1. From the date obviously the famous La Fenice which had been built by Antonio Selva from 1790 to 92. The building was destroyed by fire in 1836 as was the subsequent theatre in 1996.
2. A variation of camlet – a type of cloth or garment made thereof.
3. Mr Martin – not traced.
4. Murray gives *meanese*.

which we passed a great number of Large Houses with Extensive Gardens belonging to them –

Throughout this Country we Saw great numbers of Small Vehicles made to Carry One Person only, the Shape resembling the Back of a p^r of Stays – or Something like Half a Pedestal reversed It is put upon Two wheels & drawn by One Horse & goes with great Swiftness; being made Expressly to hold only one Person tho' we often Saw another Sitting in their Lap

114

From Fusina we went in Four Hours to Padua & Dined at the Aquila D'or, or Golden Eagle which we again found a most Comfortable House: The Floors of Composition, The Beds Clean & Good The People very Attentive & the whole much better than Any we had yet Seen in Italy

There is a Large Square in Padua in which a great number of Figures as large as life Cut in marble Surround a Plot of Grass & form a Circle & a Stream of Water Running round it.[1]

Monday Oct^br. 21st.
Left Padua at 7 in the morning being desirous of getting to Ferrara before Night – till Noon we had a Fog as thick & Damp as any I Ever Saw in London during a Nov^br month= The Road for many Posts was upon a Bank from 20 to 30 feet in Height on One Side of which was

115

Frequently a River; & on the other Cultivated Fields with Trees Planted in Rows – We came to the Po[2] just as the Sun was Sitting, but Unfortunately found the large Boat in which Carriages usually Cross the River was Broke, & we were Obliged to go Three miles further upon a High Narrow Bank Close to the River before we could get to Another Ferry, by which time it was quite Dark

---

1. The Prato della Valle laid out in 1775 to the designs of Domenico Cerato. There are 78 statues of illustrious Paduans largely by local sculptors.
2. The river Po.

However we Crossed in Safety Opposite to a Small Town Called Pont Augustin, where we could just discern Several masts of Vessels lying close to the Shore.[1]

From hence to Ferrara[2] the Road appeared to be Planted with double Rows of Trees on Each Side forming foot Paths, we Staid the Night at the Three Moors a good House but the Situation Bad, being in a very Narrow Street[3]

Tuesday Oct^{br} 22^{d}.
Left Ferrara at Noon & went towards Bologna by Sans Carlo[4] &

116

Cento, the Road continuing upon High Banks which makes it appear dangerous; after Cento the Road became Level with the Fields which were Cultivated & often resembled Large Orchards; & as the Road was continually winding it became very Pleasant. At Bologna[5] we went to the Pelegrin which we found to be a Comfortable Inn in respect to Accomodations, but the Situation Bad in a Narrow Street[6]

Wed. Octr 23.
Went after Breakfast to the Instituto [sic], A Building most admirably adapted for the Study of the Sciences in the different Branches – In Some Rooms were Plans of Architecture & Designs for Building, In Others the Human Body Anatomized & Every distinct part Shown in Wax. Chymical Experiments And Every Apparatus for the Student. In other Rooms Minerals – Fossils &c besides Lord Cowpers Collection which He had Purchased in England, & being

---

1. Pontelagoscuro?
2. Ferrara – important centre south of the river Po between Mantua and Ravenna.
3. Albergo de' Tre Mori.
4. San Carlo – between Ferrara and Cento – it can only have been a village at the time but possibly a place to change horses.
5. Bologna – town on the via Emilia and the traditional overland route to Florence.
6. The Albergo del Pellegrino – it dated from about 1500.

117

Sold at Florence where his Lordship Died.[1] They were purchased by a Gentleman of Bologna and Given to this Museum adding greatly to their former Collection of Specimens of Marble, Agate, Petrefactions[2] & Models of Ships &c. &c. but what Interested me most was the Anatomy of the Human Body, displayed in Three different points of View; First the whole Human Figure with Only the Skin taken off – Secondly the whole Figure with Every Part laid Open, Thirdly the whole Figure with Only the Bones – afterwards Every Part was Separate, The Heads were Cleft in Twain & others Cut on Cross. The Tongue, The Brains The Ears, The Eyes were all displayed Separately in Wax, and done by a Woman, who Excells[3] So greatly in the Art that Each part appears Living Flesh

In another Apartment,

118

For the Study of Acoucheurs,[4] the Child Appeared as it lies in the Womb most wonderful to behold – when most favorable to the mother, The Legs are folded across Each Other, The Hands are Over Each Eye, and the Childs Hea[d] is downward.

In more unfortunate Situations for the mother was likewise displayed in wax the different Attitudes that the Child Sometimes is in and all from Nature.

This noble and useful Institute was Founded by Marsigli[5] & Supported by Pope Benedict the 14th. who Left his whole Fortune with his Library &c for that purpose –[6]

1. George Clavering Cowper, 3rd Earl Cowper (1738–89), English peer who adopted Florence as his home – see G. Dragoni – Vicende dimenticate del mecenatismo Bolognese dell'ultimo '700: l'acquisto della collezione di strumentazioni scientifiche di Lord Cowper. Il Carobbio, 11, 1985, pp68–85.
2. Murray does not give this spelling.
3. Murray allows excell.
4. Murray does not give this spelling.
5. Count Luigi Ferdinando Marsili (1658–1730), scholar and natural scientist. He left his collections to the Istituto delle Scienze which he founded in 1711 and which is now part of the University of Bologna.
6. Benedict XIV (Prospero Lambertini) (reigned 1740–58).

The next Place we Visited was the Theatre a very Handsome Building.[1] The Boxes were Five Ranges in Height, Four of which had Stone Ballustrade[2] Fronts. The center Boxes were for the Pope's Legate[3]

119

Upon Stamping the Foot, or Speaking Loud in the Pit, The Echo and the Reverberation of the Sound was Astonishing –

We Saw afterwards the Asinelli Tower, which Leans three feet & a Half our of a Perpendicular,[4] and from thence ᵂᵉ Visited Churches & Palaces And went to the Arcade of Three Mile in Length leading to the Convent of Sᵗ. Roc,[5] And Walked to Saint Michel in Bosco to See the View of the City;[6] From Ten o Clock this morning till Five in the Afternoon we were walking about And Among the Various Palaces We Visited I think the Caprara best worth Seeing.[7] The Gallery being adorned with Turkish Spoils Given to the Marechal de Caprara at the Raising of the Siege of Vienna –[8] We observed that all the Churches at Bologna had only Brick Floors tho =Marble in great profusion upon their Altars –

120

The Theatre at Bologna had not been Opened for Exhibitions Since the present war with France being now more than 2 years.

---

1. The Teatro Comunale erected to the designs of Antonio Bibiena and opened in 1763. It still exists but with subsequent alterations.
2. Murray gives *balluster*.
3. Bologna was of course part of the Papal States at this time.
4. The Torre degli Asinelli dates to 1109–19 and leans slightly out of the perpendicular.
5. San Rocco – the Oratorio decorated by Bolognese artists still exists.
6. The ex-monastero di San Michele in Bosco on an ascent to the south of the city, and from which there is a fine view. Part of the complex is now a hospital.
7. The Palazzo Caprara – completed in 1603 to the designs of Francesco Morandi detto Terribilia but much altered later. It now houses the Prefettura di Bologna.
8. This was the second great siege of Vienna of 1683. Count Aeneas Sylvius di Caprara (1631–1701) was a field marshall in the service of the Holy Roman Empire and served in Hungary and elsewhere.

Thursday Oct^{br} 24th.

Left Bologna at half past Six & with Six Horses & Three Postillions went for Ten miles at the foot of Sandy mountains thinly Scatter'd over with Trees; & consequently having a very Barren Appearance – the next Post we began to Ascend very high & Rocky mountains which Continued Ten miles farther to Loiano which is reckon'd the Highest part of the Appenines[1] – And Here, nothing is in View but High Barren Rocks with Beds for Torrents Lying between them. Our Third Post was rather descend^g tho' Occasionally Rising to Small Eminences, with Groves of Chesnut Trees in Some Places on Each Side.

121

The Fourth Post brought us to Cubillario a Single House Situated in the midst of High Craggy mountains And it being the Close of the Day when we Arrived it was thought Advisable to Stay the Night, tho' the Accomodations were Bad, the Floors of Brick, the Rooms very Small with Two Beds in Each And no Curtains – and the Bread very Black – but as we had Allways[2] provided Ourselves with Bread, Cold Chicken & Grapes on the Days we took long Journeys that we might Dine in the Coach Or at Some Post House while Horses were Changing, It now happened that we had Some Bread left which with Our Tea & Some milk gave us a good Supper – tho' the Boiling Water was brought us in a Brown Earthen Pipkin, & the Warming Pan for the Beds was only Iron Barrs over wood Embers

122

Laid into an Earthen Dish with a very Dirty female to wait upon us but Our own Sheets was our Comfort.[3]

At Trent we had first found Brick Floors & Italian Dirt which continued at Verona, Vicenza & throughout Except at Padua where

---

1. Loiano – town in the province of Bologna now on the SS 65 and 73 kilometres from Florence.
2. Murray gives alternatives but not this one.
3. Cubillario – though Mrs Bentham found the accommodation bad, it was a popular stopping place between Bologna and Florence at this time.

the Floors were a Composition And the Inn by far the Cleanest we had Seen in Italy –

Friday Oct[br]. 25th
Left Our wretched Inn at Cubillario at Eight o Clock & went one Post & Half to Maschere,[1] where we Stopt to look at the House we Ought to have reached last Night, It being the Only tolerable Sleeping Place between Bologna and Florence; The Situation delightful, The Apartments decent & The People obliging – From Hence to Florence the Country is pleasant – and Planted with Vines – Chestnuts & Olive Trees – & the View of the City on approaching is Beautiful.

123

We Arrived at Florence[2] at 4 o Clock & went to the Hotel kept by Meggit, where we got a very good Apartment from which we had a View of the River Arno; but we had 72 Steps to Ascend to it.[3] The Apartment under Ours being Engaged by M[r]. Douglass formerly of Deal,[4] & his wife the widow of the late D[r]. Bonver of Kent,[5] And the Ground Floor was Engaged by M[r]. Berkley an English Gent[m] –[6]

This Eveng we had the Satisfaction to Receive Letters from Cha[s]. dated Brussells Oct[br] 3[d]. & likewise English Newspapers from Our Banker at London

Here we first found Nets put Over the Beds, And Curtains which we had not Seen Since Leaving Munich

Saturday Oct[br] 26[th.]
Walked before Breakfast to the Palace[7] belonging to the Grand

---

1. Le Maschere – the nearby villa is now a luxury hotel.
2. Florence – capital of what was still at that time the Grand Duchy of Tuscany.
3. Meggit's Hotel – a popular destination for British travellers at the time. It was run by an Englishman called Megit who was formerly a servant of Lord Maynard.
4. Deal – seaside town in Kent between Dover and Ramsgate.
5. Dr Bonver – not traced.
6. Nothing further is known of Mr & Mrs Douglass – see Ingamells' *Dictionary* . . . Similarly for Mr Berkley.
7. From the distance given, presumably the Villa di Poggio Imperiale.

124

Duke[1] One mile from the Town After which we passed through the Gardens belonging to the Boboli[2] At Noon went to the Academy of painting & Sculpture[3] & from thence to the Cathedral, the Campanile, the Baptistere,[4] the Lorenzo and Several Churches –[5]

Sunday Oct[br]. 27th
Went to the Palace of the Marquis de Ricardi, all the Floors were of Brick tho' the House Esteemed the best in Florence[6] We likewise went to See Pisani' manufactory of Alabaster,[7] in which were many Beautiful Vases – and Figures, Tripods &c &c. Ornamental Lamps, Ink Stands, & Plateau' for Tables &c – besides which a Sleeping Venus most Elegant in the Attitude & the Clearness & whiteness of the Alabaster which is highly Polished – from hence we Rode to the Cachino, which is a Tract of Ground adjoining the Gates[8]

125

Of the City, And being Planted forms a Circular Ride of Two miles, & In the middle of the Plantation is an Auberge or Inn Erected at the Expence of the Grand Duke where a Dinner may be had, & for that purpose is much frequented by the Tradesmen of Florence.

1. The reigning prince at the time was Ferdinand III (1769–1801) of the house of Habsburg-Lorraine. He ruled from 1790–1801 and again from 1814–24 after the Napoleonic interregnum.
2. The Boboli Gardens behind the Pitti Palace. They were laid out in the mid sixteenth century to designs by Tribolo and Buontalenti. Mrs Bentham is presumably referring to the Villa del Poggio Imperiale. It was originally a Medici villa and had been redesigned by Gaspare Paoletti in 1776.
3. Presumably the Galleria dell'Accademia founded in 1764 by Grand-duke Pietro Leopoldo. It benefited from being the depository for works of art from suppressed religious institutions and now, of course, holds Michelangelo's David and much else.
4. The Duomo, Campanile di Giotto and Battistero di Dante.
5. The church of San Lorenzo. The original church dated to the late fourth century but the present building was designed by Brunelleschi and erected from 1419 onwards.
6. Presumably the Palazzo Riccardi-Medici originally built by Michelozzo in the mid fifteenth century for Cosimo il Vecchio.
7. Fratelli Pisani – manufacturers in alabaster and marble. They are mentioned in numerous travellers' diaries, correspondence, etc and survived into the nineteenth century.
8. The Cascine – extensive gardens laid out along the bank of the Arno. It is now a public park.

We Saw many persons Riding & Others walking & Several Women making the Leghorn Hats as they Walked, in the Same manner as the English female Peasantry often go about Knitting. In the woods were a great number of Pheasants running about. And the River being the Boundary on One Side makes this Place Extremely pleasant

In the Afternoon we went to the Gardens belonging to the Boboli Palace & the Opera —[1] The Streets are all Paved with Broad Flag Stones & yet the Horses are drove with great Safety — & Florence is Certainly much Cleaner than any other City in Italy —

126

The Laquais de Place Pietro Puzzolini, whom we Hired at this Place, we found So very Intelligent that we thought it advisable to take him with us to Rome & Naples, Especially As He understood perfectly French as well as Italian & a little English, having Lived fifteen Years with Our English minister here; and had been Sent by him Twice to England on Business, & had last year been at Rome with Sir Corbet Corbet;[2] we therefore Consulted with Meggit, & likewise our Banker, who Engaged Him to go with us at Six Sequins a month to be As Courier, & Valet de Place, Jacquiae continuing to go with the Coach & to Dress M[r]. A.

Monday Oct[br]. 28th
Went to the Palace Pitti and Afterw[ds] to the Gallery; before Dinner walked over the Boboli Gardens for between the Hours of One & Three Neither Churches, Palaces nor any Publick Buildings are to be Seen in Florence, these Hours being allotted for Dinner —

127

On One Side of the Gallery we Entered the Tribune where we Saw the Celebrated Venus de Medicis & the Little Apollo = Several

---

1. Presumably the Teatro all Pergola originally constructed in 1656.
2. Sir (Andrew) Corbet Corbet (1752–1823). Whilst in Rome he was painted by both Robert Fagan and Charles Grignion. Only the Fagan is known to still exist.

beautiful Pictures of Gerrard Dou' & Meris's both favorite Painters of mine –[1]

In the Palace Pitti we observed the Beautiful Inlaid marble tables representing Shells as lying about[2] but all the Floors were Square Red Tiles and the windows double Sashed.

Tuesday Oct[br]. 29th

Left Meggits Hotel at Florence this morning for the first Post, the Hills Rise in Beautiful Forms & Shapes; but they are cheifly covered with Olive Trees which are of a Wintry Green like a Willow, & gives a barren Appearance – The Second Post was amidst High Rocks, with Houses or castles upon many of their Summits And Beds of Stony Rock between made by the Torrents of water which comes down these Precepices[3] in Winter = The Third & fourth Post

128

Which carried us to <u>Sienna</u>[4] was a more pleasing Country, the Road going through Some Plantations of Oak, and between Lands that were Cultivated – At Sun Set we Arrived at Sienna & went to the Hôtel D'Angleterre a tolerable good Inn in a Narrow Street.[5] The Town is Old, Stands upon a Hill at the Edge of a mountainous Barren Country

We observed the women of this Country had the Sleeves of their Gowns Allways tyed upon the Shoulders with different Coloured

---

1. The Tribuna of the Uffizi. The contents of the room changed over time but these are recorded in the catalogue of the *Mostra storica della Tribuna degli Uffizi*, 1970. The Medici Venus was acquired by Ferdinando I. It is an ancient work but its origins are unknown before the sixteenth century. Like the Venus, the Apollino was transferred from the Villa Medici in Rome and has always remained in the room. Gerrit Dou (1613–75) was popular in his own lifetime and remained so in the following century. The works by Frans van Mieris (1633–81) were acquired in the artist's own lifetime.
2. These are tables with shells in intarsia on a lapislazuli ground. The first was made in 1760 to a design by Giuseppe Zocchi and the following year it was sent to Vienna as a gift. In 1766 the grand-duke commissioned two further copies, those seen by Mrs Bentham. These were "stolen" by the French in 1799. One is now in the collection of the Musée du Louvre and the other is in the Hermitage in St. Petersburg – see *Splendori di pietre dure*, Florence, 1988, catalogue no.82.
3. Murray does not give this spelling.
4. Siena, the second city of Tuscany and south-west of Florence.
5. Mariana Starke gives it as the Hôtel des Armes d'Angleterre.

Ribbands, as when the Weather is Hot they wear only Shift
Sleeves –

Wednesday Oct[br] 30th
Left Sienna at 7 in the morning and went Over a Barren Country of
Sand Hills and Rocks to Radicofani[1] which is Situated upon a very
<u>High</u> mountain and at the Top is the Ruin of an Old Fortress,[2] a
Shabby dirty wretched Set of Houses form a Small Town under the
Fortress & below is the Inn, lately Built by the Grand Duke for the
Reception of Travellers,[3] It being the last Place in his Dominions
on this Side of Florence = It was a Large House

129

In Form like a long Barn & the upper Rooms divided by a Gallery;
but Only white walls, Beds without Curtains And Cold & uncomfortable but Cleaner than many we had Slept in – a Large Glass
in Shape like that we Call a Tumbler, & covered like a Flask with
Straw having a Lid or Cover to it was placed by the Sides of the
Beds for use at Night –

NB this Day a white Frost in the [morng] was Succeeded by a Thick
damp Fog till Noon.

Thursday Oct[br] 31st.
Left Our Inn at Radicofani at 7 in the morning and descending
from this very High mountain, in Six miles Crossed over the River
P[4] which Separates the Grand Dukes Dominions from the Popes'[5]
– And went through a Dirty Town Called Aqua-pendente. [6] The
Situation High and Romantic = Here Vineyards were again to be
Seen and Cultivated Land – from Hence we passed through the
Little New Town of S[t.] Lorenzo[7]

---

1. Radicofani – hill-town in southern Tuscany
2. La Rocca – it originally dates to the thirteenth century but was restored in 1565 and
   again in the late twentieth century.
3. Palazzo La Posta – it started life as a Medicean hunting lodge but later became a hos-
   tel cum customs house between Tuscany and the Papal States.
4. A space is left here for the remainder of the word. Presumably the river Paglia.
5. At the time the Grand Duchy of Tuscany and the Papal States.
6. Acquapendente – agricultural town in northern Lazio.
7. San Lorenzo Nuovo in Lazio.

130

Built upon a Hill in the Form of a Circus, and from Hence we descended through a fine Hanging wood of Oaks to Bolsena a little Town upon the Edge of a Beautiful Lake Thirty miles in Circumference, Surrounded by Woods –[1] One Post more brought us to Montefiascon a wretched Town[2] but at distance a fine Object as it Covered Entirely the Top of a Circular mountain, from which we descended into a Plain & went to Viterbo[3] a small Town where we Staid the Night & found (for Italy) good Accomodations at Albergo Reale[4]

Friday Nov^{br} 1st.
Left Viterbo in the morning & Went 44 miles to Rome which appear'd to be Situated in a Desart =[5] the Country being on One Side quite flat and resembling a dreary Heath – upon Entering Rome we immediately went to Albergo Carlando in Place D'Espagne And had a very good Apartment, consisting of a Dining Room & Two Chambers ad=joining – but a very Dirty Stone Stair Case like Every other House in Italy –[6]

131

After passing the first Post from Viterbo we had Entered a Wood at the Top of a Hill, where Four Soldiers Attended to Guard Travellers through the Wood, & till they descended into the Plain & Open Country, which Continued from Hence to the Gates of Rome[7]

The Sheep feeding on the Heath which leads to Rome were all of a dark Brown Colour with Black faces and Feet; The Lambs were Entirely Black= Instead of Hurdles, the Shepherds Here made use

---

1. Bolsena – town on the eponymous lake on the via Cassia between Viterbo and Rome.
2. Montefiascone – town on the via Cassia close to the southern tip of Lake Bolsena.
3. Viterbo – mediaeval town on the via Cassia north of Rome.
4. Albergo Reale – a notable hotel at the time, chiefly one presumes for passing travellers.
5. Murray gives this spelling.
6. Albergo Carlando – not traced.
7. The Campagna di Roma was the resort of outlaws or brigands up until the nineteenth century.

of Net work to Pen them in their Folds at Night upon the Fallow
Ground =

The Pigs in this Country were in General Black; whereas at Bologna
they were all a deep Red or Reddish Brown like the Colour we Call
Auburn The Shepherds in the Fields had Sheep Skin over their
Coats

This Day the Atmosphere was thick & Hazy & very Damp – In the
Afternoon missling Rain –[1]

At Rome we paid Half a Crown Each Day for a Fire & 3[d.] for one
Egg –

132

       Saturday Nov[br.] 2[d] –
We Went after breakfast to M[r.] Jenkins Our Banker,[2] & afterw[ds] to
See Lodgings at Margeritta' but They were Engaged=[3] We then
went to Saint Peters, The Vatican, & the Castle of S[t] Angelo –
from thence to Mont Janiculus to See the best View of the City;[4]
afterw[ds] to the Capitol, & Coloseum; Observed Arch of Severus,[5]
And Another of Vespasian, under which the Jews will never Pass –[6]
observed the 3 Arches remaining of the Temple de Paix[7] – The
Tarpeian Rock, the Senators House &c Drove through the Corso
& Saw the most Celebrated Fountains & went to the Gardens de
Medici & the Convent adjoining upon Trinité de monté Called le
Couvent de Minnimes near the Place d Espagne –[8]

1. Misling rain – to rain in very fine drops.
2. Thomas Jenkins (1722–98), painter and art dealer. Becoming very successful, Jenkins
   also acted as a banker to British and other foreign residents in Rome.
3. Margeritta's Hotel – not traced.
4. The Janiculum Hill on the western side of the river. It is still the haunt of view-
   seeking tourists and the Romans themselves.
5. The Arch of Septimius Severus dating to AD 203.
6. The Arch of Titus erected by Domitian to record the victories of Vespasian and Titus
   over the Jews and the destruction of Jerusalem.
7. The Basilica of Maxentius begun by him in 308 but completed by the Emperor
   Constantine.
8. The church of Trinità dei Monti at the summit of the Spanish Steps. It has traditionally been a French institution and has had an attached convent since 1502. The sisters
   conduct a school for French-speaking residents.

I was much disappointed in Seeing Rome = The Streets are narrow, Dirty And Filthy – Even the Palaces are a mixture of Dirt & Finery, & intermixed with wretched mean Houses. The Largest Open Places in Rome are used for

133

The Sale of Vegetables &c &c The Fountains are the Only Singular Beauties belonging to the City as a Coup d'oeil.

The Churches are magnificent within – but Saint Peters is likewise So without, nothing can Exceed the Effect it must have on Every Beholder. The Approach to it, The Profusion of marble in it, and the tout Ensemble Are beyond any thing I could beleive but, Excepting the magnificence of its Palaces & Churches, and the beauty of its Fountains, Rome has nothing within, nor without its walls to make it desirable for an English person to be an Inhabitant –

Near the Arch of Vespasian I Saw a Man with his Face Cover'd Over with a white Cloth, leaving Only Two Holes for his Eyes & he Stood in a Supplicating Posture; upon Enquiring I learnt that He was a Beggar who wished not to be known –

At Rome the Wine des pays is Called Orvietto. It is a white wine, & most pleasant Beverage.[1]

134

Sunday Nov^{br} 3^d.

The Object of Our Journey being to get to Naples As Soon as possible We left Rome at Ten in the morn'g And went 25 miles to Veletri[2] where we Staid the Night at a Very bad Inn, being obliged to eat in the Room where part of our Family Slept – Brick Floors – Beds without Curtains Dirt & nastiness, & obliged to Pay Equal to Half a Guinea Each Person for Bed & Supper – (this I Suppose is

1. The white wine from the surroundings of Orvieto, a hill town in Lazio to the north of Rome.
2. Velletri – town on the road to Naples immediately south of the Alban Hills.

the Advantage of Travelling with a Courier & an English Travelling Coach.[)]

Here we had the Gensano wine which is thought the Best on this Side of Rome = Gensano is a little Town between Albano & Veletri & the Vineyards in this Neighborhood produce a peculiar Grape=[1]

Reeds are much Cultivated in this Country they are used to Tye the Vines – And the Leaves are made use of instead of Straw to be put into the mattresses that are put nearest the Bedstead.

135

Monday Nov[br]. 4th.
Left Veletri at the break of day that we [might] not be Obliged to Sleep at the Edge of the Pontine Marshes[2] for Terracino[3] is deemed Very Unhealthy during the Summer, And the Inn at this Time of the year had not been long Open for Travellers = Upon Entring[4] the Pontine Marshes we Saw the Sun Rise – It is at the Bottom of the Hill upon which the Town of Veletri Stands that these Marshes Commence, And the Crossing them to Terracino is 24 Miles = The first part is Cultivated land, having been drained At the Expence of the present Pope Pius the Sixth=[5] The middle part is Cheifly Grass or Turf Lying under water – The latter part is Cheifly Reeds And the Road throughout Good – These Marshes are bounded on One Side by the Appenines by the Other a Forest

At Terracino The Ocean is in front And the Road turns round

---

1. A notable white wine is produced in the locality of Genzano di Roma.
2. The Pontine marshes – the low-lying area in southern Lazio bordering the coast. It was unhealthy due to the prevalence of mosquitoes though the insects were not connected to malaria at the time. Though many popes promoted drainage projects over the centuries it was a major project undertaken by Mussolini in the 1930s which really had a lasting effect on the area.
3. Terracina – port on the coast between Rome and Naples. It was within the Papal States at the time. – now the province of Lazio.
4. Murray gives "entri" as an alternative to enter.
5. Pope Pius VI (Braschi) (1717–99). His attempt to drain the marshes was largely unsuccessful.

the foot of the Appenines, & within a little Distance Enters the Neapolitan Dominions

136

152 miles from Naples; and here the mile Stones from Rome Ended at 68. At the beginning of the Neapolitan Dominions the Country immediately Changes its Appearance & you perceive Another Climate, Myrtle Hedges – Aloes – Fig Trees. Groves of Oranges & Lemons loaded with Fruit & thro' a most Beautiful Country the Road leads to Mola di Gaèta [*sic*] where we Staid the Night – at a very Comfortable Inn for this Country. The Beds had Curtains – The Floors tho' of Brick tolerably Clean & the Supper well Served; The Inn delightfully Situated being upon the Quay with the Sea dashing its Waves under Our Windows, The View Picturesque, The Town & Citadel forming One Point of the Bay – Since leaving England I had Seen nothing so pleasing & I Could have wished to have Stopt –

Tuesday Nov^{er}. 5th.
Left Mola di Gaeta[1] very Early and went 48 Miles to Naples, & immediately

137

Went to the Ville de Londres,[2] where we got an Apartment of Seven Rooms, Two Sitting Rooms & Two Bed Rooms containing Seven Windows looking upon the Bay. A very Large Room of Entrance Where Our Servant attended and Two Servants Bed Rooms with a Powdering & dressing Room – for which we were to Pay <u>Five</u> Ducats p. Day viz Eighteen Shillings And Nine Pence English, as Each Ducat was Equal to ten Carlini's a Carlini being four-pence halfpenny a Ducat reckon'd as three Shilling & Nine pence = Fire being Necessary, we Agreed for wood at Two Shilling p. day – and a Woman to Sweep the Rooms at two Carlini's a day –

---

1. Gaetà – fortified port town on the coast between Terracina and Naples. Although it lies in modern-day Lazio, the town was at the time part of the Kingdom of the Two Sicilies.
2. Ville de Londres – a notable hotel at the time.

Throughout Our Journey we found the Charges very High. The Apartments at the Inns were allways Charged as a Separate Article often Equal to a Guinea p. Night Our Dinners Five Shilling English – & between Rome and Naples a Sequin Each person which is Equal to Ten Shillings for Supper & Bed

138

tho' we never could get a Room to eat in, Separate from that we Slept in –

Nov^{br}. 6th. Wednesday
Being much fatigued with Travelling I only walked one Hour during the Day And the Coach took me for that purpose to the Villa Reale –[1]

Mr. Mackinnon Our Banker Came to Dinner with us;[2] And we found he had been Acquainted with Our Friends M^{rs}. Allen & Miss Palmer when They were at Naples –[3]

Thursday Novr 7th.
The morning Rainy, Violent Thunder and Lightning during the Night – At Two o Clock I Rode with my Dear Invalid round by the Publick Walks Called Villa Reale= We Stopt to See an Apartment at the Ville de Paris but it was to[sic] Small to be Comfortable – we likewise Visited the Crocelle but the only Apartment Vacant was at the Top of the House the Third Story, & tho' very handsomely Furnished & Extremely pleasant it was too High for an Invalid to be Carried –[4]

139

This Afternoon a very Extraordinary Procession passed before the Window of Our Inn. First one Man walked Dressed in white, with his Head & Face Covered with the Same Cloth leaving Only two-

1. The park now bounded by the via Caracciolo and the Chiaja. Its size is now somewhat curtailed by the widening of these roads for modern traffic. It was originally called the Villa Reale, then Villa Nazionale and finally becoming Villa Comunale.
2. Alexander Mackinnon – see Ingamells' *Dictionary* . . .
3. The only mention of this couple being in Italy according to Ingamells.
4. La Ville de Paris, and Le Crocelle – hotels in Naples at the time.

Holes for his Eyes, He Carried a Crucifix, & 18 other men followed
Him walking Two & Two each Dressed Exactly the Same as the
first. Then Came Twelve men in Blue Mantles with their Faces
uncovered & bare-headed walking Two & Two = then followed
Twelve men Dressed in Black like Priests walking Two & Two
with Wax Lights in their hands & Singing immediately after Came
a <u>real</u> Female Corpse Lying upon the Lid of a Coffin which was
Covered with Crimson Velvet. Her Head was adorned with a Large
Bunch of Flowers & another Bouquet lay at her Feet, Her Face &
Hands quite uncover'd. She was Dressed in a Black Silk Gown as
if Living, and the Top of the Coffin upon which the Corpse Lay
was put upon a very Rich Crimson Velvet Pall trimmed with Gold
& it flowed over the

140

mens Shoulders who were carrying the Corpse – a Plain Wooden
Coffin was carried close to follow the Procession which after going
through Some Streets Returned Singing & Chanting – nor did this
Extraordinary Sight to us appear to make any Bustle or draw any
numbers together in the Streets through which it passed –[1]

Friday Nov.[r] 8.th
I took a Walk for an Hour before breakfast upon the Pavement in
Front of the Palace where the King of Naples Resides when he
is in the City[2] It is a magnificent Building and Incloses a Large
Square or Quadrangle in which is a Large Chapel with Apartm[ts]
&c Suitable for the Residence of Royalty[3]

At Noon we Rode in a very Handsome Glass Coach which was
Hired during our Stay Here & our dear Invalid

Seemed better & we went to Portici[4] – & upon Our Return went

1. Presumably members of a confraternity.
2. Ferdinand IV, reigned 1759–99, of the House of Bourbon.
3. The Palazzo Reale adjacent to the port. It was erected in the early seventeenth century to designs by Domenico Fontana. The chapel was erected from 1660–68 to designs
   by Cosimo Fanzago. The building was damaged in WWII.
4. Portici – town on the bay of Naples immediately to the south of the city itself. It
   was the site of one of the royal palaces now housing the faculty of agriculture of the
   university.

Shopping in the Prado Toledo, [1]to Buy Black Buckles &c as it was
Expected that the English as well as Neapolitans would

141

Wear mourning upon the melancholy Event that had taken place at
Paris respect[g] the Queen of France who had been Guillotined –[2]

Saturday Nov. 9th.
Our Dear Invalid very Weak and dejected, however She went in
the Carriage at Noon & We drove through the Cavern [and Soon Came] to
the Sea Side, on the Road towards Puzzuoli = [3] The Road through
the Cavern is Paved at the Bottom, & at the Entrance you may perceive a Small Light at the End; tho' the Horses upon full Trot are
Five minutes in going through this High Rock[4]

Sunday Nov[br]. 10th.
D[r]. Nudy came by Appointment to See Our dear Invalid who was
Extremely Weak & her Spirits much affected –[5] He proposed that
She Should no longer take Laudunum[6] but a Mixture less powerful
& Ordered Asses Milk Twice a day, and Expressed his Hopes that
She would Soon be able to Ride upon an Ass which He thought an
Animal most Easy in its Pace at the Same time he Said that tho' the
Sea Air in England might agree with her

142

Yet the Climate Here was so different that He doubted whether it
might not be necessary to go more Inland –

---

1. The Via Toledo – now officially the via Roma but the original name is still used
   locally.
2. Marie Antoinette, consort of Louis XVI was guillotined on 1th October 1793.
3. Pozzuoli – town on the northern shore of the bay of Naples notable for its ancient
   remains and proximity to the sites of volcanic interest.
4. Mrs Bentham has added the following in the margin here – Pausilipo a Cavern
   In Length 2316 Feet In Breadth 22 Feet In Height 89 Feet. This is the Grotto of
   Posillipo cut by the Romans to connect Naples with Pozzuoli.
5. Dr Nudy – a Neapolitan physician – he is mentioned in other sources.
6. Laudanum – a tincture of opium. It could be obtained without a prescription and was
   widely used for many ailments.

At Noon we Rode along the Chiaia[1] by the Sea Side & afterw^ds towards Portici –

From Naples to Portici are Houses almost All the way & the Road thronged with different kind of Carriage going from One of those Places to the other the distance being Only Five miles, & the Road Side abounding in Country Houses, but the Road being paved the Noise is very great & appears like one Continued Street –

Monday Nov^br. 11th
The wind Extremely High & frequent Storms of Rain; at Noon we Rode through the Grotto towards Puzzuoli Our dear Invalid took an Emetic this morning but it had <u>no Effect</u> – Went this morning to Lady Spencer[2] who wished to part with the Apartment She Inhabited & which was Extremely pleasant being Situated Exactly opposite the Villa Reale; but it was too Small

143

Tuesday Nov^br. 12th
Our dear Invalid Only Rode One Hour Along the Chiaia = D^r. Nudy Dined with us And Assured us that He really beleived Our dear Invalid would Recover. As her Lungs were certainly not Hurt And He Should alter her Diet Entirely but it Still remained doubtful whether the Air of Rome might not be better for her, as Prince Augustus with a Similar Complaint had found more Benefit from the winter He Spent He Spent[*sic*] at Rome, than He did from the winter He Spent at Naples.[3]

My dear Farr Went in the Even'g to Sir William Hamilton' And D^r. Nudy Accompanied him[4]

---

1. The fashionable promenade to the west of the Castel dell'Ovo.
2. Margaret Georgiana, Viscountess Spencer (1737–1814).
3. Prince Augustus Frederick (1773–1843), 6th son of George III. He spent some time in Italy due to his being asthmatic.
4. The notable Sir William Hamilton (1730–1803), diplomat and antiquarian.

Wed Nov^br. 13th.

D^r. Nudy Came both morning & Evening to Attend Our dear Invalid, & Ordered her to Dine at One o Clock, on Soup Fish And Vegetables; but not meat, chicken or wine were to be Tasted = She was to Breakfast at Ten on Bread and milk with a little Souchong Tea[1] – & At Five Asses milk – which She was likewise to have at Eight Every morn^g. & a composing

144

Draught at Night going to Bed = This Day at Noon I Rode with her along the Chiaia, And while She Sat in the Coach to Breathe Sea Air, I walked upon the Pavement within Sight; And in the Evening we repeated the Ride while my dear Farr made a Visit to Lady Spencer –

Thursday Nov^br. 14th

Rode with Our dear Invalid both morning & Afternoon along the Chiaja, & in the intermediate time while She Dined I walked in the Villa Reale during which I observed a Procession going with a Corpse Exposed to View much in the Same manner as that we Saw the Day after we came to Naples.

Friday Nov^br. 15th.

Rode with Our dear Invalid to Pausilipo[2] & while She Sat in the Carriage for an Hour by the Sea-Side, I walked to & fro within her view – D^r. Nudy Dined with us & in the Evening M^r & M^rs. Mackinnon Came to drink Tea & with D^r. Nudy' Advice an Agreement was written

145

For the Apartment to be Occupied by us for Three Months Certain Viz from Novr. 5th to Feb. 5th = which being Advised by D^r. Nudy gave us great hopes that He had no doubt but that Our dear Invalid would Recover; Especially as he proposed at the Same time that we

---

1. Presumably the black China tea.
2. Posillipo – then a town on the northern shore of the bay of Naples but now part of the greater Naples.

Should take her ⁱⁿ the Summer months to Sorrentum – 18 miles from Naples –[1]

We Received to day Cards from Lord Grandison & his Daughter, Lady Gertrude Villiers & Miss Musgrave who was with Lady Gertrude[2] – L'Eveque de Winchester, & Mrs North[3]- The Earl & Countess of Besborough,[4] M^r & M^{rs}. Pinnock;[5] And in the Even'g Sir William & Lady Hamilton Came & Staid with us more than an Hour –[6]

Saturday Nov^{br}. 16th
A Clear Blue Sky with a very Hot Sun the Thermometer in the Shade 70 – We Sat in a large Room Our Windows Open to the Bay. Lady Hamilton with her mother M^{rs}. Cadogan[7] Came & most kindly offered Every Civility in

146

their power; after They left us we Rode as usual to Pausilipo – & I walked Afterw^{ds} in the Villa Reale, Received Letters from Cha' dated Dover Octr. 14th. which gave us the inexpressible Satisfactⁿ. of knowing that He was Safe arrived in England –

Sunday Nov^{br}. 17th
Rode as usual with Our dear Invalid to Pausilipo both morning & Afternoon but She appeared very Languid & weak. Dr. Nudy & M^r. & M^{rs}. Mackinnon Came to Dinner – & in the Eveng my dear Farr made a Visit to M^r. Penton the Member for Winchester who

1. Sorrento – then a village on the northern shore of the eponymous peninsular and close to Capri.
2. George Mason-Villiers (1751–1800), 2nd Earl Grandison. Miss Musgrave was a companion to Grandison's daughter Lady Gertrude Villiers and is described as a painter elsewhere – see Ingamells.
3. This was the Hon. Brownlow North (1741–1820), brother of Lord North, the Prime Minister. Mrs Bentham is perhaps being facetious because the Norths' reputation went before them – see Ingamells.
4. Frederick Ponsonby Duncannon (1758–1844), 3rd Earl of Bessborough. He married Henrietta Frances Spencer (1761–1821)
5. James Pinnock (1740–1811), a Jamaican barrister. He married Elizabeth Dehany.
6. Lady Hamilton – then, of course, the notorious Emma Hamilton (1765–1815). The couple had married in 1791.
7. Mrs Mary Cadogan (d.1810). It was not her real name.

Lodged in the Same Hotel with us – & at this time was Confined with the Gout to his Apartment –[1]

Monday Nov^br. 18th.
D^r. Nudy came this morning & persuaded us to Buy matting & Cover the whole floor of the Sitting Room; which we might remove in the Summer to Portici or Sorrentum One of which Places He Should recommend to us –[2]

147

Tuesday Nov^br. 19
D^r. Nudy Ordered Our dear Invalid to take Asses milk Three times a Day, as She had more Fever it must be her chief Nourishment. This Day we had a Strong Siroc wind and I found my Legs Tremble and was not well.[3] M^r. Clark the Antiquarian came to Visit us[4] – & my dear Farr went in the Evening to Visit M^r. Douglass.

Wed Nov^br. 20.
M^r. Douglass being greatly distressed to get lodgings near the Bay; and Our dear Invalid appearing very Weak my dear Farr desired D^r. Nudy to be Explicit and if He thought the Air of Naples did not agree, we would offer Our Lodgings to M^r. Douglass And Remove immediately: Upon which D^r. Nudy Reply'd, I Say <u>Stay</u> At Noon we Rode as usual to Pausilipo, & afterw^ds I took a melancholy Walk Tout Seul –[5] Viewing the Beautiful bay which is Said to be Thirty miles in Circumference And Eighteen in Diameter –

1. Henry Penton (1736–1812), MP.
2. Sorrento.
3. Sirocco – a hot wind from north Africa.
4. James Clark (c.1745–1800), painter and antiquary. He worked mainly in Naples where he died.
5. Tout seul – alone – properly toute seule for the feminine.

148

Thursday Nov[br]. 21st.
My dear Farr went Early this morning with M[r]. Clark the Cicirone[1]
to Pompeia[2] and Returned to a late Dinner. I attended Our dear
Invalid in a Ride towards Portici; In y[e] Evening D[r]. Nudy took Tea
with us & Observing the Extreme weakness of our dear Invalid
Ordered some wine to be mixed with Egg, & desired she might
have any thing she Liked for that He would no longer persist in a
Milk Diet –

Friday Nov[br]. 22[d]
We Rode with our dear Invalid as usual, and afterwards I took
My walk in the Villa Reale= D[r]. Nudy Dined with us. And in
the Evening my dear Farr went to Sir William Hamilton' & from
thence to the Academie of Musick –[3]

Saturday Nov[br]. 23[d]
I wrote to Cha', my dear Farr went with M[r]. Clark to Cumeæ[4] – at
Noon gave our dear Invalid Egg and wine

149

Which Seemed to give her Spirits and I Rode with her to the Castle
of S[t]. Elmo.[5] M[r] Clark Dined with us upon his Return from Cumæ
tho' it was very Late

Sunday Nov[br]. 24th
D[r]. Nudy came as usual both morn'g And Evening – at Noon we
Rode with Our dear Invalid again to the Castle of S[t]. Elmo – and in
the Eveng She Rode upon the Chiaja where we intermixed with an

---

1. Cicerone – Murray does not give this alternative spelling.
2. The modern excavations at the site had begun in 1748.
3. Possibly the Conservatorio di Musica in the ex-convent of San Pietro a Maiella.
4. Cumae – the first Greek colony on the Italian mainland and home of the eponymous sibyl.
5. The Castel Sant'Elmo – the fortress erected on the Vomero in the sixteenth century by Pedro di Toledo.

Extensive Range of Coaches; M^r & M^rs. Mackinnon Came to take Tea with us & in the Evening my dear Farr went to the Opera –[1]

Monday Nov^br 25th
My dear Farr went Early in the morn^g with M^r. Clark to Baiæ I attended Our dear Invalid:[2]

Tuesday Nov^br. 26th.
Received Letters from Cha' dated Oct^br. 25th: Our dear Invalid again very Low but went in the Coach & Stopt at the Door of Lady Hamilton to Return her Visit while my dear Farr attended her I walked to the Castle of St Elmo –[3]

150

And having asked permission went round the Inner Walls attended by a Soldier who kneeling upon One Knee Kissed My Hand with the greatest Submission when I gave him only Two Carlini^s for his Attendance = not prepared for Such a mark of Respect, I was Startled but the Instant He had paid his Complim^ts He flew like ^an Arrow from a Bow: within the Castle Walls I Saw the Duchesse de la Miranda who was Come to make her daily Visit to Her Husband the Duke, who was Confined here by Order of the King of Naples –[4]

Wed Nov^br 27th
My dear Farr went Early this morning to Portici with M^r. Clark to See the Museum in the Kings palace.[5] I attended our dear Invalid who was not disposed to go from her Apartment – M^r. Mackinnon Dined with us – –

---

1. Presumably the famous Teatro San Carlo begun in 1737 but there were other theatres at the time.
2. Baia – small port on the gulf of Pozzuoli opposite the latter town. It contains notable remains from antiquity.
3. Castel Sant'Elmo – it would have been a significant walk uphill at the time.
4. The title was bestowed on Francesco Caracciolo of Naples in 1664 by King Phillip IV of Spain. It passed to the female line in 1786 with Cayetana Caracciolo.
5. The discoveries from Pompeii were initially housed at Portici and only removed to Naples in 1822.

Thursday Nov^br. 28th
My dear Farr went Early this morning again with M^r. Clark to see the Lake[1] at Noon I Rode with our dear Invalid Two Hours – M^r. Douglass

151

And M^r. Clark (the Antiquarian) Dined with us – This Day Received Letters from England –

Friday Novr. 29th.
I Called upon Mrs Mackinnon ([2]who was An English a [sic] Lady, that had been married about Two years & now Settled here with her Husband M^r. Mackinnon who was Our Banker – at Noon I Rode with Our dear Invalid towards Portici while my dear Farr went with M^r. Pinnock a walking = Mr Pinnock had lately arrived with his Family from Jamaica & for the Education of his Children was at Naples –

Saturday Nov^br · 30th·
I Rode with Our dear Invalid to Pausilipo where we Staid an Hour to See the King of Naples Fishing – He was in an old Coat & Stood in the middle of a Common Fishing Boat Amidst the men who were taking the Net and pulling out the Fish, nor Could I believe it was the King till I Saw Sir W^m. Hamilton address Him And upon quitting the Boat Sir William

152

Came to Our Carriage, & told us, He had been Engaged in this Attendance for Some Hours & was glad to be released – Soon after Sir W^m. was gone, the King left the Fishing Boat & Entered A much handsomer ^Vessel which was in waiting with Several officers & one Lady Sitting in it – The King took the Center Seat And immediately the Boat was Rowed aCross the Bay, & from that Instant the Fishermen had Liberty to throw their Nets for their own Advantage whereas before, the Fish that was Caught was the

---

1. There is a space here left blank for the name of the lake. Presumably this is Lake Avernus beyond Baia.
2. The parenthesis is not closed.

Kings, & Sold by Him. My dear Farr went this morning with M[r]. Clark to see Drawings &c

Sunday Dec[br]. 1st

My dear Farr went very Early this morning with M[r]. Clark to Vesuvius –[1] I rode at Noon with our dear Invalid to Portici = M[r]. & M[rs]. Mackinnon and M[r.] Clark Dined with us, & D[r]. Nudy Came as usual

Monday Dec[br]. 2[d.]

D[r.] Stewart, the Husband of Lady Shelly[2] who was Come to Naples for his own health, and had been a Physician of

153

Eminence at Southampton, came this morning to See our dear Invalid & D[r]. Nudy had a Consultation with Him – at Noon we went to Capo di Monte a Palace belonging to the King at a distant part of the City And containing many things worth Seeing;[3] but Our dear Invalid appear'd too weak to be Sensible of any Pleasure In the Afternoon M[rs]. Cadogan Lady Hamilton' mother kindly Came to see us.

Tuesday Dec[r]. 3[d.]

I went in the morning to Sir William Hamiltons' & found Him & Lady H – at Breakfast. They received me in the kindest manner & I Showed them the Coat my dear Farr proposed to wear on being Presented at Court that Day, desiring their Opinion, as the Notice was So Short there was Scarcely time to have another – Sir W[m]. approved of it and at Noon my dear Farr was Presented by Sir William to the King of Naples with Several other English Gentlemen who after[ds] Staid to See the King Dine in Publick –

---

1. Vesuvius – the still active volcano overlooking the bay of Naples.

2. Dr John Stewart. He was married to Elizabeth, widow of Sir John Shelley.

3. The building remained a royal palace until 1946 and is now the Museo Nazionale di Capodimonte, housing the city's important collection of paintings. The massive palace was begun in 1738 and sits in a large park. It is indeed above the town but has now been overtaken by subsequent expansion.

154

Wed Decr. 4th.

Lady Hamilton with her mother M^{rs}. Cadogan made us a morning Visit, & likewise M^{rs}. Douglass = my dear Farr Visited Lord Grandison who having lately Lost his Lady in a Similar Situation was Extremely attentive to him – D^r. Nudy Dined with us – & in the Eveng my dear Farr went to Sir William Douglass' the British Consul –[1]

Thursday Decr. 5th.

Our dear Invalid So Extremely weak that She Slept upon a Couch the greatest part of the Day & was unwilling to move – my dear Farr went with M^r. Clark to See Some of the principal Churches Early in the morning & at his Return was much Alarmed at finding his best Beloved so Ill – D^r. Stewart And M^{rs}. Cadogan both Came to See us

Friday Decr. 6th.

My dear Invalid had her maid Sit up by her Bed side all Night – In the morng She thought herself better, came into the Sitting Room & Worked upon a Muslin Hankercheif ; my dear Farr attended her – And

155

And to relieve ^{my} mind from the melancholy Scene I took a Ride And went alone to Portici, walked through the Rooms of the Palace & the museum = at my Return I attended Our dear Invalid while my dear Farr walked & Endeavour'd to be Resigned

Saturday Decr. 7th.

I wrote Letters to my dear Cha' in England to Inform him of our melancholy Situation – Our dear Invalid having had a Bad Night, tho' She got up to Breakfast, and Seemed to be better; I Called upon Lady Hamiltons, & M^{rs}. Cadogan Shewed me Sir W^m'. English Apartment, which was the Suite of Rooms on the upper Floor,

---

1. Mrs Bentham is confusing her Douglases here. Sir James Douglas (d.1795) had formerly been consul in Naples in the 1780s and returned to the city.

Furnished in the English taste, & from one Room, was an Open Circular Alcove, Commanding the most Beautiful & Picturesque Prospect of the Bay[1]

Sunday Dec[r] 8[th.]

Our dear Invalid Rose at her usual Hour & was brought into the Sitting Room; but a Shortness of Breath came On, & it was with difficulty we got her back to her bed, where She remained Quiet the remainder of the Day –

156

Monday Dec[r]. 9th.

Our dear Invalid kept in Bed the whole Day; while my dear Farr attended her I took a melancholy Ride towards Puzzoli, and at my Return he walked –

Tuesday Dec[r]. 10th.

Our dear Invalid desired to get up & be carried into the Sitting Room where She remained the whole Day Reposing upon a Sofa – M[r]. Mackinnon Came in the Eveng –

Wed Dec[r]. 11th.

Our dear Invalid again desired to be brought into the Sitting Room to Breakfast – but Soon found it necessary to Return to her Bed – At Five in the Evening She told us, She was Dying, desired <u>me</u> to keep near her, & Expired at Nine: M[rs] Cadogan (Lady Hamilton' mother) very kindly Came to us immediately, & assisted in Every mournful office –

Thursday Dec[r]. 12[th.]

M[rs] Cadogan Came again this morning & Staid the Day with us – Lady Hamilton Called And in the Evening the Surgeons under the direction of D[r]. Nudy opened the Corpse

---

1. The view from Hamilton's residence, the Palazzo Sessa.

157

Friday Decr. 13th.

The Surgeons & D^r. Nudy upon Examining the Corpse were of opinion that the Complaint which had terminated so fatally with Our dearest had been coming on Some years; & probably owed its Existence to the delicacy of her Form: Lady Hamilton & M^{rs}. Cadogan both Came again we Read Letters from Cha' date Nov 15th

Saturday Decr. 14th

This morning the Corpse was put into a Wooden Coffin, & that was after^{wd} Inclosed in a Leaden One, & afterw^{ds} a wood Case like a Packing case, in which Shape it was Carried in the Evening on Board the Queen of Naples Captain Breaker, to be Conveyed to England=^{1} M^r. Clark & Another Gentleman went to See it Safe on Board, & Our Courier attended the Corpse to England, where by Letters we Read from Cha' dated March 28th. 1794 He Says "This Day at Noon Our dear Departed was Buried in Westm^r. Abbey & the Funeral Service performed by D^r. Bear [?],^{2} the Corpse having been carried from my dear Farr' House in Lincolns Inn Fields^3 in a Hearse with 4 Horses & Six Bearers; Cha' following in a mourning Coach, & M^{rs}. Furdale [?] in Another & my dear Farr' Coach wth Serv^{ts} followed –^{4}

158

D^r. Nudy Our Physician at Naples Either was greatly mistaken in the Complaint of our dear Invalid; or was Unwilling to lose the Advantage of having an English lady under his Care – for on the 20th. of Nov^{br}. When we most Earnestly desired his Opinion whether the Air of Naples or Rome was best for Her, He positively Said Stay Here yet on Dec^{br}. 1st. only Ten days after, to Our great Surprise He advised us to Leave Naples as he thought the Air Bad for her Complaint – this Change of Opinion disrupted us so much

---

1. A vessel with this name is listed in Lloyd's Register of Shipping for 1789 as operating between London and Naples.
2. Dr William Bell – Canon of Westminster, 1765–1816.
3. Lincolns Inn Fields – square in central London still much associated with the legal profession.
4. The burial at Westminster was probably due to the family already having connections with the abbey.

that we desired M^r. Douglass to get D^r. Stewart to Visit us – who was of opinion that it would be Extremely Cruel to have her moved from an Apartment where she had Every Convenience that could Alleviate her distressing Situation, & that her Extreme Weakness would not admit any Hopes of Recovery from any Changes of Climate; that had He been Consulted Early in the first Stage of her Complaint, He Should have advised Naples; We had tried it; more could not be done.

159

Sunday Dec^br. 15th.

M^rs. Cadogan came in the morning & took me to the Chapel in the Palace;[1] at Noon I Rode with my dear Farr to Portici where we walked, & M^r. Clark kindly came in the Evening –

The View from the Palace at Portici of the City & Bay of Naples with Pausilipo on One Side And Castello Mare[2] on the Other, with the Island of Caprea[3] in Front is Beautiful And can only be Exceeded by the View from the Castle of S^t. Elmo which may be truly called the most Picturesque imaginable nor can I conceive any View in Europe Equal to it – from S^t. Elmo the City lies Beneath, the Bay in front, Portici on One Side, and Pausilipo on the other, with Baiæ beyond. The Island of Caprea Seems in the Center of the Bay & The Convent of Camaldoli on the Top of the Highest Hill forms one of the finest Coup d'Oeil that can be conceived –[4]

In the Kings Palace[5] at Portici the Suite of Rooms are Handsome, but the Furniture

---

1. Presumably that in the Palazzo Reale. It was built from 1660–68 by Cosimo Fanzago but altered in the nineteenth century and subsequently badly damaged by a bomb in WWII.
2. Castellammare di Stabia.
3. Capri.
4. The Convent of Camádoli on a high point at the northern side of the city. It was begun in the mid sixteenth century.
5. The palace was begun in 1738 by Giovanni Antonio Medrano but continued by various architects and at the unification of Italy the building became the Faculty of Agriculture of the University of Naples. The palace housed the initial findings from Herculaneum before these were transported to the Museo Archeologico Nazionale in Naples itself in 1822.

160

Is very Indifferent. The Kings & Queens Beds were both Small & Stood Close together, the Bedsteads were of Iron the Curtains of plain white Dimity[1] & trimmed with muslin, a Blue Gawse Musqueto[2] Net hung within Side – The Suite of Rooms belonging to the Queen were hung with fine Printed Callicoe[3] And in many were Views of Naples, & Venice, and Several of London –

The Herculanean Museum is in Several Small Rooms in a Building adjoining to the Palace, and consists of Various Utensils in Bronze & Terra Cota Tuscan Vases – Antique Statues, Inscriptions but the Floors here & throughout the Palace are of Red Tiles –

The Royal Family frequently Reside Here in Summer, tho' the Situation is So near Vesuvius, from the Eruption of which, Sir W[m]. Hamilton Says, there is frequently a Noxious Vapor Called the Mosete by which both Men & Animals have often dropped down to all Appearance Dead.[4]

161

Monday Dec[r]. 16th.
Went Early this morning with my dear Farr to Caserta, from whence we went Five miles to See the Aqueduc,[5] & upon our Return Visited the Apartm[ts] in the Palace[6] = The Building is of Brick, consisting of a Center with Three Windows & Nine on Each Side with a projection again of Three windows at Each End to Correspond with the Center – Two large Inner Courts are United by an Octagon Colonade; but Only One fourth part of the Suite of Rooms are finished = The Theatre is likewise within the Palace & very Handsome

---

1. Dimity – a stout cotton fabric woven with raised stripes or motifs.
2. Murray gives this spelling along with many other alternatives.
3. Murray gives this spelling.
4. Mosete – indeed meaning noxious vapours, but it was a local idiom.
5. The Acquedotto Carolino built by Luigi Vanvitelli from 1753 to '69 to carry water from local springs to feed the Grande Cascata of the palace gardens.
6. The Reggia di Caserta – the palace was begun for the then ruling Bourbon Dynasty in 1752 by Vanvitelli and remained the largest building in Europe for some time. It is about 20 kilometres from Naples itself. The grounds of the palace are also extensive.

tho' Small; The Back Front of the Palace Communicates with the Bosquet[1] which is a Plantation of Underwood Cut into Walks, and Inhabited by a great number of Pheasants – & Peacocks which are continually crossing the Walks – [In] the Center of this Ground are large Fish Ponds gradually Ascending one above the Other & at the Top Rising allmost perpendicular from the Fish Ponds is a Hill from whence falls a Beautiful

162

Cascade, the water of which is Convey'd from the Aqueduct we had Visited this morning Five miles distant, At the Foot of this Hill very near the Cascade is the English Garden now making by M[r]. Griffith who has display'd great Taste & made Fifty Acres of Ground a little Paradise –[2]

From hence we went to See the Remains of an Amphitheatre between Caserta & Capua and near it a Circular Mausoleum or Burying Place – In the Evening we Returned to Naples –[3]

Tuesday Dec[r]. 17th
M[rs]. Cadogan & M[r]. Douglass both Called upon us in the morning – at Noon I Rode with my dear Farr through the Grotto, & from thence walked with the Carriage following – Vainly wishing for distant Friends to Soothe our Grief –

Wednesday Dec[r]. 18th.
Went with my dear Farr to Call upon D[r]. Stewart and Lady Shelly & after[ds] – Went on Board the Ship to See the last Remains were Safely Placed of Her we Loved. Dined en Famille at Sir W[m]. Hamilton'.

163

Only Sir W[m]. & lady Hamilton with her mother M[rs]. Cadogan were at Table And their Attention to us must be Ever Remembered. In

---

1. Bosquet (French) – a grove or clump of trees.
2. The garden was begun in 1772 under the direction of Johann Andreas Graeffer (1746–1802), a German horticulturalist who had been trained in England.
3. The Anfiteatro Campano at Santa Maria Cápua Vétere. It dates to the first century AD. The Mausoleum is an elliptical structure also dating to the first century.

the Afternoon they took us to the English Apartment; from the Bow window which forms occasionally an Open Alcove the View is Similar to that from the Castle of S[t]. Elmo, (under which [is] this Apartment) in respect to Situation –[1]

Among a Number of very fine Pictures are many of Lady Hamilton in different Attitudes by Romney[2] & Madame Le Brun;[3] In one Room is a Portrait of M[r]. Greville Nephew to Sir William & formerly nearly Connected with Lady Hamilton; His Countenance has a melancholy Gloom over it –[4]

The Doors in this Apartment were Made to fall into Pannels like window Shutters –

The Villa Reale lies in full View, And at this time the Gardners were taking off the Leaves from the Trees to prevent them falling on the walks & the Orange Trees & Olianders [sic] wore matting on One Side = The Fruit at Naples is without Flavour & the Peaches mealy not Juicy –

164

No lady can Walk at Naples in any of the Streets on account of the great Number of men who go about Half Naked, and many of them So disfigured in their Countenance by Sores, and So Extremely

1. This is the splendid view from a room recently built for Sir William in the Palazzo Sessa. It was famously painted by Giovanni Battista Lusieri in 1791. The large watercolour is now in the J. Paul Getty Museum, Los Angeles – see A. Weston-Lewis – *Expanding horizons: Giovanni Battista Lusieri and the panoramic landscape*. Edinburgh, 2012. The room in the palace was also drawn by Lusieri – The Interior of the bow-fronted room at Palazzo Sessa (Collection of the Earl of Elgin) and illustrated in the foregoing publication.
2. Emma Hamilton served as a muse to George Romney (1734–1802) and the artist painted many portraits of her in various guises. The pair were close friends but not known to be lovers.
3. Presumably the Emma Hamilton as a Bacchante by Elisabeth Louise Vigée Lebrun now in the Lady Lever Art Gallery. The artist painted Lady Hamilton several times whilst in Naples.
4. The Hon. Charles Francis Greville (1749–1809), politician, antiquarian and horticulturalist. He was the nephew of Sir William Hamilton and Emma Hart had been his mistress before the latter moved on to Sir William. Mrs Bentham is obviously aware of the gossip about the couple. The portrait of Greville was by George Romney and was given to his uncle by the sitter. It is now in the Kislak Collection

Filthy in their Persons that the Eye is continually disgusted by the different Objects which are continually presenting themselves.

Even upon the Chiaia which is the Ride of Parade where the Company go in Carriages and Splendid Liveries are men with their Heads lying in the Lap of women to be Cleared from Vermin And as this Ride is along the Sea Shore the Women are continually Employed in Washing of Linnen for which purpose there are Stone washing Tubs Six or Seven joined together & Lines Extended near Half a mile in Length with Linnen Hanging to Dry =

The common Carriages that are continually running about Naples are of a Singular Shape much resembling a Vase Reversed And containing only one Person who holds the Reins of the Horse, while a dirty

165

Man Stands Behind the Carriage with a whip which he is constantly using to make the Horse go –

Men Servants are generally Hired at 24 Onzes p Annum, about Twelve Guineas a year[1] – for which They Feed themselves, & Come Every morning to put On their Livery & Attend the Family but They are never allowed to Stay the Night at their masters House, nor to take their Livery away with them – the Expence of Servants being so reasonable adds to their Number, for they have often Four Servants behind a Chariot –

Naples is Supplied from England with Hard-ware, Woolen Goods of all kinds as broad Cloth – Flannel &c &c &c – Hats, Stockings, Linnen – Callicoes, Fans – Watches, Canes – Clocks – Drugs, Tea, Sugar, Cocoa –

Silk, Linnen, Ribband &c at Naples is measured by the Cane,[2] which is Equal to Two yards & Half Quarter English meas-

1. The onza (pl. onze) was in the eighteenth century a gold coin of the Kingdom of Naples but its origins date back to the mediaeval period.
2. Cane – a unit of measurement in Naples and elsewhere in Italy.

ure I paid at Naples for a p^r of Clogs – 7^s 6^d which I could have
Purchased for – 3 6^d in England – –

166

The Pound Weight both at Naples and Rome is only Twelve
Ounces – –

At Rome Tea is 24 Paoli Equal to	12^s p Pound – – – – – – – –
Loaf Sugar 3 Paoli^s. & Half – – – –	1 9^d
Powder Sug^r y^e Pound 2 Paoli^s	1 =
Coffee p pound 4 Paoli – – – –	2 =
Wax Candles 3 Paoli^s & Half	1 9
A Quiver of Letter Paper 6 Baiocchi – –	4

NB. Ten Baiocchi Equal to one Paoli –

Thursday Decr 19th.
The whole Day Engaged in Packing & preparing to Leave Naples –

Friday Decr 20th.
At half past Four this morning I entered Our Travelling Coach
with my dear Farr. And Our maid Servant Phillips – Each looking
mournfully on the Seat that Our dear departed had occupied & for
whose Sake we had Come this distance from our Native Country
& Friends – Few words passed, but with weeping Eyes we went on
Reached S^t. Agatha^1 at One o Clock & Staid Two Hours & at Seven
Arrived at Mola di Gaetæ & staid the Night –

167

Saturday Dec^{br}. 21st.
Left Mola di Gaeta at Ten & went this Day no further than
Terracina where we arrived at Four, having been persuaded at
Naples to Engage Horses to take us to Rome, our Travelling now
became very Tedious, but we found Our Inn here very Comfortable
And we passed Our time in Loitering upon the Sea Shore –

In going from Naples towards Rome, the Road for the first Sixteen

---

1. Possibly Sant'Agata dei Goti but it does not seem a very direct route north.

mile is through the Campagna Felice,[1] a Level flat Country Cheifly Corn Fields, Planted on the Sides with Fruit Trees till you arrive at Capua; from thence the Country is more open And [it still] becomes more Interesting upon coming near S[t.] Agatha where it is Varied by Hills; but from Mola di Gaeta to Terracino it is beautifully Picturesque Oranges, Lemons & Myrtle Trees grow frequently by the Side of the Road

Sunday Dec[br]. 22[d].
Left Terracino at Six, went over the Pontine Marshes to Veletri & Staid the Night.

168

Monday Dec[br]. 23
Left Velitri & our dirty Inn at Nine & going through Albano in our way to Rome we Stopt to See the Tombs of the Horatii and Curatii,[2] and at Four Arrived at L'Hôtel de Curlandie Place d'Espagne, where we Staid the Night –

Italy in its Upper Region is divided from the North of Europe by the Alps And the Appenines, which run in a S E direction and divide the Plains of Lombardy from the rest of Italy –

Polybius[3] describes this Region as a Triangle, The head of it formed by the Maritime Alps, The North Side of it Ending above Venice – The S Side Ending at Senigallie[4] upon the Adriatic, His description is Ample & Curious as to the people and produce; but it Should be observed, that the Hills of Montferrat Run through the middle of this Plain from about Turin to Modena where They fall into the Appenines

Italy is also distinguishable into Four different Regions of Two Degrees of Latitude Each, in respect of Climate.

---

1. Campagna Felice – territory to the north and east of Naples between the Appenines and the Tyrrhenian Sea.
2. A remarkable monument outside Albano usually referred to as the Tomb of the Curiatii.
3. Polybius (c200-c118 BC) – Greek historian.
4. Senigallia – town on the Adriatic coast north of Ancona.

169

The First is the Plain Country just described between the Alps & Appenines descending to about 43 & ½ Degrees of Latitude = This district produces Rice Silk-worms, & Indian wheat, but not Any Olives, Agrami,[1] or Hot-house Plants Such as Oranges, Lemons, Pomegranates grow Here in the Open Air.

The Second District Comprehends Florence and Rome & as far as Terracino, from 43½ to 41½ – Here Olives and wild oranges Stand the winter; but not Sweet Oranges, Lemons or Bergamots –

The Third which Comprehends the North part of the Kingdom of Naples from 41½ to 39½ The Agrami bears the Open Air, tho' Subject to Frost –

The Fourth Comprehends Calabria Ulterior, And Sicily, where Snow never lies= The Agrami, Palm Tree, Aloe And Indian Fig grow freely in this Region And the Aloe & Fig are used as Hedge Plants, The Aloe also yeilds[2] Cloth and the Fig Serves the People for Food – Manna,[3] and Almonds are Articles of Trade.

170

The Mineralogy of this Country is delineated Shortly by De Saussure in Memoirs prefixed to De la Lande to his Voyage en Italie;[4] and much at Length by Ferber in his Physical Letters On Italy, which are Extremely Interesting And Satisfactory[5]

The Siroc[6] Wind at Naples I found to Affect me greatly even in the month of Nov^br

1. The word should probably read *agrumi* (citrus fruits) but it is not always certain what vowel is intended.
2. Murray gives this spelling.
3. Manna – presumably used to mean a staple food.
4. That is Joseph Jérome Le Français de Lalande – *Voyage d'un François en Italie fait dans les années 1765 & 1766*. 1769. The actual book in 8 volumes does not include a preface by Saussure. Presumably Mrs Bentham had consulted a copy which had this bound in especially. The de Saussure mentioned is presumably César de Saussure (1705–83).
5. Presumably Johann Jacob Ferber's *Travels through Italy . . .*, 1776.
6. The Sirocco – a hot, oppressive and often dusty wind blowing over the Mediterranean from north Africa.

At Rome the Sky even during the Winter months was frequently Clear And Cloudless. And the Sun Hot, but the Air Cold – In Jany we had Rain for Three weeks, but it Seldom continued many Hours together – The month of Feby was dry & mild, & Some days very Hot. March Dry, but often the Wind very Cold.

At Florence we found the Atmosphere in March Hazy & Thick, the Air Cold And No Sun; the Weather much like Such as we know at that Season in England and the Men wrapped in Cloaks.

Tuesday Decr 24th.

Went to See the Apartments at Margeritta' in Place d'Espagne and Agreed to Give Thirty Sequins a month for a Ground Floor.

171

Consisting of a Room of Entrance where the Servants Sitg, a Dining parlour, a Sitting Room Two Large bed Rooms a Dressing Room & Servants Room in the whole Seven good Sized Rooms with Four good Beds and Two of the Rooms Covered with Carpet – a Small but Neat Garden with Coach House & Serv^ts Room in a Front Court – In the Garden were Oranges & Lemons upon the Trees which Stood the winter –

Wenesday Decr. 25th.

Went with my dear Farr in the morning to S^t. Peters and Saw the Pope[1] in full Splendor officiate at High Mass with his Golden Mitre upon his Head, & after the Celebration of Mass we saw Him Carried from the Altar on a Palanquin, Blessing the People on Each Side as He was carried through the Church. His Dress was a white Silk Robe Ornamented with Gold, & when He Walked the Train was Supported – from St Peters we drove to lady Knights who Returned our Visit in the Even^g & we went with her & her Daughter Miss Cornelia to Angelica Kauffman'.[2]

---

1. At the time, Pius VI (Braschi), reigned 1775–99.
2. Lady Phillipina Knight (1726–99) – she lived abroad with her daughter Cornelia (1757–1837) for financial reasons. The latter was something of a blue-stocking and returned to England with the Hamiltons in 1800. Angelica Kaufmann (1741–1807) was the notable Swiss artist. She spent her last years in Rome.

Thursday Dec^br. 26th.

Walked before Breakfast upon the Hill Called Trinité de Monté, to
which we Ascended by a private Stair Case which belonged to Our
House, & was in a Small Building in the Front Court – & by which
we were in Two minutes at the Palais des Medicis,[1] & could walk
at any time in the Gardens from which was a very fine View of the
City and adjacent Country[2]

At Noon Rode to the Villa Borghese, not more than a Mile from
the City, & walked in the Gardens which are allways Open and
are very pleasant as well as Extensive; the Ground being much
diversifyed,[3] One part being laid out in the manner of an English
Garden the other in wood walks, & Park like with a Carriage Road
going through[4] – In the Afternoon we went to the Church Saint
Marie in Araceli,[5] where we saw the Representation of ^the Nativity of Our
Saviour Lying in the Manger; It was very Picturesque And had a
good Stage Effect, by Lights being Placed behind the Exhibition;
which was the Virgin with the Child in Swaddling Cloaths, & the
Shepherds & Flocks attending –

Friday Decr. 27th.

Went in the morning to M^r. Jenkins our Banker, Afterwards to
the Villa Pamphili And walked in the Gardens which are laid
out in Strait walks, & ornamented with a great Number of Jet

---

1. The Villa Medici, now the French Academy in Rome. A pre-existing building was
   transformed in 1564–75 by Nanni di Baccio Bigio for Cardinal Giovanni Ricci, but
   the villa was subsequently acquired by Cardinal Ferdinando de' Medici and consid-
   erably embellished again. It became the seat of the French Academy in 1804.
2. The Viale Trinità dei Monti leading from the summit of the Spanish Steps, passed
   the Villa Medici towards the Pincio.
3. Murray gives this spelling.
4. Part of the grounds of the villa had recently been laid out in the naturalistic English
   style by the then prince Marcantonio IV Borghese.
5. The church of Santa Maria in Aracoeli. The practice of having a Christmas crib or
   presepio was of course widespread.

d'eau^s;[1] M^r· Grignon went with us,[2] and afterwards took us to his Home to See a Picture he had finished of Sir Corbet Corbet, it appeared a good Likeness and the Attitude was pleasing of Sir Corbet, who was Sitting under an Oak Tree – we likewise went to See Mr Fagens[3] Pictures and M^r. Deare' Sculpture;[4] upon Our Return Mr Grignon Dined with us And we Afterwards went to See the Church of Saint Maria Maggiore –[5]

Saturday Dec^{br}. 28th·
Went in the morning to visit lady Knight, at Noon went to S^t. Peters to see the pope who constantly comes there between One & Two o Clock to say his Prayers – When He Entered the Church He was Attended only by Three Persons, one of whom in the Habit of an Abbé walked before Him, & as his Holiness passed us He Waved his Right Hand by way of Benediction and immediately went on to

174

The Bronze Figure of Saint Peter,[6] the Foot of which He Kissed with great Devotion, and putting his Head under the Foot in Such a manner as gave the appearance of the Foot pressing his Head He Prayed a considerable time in a Stooping Attitude; from thence he walked to the upper End of the Church where He Knelt before a Small Desk and Prayed still longer, His Attendants Three Abbee^s [sic] Standing behind him at a little distance = The Pope was Dressed in a Brown Camlet Banyan[7] or Robe de Chambre His Slippers were Crimson Velvet, He lookd about Seventy years of Age with a Countenance mild & Serene = M^r· Grignon Dined with us, & Lady Knight with Miss Cornelia Came in the Evening to Tea

---

1. The Villa Doria Pamphilj, a large suburban villa, like Villa Borghese just beyond the Aurelian Walls. It too has a casino known as Bel Respiro created for Camillo Pamphilj, nephew of Innocent X.
2. Charles Grignion the Younger (1754–1804), British artist of Huguenot descent.
3. Robert Fagan (c.1761–1816), English painter, archæologist and diplomat. He spent most of his career in Rome and Sicily, painting a great many portraits of British visitors to Italy.
4. John Deare (1759–98), English neo-classical sculptor. He died in Rome.
5. Santa Maria Maggiore, one of the seven basilicas of Rome.
6. The bronze statue of the apostle immediately to the right of the high altar. It was long thought to date from the fifth century but is now thought to belong to the thirteenth and possibly the work of Arnolfo di Cambio.
7. Banyan – a loose shirt.

Sunday Dec[br]. 29th.

M[r]. Grignon Came in the morning & took us to See Mr Robinson' Pictures,[1] amongst which, were the Duchess of Devonshire, Lady Elizabeth Forster, Lord Bruce, Lord Dalkeith, and D[r]. North Bishop of Winchester. –[2] Afterwards we went to the Church of Saint John de Lateran, & the Baptistery adjoining[3] = from Hence went to

175

The Church Saint Gregoire from which we had a good View of many of the principal Ruins =[4] In the Evening went to Lady Knights where we met Several of the Inhabitants of Rome, both Gentlemen and Ladies, upon our Return We made a Visit to M[r]. & M[rs]. Montague Wilkinson,[5] who Lived in the Apartment above Ours at Margaritta' met there M[rs]. Canning[6] an English Lady who is Aunt to lady Throgmorton, and a M[r]. Ashe who was lately arrived from Geneva and going to Naples Having a Travelling Fellowship of D[r]. Radcliffe'[7]

Monday Dec[br]. 30th.

M[r]. Grignon Came in the morning and took us to the Museum in the Vatican where the Collection of Sculptur is most admirably disposed in different Rooms which Communicate with Each Other in a manner that renders the whole One Assemblage of the most Extraordinary and Valuable works of Art. The disposition of them was under the Order and Direction of the present Pope Pius the

1. Hugh Robinson (1756–96), painter. He probably went to Italy in 1783 and died in Rome. His Italian paintings were probably lost at sea and the only surviving works are those completed before he left England.
2. Georgiana, Duchess of Devonshire (1757–1806); Lady Elizabeth Foster (1758–1824), novelist and later Duchess of Devonshire, Lord Bruce – not traced; Charles Montagu-Scott, 4th Duke of Buccleugh (1772–1819), Earl of Dalkeith until he succeeded his father; Brownlow North (1741–1820), Bishop of Winchester.
3. The Basilica of San Giovanni in Laterano.
4. San Gregorio al Celio – the church overlooks the Palatine Hill.
5. Montagu Wilkinson – he married Anne Catherine Hobart in 1784 – see Ingamells' *Dictionary* . . .
6. Catherine Canning (née Gifford) (b.1734). She married Francis Canning. The family were Roman Catholics.
7. Edward Ashe received one of the Radcliffe Travelling Fellowships of the University of Oxford funded by Dr John Radcliffe.

Sixth – and from the Long Gallery leading to this museum is a very fine View of Rome –[1]

176

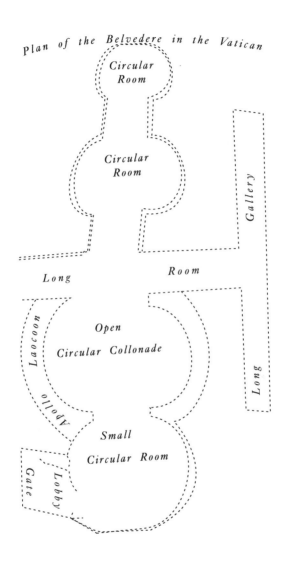

Plan of the Belvedere in the Vatican

Circular Room

Circular Room

Gallery

Long   Room

Laocoon

Open

Circular Collonade

Apollo

Long

Small

Circular Room

Gate   Lobby

177

After Staying Some Hours in the museum we went to the Four Rooms Called Raphael' Chambers to See his Pictures of the History of Constantine[2] – afterwards we Went to the Farnese & Farnesian

---

1. The suite of rooms known as the Museo Pio–Clementino having been begun by Clement XIV and completed by the then reigning Pius VI.
2. Of course, Raphael's Stanze, however the Sala di Constantino particularly mentioned by Mrs Bentham was actually painted by Giulio Romano after Raphael's death.

Palaces, both belonging to the King of Naples, but neither Inhabited –[1] In the First is a Saloon or Gallery painted by Annibal Carrache for which having receivd Only 500 Crowns, and having Expected more in the Purchase of Colours &c for it It affected him So much that He Sickened And Died in Three weeks after –[2]

Tuesday Dec[br]. 31st.
Walked in the morning in the Gardens de Medici =[3] afterw[ds] went with Miss Knight to the Church Saint Jesu,[4] where we heard Two Correspondent Organs Playing The Musick and Singing were allowed to be very good, It being to Commemorate the Close of the Year – The Three Altars in this Church are remarkable for their Riches in Silver Figures – Saint Ignatius is Seven Feet in Height all of Silver & Ornamented with precious Stones.[5] Lady and Miss Knight Dined with us –

178

1794

Wednesday Jany 1st
Monsieur Abbé Giuntotardi[6] Came to Breakfast with us & afterw[ds] took us to the Sistine Chapel, where we Saw the Pope assist at Mass = Many Cardinals were Present and received his Benediction after which They Gave the Kiss of Peace to Each Other – We went

---

1. The Palazzo Farnese and Villa Farnesina, both at the time the property of the Kings of Naples by descent. The palace was usually occupied by the Neapolitan Ambassador at the time. The vast palace in its eponymous piazza was begun by Antonio da Sangallo for Cardinal Alessandro Farnese in 1517 but the plans became more grandiose when he was elected pope as Paul III in 1534. The Villa Farnesina on the other side of the river was actually begun for Agostino Chigi, the banker, by Baldassare Peruzzi, only passing to the Farnese in 1590.
2. The Galleria of the palace frescoed by Annibale Carracci between 1597–1604.
3. The gardens adjacent to the Villa Medici.
4. Chiesa del Gesù – after a long period of gestation, the church was eventually built to a design by Vignola and consecrated in 1584. Both the design and the famous façade designed by Giacomo della Porta were enormously influential in subsequent church building. It is, of course, the mother church of the Jesuit Order.
5. The Chapel of St Ignatius of Loyola in the left transept. It was designed by Andrea Pozzo but the silver statue of the saint by Pierre Legros was melted down during the French invasion 4 years later and replaced by a stucco copy.
6. Probably Abate Luigi Giuntotardi.

Afterwards to the Library, & Saw many Manuscripts, & the Cloth
Spun from a Stone which they formerly wrapped round the Dead;
It resists Fire, and therefore preserved the Ashes – we likewise Saw
the Collection of Gems Pearls and marbles, with the Etruscan Vases
– These Rooms were large and Well proportioned & Ornamented
with painting And were Built by the present Pope – Pius the Sixth[1]
– We afterw[ds] took a Ride to the Ponte Molle[2] & Returned to a late
Dinner – In the Evening went to M[rs]. Hollands Party, we found
Four Card Tables & a great many English;[3]

NB M[r] Holland was Son of the Architect of that Name in England
& had married a Sister of Sir Fred. Edens & They both had
Resided at Rome Some years –[4]

179

Thursday Jan[y]. 2[d.]
M[r]. Fagen Came to Breakfast with us and Afterw[ds] took us to the
Palace Borghese which is Built in the Shape of a Harpsichord,[5]
And the Rooms at the Narrow End are fronting the Tiber, The
Long Suite of Rooms are magnificent; The windows are Singular,
having a Row of M[6] over the Others in the Same Room, nor would
the Rooms be otherwise Sufficiently Light as the Ceilings are very
Lofty, and there is a great Depth between the Small window &
the large but the panes of Glass in Both are of Equal Size[7] – & the
Depth of wainscot between is formed Slanting to Admit the Light
more fully – All the Rooms are Covered on the Sides with Pictures
in Gold Frames; but the Rooms being in general, hung with yel-

---

1. The main room of the library, the Salone Sistino was built for Sixtus V but several
   later pontiffs made additions including the then pope, Pius VI (Braschi). The latter
   also completed the Museo Profano seen by Mrs Bentham.
2. The Ponte Molle, or Milvio – the bridge across the Tiber to the north of the city and the
   site of the famous battle between Maxentius and the Emperor Constantine in 312 AD.
3. John Holland (b.c.1762) married Catherine Eden (b.c.1767). Mr Holland was indeed
   the brother of the architect Henry Holland – see Ingamells' *Dictionary* . . .
4. Sir Frederick Morton Eden (1766–1809), 2nd Bt.
5. The palace is referred to as "il cembalo" because of the awkward shape of the site.
   The building was probably begun to a design by Vignola but was completed for
   Cardinal Camillo Borghese by Flaminio Ponzio from 1605–14.
6. There is a space here for the rest of the word – presumably mirrors – ed.
7. The three storeys of the palace each have further openings above the main windows.

low Silk Spoils the Effect which the Richness of the Frames would otherwise have. The Pictures are from the hands of the Best Artists viz Raffaello Titian^s &c &c^1 – The Floors throughout were

180

Square Red Tiles and kept very Glossy by Rubbing =^{2} Over the State Apartments were Another very Comfortable Suite of Family Rooms; and in Front of the Chairs which were placed round the Room, Skins of Bears were put to keep the Feet from the Cold Tiles; for there is not any Fire Places in the Rooms

From hence we went to the Colonna Palace In which is One most Spacious Room being in Length 139 Feet, and 34^{ft} wide, & 70^{ft} High besides many other very Large Rooms And the whole filled with Pictures and Statues &c^3 but the most Elegant Collection of Statues and Marbles &c is at the Villa Borghese to which we went & found this Villa Entirely devoted for The purpose of Containing them, as there are no Rooms in it for a Family to Occupy, but it is One Compleat Museum.^{4} Standing in the Center of a Park, which likewise Includes a Beautiful Garden at the End, with An Island in the Center Ornamented with Sculpture – M^r. Fagan Dined with us, & Miss Carr from Newcastle^5

181

Made us a Visit in the Evening & afterw^{ds} We went with her to Mrs Cannings Party Four Card Tables & a great Number of Persons, amongst them Prince Czernichef from Russia^6 & a Prussian Baron –

---

1. The pictures were later transferred to the Casino of Villa Borghese where they remain.
2. The main suite of rooms, the Galleria Terrena, were renovated by Antonio Asprucci for Prince Marcantonio IV Borghese between 1768 and '75.
3. The Galleria of the Colonna palace. Despite a forced sale of some works to the French in 1798, the collection still contains notable works of art and is open to the public. A catalogue of the paintings has recently been published – see *Galleria Colonna in Rome: catalogo dei dipinti*. Rome, De Luca, 2015.
4. Of course, the Casino of the Villa Borghese. The collection is largely intact as Prince Borghese was married to Napoleon's sister Pauline, and thus protected from pillage during the Napoleonic occupation of the city.
5. Harriet Carr the sister of John Carr. She was an amateur artist of some repute.
6. Almost certainly Ivan Grigoryevich Chernyshev (1726–97), a Russian Field Marshal. He died in Rome.

Friday Jany 3^d–

Walked Two Hours in the Garden belonging to the Palais de Medici – Dined Chez lady Knight & met Mr. Talbot there whom we had known at Spa – In the Evening went with Miss Knight to a Concert of Gentlemen Performers – & heard Two young Ladies Sing, & we were Introduced to the Princess Santa Croce[1] from Hence we went to a Conversatione[2] at the Palais Borghese we passed thro a Suite of Seven Rooms well Lighted and Card Tables Set – where after the Company had Chatted & taken Refreshments they formed their own Parties for Play – Three Servants attended with Tea & Coffee The first Servant held a large Waiter containing about a dozen Cups & Saucers of China resembling Wedgewoods [*sic*] Staffordshire Ware,[3] with very fine Sugar Candy Pounded very Smooth – The Second Servant followed Close to him with a Large Silver Coffee

182

Pot in One hand, and a large Silver Tea Pot in the other to Give you which you Chose, while a Third Servt. attended Close to him with a large Silver Jug like another Coffee Pot but filled with Cream = At Ten o Clock Ice of Various Sort was handed about = The Company were numerous & Splendid in Dress The Gentlemen were all in full Dress with Bag & Sword – The Ladies had Cheifly Turban Caps and the Sleeves of their Gowns were as Fancy directed Some Long other Short. The Shape like a Vest with a Band round the waist –

The Floors were Covered with Carpets but it was Brick underneath. The Serv^{ts.} that belonged to the Company waited in the First Room of Entrance Each that attended the English had a Flambeau ready to Light upon Leaving the House, for the City is not Lighted and the Roman Serv^{ts.} carry behind the Coaches only a Small Lanthorn, very like such as we Call dark Lanthorns, having only a Small candle in them

The Gentlemen & Ladies in general take a great deal of Snuff and Spit very frequently upon the Carpets –

---

1. The Santacroce Pubblicola were a noble Roman family – now extinct.
2. *Conversazione* in modern Italian.
3. Presumably meaning the ware that Wedgwood produced in imitation of the bone china teaware imported from China.

183

Saturday Jany. 4th.

M^r. Fagan Breakfasted with us, and afterw^{ds}. took us to the Palace Barberini On the Quirinal Hill[1] where among a very great Collection was the Famous Magdalene by Guido[2] – and the Two Mary^s. Called Modesty and Virtue by Leonardo da Vinci –[3] The young Man Cheated by Gamesters by Michael Angelo da Caravaggio[4] – and among the Statues The Drunken Faun Asleep –[5]

From the Barberini Palace We went to the Rospigliosi Palace on the Same Hill to See the Pictures And Sculptur [*sic*] not Omitting the Aurora of Guido upon the Ceiling of the Pavilion in the Garden.[6]

From Hence we went to the Palace Pamfili or Doria, the best Furnished of Any in Rome;[7] The Gallery Surrounds the Inner Court & consists of Four Rooms united as One, filled with Pictures of the best masters, many of Claude Lorrain^s. & Poussins,[8] and one Extremely Beautiful of Raphaels, viz

---

1. The site was obtained by Cardinal Francesco Barberini in 1625 and the building much aggrandized. The palace now contains the Galleria Nazionale d'Arte antica.
2. Reni painted the subject several times but that to which Mrs Bentham refers is now in the Galleria Nazionale (Palazzo Barberini), Rome and dates to 1631/2. It was originally owned by Cardinal Valerio Santa Croce but was given by him to Antonio Barberini in 1641. It was sold in 1891/2 and subsequently entered the national collection.
3. The painting of Martha and Mary Magdalene is now given to Bernardino Luini and dated to *c.*1520. It is now in the San Diego Museum of Art.
4. The celebrated *Cardsharps* by Caravaggio was originally owned by his early patron Cardinal Francesco Maria del Monte but was bought in 1628 by Cardinal Antonio Barberini. The painting subsequently disappeared and on resurfacing in the twentieth century was purchased by the Kimbell Museum of Art, Fort Worth, Texas.
5. The famous Barberini Faun probably discovered in the grounds of the Castel Sant'Angelo. It was sold to Crown Prince Ludwig of Bavaria in 1814 and is now in the Glyptothek at Munich.
6. The Aurora was originally commissioned in 1614 by Cardinal Scipione Borghese for the garden pavilion of his palace (now Palazzo Pallavicini Rospigliosi).
7. The huge complex on the via del Corso largely dates from work in the seventeenth & eighteenth centuries. The palace, of course, still exists and is open to the public.
8. The collection still includes *Landscape with the Rest on the flight into Egypt*, *c.*1639, and others by Claude.

184

The Virgin with the Child Jesus, Standing at her Knee, and the Child John Kissing Our Saviour.[1]

The Floors of this palace are Only Square Red Tiles kept well Rubbed – The windows were very Large Panes of Glass & cemented together without any Frame work between the Glass –

When the Arch-Duke and the Arch Dutchess of Austria[2] were Here in the year 1780 Prince Doria[3] Entertained Four Thousand Persons in this Palace

After Seeing these Palaces we Rode to the Villa Borghese & walked by the Side of the Lake; The Day Fine with a warm Sun

In the Evening went with Miss Knight to See Two different Presepias[4] One at a Private House, the Other in the Church Araceli,[5] and both very Picturesque It was the Child Jesus Lying in the manger with the Wise men making their offerings. Exhibited like Scenery & the Perspective very good – we afterw[ds] went to the Convent of Capuchins to See the Celebrated Picture of Saint Michael by Guido[6]

185

Sunday Jany 5th
Abbée [sic] Giuntotardi Breakfasted with us, And took us afterwards to the Capitol Where we Saw the she Wolf in Bronze with

1. This is the Madonna & Child with St John known as the Madonna del Passeggio. A number of copies of the painting exist. The invention of the group was probably Raphael's but the copies are by his assistants notably Gianfrancesco Penni. The Doria-Pamphilj version is no.317 in the collection.
2. Archduke Ferdinand (1754–1806), governor of the Duchy of Milan, 1765–96. He married Maria Beatrice d'Este (1756–1828) in 1771.
3. Prince Giovanni Andrea Doria Pamphili Landi (1747–1820)
4. Properly – presepio or presepe, pl. presepi.
5. Santa Maria in Aracoeli.
6. The painting was commissioned from Guido Reni by Cardinal Antonio Barberini in the 1630s. He was protector of the Capuchin church of Santa Maria Della Concezione. The picture still remains in situ.

Romulus and Remus in the Attitude of Sucking,[1] And many other celebrated Figures in Bronze & Marble – went to the Tarpeian Rock[2] – The Ruins of the Temple of Jupiter – Temple of Concord – Arch of Severus – Temple of Peace – The Arch of Vespasian through which the Jews will never Walk but allways go on One Side by a Narrow & dirty path[3]

Went to the Palatine Hill, now made use of as a Garden for Vegetables Examined the Ruins of the Palace & Went with Torches into a Subterranean Vault where we could perceive the remains of Gilding upon the Ceiling; for tho' now, it lay deep below the Surface of the Earth, yet it was formerly a Splendid Apartment –[4]

In the Evening went with Miss Knight to a Concert at the Duc de Ceres,[5] where the principal Nobility of Rome were Assembled = In Conversation, I heard the Duke Say "the Perfumes used by

186

many English ladies were So very disagreable to the Roman[s]. that He had often known the Dutchess Ill after She had been in Company with Ladies that made use of them –

Monday Jan. 6th.
At Noon Received Letters from Cha[s]. dated Dec[br]. 10th. – Went this morning to the Sestine [sic] Chapel at Saint Peters, where I Saw the Pope in all his Splendor Assisting at the Celebration of this Day.[6] His Dress a Robe of white & Gold, Shoes of Crimson Velvet Embroidered, And his Mitre (which was frequently put on & taken from his Head) resembled Gold; & had Two broad

1. The bronze Wolf in the Capitoline Museum. Both Winckelmann and Helbig attribute it to be of Etruscan origin but the figures of Romulus and Remus were added later, an addition that probably cemented both its fame and survival.
2. The Rupe Tarpea – a point on the Capitoline Hill from which, as legend has it, that in antiquity traitors were thrown to their deaths.
3. The Arch of Titus in the Forum erected by Domitian to celebrate the victories of Vespasian & Titus over the Jews and the destruction of Jerusalem. It was only completely liberated from later accretions by Valadier in 1821.
4. The remains of the imperial palace on the Palatine Hill are extensive. It is difficult to pinpoint to which part Mrs Bentham may be referring.
5. Possibly Baldassare Odescalchi, Duca di Ceri (1748–1810).
6. The Feast of the Epiphany.

pieces of the Same hanging from the Mitre behind – He Gave his Benediction in a most graceful manner – and repeated it Several Times; besides doing it ^{at his Entrance and} upon Quitting the Church = more than Twenty Cardinals were Present; Each in a Robe of Scarlet Silk with an Ermine Mantle covering the Breast and Tyed at the Shoulders= The principal Priest that officiated at the Altar was a cardinal and He

187

He had likewise a Mitre, resembling Silver which He wore upon his Head when He was not at the Altar= Each Cardinal had a Priest Sitting at his Feet; whose Business Seemed to consist in adjusting their Robes, and Occasionally holding their Cap= In front of the Altar Sat Twenty Four Priests, and on Each Side the Choir the cardinals sat on a Bench raised by Two Steps = The Popes Seat was Elevated by Six Steps with a Canopy over it, & nearby in the Same part of the Choir as the Pulpit is placed with us –

Tuesday Jan 7th
Walked before Breakfast in the Garden de Medicis, & afterwards went to S^t. Peters And with Book in Hand Examined the mosaic Representations of the Miracles performed by Our Saviour[1] = And the Wonderful Effect of the Sculpture &c &c throughout the whole

In the Evening went with Miss Knight to a Conversatione at the Prince Doria^s. Several Rooms were Illuminated but no Card Tables= The Ladies were Seated round a very Large Room, in the

188

Middle of which the Gentlemen Stood – One Servant Carried a number of Silver Plates of a very Small Size, which He offered to the Company, and upon Acceptance Another Servant immediately offerd Ice of Various Sorts with Tea Spoon^s & another Servant

---

1. The mosaics in the new basilica generally depict scenes from the Old Testament rather than the new – see F. DiFederico – The mosaics of Saint Peter's: decorating the new basilica. London, 1983.

followed with a Variety of Cakes. After Staying about an Hour we took Leave of the Princess Doria[1] & went to Another Conversatione at the Princess Santa Croce where we found a great Number of Card Tables but not any Refreshments –[2]

The Princess Doria allways[3] has her Conversatione at the Prima Serra [sic] viz from 5 to 7 – & the Princess Santa Croce from 7 to 10 –

Wed Jan 8th.

M[r]. Fagan came to Breakfast with us And we went with him to the Palace Ghigi[4] where we Saw Several fine Pictures of Claude[s] & Salvator Rosa;[5] but the Furniture was Old & the Floors of Coarse Brick – From thence we Went to the Palace Giustiniani, where the Staircase as well as the Rooms is crowded with Sculpture but all very Dirty.[6]

189

Went to the Palace Altieri[7] in which were a Suite of Apartments newly Furnished in a Style resembling the English manner and very Elegant;[8] The Doors to the Rooms were white and Ornamented with Gold, the Pannels of Alabaster – The Floors tho' of Square

1. Princess Leopoldina di Savoia Carignano (1744–1807). She married Prince Doria in 1767.
2. Giuliana Pubblicola Santacroce (1746–1814). She married the Prince Antonio in 1767.
3. Murray gives several variant spellings but not this one.
4. Presumably that in Piazza Colonna, now the seat of the Presidenza del Consiglio dei Ministri, i.e. the prime minister's office. Part of the palace already existed when it was acquired by the Chigi in 1659.
5. Two large canvases by Claude and Rosa were part of the collection at the time. They were not a pair but were of similar size. They were sold in 1799 to the English Banker Robert Sloane. The Claude eventually entered the National Gallery, London and the Rosa went to Kansas City – see B. Fredericksen- A pair of pendant pictures by Claude Lorrain and Salvator Rosa from the Chigi Collection, *Burlington Magazine*, August, 1991, pp.543–6.
6. Palazzo Giustiniani – begun in 1585 by the Fontanas but carried on by other architects into the next century. It now houses the offices of the Italian Senate. Vincenzo Giustiniani, the last of his line, died in 1826. The collection of sculpture and paintings was dispersed.
7. The vast palace opposite the church of the Gesù was constructed during the reign of the Altieri pope Clement X by Giovanni Antonio de' Rossi (1650–55) and continued by others into the following century. The building now houses a bank.
8. Probably the suite of rooms decorated by Giuseppe Barberi (1746–1809) in 1787 for the marriage of Prince Paluzzo Altieri.

Tiles were painted over in Various Colours & Patterns – In the Corners of the Rooms were Small Circular Tables Supported on three Pillars,[1] the Tops of beautiful marble a great Collection of fine Pictures particularly Two of Claude Lorrains[2]

From hence we went to the Capitol & looked in the Museum for Sculpture which is fully particulariz'd in descrip^ts de Rome – afterw^ds went to See the Collection of Antiques Purchased of Mr Hamilton. & now placed in a Building in the Garden de Borgheses, They were brought from Gabia –[3]we afterw^ds drove to the Villa Albani Two miles distant,[4] the Situation very fine Commanding the Sabine & Latian Hills, with a distant View of

190

Frescati [sic] and Tivoli. The Gardens are laid out in the Dutch Taste, but the Front of the House towards them is very fine, the Lower part forms an Open Gallery for walking under Cover, being Supported by Pillars of Granites and is filled ^with Statues, vases &c. & is terminated at Each End by a Circular Low Building divided into a number of Small Rooms that are filled with Antiques, collected at an Immense Expence during a research of Fifty years by the late Cardinal Alexander Albani –[5] and this Villa is now Esteemed to be the most Elegant One in Italy – tho' I think Villa Borghese is in many respects preferable as from its Situation it takes in View great part of

1. These still exist.
2. The notable Altieri Claudes. The two paintings date to 1662 and 1675 and remained in the family collection until the French domination of Rome. They were then sold to Robert Fagan and Charles Grignion and shipped with some difficulty to England where they passed through many collections before being bought by Lord Fairhaven in 1947.
3. The painter and dealer in antiquities, Gavin Hamilton (1730–97) undertook excavations at Gabii in conjunction with Prince Marcantonio Borghese in 1792. Their discoveries were then housed in the Casino dell'Orologio in the Villa Borghese which had an interior especially designed for the collection. The prince's son, Camillo Borghese sold the collection along with many other antiquities to Napoleon in 1807 and all these remain in the collection of the Louvre in Paris – see A. Campitelli, The Museo di Gabii at the Villa Borghese: drawings for the prince's new museum, In Paul, Carole – *Making a prince's museum: drawings for the late-eighteenth-century redecoration of the Villa Borghese*, Los Angeles, Getty Research Institute, 2000, pp.145–165.
4. The Villa Albani on the via Salaria built between 1747–67 for Cardinal Alessandro Albani by Carlo Marchionni to house his notable collection of antique sculpture. It was acquired by the Torlonia family in 1866 and is not generally open to the public.
5. Cardinal Alessandro Albani (1692–1779), antiquarian and art collector.

Rome, & the Gardens are more extensive, with a park Three miles in Circumference full of inequalities, & woods of Evergreen Oaks

Thursday Jan 9th.
Walked in the Gardens de Medicis, which is finely Situated on the Pincian Hill & from the walks is a very good View of Rome –

191

The Garden is laid out in straight Lines but many of the walks are Shady, & tho' there are no Inequalities yet from the great Height above the City it is very pleasant – In the Evening went to a Large Party at M[rs]. Cannings were [sic] we found many English viz the St Pinnochs, Holland, Madame Ciciporci &c & c

Friday Jan 10th.
Abbée Giuntotardi came in the morn'g to give Lessons in the Italien [sic] Language at Noon I went to St Peters and attentively Examined the mosaic[s] which have all the Appearance of Paintings.[1] In the Evening went with Miss Knight to the Cardinal de Bernis,[2] who Receiv'd us with great Politeness Speaking only in French = On our Names being Announced before we left our Carriage Two Servants in pompous Livery descended the Great Stair case & each with a Lighted Flambeaux went before us to the Entrance of the Anti [sic] Chamber where a gentleman in a full Suit of Black made us a profound Bow.

192

And walking before us, Conducted us thro' Two Rooms, at the End of which Another Gentleman waited to Conduct us through Three Rooms further, all well Lighted: at the End of these Five Rooms we Entered Another, where the Cardinal was Sitting in a Circle of

1. The new basilica was found to be too damp to house traditional altarpieces on canvas and beginning in the early seventeenth century these were either replaced by mosaic copies or new works were copied in mosaic from cartoons – see again DiFederico, F – *The mosaics of Saint Peter's: decorating the new basilica*, London, 1983.
2. François-Joachim de Pierre de Bernis (1715–94), French diplomat and man of letters. He was the French ambassador in Rome and was created cardinal by Clement XIII in 1758. He lived at the Palazzo di Carolis built by Alessandro Specchi from 1714–24 but at this time the seat of the French Embassy.

Twelve Chairs; but only Two Gentlemen with Him; One of whom quitted the Room on Our Entering, as the other did immediately upon the Entrance of Another Gentleman; and we did the Same upon another Name being Announced – The Cardinal appeared to be a Tall Handsome man, well made, a good Countenance & about Sixty years of Age; from hence we went to Another Conversatione and afterwards Ended our Evening with M^r. & M^rs. Montague Wilkinson who had the Apartment at Margeritta^s above Our own, And found most of the English who were at Rome assembled together, Some at Cards – others attending to the Harpsichord on which M^rs. W. Played.

193

Saturday Jany 11th
Made a morning Visit to Madame Ciciporci, and afterwards Walked in the Gardens de Medicis : M^r. Hill[1] (Brother to M^rs. Walker of Southgate) Dined with us, and likewise M^r. Holland; but M^rs. Holland declining all Dinner Invitations Came only to take Tea with us, & go afterw^ds to a Party at Miss Carr^s. an English Lady from the Neighbourhood of Newcastle. I Conversed the greatest part of the Evening with M^rs. Harrison a Lady from Yorkshire who with her Husband And Daughter have been Travelling near Four years: their family Seat near Durham[2]

Sunday Jany 12th.
Abbé Giuntotardi Breakfasted & Staid the day with us; we went with Him to the Church of St Pauolo[3] Two Miles Out of the City & remarkable for the Pillars which were formerly at the Castle St Angelo, And for the Portraits of <u>All</u> the Popes = The present Pope's Portrait filling up

---

1. Ingamells' *Dictionary* furnishes no further details of this individual.
2. Ingamells' *Dictionary* gives the family as coming from Walworth but with no further details as to their forenames and dates.
3. San Paolo fuori le mura – the ancient basilica was almost totally destroyed by fire in 1823 and rebuilt. Mrs Bentham is of course describing the palæo-Christian building notable for its columns of antique marbles.

194

the Only Space left= We went to the Burying Ground Set apart
for Protestants[1] – & took a Ride to the Arch of Constantine – The
Coliseum – Arch of Titus Vespasian Arch of Severus = The
Temple of Jupiter – The Capitol &c &c – Returned to Dress, Dine
and take a Lesson de L'Italinnæ In the Evening went with Miss
Knight to the Giustiani [*sic*] Palace – It was the Second Sunday
Evening Concert given by the Roman Nobility this winter –[2]

At the Entrance of the Concert Room (having passed through
Several very Handsome Rooms before we Came to this) The Prince
himself was Standg And immediately gave me his Hand And lead
me to a Chair; and at the End of the First Act The Princess Santa
Croce came to Miss Knight And desired She would bring me the
following Sunday to her House where the Concert was to be =
The Concert Room here had a High Cove Ceiling the Sides of the
Room Covered with

195

Pictures of the most Celebrated Artists[3] / This Palace being allowed
to have the greatest Collection of fine Paintings, And Sculptures

At the Upper End of the Room the Performers Sat upon an
Elevated Floor – The Company on Each Side, And before each
Chair were Bear Skins to keep the feet warm – The Room was
filled with the Nobility of Rome – All full Dressed And many of
their Coats most beautifully Embroidered = The Concert began at
Ten, many Vocal as Well as Instrumental Performers.

Monday Jan[y] 13
M[r]. Harrison Visited us this morning And gave us much useful
Information relative to Switzerland where He And his Family had

---

1. The Protestant Cemetery, or Cimitero acattolico was created in the eighteenth century to house the remains of non-catholics and is notable for the tombs of Keats and
   Shelley, etc.
2. Palazzo Giustiniani – begun in the late sixteenth century but brought to completion
   by Francesco Borromini. It is now occupied by the offices of the Italian Senate.
3. Presumably the Grande Galleria decorated by Tempesta, Giovanni Ricci, Ventura
   Salimbeni and others in the late sixteenth century.

Resided Some time – At Noon I walked upon the Terrace Called Trinité de Monté And in the Evening went with Miss Knight to the Venetian Ambassadors Conversatione[1] which He gave Every

196

Monday, upon Driving through a large Court and Stopping at the Foot of a Great Staircase, Two Servants in magnificent Liveries & Lighted Flambeaux in their Hands went before us to the Top, where we found Six other Servants Stand[g] on Each Side of an Anti Room And One of the Ambassadors Gentlemen Waiting to Receive us which he did by making a Low Bow & walking before us through Two Rooms, At the Entrance of the Third Room Stood the Ambassador who paid his Comp[s]. to Each Person as They Entered – The ladies Sat in Chairs round the Room, in the Center Stood the Gentlemen Conversing with Each other, and Occasionally Chatting with the Ladies when they found a Chair Vacant; but immediatly[2] Quitting it upon a Lady[s] Entering as no Lady ever Stands in the Room. Coffee & Tea were offered to Each Person by Servants, One of which went

197

with a Coffee Pot in his Hand, follow'g Another Servant who carried a Large Square Tray filled with Tea Cups Sugar & Milk, Another brought Three Sorts of Ice, Cut in Square Pieces & put into Saucers with Spoons, viz lemon Ice – Currant Ice, & Milk ice with Chocolate upon it – And great Variety of Cakes – The Company began to Assemble at Six and Separated before Eleven – many Played at Cards & many were continually Coming and Going –

The Floors were Carpeted and were frequently Spit upon by the Men who Scraped their feet upon it, And all took Snuff in great Quantitys. [sic] The Rooms were hung with Rich Silk. The Chairs of different Sorts Some Silk others Cane Bottoms. The morning

---

1. Presumably at Palazzo Venezia which had been the Venetian ambassador's residence since Pope Pius IV presented part of it to the Republic in 1564, and remained so until 1797 when it was confiscated by the French. The ambassador at that time (1789–94) was Antonio Cappello (1736–1807), diplomat. He had also served in France.
2. Murray gives immediat.

after having been at Any of these Conversatione[s] a Serv[t] Calls for a Gratuity which is generally Three Paolis; and this Demand is Only made once in the year –

198

In many Rooms there are not Any Fire Places, And when there is, a Low Screen is allways put before the Chimney, to prevent the Fire being Seen –

Tuesday Jan[y] 14th.
Returned M[r]. Harrison' Visit & afterw[ds] Rode to the Villa Borghese and walked in the Shrubbery by the Lake – before Dinner Rode thro' the principal Streets in Rome, observed in many that there was Linnen Hanging to Dry upon Cords fasten'd from House to House on the opposite Sides of the Street & Our Coachman was frequently obliged to Stoop as He drove under the wet Linnen. We went through the Quarter of the City destined for the Habitation of Jews, it is Called the Gæta, & Consists of Several very Narrow Streets only Sufficiently wide for a Carriage to be drove through, & the Houses on Each Side are very High & the whole Inclosed within High Walls And Shut by Gates, one to Enter,[1]

199

Another to go Out – The weather at this time was So Cold that we observed All the Female Servants in the Streets had a Round Pot filled with Wood Embers hanging upon their Arms to keep them warm – – In the Evening we took Tea at M[rs]. Hollands And there met the Family of Pinnocks' lately Come from Jamaica

Wed Jan[y] 15th
Rode & walked in the Grounds of the Villa Borghese which are delightfull [sic] – from thence Rode Over the Three Bridges which

---

1. Rome's Jewish population had for centuries congregated close to the river towards the Ponte Fabricio. Paul IV obliged them to live in an enclosed community with a bull of 1555 and that area surrounding the present-day Synagogue became the Ghetto. With the arrival of the united Italy in 1870, Jews obtained the same rights as every Italian. The ghetto was demolished and the new synagogue inaugurated in 1904. There has been something of a revival of overt Jewish presence in the area in recent years.

Cross the Tiber in different parts of Rome,[1] & finished the morning by looking into Some Churches In the Evening went to M[rs].
Leslie[s] Party,[2] & Chatted Cheifly w' M[rs]. Harrison.

Thursday Jan[y] 16th
At Noon walked in the Gardens of the Villa Borghese & there met
M[r]. & M[rs]. & Three Miss Pinnocks – And

200

M[r]. M[rs]. & Miss Harrison with M[r] & M[rs]. Holland – M[r]. Leason[3]
[sic] &c &c with whom We agreed to go to the Vatican in the Evening
to See the Clementine Museum by Torch Light[4] – which we did
and Observed the Shade thrown on the Apollo Belvedere to See
his Attitude to Advantage –[5] And the no less admired Laocoon;[6]
the first Said to be the finest Single Figure And the latter the finest
Groupe[7] in the World – Apollo is Suppos'd to have just discharged
the Arrow at the Python & his Attitude is Beautiful and Natural
– His Countenance Composed and Elegant – In the Laocoon
Every Feature Shews the deepest Anguish, The Fathers flesh is
Contracted in Consequence of Poison. The Youngest Son is fallen
down in the Agonies of Death, The Other Son, Looking towards
the Father Wishing to Help him, yet wanting Help himself = And
many other Figures Appeared to great Advantage by the

201

Light & Shade thrown upon them by the Torches – And we were
all much pleased with our Evenings Amusement tho' we found the
Place we were in very Cold –

---

1. The Ponte Sant'Angelo, the Ponte Sisto, and the Ponti Cestio & Fabricio the latter
   crossing the river each side of the Tiber island.
2. Mrs Laura Leslie was in Italy with her two daughters – see Ingamells' *Dictionary* . . .
3. Either the Hon William or the Hon Robert Leeson, sons of the 1st earl of Milltown.
4. The practice was popular in the eighteenth century.
5. The discovery of the Apollo Belvedere is uncertain but it was in the collection of
   Giuliano della Rovere and entered the Vatican Collection when the cardinal became
   pope as Julius II. It has remained one of the treasures of the museum ever since.
6. The Laocoon was discovered in a garden in Rome in 1506 and instantly distinguished
   as the famous sculpture of antiquity recorded by Pliny. It was soon after purchased
   by Julius II and entered the Vatican Collection.
7. Murray gives this spelling.

Friday Jan[y] 17th
We went at Noon to Saint Antonio where there is Annually upon this Day a Blessing Given to the Horses in Rome[1] – In a Small Room, Called a Chapel fronting the Street, Two Priests Attended, and As the Horses were brought near to them, They Dipped a Small brush into Holy Water & Sprinkled each Horse, upon which Wax Candles or Flambeaux were presented – and in Return a piece of Paper with the Portrait of the Saint is given to the Servant who Drives or Leads the Horses – from hence I went with M[rs] Holland in her New Carriage resembling a Laundelet [*sic*] to the Villa Borghese & M[rs]. Holland was the Driver – – M[r] & M[rs]-

202

Montague Wilkinson, M[r]. & M[rs]. Canning with their Son, & M[r]. Talbot Came to Dine with us –

Saturday Jan[y] 18th
Nine o Clock – morn[g]. Ther – 41.

Clear Sky and Bright Sun –

Before Breakfast Walked (as usual) upon the Monte Pincio which is 135 Steps above the level of the Street – And the Garden De Medici being 75 Steps above this Terrace makes the Height 210 Steps from the Level of the City – And Here I generally walked Every Day, Amusing Myself with the distinct View of the Streets and many of the Build[gs] in Rome – with the Country beyond Regretting at the Same time the Distance I was from my Native Land, & those So Dear to me –

At Noon went to S[t]. Peters to hear Some very fine Solemn Musick – & in y[e] Evening to a Party at Miss Carr' –

---

1. Sant'Antonio Abate close to the basilica of Santa Maria Maggiore. The ceremony continued in front of the church up until the unification in 1870 but the square was later altered and the event now takes place nearby. Although the ceremony was decried by many British commentators, such events are popular in Britain today.

203

Sunday Jany 19.
Abbé Giuntotardi Breakfasted with us & afterw^ds took us to the
Churches of Saint Bernardo & Saint Susanna[1] – from thence to
the most magnificent Church in Rome (except Saint Peters) Saint
Maria degli Angeli Built by Michael Angelo or rather formed by
Him from Diocletian^s Thermæ –[2] It was the Room in which the
youths performed their Exercises in Bad Weather – The Columns
are of Granite 40 feet in Height, & the Church is in the Form of
a Greek Cross, Benedict the 14th. fitted it up; upon the Pavement
is Traced the Meridian Line by Bianchini –[3] On Each Side the
Entrance are the Tombs of Carlo Maratti and Salvator Rosa –[4] We
afterw^ds Visited Saint Maria della Vittoria[5] And Saint Agnes fuori
della mura, this Last is a mile from the City And Allmost Under
Ground for the Descent to it is by a long flight of Steps – Four
Pillars of Porphyry Support the Great Altar and are Esteemed the

204

the most Curious in Rome,[6] very near to this Church is a Rotunda
now Called the Church of S^t. Costanza It is Supposed to have been

1. San Bernardo alle Terme formed from one of the corner towers of the baths of
   Diocletian complex from 1598, and Santa Susanna (opposite), a building of early
   Christian origins but radically altered by Carlo Maderno in 1603.
2. The basilica of Santa Maria degli Angeli. It was initiated by Michelangelo, trans-
   forming the tepidarium of Diocletian's Baths, but actually carried out by Giacomo
   del Duca from 1566.
3. A meridian line set in the pavement and called the Linea Clementina in honour of
   Clement XI. It was carried out by Francesco Bianchini and Giacomo Maraldi in 1702.
4. The tomb of Carlo Maratta is by himself with a bust by Francesco Maratta, and that
   of Salvator Rosa is by Bernardino Fioriti.
5. Santa Maria della Vittoria – church designed by Maderno with a façade by G.B. Soria
   of 1626. It is now chiefly notable for the Cappella Cornaro containing the famous (or
   infamous) Ecstasy of Saint Teresa by Bernini.
6. Sant'Agnese fuori le mura is indeed outside the town on the via Nomentana and
   some distance from the three churches previously described. It was erected in the
   fourth century by Costanza, daughter (?) of the Emperor Constantine on the site of
   the supposed burial place of the eponymous saint. The ciborium is supported by four
   porphyry columns which probably originated from the first church on the site. The
   nave arcade and galleries also contain columns and other architectural elements from
   the imperial period.

the Temple of Bacchus, because the Sarcophagus has Carvings of Children Playing with Bunches of Grapes –[1]

We next went to L'Hyppodromo di Constantine[2] Il Pont Salaro[3] – Il Monte Sacro[4] and La Fontana di Acqua Acetosa –[5]

In the Evening Went to the Third Concert at the Princess Santa Croce, who was herself Dressed in a Robe of white Gawse with Sattin[6] Stripes & Gold Spangles Crossing in Lines from Stripe to Stripe – –

Monday Jan[y] 20th.
At Noon took M[rs]. Montague Wilkinson to the Villa Borghese And Afterw[ds] to the Gardens of the Villa Doria = where it is Said that Raphael Lived[7] – upon our Return went together Shopping – M[r] Grignon the Artist Came to Dinner with us – a Sensible pleasing man & Strongly Recommended to us by Sir Corbet Corbet

205

Tuesday Jan[y] 21st
At Noon Rode Over the Bridge S[t]. Angelo and turning Short on the Left went to the Villa Lanti –[8] which being Situated on an Eminence Commands an fine & Extensive View of Rome – after-

---

1. This is the mausoleum of Sta Costanza erected in 342 AD and later transformed into a church. The red porphyry sarcophagus was probably made to house the remains of Constantia, daughter of Constantine, who died in 354 AD. It was moved to the piazza San Marco between 1467 and 71 and in 1790 placed in the Vatican Museum. It was replaced in the church by a plaster copy.
2. The so-called hippodrome of Constantine is actually the remains of a basilica built adjacent to Sta Costanza. It was 98 metres long and shaped like a circus for racing.
3. Ponte Salario – the bridge over the Aniene where the via Salaria crosses this river.
4. Monte Sacro – the ancient mons Sacer. It is now surrounded by modern suburbs.
5. The Fontana dell'Acqua Acetosa is a mineral spring to the north of the city close to the Tiber. The fountain was originally built by Pius V in 1616 and was very popular with the Romans for its therapeutic value.
6. Murray gives this spelling.
7. Not the Villa Doria-Pamphilj but a small building known as the Villetta Doria which stood in the area of the Galoppatoio which was destroyed in 1849. Raphael never lived there.
8. Villa Lante al Gianicolo – built by Giulio Romano from 1518–27, and passing to the Lante in 1551. The small building was the home of the Helbigs in the nineteenth century and became through them the seat of the Finnish Embassy to the Holy See.

w^{ds}. Went to the Villa Borghese – and in the Evening Called On Miss Knight & went with her to Prince Doria^s where at the Door we were Received by the Gentleman Usher belonging to the Prince who meeting us at the Door of the Anti Chamber – made a Bow And Conducted us through Three Rooms – At the Fourth the Princess Sitting near the Door Rose to Receive us and after the usual Compliments were Exchang'd we mix'd with the Company; The Gentlemen Standing, the Ladies Sitting= Apricot Ice & Various others in Small Glasses with Silver Saucers, & Cakes Lemonade &c were Continually offer'd = The Room was Carpetted

206

And a Low Screen (as usual) placed before the Fire, for the Italians never like to Look at One. From Six to Eight the Company are Coming but by Nine all are Gone as the Conversationné at this Palace is only at the Prima Sera – or first part of the Evening – we went after- w^{ds} – to the Princess Santa Croce where Company were beginning to assemble And many Parties at Cards were Soon made – for here the Company do not Come till after Eight & Say till after Ten –

Wed Jany 22^d.
Went this morning to the Church of Saint Giovanni in Laterano, In which the Annual Commemoration of the Death of the Late King of France[1] was Celebrating by throwing Incense, and Sprinkling with Holy water a Tomb Erected for that purpose having a Bust of

207

Of the Late King place upon it The Musick was Fine; but not so Solemn as I Expected = Both the Kings Aunts were there in a Tribune placed for the purpose near the Altar – And I was in Another Tribune with Several Ladies belonging to their Suite; Le Comtesse de Narbonne who is a Dame d'Honneur Shewed me the Mesdames as they walked by me Out of the Church[2] = Six Soldiers walking Two & Two together went before them, Madame Adelaide

1. Louis XVI who had been guillotined on 21st January 1793.
2. Françoise de Chalus, Duchesse de Narbonne (1734–1821). She was a lady-in-waiting to Madame Adelaide and promoted to *dame d'honneur* in 1781.

followed the Soldiers & Madame Victoire walked next[1] – then Two ladies Singly and Two Gentlemen M[r]. Hill an English Gentleman was with me & Shewed me afterwards the Corsini Chapel which is on One Side the Aisle & is Esteemed the most Elegant in Europe; both for its Proportions and the disposition of the Marbles and a Beautiful Porphyry Sarcophagus under the

208

Statue of Clement the 12th. It was found in the Pantheon & Supposed to have contained the Ashes of Agrippa.[2]

There is a very Fine Picture of the Founder of the Corsini Family Over the Altar. It is in Mosaic[3] – We went from hence to the Villa Borghese our favorite Place for Exercise by walking And Enjoying the Clear Sky & Bright Sun, which we had, but the wind was rather Cold In the Evening went to a party at M[rs]. Pinnocks where most of the English here were Assembled –

Thursday Jan[y] 23[d]
At Noon Rode to the Villa Borghese walked there as usual and Afterw[ds] went Shopping – Messieurs Prevot,[4] Angerstein,[5] Brand[6] & M[r]. Kuittner[7] (who is Travelling with Lord Tyrone)[8] Dined with us & in the Evening we all went together to a Party at M[rs]. Cannings –

1. Marie Louise Thérèse Victoire (1733–99) and Marie Adelaïde (1732–1800), daughters of Louis XV of France.
2. Presumably because Agrippa was thought at this time to have been responsible for the construction of the temple.
3. The chapel was added to the church for the Corsini pope, Clement XII by Alessandro Galilei between 1732–5. The porphyry sarcophagus came from the atrium of the Pantheon and the mosaic altarpiece is a copy of that by Guido Reni of Sant'Andrea Corsini. The statue of the pope is a bronze by Giovanni Battista Maini.
4. Signor Prevot – not traced.
5. Ingamells' *Dictionary* gives him as possibly John Angerstein (1773–1858), son of John Julius Angerstein.
6. Thomas Brand (1774–1851) of the Hoo, Kimpton, Herts. He was attracted to Jacobinism as a young man.
7. Possibly Carl Gottlieb Küttner (1753–1803) who had been in England and Ireland.
8. Henry de la Poer Beresford, Earl of Tyrone (1772–1826).

209

Friday Jany 24th.
This morning we Saw Icicles hanging Seven Inches in Length from
the Top of the Fountain that is upon the Hill on which the Palais de
Medicis is Situated –[1] And the Fountain being immediately under
Some Large Ever-Green Trees the water thus froze had a very fine
Effect – At Noon Rode to the Villa Borghese and there Walked
with M^r & M^rs. Holland, M^r. Leeson Brother to Lord Miltons,[sic][2]
M^r. Brand of the Hoo, in Hertfordshire, M^r. Dawkins of Portman
Square,[3] & the Family of Pinnocks, with Several Other English – In
the Evening Went with Miss Knight to Cardinal Bernis where Two
Servants met us (as usual) at the Bottom of the Great Stairs with
Lighted Flambeaux^s And walked before us to the Anti-Chamber
where the Cardinal^s Gentleman met us, & having made us a very
Low Bow, Walked before us through Six Rooms. In the Seventh
was found the Cardinal Sitting with a Circle of Twelve Chairs

210

Before him, but only Four Persons with him who appeared to
be Abbé^s. We made a Short Visit & went afterwards to a Private
Concert – where we found most of the English

Saturday Jany 25th
M^r. Fagan Breakfasted with us & we went with him to the Villa
Ludovisi on the Pincian Hill – the Garden is a mile & Half in compass And in it are a great number of Statues & Busts = The Ruins
of the City Wall forms one Boundary, and from Another part of
the Garden is a delightful View of the City which appears in a
Semi-Circular Form with the Hill Janiculum forming the Back

---

1. The fountain in front of the Villa Medici. It was designed by Annibale Lippi (1589?)
   and consists of a bowl of red granite.
2. Joseph Leeson (1730–1801), 2nd Earl of Milltown.
3. On her return journey we see that Mrs Bentham dined again with a Mr George
   Dawkins of Portman Square. This was probably George Hay Dawkins-Pennant
   (1764–1840). He later inherited the estate of Richard Pennant and added that surname to his own. He had estates in Jamaica and was later an MP.

Ground –[1] In the Garden is a Casino with many fine Statues particularly Papirius & his mother, Esteemed the Best Groupe[2] in Rome next to the Laocoon which is in the Museum at the Vatican – And Here are Several Pictures by Guerchino [*sic*][3]

From hence we went to Monte Cavallo, The Pope[s] Summer Palace on the Quirinal Hill = The Name

211

Was Given it from Two Colossal Statues being there with Each a Horse And the present Pope has placed an Obelisk between them –[4] We walked round the Garden, which is a mile in compass, And in it is a Grotto with an Organ, which Plays by means of Water – And there are many whimsical Jet d'Eau[s]. in the Garden, and likewise An Elegant Room called the Coffee Room in which are Two very fine Large Views of Rome by Paolo Pannini of Narne –[5] We went afterw[ds] to the Mausoleum of Adrian, now the Castle of S[t] Angelo and now the Citadel of Rome – The Arsenal – The Treasury And the State Prison in which at this Time were many French men –[6]

1. Villa Ludovisi – the villa built between 1621–22 for Cardinal Ludovico Ludovisi, nephew of Gregory XV, was one of the great losses of the post–1870 transformation of the city. It was torn down and the gardens divided into building lots between 1883–5. The via Veneto passes through what were once the grounds of the villa.
2. The group first appeared in the records of the Ludovisi Collection in 1623 and it is presumed that it was found on the site of the villa when it was being built. The statue with much of the remainder of the collection was purchased by the State in 1901 and is now in the Museo Nazionale.
3. The Casino of the Villa Ludovisi is the only part of the Villa Ludovisi surviving and contains the famous fresco of Aurora by Guercino.
4. The two colossal statues of Castor and Pollux forming part of the fountain in the Piazza del Quirinale came from the Baths of Constantine and were brought to the Quirinale Hill by Sixtus V. An obelisk from the Mausoleum of Augustus was added by Giovanni Antinori for Pius VI and finally the fountain by Raffaelle Stern was commissioned by Pius VII in 1810, using a basin found in the Forum.
5. The Coffee House was begun by Ferdinando Fuga in 1741 and contains two views of Rome by Giovanni Paolo Pannini of Piacenza.
6. The Mausoleum of Hadrian – the huge tomb was initiated by the Emperor Hadrian about 123 AD as a family mausoleum but was completed by Antoninus Pius (reigned 138–161 AD). The Ponte Sant'Angelo was built subsequently to provide access from the city proper. The structure was added to over the centuries and became the fortress of the popes and finally a museum. The original function of the building was eventually forgotten and the entrance was only rediscovered in the early nineteenth century. After 1870 further explorations were undertaken by Mariano Borgatti (b.1853) who found himself working for the Ministry of Defence, the building being then considered a fortress, rather than as an historic monument.

The View from the Top of the Castle is very fine – The Tiber winding at the Foot and the City, Surrounded by a Circular Chain of Hills – from Hence we went to the Villa Pamfili and walked in the Garden with the Pinnocks and Several more English – In the

212

Evening took Tea with Our Banker M[r]. Jenkins And his Neice[1] of the Same Name, who Came from Sidmouth in Devonshire to Live with her Uncle And who is going Soon to be married to an Italian for whose Sake She proposes to become a Roman –[2]

Sunday Jany 26th.
Abbé Giuntotardi Breakfasted with us And the Day being Rainy He Gave us double Lesson[s] in the Italian Language At Three we Calld upon M[r]. Jenkins & went with him & his Neice to the Academiæ,[3] where a great number of Persons were Assembled to hear Madame Bandinini[4] from Lucca Speak & Recite Verses; this Lady was Called a L'Improvisitore And what She Recited was in a Tone like Chanting & Said to Resemble the manner of the Ancient Poets who from memory Recited the History of Past Ages in Verse = Several Monks and Abbé[s] Spoke, & Some Read their Compositions = but in general it was Extempore –

213

In the Evening Called upon Miss Knight And went with her to the Fourth Concert which was at La Marchesa Patrizie Montoro;[5] we passed through Five Rooms handsomely Furnished before we came to the Concert Room which was hung with Crimson Velvet formed into Pannels by Gold Lace & Lighted by Lustres – After the Concert there was a good number of Card Tables in different Rooms.[6]

---

1. Murray gives this spelling.
2. Anna Maria Jenkins. She married Giovanni Martinez later that year. Presumably becoming a Roman means becoming a Roman Catholic.
3. Possibly the Accademia dei Lincei founded by Federico Cesi in 1603 and still an important cultural institution today.
4. Teresa Bandettini (1763–1819).
5. The Marchesa Patrizi Naro Montoro – probably Cunegonda di Sassonia who married Marchese Giovanni Patrizi Naro Montoro.
6. The Palazzo Montoro in via di Montoro was built in the sixteenth century.

Monday Jany 27th

Within the last Twenty Four Hours there has been Violent
Thunder & Lightning, which was Succeeded by Rain, Hail, and
Snow that laid Some Hours upon the Ground –

At Noon we went to Saint Peters & Staid Two Hours. The Pope
Came as usual to his Prayers and the Ceremony the Same as before
describ'd

Lord Tyrone Eldest Son to the Earl of Waterford, Mr. Douglass[1]
the Eldest Son of Lord Douglass, M^{r.}

214

Ballard,[2] M^{r.} M^{rs.} & Miss Pinnock Dined with us, & And [*sic*] we
went together in the Evening to the Venetian Ambassadors, where
there was a Large Wood Fire = The Refreshm^{ts} were Coffee, Tea
& Chocolate Ice

Tuesday Jany 28th

At Noon went to the Piazza Navona to Observe the Fountain
which is Esteemed the most Magnificent in Rome – It Resembles
a vast Rock pierced through and Through, So as to be divided into
Four Parts which Unite at the Top, where an Obelisk is placed:
Toward the Bottom of the Rock Are Seated Four Colossal Figures
Representing the Principal Rivers;[3] We went afterw^{ds}. To Lady
Knight^s And took her Ladyship for a Ride to the Church of Saint
Giovanni in Laterano, and Returned by Saint Maria Maggiore,
which is Situated On the highest part of the Esquiline Hill – Before
Dinner Walked upon Monte Pincio, or as many Call it

215

Trinité de Monte = We Dined with M^{r.} & Mrs. Montague
Wilkinson and met Mr. Ashe, a Gentleman who was Travelling
upon Dr. Radcliffe' medical Fellowship. He is of Christ Church

---

1. Hon. Archibald Douglas (1773–1844)
2. Charles Ballard – he was in Italy as tutor to the Hon. Archibald Douglas.
3. The Four Rivers Fountain erected by Bernini for Innocent X in 1651. The obelisk at
   the summit is ancient but is a local production, not Egyptian.

Oxford and had now been more than Two Years in Germany and Italy[1] – In the Evening M^r. Prevot with M^r. Angerstein, And M^rs. Hill & M^rs. Canning & Family were added to Our Party

Wed Jany 29th.
Walked in the Borghese Gardens & Afterwards Rode to the Coliseum And S^t. Giovanni in Laterno [sic] – and went to the Scala Santa which is nearly Opposite where we found Several Persons Ascending the Stairs upon their Knees. At the Top we found A Small Dark Chapel = There were Three paralel[2] flights of Stairs, the Middle one never Ascended but upon the Knees, on Either Side Any Person may walk up or go Down.[3] In the Afternoon took a Lesson in Italien & in the Evening went to Lady Knights.

216

Thursday Jany. 30th
Went in the morning to the Church of Saint Marie del Popolo[4] and Afterwards to S^t. Carlo, where upon the High Altar is a painting Representing the Procession of Saint Carlo at the time the Plague was at Milan[5] – from hence we Went to the Piazza Navona, to See the Church of Saint Agnese[6] On Our Return went to the Villa Borghese And in the Evening to a party at M^rs. Cannings –

Friday Jany 31st
Clear Sky with a very warm Sun we went this morning to Saint Pietro in Montorio,[7] on the Top of the Hill S^t. Janiculum, to See The Picture of Raphael of the Transfiguration of Christ; which is

1. Edward Ash (c.1765–1829). He was elected to a Radcliffe travelling fellowship in 1790.
2. Murray gives this spelling.
3. On rebuilding the Lateran Palace Sixtus V commissioned this shrine from Domenico Fontana to house the private chapel of the popes, or Sancta Sanctorum. The stairs leading up to the chapel, also reused from the old palace, were long thought to be those of the house of Pontius Pilate in Jerusalem, hence the procession of supplicants. The practice continues to this day.
4. Santa Maria del Popolo in the eponymous piazza.
5. San Carlo ai Catinari – the painting of San Carlo Borromeo in procession over the high altar is by Pietro da Cortona and dates to 1650. It is still in situ.
6. Sant'Agnese in Agone in Piazza Navona. It was begun by Carlo Rainaldi in 1652 for Innocent X and completed by Borromini.
7. San Pietro in Montorio – church built on the site of the supposed Crucifixion of St Peter.

Esteemed to be the first Easel painting in the World,[1] and in the Court of the Convent is the Round Doric Temple of Bramante[s] Built

217

Of Tivertine Stone,[2] and Surrounded by a Portico of Sixteen Columns of Oriental Granite, remarkable for its Elegance and Simplicity[3] = From this Church is the finest View of Rome, Commanding the whole City And the principal Ruins – from hence We went to the Villa Corsini,[4] and to Monte Mariæ at the Top of which is a good View of the Ponte Molle with the Bend of the River Tiber – –[5]

In the Evening went with Miss Knight to the Borghese palace where Six Rooms were Opened And many Card tables in Each – Servants as usual attended with Tea & Coffee, And both at our Entrance & Return Two attended us with Lighted Flambeaux while we Ascended And Descended the Great Stair Case.

Saturday Feb[y] 1st
Received letters from Cha' in Answer to those which had Announced Our

218

Irreparable Loss at Naples – And the melancholy Impression Renewed by the receipt of these Letters rendered us unfit for Society the whole Day but M[r]. Fagan having been Engag'd to

---

1. Raphael's Transfiguration originally stood over the high altar but was transferred to the Vatican Picture Gallery in 1809.
2. Travertine – a limestone the deposits of which are usually associated with the presence of sulphurous springs, hence the derivation of the Italian name *travertino* from those deposits between Rome and Tivoli, where such springs still exist, and in use since antiquity.
3. The Tempietto by Donato Bramante probably erected between 1502–7.
4. The Palazzo Corsini on the via della Lungara. It was built in the early sixteenth century and was later the home of Queen Cristina of Sweden. It became the property of the Corsini family in 1736 and is now a picture gallery largely housing the collection of the family.
5. Monte Mario – overlooking the Tiber valley to the north of the city. Presumably the outing was a carriage drive as it is some distance from the Palazzo Corsini.

Attend us to different Artists we went with him to See Specimens in mosaic; And afterwards Sculpture And Prints –

Sunday Feb.ᵧ 2ᵈ
Walked before Breakfast (as we usually did) upon Trinité de Monte & met Mʳ. Grigby an English Gentleman of Suffolk[1] – Afterwards we went to the Sistine Chapel where the Pope Dressed in Crimson & Gold & Seated upon his Throne, Gave a large Wax Candle to Each Cardinal, and then Descending from his Seat under the Canopy, went into his Chair, which being immediately Elevated On Poles,[2] and Supported on the Shoulders of Ten men, He holding a Large Wax Candle in his Hand was Carried in Procession Round a

219

Large Hall adjoining to the Chapel,[3] The Cardinals Walked in the Procession Two together before the Pope, And Two Priests with Lighted Candles went between –

At the Return of the Procession into the Chapel, Each Cardinal had his Silk Dress which was Embroider'd With Gold taken off, but the Robe of Scarlet Cloth trimmed with Ermine which was under the Silk Dress remained – The Pope continued in the Chair till his Fine Garment of Red Silk richly Covered with Gold was taken off, and Another of white And Gold put on, and the mitre of white Changed for one of Gold –

From hence we went with Mʳˢ. Hill to See the Ruins of Caracalla' Baths, Went through the Arch of Drusus,[4] and the Gate of Saint Sebastian[5] to Capo di Bove, the Tomb of Cecilia Metella the wife

1. A Mr Grigby is listed in Ingamells' *Dictionary* but no further details are given. However, this Mr Grigby is almost certainly Joshua Grigby although Mr Joshua senior died in 1798 and his son in 1829.
2. The Sedia gestatoria – the ceremonial throne on which popes were carried until 1978. It was supported by 12 footmen (palafrenieri).
3. Presumably the Sala Regia – once the reception chamber for the papacy but now reduced, more or less, to the function of antechamber to the Sistine Chapel. It was built by Antonio da Sangallo for Paul III (Farnese) and decorated extremely lavishly by numerous artists.
4. Although called the Arch of Drusus, the monument was actually built to carry the Acqua Antoniniana over the via Appia Antica to the nearby Baths of Caracalla.
5. The Porta San Sebastiano in the Aurelian Wall.

of Crassus = It is Called Capo di Bove from the Frieze Ornament which is the Heads of Bulls in Releivo –[1]

220

We then went to the Inclosed Ground Called the Circus of Caracalla,[2] & afterw^ds to the Fountain of Egeria,[3] and from thence to the Convent of Saint Gregoire upon Mount Celias[4] – where We Saw the Fine Picture by Annibal Carache –[5]

M^r. Hill Dined with us and we went in the Evening to a Conversatione at Madame Ciciporci.

Monday Feby 3^d.
Rode with M^rs. Montague Wilkinson to the Monte Aventine, and walked in the Gardens of the Priorato which Commands a fine Prospect –[6] from thence went to Monte Testacio,[7] which is a Hill composed of Potsherds, And near it is the Tomb of Caius Cestius,[8] a beautiful Pyramid, And the only One in Europe; It Stands Half within and Half without the City walls; Within it is a Room 20 f^t in Length & 14 in Breadth & 13 ft in Heighth – The Door of Entrance was very Low & we were obligd to

1. The mausoleum dates to the 1st century AD and survived destruction by being used as a fortress. It was known as Capo di Bove because of the ox heads (bucrania) in its frieze.
2. Actually the Circus of Maxentius and the best preserved of such structures in Rome. It was built in 309 AD.
3. The so-called Grotto of Egeria, a favourite resort of tourists at this time but actually a nymphaeum dating to the 2nd century AD.
4. San Gregorio Magno, or, al Celio.
5. The altarpiece of St Gregory for the Cappella Salviati in San Gregorio by Annibale Carracci was subsequently part of the Bridgewater House Collection but was destroyed in WWII – see Posner (1971), no.130.
6. Presumably the gardens of the Villa Malta built as the residence of the Grand Master of the Knights of Malta. The church of the order, Santa Maria del Priorato, adjoins it.
7. Monte Testaccio – an artificial mound of broken pots formed by the dumping of pottery from the warehouses of the neighbouring river port on the Tiber.
8. Tomb of Caius Cestius – the famous pyramidal tomb built in the reign of Augustus, its base now well below street level. The chamber within is not now usually accessible to the general public but it is a rectangular space with a barrel vault and simply decorated.

221

Stoop to gain Admittance And a woman Carried a Torch before us. Two Antique Columns Stand near.

Adjoining to a Burying Ground Allotted for Protestants, and upon a Stone Thrown on the Ground was Inscribed as follows –

To the Memory
Of M^r. James
Of Canterbury
And Fellow of Trin – Coll
Cambridge
An Elegant Poet
An Amiable Philosopher
And
He Died at Rome
December 1706

NB. Where the Omissions appear in the Inscription, the Stone had been defaced with a Chissel & was most Roughly Hacked –

NB. It is Supposed to be M^r. James Six,[1] who Travelled with Sir J. Stanly^s Eldest Son[2]

222

In the Evening We Went to the Venetian Ambassadors, and (as usual) found Two Servants attending with Lighted Flambeauxs [sic] to go before us as we Ascended & Descended the Great Stair Case – In the Rooms were Several Card Tables, and Coffee, Tea & Various Sorts of Ice were offered to Each Person from Eight o Clock till after Ten –

Tuesday Feby. 4th.
Rec^d. Letters from Cha'. Dated Jany 14. Before Breakfast we walked upon Trinite de Monte – At Noon went with M^r. Hill to See the

1. James Six (c.1758–86), a young scholar who died in Rome. His tomb which had been defaced has been restored according to Ingamells' Dictionary . . .
2. John Thomas Stanley, the Younger (1766–1850).

Mausoleum of Augustus[1] near the Church of Saint Carlo[2] between the Corso and the River = The Inner wall is Entire And is Circular, we saw it from the Apartments lately taken for the Residence of Prince Augustus,[3] in a House that is in a Narrow Dirty Street – We went from thence to a Church Called Saint Croce in Gerusalemme[4] and from

223

thence to the Picturesque Ruin of the Temple of Minerva Medica,[5] now Situated in a Vineyard near the Aqueducts adjoining to the Arches of Nero – At Our Return We Dined with M[r]. & M[rs]. Pinnock & there met Sir Lionel Copley[6] and M[r]. Rushout –[7]

Wed – Feb[y] 5th.

At Noon went with Miss Knight to the Senators, who gave the Fifth Concert at his Apartments in the Capitol – which are the whole Suite of Rooms in the Upper part of the Center Building[8] The Lower part being a Court of Justice – From these Apartments the Coliseum and the Various Surrounding Ruins with the Sabine And Latium Hill form a most Interesting Scene – The Suite of Rooms are near twenty, rather Small, but Elegantly fitted up, and at the End a very Large Rooms for Musick – No Roman can be Elected Senator – He must be a Foreigner, And the present is a

---

1. The Mausoleum of Augustus was begun by the emperor for himself and his successors in 27 AD but was already being used as a source for building materials by late Antiquity. The monument was later used for various purposes and became hemmed about by later buildings. The structure remaining was only "liberated " from these later accretions between 1936–38 during the Fascist period. It has recently been announced that a (much needed) refurbishment is to be undertaken – ed.
2. San Carlo al Corso.
3. Prince Augustus Frederick had met Lady Augusta Murray in Rome and they had secretly married in April 1793.
4. Santa Croce in Gerusalemme – the ancient basilica is thought to have been built on the site of an imperial villa and is now close to the Aurelian Wall. The building has been much altered over the centuries including the addition of a Baroque façade and a fascist-style chapel for the relics of the True Cross only completed in 1952.
5. The so-called Temple of Minerva Medica is actually thought to have been a garden building. It is now rather "buried" in subsequent developments close to the main railway line into the city. Most of the vault of the surviving structure collapsed in 1828.
6. Sir Lionel Copley, 2nd Bt. (c.1767–1806)
7. John Rushout (1770–1859) – see Ingamells' *Dictionary* . . .
8. Palazzo Senatorio erected in the late sixteenth century and based on a project of Michelangelo.

224

Venetian And has held this Office Twenty Years, And in respect to Age may continue as many more The Office being for Life And from Appearance He is not Fifty.[1]

Between the Selection of Musick We had La Signora Teresia Bandettini Landucci – an Improvisa who was said to perform Extremely Well – The Subject was given her by the Senator, Viz the Mother of Coriolanus[2] And afterw^{ds}. Two Other Subjects were given by different persons, upon Each of which She made a Declamation Either in Prose or verse in a kind of Voice that was between Singing and Speaking like Recitative this manner is Supposed to resemble the Antient Poets Rehearsing the History of their Country.

In the Evening we took Tea with M^r. & M^{rs}. Montague Wilkinson

225

Thursday Feb. 6th
Walked at Noon in the Borghese Gardens with M^r. & M^{rs}. & Miss Harrison And M^{rs}. & Miss Leslie & Miss Freeman. In the Evening went with Miss Knight to the Sixth Concert, given by the Governor of the Castle of S^t. Angelo,[3] at his Sisters, The Palais de Fiani – The Concert Room was large and had more than 200 Wax Lights, but the Other Rooms about Ten in number, were Small And after the Concert were filled with Card Tables –[4]

Friday Feby 7th
At Six o Clock we Called on M^r & M^{rs}. Fagan & took them with us to Tivoli – We put 4 Post Horses to Our Travelling Coach

1. Between 1191 and the mid nineteenth century only one person was ever elected at a time to serve as senator of the city.
2. Mother of Coriolanus – presumably referring to Volumnia the character in Shakespeare's play of *Coriolanus*.
3. Properly the *castellano* of Castel Sant'Angelo. However, Mrs Bentham is referring to the *vice-castellano* at that time, namely Marco Boncompagni Ludovisi Ottoboni (1741–1818). He was raised to the post in 1789 and succeeded his brother as Duke of Fiano in 1806. Presumably the princess mentioned here was his sister-in-law.
4. The Palazzo Fiano in via del Corso. The room specified by Mrs Bentham is probably the Salone frescoed by Baldassare Croce (1558–1628).

the Distance being Eighteen miles from Rome. We Saw many Sepulchral monuments On Each Side the Road, And at Four miles from Rome we Crossed the River Teverone, and at Eight

226

The Solfatare, the Water of which is like the Colour of Milk & feels Warm[1] – The whole Country here has a Fetid disagreable Smell – from Hence we Soon Came to the Beautiful Tomb of Plautius of A Circular Form like that of Mettella's .[2] We then went on to See the Ruins of Adrian's Villa[3] which Spread over a large Tract of Ground – we observed the remains of an Amphitheatre – Ruins of the Barracks intended for Soldiers – Baths – Temples &c &c – likewise a Very High Wall of great length On Each Side of which was formerly a Colonade to walk under as Either the Sun or moon made it desirable – It is Supposed that the Circle inclosing these different Buildings & the Ground belonging to Adrian[s]. Villa was Seven miles.

At Tivoli, upon the Edge of a High Rock, fronting a Beautiful

227

Cascade, Stands the Temple of the Sibyl – One of the most Elegant Remains of Grecian Architecture – Its Situation is Uncommonly Picturesque, & very near it at the Bottom is the Grotto of Neptune, to which we Descended by a very narrow And allmost Perpendicular Path; but Was Amply repaid by the magnificent Scenery of the Grotto and Cascades. The Water falling from an Amazing Height, and Tumbling through the different Arches of the Cavern Rises again with a Foam Shining like Silver. – From this Place We walked near a mile amidst the most Interesting Scenery of Wood, Composed Cheifly of Olive Tree[s] at this time loaded with Fruit – It

---

1. The lake of Solfatare the waters of which are sulphurous and supply the baths at Bagni di Tivoli.
2. The Tomb of the Plautii dating to the time of Augustus.
3. Villa Adriana – the large palace (almost a town) built below the town of Tivoli by the Emperor Hadrian. It became the object of study from the fifteenth century onwards, at first mainly as a source for sculptures, etc. From the nineteenth century research became more scientific and systematic and in the twentieth century the site became public property.

being the Black Olive which the People were now Gathering – We
went afterw[ds] to See the Cascadelle, which is the Fall

228

Of the River Anio, now Called Teverone – This River Falls fifty
Feet down a Rock & then forms a Second Cascade Amidst Other
Rocks,[1] And within View are Some fine Remains of the Villa of
Mecæneas,[2] And the Temple of the Sibyl, or rather of Vesta[3] –
We Went from hence to the Villa D'Este, at which is a Curious
Specimen of Gardens in former Days. Terraces one above Another
Clipt Tree's & Water Works from a Variety of different Figures[4] –
We had taken with us Cold Chicken And with the addition of Fish
& Pigeons of Tivoli we were greatly Refreshed, And found the Inn
were [sic] we Dined tolerably Decent – At Seven in the Evening we
arrived at Rome having passed a very pleasant Day with the Air as
Warm as it usually is in June in England –

229

Saturday Feb[y] 8th.
Received Letters from England and Answered them – Walked in the
Gardens de Medicis & in the Even'[g] Went to Miss Carr's Party –

1. The situation of the falls at Tivoli changed dramatically in the 1830s. After a serious
   flood in the town in 1826 Gregory XVI ordered a tunnel to be constructed taking the
   waters of the Aniene under the town to a new "grande cascata" but still below the two
   temples at the edge of the locality. There are walks remaining below this in what is
   now known as the Villa Gregoriana.
2. Villa of Maecenas – an imposing complex of ruins thought to be the Villa of Maecenas
   and painted as such by many artists. In 1849 it was established as the Sanctuary of
   Hercules Victor.
3. The notable circular temple with a Corinthian colonnade is known as the temple of
   Vesta. The rectangular temple close by is known as the Temple of the Sibyl though
   both attributions are uncertain.
4. Villa d'Este – the villa and famous garden laid out by Pirro Ligorio (1510–83) for
   Cardinal Ippolito d'Este and noted for its descending terraces of water features.

Sunday Feby 9th

Monsr. Giuntotardi Breakfasted and Staid the Day with us, and with him we went to the Church of Saint Pietro in Vinicoli,[1] to See the famous Statue of Moses between the Cardinal Virtues beneath the Monument of the Pope Julius the Eleventh[2] by Michelangelo from hence we went to the Coliseum, The Arch of Constantine, The Arch of Titus, The Arch of Severus, The Temple of Peace, The Three Beautiful Fluted Corinthian Colums [sic] at the foot of the Capitoline Hill, Supposed to be part of the Temple of Jupiter Tonans, Built by Augustus.[3] The Eight Column part of the Portico

230

Of the Temple of Concord[4] – The Single Pillar with a Corinthian Capital –[5]

The Ten Columns belonging to the Temple of Antoninus and Faustina now Standing before the Church of Saint Lorenzo –[6] The Temple of Romulus and Remus now the Church of Saint Cosmo & Damiano,[7] The Doors of which were the Old Bronze Doors of the Temple and are now Entire.[8]

After Staying a Considerable Time Viewing the different Ruins in the Campo Vachino[9] we went to Monte Testacio which is 160 feet in Height and half a mile in Circumference, Composed wholly of

---

1. San Pietro in Vincoli – one of the ancient basilicas of the city, the church is famous for housing the chains used to imprison St Peter and perhaps more so today as the location of Michelangelo's Tomb for Julius II which includes his "Moses" of 1514–16.
2. This should read Julius 2nd – ed.
3. The Temple of the deified Vespasian and Titus – it was erected about AD80.
4. The Temple of Saturn – as its inscription relates it was restored in the late fourth century.
5. The Column of Phocas. The actual monument predates this dedication when in 608 AD a statue of the aforesaid eastern emperor was placed on top of the column.
6. The Temple of the Divus Antoninus Pius and Diva Faustina – it was originally dedicated to the empress alone in 140 AD.
7. The basilica of SS. Cosma and Damiano formed from the fusion of two buildings from antiquity. It was restored in the reign of Urban VIII but still retains much work of earlier periods.
8. The bronze doors were a rare survival from antiquity.
9. Properly, the Campo vaccino – the name given to the forum when it was used to pasture cattle in post-classical times.

Potsherds. from hence we Went to the Gardens of the Priorato on the Aventine Hill And to See the Candelabria in the Chapel –[1]

In the Evening we went to the Concert at the Duke de Fianis NB the Same palace we were at on Thursday last – –

231

Monday Feb[y] 10th
Went to See the Pope go in his State Carriage to Visit a Convent. The Coach was drawn by Six Horses with only Two Postillions, the middle Horses being without a Rider. The Postillions were Dressed in a loose flowing Jacket of Crimson Velvet, & Sleeves of Sattin, the Hair Curled & Powdered flowing on their Shoulders, & no Hat or Cap upon their Heads. From the Convent the Pope walked to an adjacent Palace attended by Two Prelates

From hence we went to the Borghese Gardens & walked near & about the Beautiful Lake where the great number of Ever Green Oaks[2] with Birds Singing gave all the appearance of Summer And upon the Lake were a great Variety of Muscovy[3] & other Ducks And an Extensive View of Country

We Dined at M[r]. Cannings & met Madame Norton an English

232

Lady who had been Educated in France, and had been une Dame

---

1. The elaborate candelabrum designed by Piranesi for his own tomb in Sta Maria del Priorato. It was a confection of antique and "modern" pieces and is now in the Musée du Louvre having been replaced by a statue of the artist.
2. Evergreen oak – the Holm Oak (Quercus ilex).
3. Muscovy ducks (Cairina moschata) – not Russian at all but native to north America and imported to Europe.

d'Honneur to Le Comtesse d'Albani[1] there was likewise Sir Lionel Copley, Messrs. Ker[2] & Plunket[3] & an Abbée Monsr. Green[4]

In the Evening went (as usual[5] to the Venetian Ambassadors where the Refreshments were Coffee Tea, Cedrata[6] & Chocolate Ice – The Coffee & Ice[s] were brought into the Room from 8 to 9 and at Ten tea –

Tuesday Feby 11th.
Walked only in the Gardens de Medici, & afterw[ds] went Shopping with M[rs]. Montague Wilkinson who with M[r]. Wilkinson, M[rs.] Dawkins and M[r]. Hill Dined with us –

This morning my dear Farr Purchased the Views of Rome[7] – Some Coloured Drawings and Mosaics[8]

Wed Feb[y] 12.
Walked upon the Banks of the Tiber in the morning[9] – In the Even[g] at M[rs]. Pinnocks

233

Thursday Feb[y] 13th.
Went with M[r]. & M[rs]. Pinnock to the Church of Saint Cecilia in Trastevere, where we saw the Elegant marble Figure of Cecilia in

1. Miss Norton originally came to Rome in 1788 as the companion of the Duchess of Albany who died the following year. At the time of Mrs Bentham's visit she was living in the household of Cardinal York. Charlotte Stuart, later Duchess of Albany, died in 1789.
2. David Ker (1742–1811). He was a widower and in Italy with his three daughters and their governess having been married to a Venetian singer.
3. Little else is known of Mr Plunket – see Ingamells' *Dictionary* . . .
4. It is presumed the Abbé James Green who trained at Douai.
5. The bracket is not closed – ed.
6. Cedrata – a citron flavoured drink.
7. Presumably Piranesi's Vedute di Roma which were published from 1760 onwards. Purchasers could buy their own selection.
8. Presumably further views of the city in micro mosaics which were widely produced at the time and sold to tourists.
9. We are not told where but should bear in mind that the river Tiber at that time was not embanked, such work only beginning in the late nineteenth century.

a Recumbent Posture[1] & a good Picture of the Virgin by Annibal Carraci [sic][2] – and Another of the Executioner Cutting off Saint Cecilia[s] Head, by Guido –[3]

Went afterw[ds] to the manufactory of Tapestry,[4] where they had Worked a fine Portrait of Saint Peter, & likewise Hangings for a Room, in which the Colours were little Inferior to the Gobelins at Paris[5]

From hence we walked through the Portus Ripæ Majoris[6] & went upon the Bank of the Tiber till we Came opposite the Church of Saint Paoli fuori[7] – & at our Return Stopt at the Capitol to Examine the Ruins in the Campo Vachino – – We Dined with M[r] & M[rs]. Montague Wilkinson to

234

to meet Sir Robert Herries,[8] and a M[r]. Ker, who has a Large Estate in the North of Ireland –[9] In the Evening Madame Norton, M[rs]. Hill, & Coll Rooke Came to Tea.[10]

Friday 14th.
Went with my dear Farr & Coll Rooke to See Cameo[s] &c afterw[ds] to Saint Peters – from thence to a Bookseller in Piazza di Pasquino who Shewed us the Antique mutilated Statue of Pasquin.[11] We then

1. The statue of St Cecilia by Stefano Maderno dating to 1600. It replicated the posture of the saint's body which had recently been rediscovered.
2. Not traced – there is a painting of the Virgin and Child with St. Agnes by Giovanni Baglione in the convent according to Erwee (2014).
3. The painting is the altarpiece in the calidarium and dates to 1603. It is still in situ.
4. A manufactory had been founded by Cardinal Barberini in 1625. After this venture folded another was started in 1710 by Clement XI at San Francesco a Ripa in Trastevere with the intention of giving work to poor youngsters. This closed in 1798 during the French occupation of the city. It was known as the Arazzeria del San Michele or Arazzeria Albani (the family name of Clement XI).
5. Gobelins – the famous tapestry manufactory in Paris. It still exists.
6. The Ripa Grande, the former river port on the Tiber opposite the Aventine Hill.
7. San Paolo fuori le mura.
8. Sir Robert Herries (1730–1815), banker and founder of Herries Bank.
9. David Ker (1742–1811) of County Down. He was travelling with his three daughters and their governess.
10. Colonel Henry Rooke according to Ingamells' *Dictionary* . . .
11. Pasquino – a mutilated classical group which served as the best known of Rome's "talking" statues hence the word "pasquinade"

went to Monte Citorio a Small Square in which is a Handsome Building for the Courts of Law,[1] the Situation is Almost adjoining The Piazza de Colonna where the Antonine Column is[2] – In the Evening we took our Tea with M[r]. Wilkinson who gave us much Information relative to going over Mount St Gothard –

Saturday Feby 15th.
Walked before Breakfast (as usual) upon Trinité di Monti – at Noon Rode to the Capitol & went to the

235

Top of the Tower,[3] from whence is the <u>finest View</u> of Rome – Every Part of the City is distinctly Seen, and the Ruins of the Colisseum & Every other appear to much advantage, – after Continuing a considerable time in attentively Examining the different objects we Descended & walked through the Forum to the Colisseum where We Staid till near the Hour of Dinner – In the Evening Settled Our Plan of going to Frescati [sic] –[4]

Sunday Feb[y] 16th
Left Rome at Six o Clock & took M[r]. & M[rs]. Fagan with us in Our Travelling Coach to Frescati, as Soon as we Arrived there went into the Church & Looked at the Monument Erected to the —[5] who Died in 1788 – we then walked to the Villa Aldobrandini[6] which belongs to the Prince de Borghese where the water works Play'd in

236

Various Shapes, Some Figures were Sounding French Horns &

1. Piazza di Monte Citorio – the palace facing now houses the Italian Chamber of Deputies.
2. Piazza Colonna containing the column of Marcus Aurelius erected between 180–93 AD.
3. The Torre Campanaria of the Palazzo Senatorio. It was erected by Martino Longhi the Elder in 1578–82 to replace a mediæval structure.
4. Frascati.
5. A diplomatic blank space is left here for the name as the monument was to Charles Edward Stuart (Young Pretender) who had died in 1788. Perhaps Mrs Bentham was unsure as to how she should describe him. The tablet is in the cathedral.
6. The Villa Aldobrandini was acquired by Clement VIII for his nephew Cardinal Pietro in 1597 and is surrounded by beautiful gardens.

Others Playing on Reeds, & Jet d'eau^s in abundance – In one of the Rooms in the House was a Representation of Mont Parnassus on which the Muses were Playing upon different Instruments & we heard Several Tunes Played by means of water – The Room was painted by Dominiquin –[1]

From hence we went to the Villa Conti,[2] & through a fine Avenue of Wood of the Duke de Ceres whose Villa is the best Situated of any at Frescati –[3]

The Name Frescati was given on account of the Town being Destroyed in the year 1191 and the Inhabitants Sheltering them-Selves in Huts which they Covered with Branches of Trees, Called in Italian Frasche – This Town is now the Seat of a Cardinal Bishop

237

And the cardinal of York Resides here at present –[4]

From hence we went to Grotta ferrata, Supposed to be the Cite[5] of Cicero^s Tuscan Villa, now a Convent of Capuchin^s – In this Abbey is a Chapel Painted in Fresco by Domenichino –[6]

We went afterw^{ds} to <u>Marino</u>[7] Upon a fine Eminence, behind which is the Lofty Mont Carro[8] with the Picturesque Hill of Rocca de la Papé Covered with Houses rising One above the Other like the Steps of a Ladder –[9]

1. Seven out of ten frescoes painted by Domenichino and assistants between 1616–18 depicting scenes from the story of Apollo, were detached and are now in the National Gallery, London.
2. The Villa Conti was designed by Carlo Maderno but largely destroyed in WWII.
3. Presumably Duca di Ceri.
4. Prince Henry Benedict Stuart, Duke of York (1725–1807), younger son of James III. He was created cardinal by Benedict XIV in 1747.
5. Murray gives this spelling.
6. Grottaferrata – town famous for its eponymous abbey founded in 1004. The latter was built on the site of a Roman villa but whether this belonged to Cicero is open to question. Domenichino decorated the Chapel of St. Nilo in the abbey in 1610.
7. Marino – town in the Alban Hills close to Lake Albano
8. Monte Cavo – 949 metres.
9. Rocca di Papa – town to the north of Monte Cavo.

The Situation of <u>Marino</u> I think more delightful than Even Frescati, as it Commands not only a fine View of Rome, and likewise the Mediterranean Sea; but between Marino & the Mountain which forms the Back Ground is a delightful Wood, through which the Road Winds to Castel Gondolfo –[1] where the Pope has a House for the Autumnal Months. It Stands High & at the

238

Bottom is a very Beautiful Lake

We Returned to Rome in the Evening – The Eigth [sic] Concert was to Night at the Palace of Prince Giustiani [sic] where the Second Concert was given – These Concerts began Jan 5th. & Continued to March 2d – They were given by the Roman Nobility as the Theatres were not allowed to be Open this year –

Monday Feby 17th.
Went Shopping & afterwds. Walked in the Villa de Medicis – In the Evening went with Mr- & Mrs. Harrison to the Venetian Ambassadors –

Tuesday 18th.
Walked in the Borghese Gardens & about the Beautiful Lake which being Surrounded with Ever Green Oaks gives the appearance of Summer Even at this Season of the Year – Mr. & Mrs. Montague Wilkinson Dined with us & in the Eveng Coll Rooke[2] & Monseigneur Le Cardinal Albani Came[3]

239

Wed Feby 19th-
Went with Mr. & Mrs. Montague Wilkinson this morning to Saint Peters, the Heigth[4] of which to the Top of the Cross is Said to be 435

---

1. Castel Gandolfo – town overlooking Lake Albano. The pope traditionally stays at the papal palace during the summer months.
2. Colonel Henry Rooke (no dates known).
3. Not the celebrated cardinal-collector but Giovanni Francesco (1720–1803). He was created cardinal in 1747.
4. Murray gives this spelling.

^{feet} English Measure – The Length on the Outside 704 feet – within 622 feet – the Breadth within side 291 feet And the length of the Cross Aisle 493 feet – The Immense Area The Circular Peristyle or double Colonnade –[1] The Two magnificent Fountains,[2] and the Egyptian Obelisk All together, form an Amazing fine Coup d'oeil on the approach to this noble Building; –[3] from the Entrance into the Area, to the End , is above One Third of a mile[4]

We Went to the Top of the Church, Ascending gradually (but not by Steps) a winding Stair Case till we came to the Roof of the center Aisle of the Church – We then walked upon the Leads

240

On which the Large Figures are ^{Placed} Over the Front Portico[5] – from thence, we Entered again, by a Door on the Outside, which Communicated with a Stair case leading to the first Gallery within the Church, going round the Center Cupulo, resembling the whispering Gallery at Saint Pauls in London[6] & from this Place we could Observe the Rough manner in which the Mosaic Pictures in this noble Cathedral were Executed –

We then began to Ascend where the Cupulo becomes Double, And Entered a Second Circular Gallery, which went round the Bottom of the Highest Cupulo – Here the Heigth from the Bottom of the Church appeared Prodigious; And it was with a degree of Pain rather than Pleasure, that we looked at the Objects in the Church. From Hence, the Ascent to the

---

1. The colonnades erected by Bernini between 1656–67.
2. The fountains were erected by Carlo Maderno in 1613 and Carlo Fontana in 1677.
3. Domenico Fontana famously moved the Egyptian obelisk to the site in 1586.
4. The present via della Conciliazione, of course, was only opened up after Mussolini's Concordat with the Vatican of 1929 thus "ruining" Mrs Bentham's surprise view.
5. The thirteen statues above the façade of the basilica. They represent Christ and the Apostles (less St Peter) but including St John the Baptist. These are 5.70 metres high.
6. The gallery beneath the dome of St Paul's Cathedral in London erected by Sir Christopher Wren.

241

Ball is by very Narrow & Steep Stone Steps Ending at a Ladder which rises almost Perpendicular.

We Ascended the Stone Steps, & great part of the Ladder, but at the Top of the Ladder, we found the Small Iron Ladder leading directly into the Ball Was gone And Tho' we Saw the Inside of the ball, we could not actually Enter into it; which we Otherwise Should certainly have done, for at this last Ascent, the Neck leading into the Ball, is So very Narrow, that there did not appear to be the least danger of Falling

At the different heights we found very Interesting & Extensive Views of the City, And in Some places the <u>whole</u> City appeared under the Eye, And not a Chimney Issued any Smoke; nor had we any Wind – The Sun Shone bright – And warm – all was Calm & Serene But, tho from hence is the most

242

Comprehensive View of Rome; yet from the Tower of the Capitol, is the most Picturesque View of the Antient Ruins, Viz the Coliseum &c &c &c &c &c &c &c &c

Thursday Feby 20th.
Went with M^rs. Montague Wilkinson a Shopping, Bought Blankets for Travelling – And Leather Sheets, a very Comfortable Accomodation, as Vermin (with which Italy abounds) cannot teaze[1] you – went afterds to the Villa Borghese. And in the Evening went with Miss Knight to the Ninth Concert at the Marchesa Massini – NB This lady had Our Friend M^r. Banks for her Cavalier Servente[2] when he was at Rome. And it was Supposed to be on her account, that he Left England a Second time, & Came in Nineteen Days to Rome –[3]

---

1. Murray gives this spelling.
2. Cavaliere servente – a gentleman who attended a lady who was not his wife. The relationship was supposedly innocent but many English visitors thought otherwise and frowned upon the practice.
3. This was Henry Bankes of Kingston Lacy (1756–1834). He went to Rome for a second visit in 1782.

243

    Friday Feby 21
Went to See the Ruins of the Baths of Caracalla at the Foot of the
Aventine Mount, They Appeared of great Extent and are Said to con-
tain 23000 Cells where as many Persons might Bathe In the Evening
took M^r. & M^rs. Fagan in the Coach & Drove through the Principal
Street in Rome to See the Illuminations On account of Eight New
made Cardinals =[1] The principal Palaces were Illuminated with
Large wax Candles placed without Side of the windows, and they
Burnt in the Open Air, as Steady as if they had been in a Room –
Before the Lower Apartments were Flambeaux^s [sic] – Or Oyl[2] put
into Open Bason^s[3] of Tin and put upon high Poles

The Governor of Rome being One of the New made Cardinals[4]

244

Opened his House for the Reception of Company, And before
the Front of his House in the middle of the Street were Erected
Two Stages for Musick, And when One Band ceased Playing the
Other immediately Begun – The Court Yard (through which the
Carriages drove after Setting the Company Down at the Foot of the
Great Stairs) was likewise Illuminated with Candles & the Gallery
which went round the Court Yard – At Two of the Corners of the
Court, were Stages for Musick, with the Bands Playing Alternately
– The Croud of People before the Palace and within the Court
was great; Scarcely leaving a Passage for the Carriages to Drive
through, yet not the least Noise, but Soldiers on Each Side kept
the Passages Clear –

1. Pius VI created eight new cardinals on 21st Fenruary 1794, viz- Antonio Dugnani,
 Ippolito Mareri, Jean-Sifrein Maury, Giovanni Battista Bussi de Pretis, Francesco
 Maria Pignatelli, Aurelio Roverella, Giovanni Rinuccini and Filippo Lancelloti.
2. Murray gives this spelling.
3. Murray gives this spelling.
4. Giovanni Rinuccini (1743–1801) was made governor of Rome in 1789 before being
 created cardinal in 1794.

245

Saturday Feby 22^d

This morning we received a Note from the Popes Secretary with permission to go with M^r. Giuntotardi to the Souterrain under Saint Peters, now made use of as a Mausoleum[1] – Among the Tombs was a Large Sacercophagus [sic] including the Remains of King James the Third (as He was there called) King of Great Britain &c and his Death in the year 1777-[2] Among many very Fine Bas releifs[3] in marble was One representing Adam in Paradise Sleeping, with Eve coming forth from his Rib – Her Body entirely Out And the appearance of the Leg coming, with the Deity above Looking down upon our first Parent.[4] There were many Small Chapels in this Soutterain in which by Torch Light the Paintings ^appeared quite fresh. In One was the Tomb of St Peter

246

Made in the Form of an Altar And used as Such –[5] upon our Return from Our mornings Amusement we had Sir Lionel Copley, Colonel Rooke & Mr Rushout to Dine with us and in the Evening we again Drove the Streets of Rome to See a Second Illumination –

---

1. The crypt of St. Peter's Basilica is still open to the public and is popular with tourists and of course those seeking more spiritual inspiration.
2. James Francis Edward Stuart, the "Old Pretender". He actually died in 1766 at the age of 77.
3. Murray gives this spelling.
4. Such an image is mentioned as belonging to part of the sarcophagus of Paul II (Pietro Barbo) (1417–71) – see Giovanni Pietro Pinaroli – *Trattato delle cose più memorabili di Roma* , Rome, 1725, p.49. The tomb was moved during the construction of the new basilica and only parts were returned to the Vatican Grotte. However, the tomb by Giovanni Dalmata (Ivan Duknović) (*c*.1440–*c*.1514), has now been reconstructed and since 1994, placed in the Ottagono di San Basilio in St Peter's Basilica – see Johannes Röll, *Giovanni Dalmata* (Römische Studien der Bibliotheca Hertziana, 10), Worms, 1994, pp.60–84.
5. The Vatican grottoes are still much visited but the area was systematized by Pius XII beginning in 1940.

Sunday Feby 23^d.

Went with Miss Knight to the Tour de Specca[1] to See a Nun take the Veil – The Chapel tho' Small was magnificent in Ornaments of Silver, And a Cardinal Bishop Officiated – The Nun Entered the Chapel in a Black Silk Gown, Her Long Hair flowing down her Back And upon her Head yellow Gawse Plaited & hanging loose to the waist – with her Right Hand She Led a pretty Child about Six years of Age, Cloathed in Gawse of Flesh Colour, & Stretched

247

So Close upon the Body and Limbs as to resemble a Naked Figure – Round the Waist was a Short flounce of Blue Sattin, tyed with a Knot upon the Right Shoulder And at the back part of the Shoulder were Two wings of different Coloured Feathers – upon the Feet were Sandals tyed with Blue Ribband, which afterwards was Crossed above the Ancle[2] – Two wreaths of Rose Coloured Ribban Ornamented the Body of this Child whose whole Figure I thought resembled a Cupid, But I was informed that the Intention was to Represent an Angel – This little Creature Accompanied the Nun to the Altar And Stood Close to her Side during the whole Ceremony – After the cardinal had Presented to the Nun the Crucifixion in Silver And She had most devoutly Prayed Kneeling before the Altar – She Turned round to the Spectators and

248

In a most Solemn manner Renounced the Pomp of this World = Two Nuns then Came to her And took off the Yellow Gawse from her Head, then took off her Gown And put on a Coarse Black Woolen Robe with the Cord round the waist They then began to Cut off her fine long Hair And one of the Priests held a Silver Dish to Receive it – The Organ Played Solemn Musick And the Nuns of the Convent Sang behind their Grated Windows above the Choir. After the Ceremony at the Altar was over, the Nun walked to the Bottom of the Choir Attended by Two Nuns and the Little Child – Then turning

---

1. Presumably the Monastero di Tor de' Specchi. It was founded by Sta Francesca Romana in 1433 and still functions as such to this day.
2. Murray gives this spelling.

her Face to the Altar She laid herself down upon a Carpet (which was put upon the Ground for that purpose) and with her Face

249

To the Ground remained Stretched at full Length for a considerable time, while Solemn Musick, Called the Misere [sic] was Playing and the Nuns Singing behind their Latticed Windows – Upon her Rising from the Ground the Cardinal Bishop (who during the Ceremony had twice Changed his Dress) Gave the Benediction And Every One left the Chapel, but before we left the Convent we Saw Several of the Nuns bed Rooms, which were adjoining Each other in a long Gallery, having in Each a Small Bed, one Chair and one Table and One Window

In the Evening we went with Miss Knight to the Ghigi Palace, One Front of which was to the Corso, the other to the Piazza Colona – Soldiers Stood at Each Gate as Centinels, and Large Burning Lamps Announced it to be Open for Visitors – After Ascending a Great Stair Case and

250

Passing through Six Rooms (in which were Servants Out of Livery) we came to the Concert Room filled with the first of the Roman Nobility – About the middle of the first Act there was a great Noise, And the Musick was Stopped by Some of the Nobility who had Observed a Man Standing in the Room with his Hair close Cropped round his Head, and a dirty frock Coat with a Large undress Collar to it; They immediately Supposed him a French Democrat, and would certainly have turned him out of the Room, had not Some English Gentleman declared that his Name was <u>Brand</u> & that He was nearly Related to M^r. Trevor the English Minister at Turin[1] – upon which he was permitted to Remain, but he went Away as Soon as the first Act of the Concert was over – while

---

1. Hon. John Trevor (1749–1824), envoy extraordinary at Turin, 1783–99.

251

While M^r. Brand was at Naples he had in a Drunken Frolic had his Hair Cropped, And now in defiance of all Propriety determined to Come to a Roman Concert in a Dirty Dress, tho' he knew that the Romans are never accustomed to go into Publick Company but in Full Dress, And Every English Gentleman wears a Bag & Sword when they attend Even a Conversatione at Rome; but this young man had for Some time been known to be a great Democrat, and was at this time Travelling with M^r. Leeson an Irish Gentleman Brother to Lord Miltown; Both thoughtless and Dissipated and both declaring they would go together in future to Every Roman Conversationé in the Same kind of Dress; but they were Soon given to understand how much Such an Appearance would displease Every

252

Englishman as well as the Romans And therefore they relinquished their Intention And allways appeared in a Full Dress Coat at the Assembly^s tho' they could not wear a Bag to their Cropped Hair NB. This was the Tenth Concert

Monday Feby 24th.
Walked at Noon in the Borghese Gardens with the Harrison^s and Leslie^s. &c – In the Evening went to the Venetian Ambassadors where there was Eight Card Tables and various Sorts of Ice with Coffee, Tea &c &c – – –

Tuesday Feby 25th.
We went to Monte Cavallo, the Pope^s Summer palace on the Quirinal Hill[1] and took M^r. & M^rs. Montague Wilkinson with us – The Chapel in the Palace is very Handsome,[2] but the Apartments

253

Were totally Unfurnished, Except having a few Chairs in Some of

1. Palazzo Quirinale – the popes traditionally retired here in the hot summer months. The palace now serves as the residence of the President of Italy.
2. There are two chapels in the palace, the Cappella Paolina by Maderno of 1617 and the Cappella dell'Annunciata by Ponzio of 1610.

the Rooms, from hence we went to the Villa Lantri [*sic*] from which is a Comprehensive View of the City of Rome;[1] but no Situation is Equal to the Tower of the Capitol for a View of the Ruins of Ancient Rome – In the Villa Lantri the Bedsteads for the Servants were put upon Castors & went under Large Deal Tables, And if they were made of Iron And Painted, might be of great use in Sickness as they could be put under a Toilet Table with a Matrass[2] and Bed Cloaths ready to be used by a Nurse in the Night.

From hence we went to the Palace Spada by Piazza Farnese,[3] remarkable for an Antique Colossal Statue of Pompey –[4]

254

Amongst the Pictures is One of Dido Sitting upon her Funeral Pile of Wood –[5] We Dined at our Return with Mr. & Mrs. Wilkinson And met Mr Rushout the Eldest Son of Sir John Rushout, He had been Four years from England And had Visited Several Countries.

Wed Feby 26th.
Went with Mrs. & Miss Harrison to See La Madona de Sept Dolores a Convent, in which Mr. Bischi had a Sister – who Shewed us Every part of the Convent.[6] In the Refectory we saw the Nuns at Dinner – upon Soup & made Dishes, & in passing we saw the Kitchen & Laundry – The Bed Rooms were on One Side of a Long Gallery, consisting of Small Rooms with white washed Walls hung round with Prints of Piety.[7]

---

1. The Villa Lante on the Janiculum Hill already mentioned.
2. Murray gives this spelling.
3. Palazzo Spada was built for Cardinal Girolamo Capodiferro in the mid sixteenth century, passing to Cardinal Bernardino Spada in the following century. It now houses offices of the state.
4. The statue of Pompey, still in situ, was probably given to Cardinal Capodiferro by Pope Julius III.
5. The Death of Dido by Guercino – the painting is still in the Spada Collection in the palace.
6. Possibly Nicola Bischi, born Tivoli c,1730, or his son Settimio.
7. The Church and Convent of Santa Maria dei Sette Dolore now in via Garibaldi. Borromini had a hand in its construction in the 1640s.

255

In One Corner of these Rooms And near the Bed, there was a Large wax Candle Painted Over with Flowers which had been Blessed by the Pope – The Chapel was Neat and Handsome.

Before we left the Convent we Entered a Parlour were [*sic*] the Gentlemen of Our Party waited for us, as They had not been permitted to go through the different Apartments with us, Here we found a very Elegant Collation, consisting of a Large Cake of Milk Ice in the Center Cold Ham & Sausages in Slices Cakes & Sweetmeats with a Bowl of Orangead [*sic*] And Another with Punch

In the Evening went to the Eleventh Concert at the Palace Di Fiano with Miss Knight.

256

Eight Rooms were Opened for Cards And the Saloon had a Carpet. The Other Rooms were Paved with Square Red Tiles highly Polished – The Saloon was Ornamented with very fine Lustres, and Tables of beautiful marble, the Hangings of white Sattin, Embroidered with Flowers in the form of Pannels in the middle of which were Circles of Flowers, all Said to be Worked by the Lady of the House

Thursday Feby 27th
At Nine o Clock went with M^rs. Wilkinson to the Chapel in the Vatican, where the Pope made Eight New Cardinals – as They advanced towards the Altar Each making a Low Reverence They first Kissed the Popes Foot then his Hand and then Embraced him – Then Leaving the Chapel were again brought in by an

257

Equal Number of the former Cardinals. And Each Kneeling at the Pope^s Foot, the Cowl of the Purple Hood was drawn over his Head, And the Pope holding a Large Red Cardinals Hat over his Head Blessed it.

In the Evening went to a Party at M^rs. Canning^s –

Friday Feby 28th.

Walked as usual before Breakfast upon Trinité de Monte, afterw^ds Called upon Lady Knight And from her went to the Hill of St Janiculum & walked to the Fountain of Pope Paul the Fifth near the Church of Saint Pietro Monterio[1] – The water Came with great Velocity and the Sight was pleasing –[2]

From hence went to Saint Peters and Saw the Pope at

258

His Usual Prayers, from hence went to the Vatican and Saw for the Third time the Belvedere that noble Repository of Antique Sculpture Called the Clementine Museum – I walked attentively through the different Rooms and for the last time observed the famous Apollo and the Laocoon the First Supposed to be the finest Single Figure , and the Last the Noblest Groupe in the World – and are thus described "Apollo is Supposed to have just discharged his Arrow at the Python His Attitude is Beautiful and Natural, His Countenance Composed and Elegant – The Laocoon has not a Feature – or muscle which does not Shew the deepest Anguish – The Fathers Flesh is all Contracted in consequence of the Poison, and the Youngest Son

259

Is fallen down in the Agonies of Death, the Other not yet hurt is looking towards his Father wishing to Assist him & at the Same time wanting help himself – from hence we went to the Villa Borghese –

M^r. Ker (whose Estate lies near Port Patrick in Ireland) M^r. Montague Wilkinson & M^r. Hill Dined with us –

Saturday March 1st.

at Noon went to the Villa Borghese were [sic] to my great Surprise I met M^rs. Motte, (formerly Miss Touchet) who was Travelling through Italy, accompanied only by her Female Servant –[3]

---

1. San Pietro in Montorio already mentioned.
2. The Fontana dell'Acqua Paola erected in the reign of Paul V (Borghese).
3. Mrs Maria Motte.

In the Evening went to a Ball given by M^r. Kerr, met there the
Stewarts – the Harrisons Miss Grimstone Neice to M^rs. Harrison,[1]
The Pinnocks, Cannings, Hollands &

260

Ciciporcia, Messrs. Leeson, Brand & Grigby with many Italians
– Twelve Couples Danced and Three Rooms were Opened for
Cards –

At the End of Every Second Dance Teas, Cakes & Negus with
Ice of Various Sorts were offered and at Eleven a Side Board was
Opened with Cold Chickens, Ham, Oranges & Sweet meats –

Sunday March 2^d.
Called on M^rs. Motte & took her to the Borghese Gardens were [sic]
we Walked – In the Evening went with Miss Knight to Princessa
[sic] Santa Croci at whose Palace was the Twelfth and Last Concert
for this year – met there the Leslie^s Pinnocks Harrisons & Hollands
with Coll Rooke Mr Douglass & Hill And a numerous Company
of Italians

261

Monday March 3^d.
Went Shopping And to the Villa Borghese – M^rs. Motte Dined with
us, And we took her in the Evening to a Concert at the Nazarene
College,[2] and afterw^ds. to the Venetian Ambassadors. Where we
met many English and more Italians & were offered the usual
Refreshments of Ice, Coffee & Tea – In the Inner Room were Five
Card Tables –

Tuesday March 4th.
Went to the Church of Saint Bernardo, which is Circular, and
was part of the Baths of Dioclesian afterw^ds. went to the Corsini

---

1. Either Maria or Emily Grimston, the wards of Sir John Legard.
2. The Collegio Nazareno – an institution founded by Michelangelo Tonti, archbishop of
   Nazareth (hence the name), which has been in the present Palazzo Tonti since 1689.

Garden[1] – And from the Casino at the Top of the Hill, is the most Comprehensive View of Rome; & from this Place was taken Some of the best Views

We Dined with M[r]. & M[rs]. Montague Wilkinson & met M[ss] Canning & Hill.

262

Wed[y]. March 5th

Went this morning with M[r]. Hill to the Sistine Chapel in the Vatican, where the Pope assisted at Mass, and it being Ash. Wednesd[y] He put Ashes on Every Cardinals Hand, by having a Bason with Ashes held by a Priest, in which the Pope put his Hand as each Cardinal Knelt before Him, and made a Cross with the Ashes on their Forehead – Twenty Four Cardinals were at the Chapel And to Day their Robes were Purple instead of Scarlet

After the Cardinals, and the Priests, And One of Every Order of the Monks had received the Sign of the Cross made with Ashes on their Foreheads, The Pope washed his Hands and descended from his Throne to Pray before the Altar And then Gave his Benediction –

263

At Noon I left Cards to take Leave of the English we had Visited during our Stay at Rome, and afterw[ds] walked in the Borghese M[r]. & M[rs]. Montague Wilkinson took Tea with us for the last time, it being Our Intention to Quit Rome in the morning and begin our Journey to Florence

Our Stay at Rome had been made pleasant by agreable Society, we having allways had Company at Home or been Engaged Every Even[g] (Except Two) in Concerts or Conversatione abroad –

We observed the Roman ladies walked in the Villa Borghese in Great Coats made of Coloured Sattin and trimmed with Fur –

---

1. The garden behind the Palazzo Corsini is now the Orto Botanico.

The Men in Cloaks Called a <u>Fariola</u> which Completely Covers them, And often they have only a Waistcoat underneath –[1]

264

Painters most Esteemed

Claude for	Landscapes
Poussin	D° –
Teniers	Village Feasts
Meyris	D° & Cottages
Vernet	Sea Views
Vanderwerf	Dutch Rivers
Schalcken	Candle Light
Woenix	Wild beasts
Wooverman	Hunting Pieces
Bourgignon	Battle Pieces
Guido for	Softness
Titian for	Colouring
Guercino	Light & Shade
Gerard de la Notte	Candle Light
Salvator Rosa	Rocks and Banditti –[2]

265

A Few Observations

At Rome the Common People Carry a Pot of Embers in their Hand when they go into the Street in Winter – at Margaritta's in the Place d'Espagne where we had Lodgings, Our Servant Madelaine never went on an Errand without taking her Pot of Hot wood Ashes in her Hand –

In making Visits the Servant Allways Enquiries if the Lady is

---

1. Fariola – a full-length cloak usually worn by clerics.
2. Claude Lorrain (1604/5?–82), Nicolas Poussin (1594–1665), David Teniers the Younger (1610–90), Adriaen van der Werff (1659–1722)?, Frans van Mieris (1635–81), Joseph Vernet (1714–89), Godfried Schalcken (1643–1706), probably Jan Weenix the Younger (1642–1719), Philips Wouwerman (1619–68), Pierre Bourguignon (1630–98)?, Guido Reni (1575–1642) Titian (1485/90–1576), Guercino (1591–1666), Gerrit van Honthorst (1592–1656), Salvator Rosa (1615–73).

<u>Visible</u> Qu^y is not this better than asking if the Lady is at Home –
frequently Skins of Bears are laid for the Feet before ^{ye} Chairs

266

Curtains are hung over the Doors of the Apartments and look well
when they are hung within the Architrave of the Door & the Rod
Covered by a Vallan[1] which is hung in drapery on Each Side

The Houses in Italy are Cold & the Atmosphere warm

In England the Houses are Warm and the Atmosphere Cold

At Naples & Rome the Sky very Clear & in general of a fine Azure
Blue –

At Florence the Atmosphere is often Hazy & thick as in England

The Houses in Italy are in general Built of rough Stones &
Plaister'd over & the Plaister is Painted of Various Colours; but as
that frequently Breaks the Houses often look Shabby – Excepting
those which belong to Persons of Large Fortune –

267

For an Invalid who cannot take Exercise, Naples is more Amusing
than Rome, and Portici a good Summer Residence –

At Naples the Countenance of the Common People is often much
disfigured by Sores & Scars, And Sometimes they have only Half a
Nose. And in general are very disgusting Objects to Look upon

At Rome the Countenance is more Healthy, And Still more So at
Florence, but throughout Italy Sore Eyes are frequent

At Rome the Beef & Pork very good – but mutton is Indifferent
Soles are the best Fish – no other very good –

---

1. Murray gives various alternative forms for valance, including the use of the double
"l", but not this one.

At Naples & at Rome Silk & Linnen is Sold by the Canne which is Two y^{ds} & a Q^r. English Measure –[1]

At Florence by the Palm. Viz 24 Inches –

268

Travelling throughout Italy is much more Expensive than in England. At the Inns Bed Rooms with a Sitting Room were Charged a Sequin Each Night – Ten Paoli Each Persons Dinner –

Postillions not Satisfied with less than Four paoli each Post of 7 or 9 miles.

The Good Inns are only in Capital Towns, which are at a very great distance from Each Other, And the intermediate Inns have only Small Rooms – Clay or Tile Floor – Beds without Curtains, And no Room to Eat in but a Bed Room, but they Charge Equal to Half a Guinea English for Each Person^s Supper & Bed –

The Oxen at Rome & Naples of a Grey Colour & likewise at Florence but at Modena many were Red, and at Bologna the Pigs were all Red.

269

Left Rome at Seven o Clock this morning having Agreed to go by Veturino[2] [sic] to Florence for Thirty Sequins, for which we were to be Supplied with Provisions & Lodgings at the Inns upon the Road – on going through the Porta del Popolo we went on to Ponte Molle, the Road being between the Pincian Hill and Monte Maria, but a Wall & Buildings are on Each Side the greatest part of the Way: From Ponte Molle the Country rises in pleasing Inequalities, but there are no Trees upon the Hills till Monte Rosi 25 Mile from Rome Nor are there any Trees on the Other Side of Rome nearer than Frescati which [is] 12 Miles distant, And therefore Rome

---

1. Canna – measurement of length especially in the Kingdom of the Two Sicilies. One canna is just over two metres.
2. Vetturino – a driver or coachman.

270

Appears to be Situated in a Desert

Monte Rosi[1] is a Small Place with an Indifferent Inn & few other Houses, from hence it is 13 Mile through a Woody Country to Civita Castellana where we Staid the Night – & found One good Bed Room with Two Beds in it & a Fire Place[2]

Friday March 7th.
Left Civita Castellana at Six this Morning – The Town Standing upon a Hill looked Picturesque And from being Surrounded by a Ditch & having a Castle adjoining Appeared to be a Place of Strength It is Said to be the Antient Veii[3]

Upon Leaving it we Crossed the Tiber by a Handsome Bridge[4] & the Road immediately Ascended And Winding round high Hills Cover'd with Ever green oaks & Firs, and

271

Frequently having castles or Small Towns on the Top we Came to Otricoli[5] where we quitted <u>Sabinæ</u>[6] And Entered <u>Umbria</u>. The Road continuing to Wind round the Hills to Narni which is a very Poor Town in a Beautiful Situation being upon a high Hill Covered with Wood & fronting a fine Valley in which is the Remains of a Bridge Built by Augustus with Blocks of Marble.[7]

1. Monterosi – village on the via Cassia between Rome and Viterbo.
2. Città Castellana – town southeast of Viterbo. It is now bypassed by the Rome–Florence motorway.
3. The castle or Rocca – it was built by Antonio da Sangallo the Elder for Pope Alexander VI (Borgia). The town was the site of the ancient Falerii Veteres destroyed in AD 241.
4. Presumably the Ponte Felice erected by Sixtus V.
5. Otricoli – town in southern Umbria between Città Castellana and Narni.
6. Sabinium – the area of the Sabine Hills in northern Lazio named after its ancient inhabitants.
7. Narni's chief claim to fame is the nearby Ponte Augusto built over the river Nera by the Emperor Augustus in 27 BC. It is now a ruin and was the subject of paintings by many artists.

At the farther End of this Valley is Terni,[1] where we Staid the Night at a very Comfortable Inn; but before we Dined we Went in a Calash with Three Horses & Two Postillions and a Third man who walked Occasionally to guide the Calash upon the Side of the Mountain which we Ascended to See the Fall of the River Velino into the Nera being 1364 Feet from the

272

Level, And Four miles from Terni[2] – we had now Travelled 30 Miles from Civita Castellana

Saturday March 8th.
Left Terni at Six this morning And Soon begun again to Ascend Very High Mountains Covered with Ever green Oaks & Firs till We Arrived at Somma the Highest Point of the Appenines[3]

The Road generally Winding between Mountains Separated from Other Mountains Only by a narrow Dell where a torrent of water Seemed to have made the Separation

This Country very much resembled the Tyrol Except that at this time there was not any Water in the Torrent Beds

At the Extremity of these Mountains we Came to Spoleto.[4]

273

The Capital of Umbria which Stands upon a great Eminence And Commands an Extensive Valley in Front – The Streets are very Narrow and through the middle of Each Street is a paved Gutter for the water to descend, and all are too Steep for any Carriage

---

1. Terni – town in southern Umbria, now an industrial centre.
2. The Cascata delle Marmore – a waterfall created by the Romans close to Terni. The waters of the Velino fall 541 feet into the river Nera. It is now harnessed to create electricity.
3. Valico della Somma – pass on the road between Terni and Spoleto. It is 680 metres above sea level.
4. Spoleto – town in Umbria now chiefly known for its international festival.

We Walked to the Cathedral[1] And about the Town while the Horses were Refreshed and then went on to Foligno and Staid the Night at a miserable Inn. It was 33 miles from Terni to Foligno[2]

Sunday March 9[th.]
Left Foligno & our wretched Inn at Seven this morning & went Twenty Miles to Perrugia The Horses having literally Walked without trotting once the whole way tho' the Road was good & chiefly through a Valley divided into

274

Corn Fields and Planted with Pollards to Support Vines –

Perrugia is Situated upon a high mountain and is a Large Town, the best Inn is very Dirty tho' tolerable for Italy We Dined Early & went afterw[ds] to the Cathedral[3] & Several other Churches to See the Paintings by Pietro Perugino[4] – from Foligno to Perrugia 22 Miles –

Monday March 10th
Left Perrugio at Seven this Morning, and descended immediately into the Valley which is Encircled by a Chain of Mountains, On One of which this Town is Situated

In going through Umbria we Saw the best Cultivated part of the Apennines; the Valley through which we passed was Cultivated

275

As Corn Fields with Pollards planted in Rows for Vines, and likewise many Olive Trees

At Ten o Clock Our Vetturino Stopt at a Wretched House

---

1. The twelth century Duomo retains much of its external appearance though the interior was remodelled in the seventeenth century.
2. Foligno – town in Umbria midway between Spoleto and Perugia.
3. Duomo – a gothic structure most notable for Barocci's Descent from the Cross (not mentioned here) but still in situ.
4. Probably those in the Collegio del Cambio completed in 1500 and still in situ.

(tho Called the Post-House) at Torricella[1] where we Staid Two Hours – fortunately for us the Weather was Dry, and we Amused Ourselves by walking on the Shore of the Lake of Perrugia which was Opposite to this House – This lake was Antiently Called Thrasymene And made famous by the Defeat of the Consul Flaminius by Hannibal –[2] It is Said to be Thirty Miles in Circumference and to have abundance of Fish, There are Three Islands upon it –[3]

From hence we went through a pleasant Country to Camocia

276

Distant 23 miles;[4] And about Five beyond the Popes Territory having at that distance Entered Tuscany We Staid the Night at a very Indiffeent Inn, tho much Cleaner than that ^{at} Perrugia

Tuesday March 11th

Left Camocia at Seven this morning and at 15 miles distance arrived at Arrezo,[5] famous for being the Birth place of Petrach [sic] in the year 1304 –[6] From hence we went 13 miles to a decent Clean House Situated in the Midst of a Forest Called Amagiore[7] where we Dined and afterwards Went 12 Miles to a most wretched Inn, with only Paper and Canvass Windows at a Small Town Called Giovani where our Veturino obliged us to Stay the Night; and we determined never more to Travel by Such Conveyance –[8]

---

1. Torricella – village on the eastern shore of Lake Trasimeno.
2. The battle took place on the 24th June 217 BC.
3. The lake is 28 miles in circumference and is the largest in central and southern Italy.
4. Camucia – village close to Cortona in southern Tuscany.
5. Arezzo – town in Tuscany between Perugia and Florence.
6. Francesco Petrarca (1304–74), scholar and poet.
7. Amagiore – not traced.
8. Presumably San Giovanni Valdarno, – as its name suggests in the valley of the river Arno. It was originally called Castel San Giovanni.

277

Wed^y March 12th.
Having Left Giovani at Seven this morning we Travelled for 24
miles through a mountainous but Cultivatd Country, Intermixed
with Olive Trees and Vineyards till we arrived at Florence, And
at the Request of M^r. Montague Wilkinson we went to Vannini^s.
Hotel[1] upon the Bank of the Arno, and almost Opposite to Meggits
Hotel which we had been at last year and Should have certainly
gone to again, had we been Blessed with her we Lost[2]

The Sun to Day very Hot but the Wind Cold – The Almond Tree^s
in full Bloom but no Other, in Every respect Vegetation Appeared
in a Similar State to what it is in England at this Season of the year
– and the

278

Atmosphere appeared as thick as in London

Thursday March 13th.
We went this morning to Our Banker Messrs Orri[3] & afterw^{ds}
left Cards at Lord Hervey^s –[4] then went to Pisani^s Manufactory
of Alabaster And Purchased Two Beautiful Vases. One of them
designed for a Present to M^{rs}. Justice Buller –[5] afterw^{ds}. Drove to
the Boboli Gardens where we walked Two Hours in Walks Covered
with Ever-greens, giving the appearance of Summer. From the
upper part of this Garden is a very Comprehensive View of the City
of Florence and the Surrounding Hills, but the Atmosphere was as
thick & the Air as Cold as it ever is in England in this month

1. Albergo Vannini had been in existence since mid-century. The original proprietor,
   Maria Vannini was English making the hotel popular with British visitors.
2. Meaning the death of her daughter-in-law at Naples.
3. Messrs Orri – not traced.
4. This was John Augustus Hervey, Lord Hervey (1757–96), son of the notable travelling Earl of Bristol. Lord Hervey was expelled from Florence in March 1795 having
   been involved in a duel.
5. Susanna Yarde (1740–1810), wife of Sir Francis Buller (1746–1800), judge.

Friday March 14th

Rain all Day, and very Cold, we Went after Breakfast again to Pisani^s

279

Manufactory and Purchased a Sleeping Venus & Two Beautiful Small Vases for Lamps to a Side Board, & Several other things afterwards went to the Gallery[1] and Staid till One o Clock, when we Entered the Tribune, which is a Room in the form of an Octagon & Lighted by a Cupola, the Cove of which is painted Red and Indented with Silver in Imitation of Oyster Shells; The Pavement of Coloured Marble – In this Room is the Celebrated Venus di Medici Beautiful in Every Point of View And in delicacy of Character Exceeds Every other Venus Either at Rome or Elsewhere = But the Apollo is not Equal to that in the Belvedere at Rome – The Wrestlers Shew great Muscular Exertion = The Arrotino Employ'd

280

In Whetting a Knife, and in the Attitude of List'ning, and the Dancing Faun, form very Interest^g Objects; Besides this Cabinet We Visited Twelve others, Amongst which was that of Niobe, a Handsome Saloon fitted up by the late Grand Duke for the Statue of Niobe and her Fourteen Children The Statues were by Grecian Artists This Room has a Dome in the Center of the Ceiling and a Cove on Each Side & all Rich in Gilding –[2] We walked afterw^{ds} in the Corridores consisting of Two Narrow Galleries 400 Feet in Length and Connected at the End by Another Gallery 130 Feet long which Unites the Two former, and all are 22 Feet in Breadth = And Underneath the Piazza forms an Open Walk –[3]

---

1. Galleria degli Uffizi.
2. The Niobe group were discovered in Rome in 1583 and purchased by Cardinal Ferdinando de' Medici in the same year. Initially the statues were displayed in the garden of the Villa Medici but were moved to Florence in 1770 where subsequently a room was especially designed in the Uffizi to house them. Originally thought to be Greek sculptures, they are almost certainly Roman copies.
3. The Palazzo degli Uffizi – originally designed by Vasari in 1560 as offices, the palace is now, of course used to house the magnificent Medici art collections.

In the Afternoon went to the Cathedral, the Outside of which

281

Is Incrusted with Black & White Marble in Compartments = The Campanile Or Steeple almost adjoins, and is Built of the Same materials, and very near both, is the Baptistery; which is Built in the Form of An Octagon, and greatly Admired for the Bronze Gates belonging to it. Michael Angelo used to Say, They were fit to be the Doors of paradise =[1] The Inside of the Cathedral is very Gloomy, and appears to have nothing worth Attention but the Painted Glass Windows =[2] From hence went to the Church of the Annunciation[3] belonging to a Convent of Monks In the Little Cloister which Serves as a vestibule to the Church, there are Some Paintings in Fresco by Andrea del Sarto,[4] and the Chapel is Rich in Ornaments of Gilding and Silver at the different Altars –

282

Saturday March 15th
Went this morning to See the Museum of Natural History & Philosophy, for which, Our Valet de Place got the Order from the Grand Duke;[5] We met M[r]. Ferguson there; this Gentleman we had Seen before both at Verona and Rome – He was now Accompanied by the Marquis Manfredini major Duomo majori to the Grand Duke, and likewise a general in the Emperors Service – and Supposed by the Florentines to have Influenced the Grand Duke lately in favour of the French –[6]

1. The three bronze doors of the Baptistery – the first was designed by Andrea Pisano in the early fourteenth century, followed by those by Lorenzo Ghiberti 100 years later. The east door by Ghiberti is that to which Michelangelo gave the epithet "del Paradiso".
2. The windows of the cathedral were designed by numerous artists.
3. Church of the Santissima Annunziata – it was reconstructed between 1444 and 1481 by Michelozzo.
4. The forecourt or small cloister contains frescoes by Andrea del Sarto and his associates dating to the second decade of the sixteenth century.
5. Presumably the Museo di Fisica e Storia Naturale. It developed from the collections of the grand dukes and was originally housed in the Uffizi but was given its own "identity" in 1775 by Pietro Leopoldo I.
6. Federico Manfredini (1743–1829), prime minister of Tuscany, 1791–6.

However it was fortunate for us to meet him, as the Director of the Museum attended him through all the Rooms which were near Forty, and full of a Series of most Curious Anatomical Preparations in Wax, besides,

283

Quadrupeds, Birds, Fishes, Shells, Petrefactions, Minerals, Stones Materia Medica, Woods &c &c &c.

The Director (who attended us) Observed, that the Grand Duke had great Advantages in making Such a Collection from the Situation of his Teritories being near The Alps, & The Apennines And the Mediterranean Sea on One Side, And the Adriatick On the Other= We afterwards took a Ride through the Cachino, which is a very pretty Plantation divided into Rides & Promenades upon the Banks of the Arno – Here we got Out of Our Carriage And Walked; Returned to a Five o Clock Dinner And in the Evening wrote Letters &c.

284

Sunday March 16th.
Went in the Morning to See the Corsini Palace on the Side of the Arno[1] – In the principal Room were Three large Turky Carpets Sewed together, which Cover'd the whole Room –

Amongst a great Number of Pictures were Two Excellent ones by Albano, viz Children Dancing= Two of the Vintage by Bassano, And the Head of a Woman by Carlo Dolci[2]

From hence we went to the Boboli Gardens & Returned to an Early Dinner that we might go between Four & Five o Clock to the Porta Sains Gala,[3] where the Grand Duke in his Carriage Attended by One Gentleman And the Grand Dutchess in Another Carriage

---

1. Palazzo Corsini sul lungarno. The palace dates to 1648–56.
2. The collection was begun by Lorenzo Corsini, nephew of Clement XII in 1765 and still exists.
3. The Porta San Gallo – it dates from 1284 and was originally part of the city walls. It is now isolated in what is called the Piazza della Libertà.

Attended by a lady, Exhibited themselves by Riding up & down the Street with a great number of

285

Carriages following, like the Scene in Hyde Park[1] in England on a Sunday at Noon

In the Evening went with M[r]. & Miss Gascoyne to the Opera;[2] We had Accidentally met them last Friday at the Gallery, when Miss Gascoyne Recollected having Seen me at her Aunt[s]. M[rs]. Chandlers in Bruton Street, And we now Commenced an Acquaintance. And Spent together a very pleasant Evening[3]

The Opera was filled with the principal Florentines the Grand Duke & Dutchess being there – The Stage Effect Good, The Scenery Fine, but in other respects the House was Dark and Gloomy[4]

Monday March 17th.
Went in the morning to Palazzo Pitti, the Residence of the Grand

286

Duke, The Rustic Front, tho' Heavy looks very Handsome, And the Court of Entrance is noble.[5]

The Furniture within Handsome, And a great number of Beautiful marble Tables were Inlaid So as to represent Shells Scattered upon the Top =[6] many very Fine Pictures, particularly the Holy Family

---

1. Hyde Park in London.
2. Little is known of the Gascoynes beyond the fact that they came from Sunbury in Middlesex.
3. Probably George Chandler (1721–79?). His wife's name was Sarah. Bruton Street – then a residential street in fashionable Mayfair, London.
4. Presumably the Teatro alla Pergola – originally built in 1656 but radically renewed in the nineteenth century.
5. The Palazzo Pitti was begun for Luca Pitti in the mid-quattrocento but became the home of the Grand-Duchess Eleanora of Toledo in the following century and greatly enlarged.
6. See note to page 127.

Called <u>Madonna</u> <u>della</u> <u>Sedia</u> by Raphael[1] & One of Pope Paul 3ᵈ by Titian[2]

We Rode afterwᵈˢ. To the Cachino, and at Our Return Mʳ. & Miss Gascoyne Came & Dined with us, & told us their Intention of going in a few Days to Rome & from thence to Naples – & to Continue in Italy one year longer as they left England only in Janʸ last –

NB. At the Palace Pitti all the Floors were Square Red Tiles

287

Tuesday March 18ᵗʰ

Went this morning to See the Palace Poggia, or, as it is Sometimes Called The Villa Imperiale,[3] one Mile and Half out of Town, It is a favorite Residence of the Grand Dukes, And Five Rooms in it, were lately Furnished for the Dutchess with Chinese Paper and Beautiful Chintz Furniture – The Other Rooms were Furnished with Silk; All the Floors were Square Red Tiles and kept very nicely Rubbed – we went Afterwards to See a House about Two miles from the Porta Saint Gala, where Sir Corbet Corbet had Resided Some month last Summer –[4] And from thence to the Cachino here we walked near Two Hours The Black Birds were Singing in the woods, And the Pheasants were running about in great numbers The Trees beginning to bear leaves And the yellow Flower of the Furze

288

looked delightful – At Five o Clock went to Dine with Mʳ. & Miss Gascoyne at ᵗʰᵉ Aquila Nera kept by Pio –[5] Their Apartments were Extremely Neat & rather Elegant, consisting of a very Large Room

1. The Madonna della Sedia – a tondo of the Mother & Child by Raphael dating to c.1513–14. It is still in the collection at the Pitti Palace.
2. Titian's Portrait of Pope Paul III (Farnese) is in the collection of the Museo di Capodimonte, Naples. The Pitti painting is a copy of which there are several.
3. Poggio Imperiale – already noted above.
4. Possibly the Villa la Pietra once also the home of Sir Harold Acton and now an outpost of New York University. The villa was largely given its present form in the seventeenth century.
5. At the time the Aquila Nera was at Borgo Ognissanti, 8. It was a popular locale, Mozart had also stayed there.

with a Fire Place and the Furniture of Silk, Two good Bed Rooms, Two Dressing Rooms & Two Servants Rooms, The Price was Ten Paoli[s] or Five Shilligs [*sic*] a Day – whereas we paid at Vannini[s] Fifteen Shillings or Seven Shillings & Sixpence p Day for a very dirty Apartment & the Rooms Small tho' Convenient –

Florence is certainly a much Cleaner Town than any Other in Italy – The Streets are all Paved with Broad Flag Stones tho' they are in general Narrow – The Shops appear Clean, and the People Civil with the appearance

289

Of Honesty, The Environs of Florence are Pleasant, The River Arno divides the City by Four Stone Bridges, and running through the Valley which is Surrounded by Small Hills, well Cultivated with Vineyards and Adorned with innumerable white Houses forms a very Pictureque Scenery –

The Autumn here is frequently Rainy, but the Climate in Summer is esteemed Healthy, tho' the Atmosphere at this Season is often Thick and Hazy –

Wed[y] March 19th

Went Shopping this morning with Miss Gascoyne & at Noon went to the Palace Ricardi,[1] in which is One Gallery or Saloon Paved with marble, And richly Ornamented with Gilding, And Two cases filled with Cameo[s] – Intaglio[s] Chrystals & Gems And a Library of Three Rooms, but in other respects the Furniture

290

was Old, And the Floors of Coarse Brick – from hence we went to See the House where Michael Angelo Lived, in which were Some

---

1. Presumably the Palazzo Riccardi–Medici originally built by Michelozzo for Cosimo il Vecchio in the mid fifteenth century. It contains a library and once housed a small museum, the material now transferred elsewhere.

paintings representing the principal Actions of his Life Said to be done by himself –[1]

We went afterw^ds. to the Boboli Gardens with M^r. & Miss Gascoyne And after walking with them a Considerable time took Leave As we proposed quitting Florence the next morning –

M^r. Wyndham[2] arrived this morning at Meggitts Hotel, being to Succeed Lord Harvey [sic] as minister to this Court – And certainly the Accomodations at Meggits are preferable to Any Other Hotel in Florence, tho' the Loss of the dear Companion we had been with there rendered it now unpleasant for us

291

Thursday March 20th.

We Left Florence this morning And the Road during the first Post was winding near High Picturesque Hills Covered with Olive Trees, And many white Houses were Scattered about – at the bottom of these Hills were Corn Fields & many of them planted with Trees from which Vines were Suspended in festoons = Other Fields Covered with Vegetables and at this time the Pease and beans were in full Bloom, So that it might with great Truth be Said, that Corn Wine and Oyl abounds in this Country

In the different Villages we passed through the women were Employed in making those Hats, we Call Leghorn[3] – during the Second Post we found the Hills were in general Quarries of Slate and Stone

---

1. The Casa Buonarroti. It was originally purchased by the artist for his nephew Leonardo but decorated by Michelangelo il Giovane. It was left to the state in 1858 by the last surviving member of the family.
2. Hon. William Frederick Wyndham (1767–1828). He was appointed envoy extraordinary to the Tuscan Court in 1794, arriving on the 20th March. He had a somewhat colourful private life.
3. Leghorn hat – a wide-brimmed straw hat often decorated with muslin and artificial flowers.

292

And we saw many men Employ'd in Digging, And Sometimes between the Hills the Arno filled the whole Space Except the Road which kept winding round the Bottom of these mountains = the whole View was Romantic

At the Third Post the Hills began to be more distant and the Valley became more wide & So continued till we Came to Pisa[1] but were thickly Planted with Trees made Pollards & Cut round like a Cup with the Vines hanging (as before) in Festoons, & Corn feilds between Cheifly wheat – The Women were frequently Digging in the Fields with the men.

We Arrived at Pisa about Four & went immediately to the Tre Donzelles, or Three Damsels An Inn very pleasantly Situated upon the Bank of the Arno where we had an Eating Room

293

Opening into a balcony fronting the River & a Dressing Room for One Sequin a Day – And our Dinners were to be Eight Paoli's Each Person –[2]

The Hussar is said to be the principal Inn, but being in a narrow Street we declined going to it[3]

Friday March 21st
Went in the morning to the Cathedral in which are Some fine Columns of Marble, And Some good Pictures – The bronze gates are likewise very Curious.[4]

---

1. Pisa – city west of Florence and close to the Tuscan coast.
2. Albergo delle Tre Donzelle – the building still exists.
3. The Albergo dell'Ussero, or Hussar. It appears to have been popular with visitors into the following century.
4. The Duomo begun in 1064 in the Pisan Romanesque style. The original doors of the façade were destroyed in a fire in 1595 and reconstructed by various Tuscan artists in the seventeenth century. Only the transept door facing the campanile survived and are by Bonanno Pisano of c.1180. The columns to which Mrs Bentham refers are probably those granite Corinthian between the nave and apse which came from the mosque of Palermo.

Allmost adjoining is the leaning Tower, or Campanile 150 Feet in Height and 15 Feet out of the Perpendicular – The Six Rows of Gothic Arches, or Pillars which wreath round the Tower appear very Light & Elegant.

294

From the Top of this Tower is a fine View of the Town And Country –[1]

From hence we Rode Four Miles to the Baths, which are close under the mountains. Here is a large Building, the Center consists of a Ball Room And a Card Room, on Each Side And Adjoining is a Range of Apartments, with a Covered Gallery at the Back, into which they all Open – Each Apartment consists of One Sitting Room and Three Bed Rooms, with a Kitchen and Servants Bed Rooms underneath = The Price is Eight Paoli[s] a Day for the Apartments And Two more for the Four Beds – The Linnen to be paid for Separately – and Provisions Either from a Traitear or to be Cooked by your Servants – There are Doors of Communication between the Separate Apartments.

Page 295

So that if One is not Sufficiently Large for a Family, more may be had, and all will Communicate with each other –

The Water of the Bath is Warm & temperate and there are Small Dressing Rooms adjoining about the Size of the Kingston bath at Bath in England[2]

At Our Return to Pisa we visited the House Inhabited by the Grand Duke when he Resides at this Place It is Situated upon Side of the

---

1. The Campanile or leaning tower of the Duomo of Pisa. It was begun in 1173 but building was suspended after the 3rd storey when the foundations were found to be faulty. Subsequent building tried to rectify the lean to no avail.
2. Presumably those at San Giuliano Terme. The baths were built over the spring in the eighteenth century by Ignazio Pellegrini. Such health facilities remain popular with Italians. The Kingston Baths at Bath in Somerset were built in 1762 by Thomas Jelly over the remains of the Roman baths discovered a few years previously. They were demolished about 1885.

River Arno & very near the Inn we were at – It had a Large Hall of Entrance with a Coach Way through it, and the Great Staircase in the Center led to the principal Apartment which consisted of Five Rooms all fronting the River besides a Ball Room & Eating

296

Room in the Back front towards a Court yard, The Rooms neatly Furnished with Silk Hangings, Inlaid Tables &c &c &c [1]

In the Evening Miss Starke (to whom I had brought Letters from Miss Knight) made us a Visit; but having very lately Lost her Father She was going next day to Quit Pisa & therefore desired to Introduce us to her Friend Lady Bolingbroke[2]

Pisa is a Considerable City many of the Streets are wide with a foot Pavement a little Elevated, It is divided like Florence by the River Arno, over which there are Three Bridges, and a Broad Street one each Side the River gives it a very Chearful appearance = The Country Around is Flat, & tho Cultivated with Corn looks Marshy –

297

Pisa is Said to be preferable to most City[s] in Italy for a Winters Residence on Account of the mildness of the Climate but in Summer the Stagnation of Water about it must render it Unhealthy – We found the Bread here remarkably good –

---

1. The Palazzo Reale on the Lungarno Pacinotti. It was begun for Cosimo I by Baccio Bandinelli in 1559 and subsequently much enlarged. Used as winter quarters, it was much damaged during WWII.
2. Mariana Starke (1761/2–1838), writer and traveller. She is chiefly remembered for her *Letters from Italy* . . . *The Poor Soldier* dates to 1789 and the *Widow of Malabar* to 1790. Charlotte Collins, Lady Bolingbroke (d.1803) was the unfortunate wife of George, 3rd Viscount Bolingbroke. The latter had a notorious incestuous affair with his half-sister.

Saturday March 22ᵈ

We went this morning 14 miles to Lucca in a Cabriolet¹ – The Capital of this little Republick² is Said to be for its Extent, the Richest in Italy – The Town is very indifferently Built – and the Only pleasant part is the Ramparts which forms a good Ride and walk of Three miles in a Circle And here the Inhabitants Amuse themselves, & the Prospect of the Country is finely diversified being Pasture Grounds Surrounded by High Hills rising one above the other

298

The Lowest of these Hills are Picturesque having many white Houses upon them in the midst of Woods of Olive Trees –³

We went to See the Pallazzo [sic] Publico, or Town Hall where the principal Magistrate Resides, The Rooms were neatly fitted up with Silk Hangings, but the Floors (as usual) of Brick and no Chimnies –⁴

The Habit of Ceremony worn in this Town is Black, but we met One of the principal Inhabitants of the City in a Coloured Sattin Coat Lined with Fur, Long Sleaves & a Large Fur Cape tho we thought the weather very Hot, yet almost Every Person we met had had a Fariola thrown over his Coat.⁵ We visited the Armoury which is kept very neat And said to Contain Sufficient

299

To Arm 25, 000 Men –⁶

The Cathedral is Old and not worth Seeing –⁷

---

1. Lucca – town north-east of Pisa. It was at the time ruled by an oligarchy and thus not democratic in the true sense.
2. Murray gives this spelling.
3. The ramparts built between 1504 and 1645 still exist and were never actually used for defence. They are still used for walking, etc.
4. Now the Palazzo della Provincia – it also houses the local picture gallery. It was begun by Ammanati in 1578 but much enlarged later.
5. Italians are still noted for their valetudinarianism.
6. Probably the Palazzo Ducale rebuilt by Bartolomeo Ammannati from 1577 after a fire destroyed the original building.
7. The Duomo was probably founded in the sixth century but the present façade dates to the mid eleventh century. The Romanesque was obviously not to Mrs Bentham's taste!

The Neighbouring Mountains are Planted to a great height with Olive Trees, and in the Fields are abundance of Vines hanging in Festoons from Tree to Tree – Towards the Sea the Ground is Marshy and the Cattle feed there in great numbers

The Olives, And the Oyl of this Place is in great Estimation

We took Some refreshment at the Cross of Malta[1] & the Apartments in the Inn appeared Clean and the Beds Excellent but we Returned to a late Dinner at Pisa which is a much more Chearful & Pleasant City – In the Evening received a Note from Miss Starke with an English Newspaper dated Feb. 22[d] –

300

Sunday March 23[d].
This morning Lady Bolingbroke with her Sister Miss Collins made us a Visit and Engaged us to Accompany [them] in the Evening to Lady Mary Eyres –[2]

At Noon we Rode to the Cascino [sic][3] and Saw a great many Camels, Some in the Stables and Others Feeding in the wood, They are used to carry the Wood belonging to the Grand Duke into Pisa where it Sells at a great Price, Fuel being very Dear in this Country[4] – we went from hence to the Aqueduct which Conveys water from the Adjacent Mountains into the City for the use of the Inhabitants As the water of the Arno is not Clear –[5] upon our Return we went to the Baptistery in which is a most Surprising Echo that Repeats the Sound Several times

1. Croce di Malta not traced but there remains a Vicolo della Croce di Malta in the town.
2. Lady Mary Eyre (1732–98), wife of Francis Eyre.
3. The cascine no longer exist as such but there remains a suburb of Pisa called Cascine Vecchie.
4. Camels were first kept near Pisa by Grand-duke Ferdinand II (Medici), they being a gift of the ruler of Tunisia. Thereafter camels were bred locally, the last dying in 1976.
5. The Medici aqueduct bringing water from the Pisan mountains to the city. It was begun 1592 by Cosimo I but most of the work was carried out under Ferdinando I. It still largely exists though the water supply is now piped underground.

301

The Baptistery is a Rotunda & within it is Eight Columns of Granite in a Circle, and Another Row of Pillars over them, Supporting the Cupulo – In the Center is a Large Octagon Marble Font, And on One Side a very magnificent Pulpit with Bas relief in marble[1]

Very near the Baptistery is the Campo Santo or Burial Place, It is a long Cloister Surrounded by a Portico of Sixty Arches in the Gothic Style The middle is a Grass Plot The Walls of the Cloyster are Painted in Fresco with Sacred History, And there are many Monuments[2]

In the Evening we went with Lady Bolingbroke & Miss Collins to Lady Mary Eyres a Sister of the present L[d] Faconberg[3]

302

Where we met M[r]. Collins (Lady Bolingbrokes Father)[4] and Governor Ellis,[5] with a M[r]. & M[rs]. Green lately come from Genoa and M[r]. Green had been Resident Consul at Nice –[6]

Monday March 24th.
Left Pisa this morning & went Fourteen Miles to Leghorn, the Road good & the greatest part of it through a wood, or rather a rough kind of Park with underwood – The Hills on Our Left within Three or Four Miles, [and] continued to the Entrance of Leghorn,[7] we went directly to Corri,[s] Hotel & got a very Comfortable Apartment of Six Rooms, Two of which had a full View of the Sea – the Dock yard and Harbour

---

1. The circular Baptistery was begun in 1152 and does indeed have a remarkable echo. The large octagonal font is by Guido Bigarelli of Como and dates to 1246. The famous *pergamo* or pulpit is by Nicola Pisano and dates to 1260.
2. The famous Camposanto of Pisa. It was founded in the twelfth century, legend has it with earth brought from Calvary by the Crusaders. It was badly damaged by Allied bombing in WWII.
3. Lord Faconberg or Falconberg – not traced.
4. Rev. Thomas Collins, father of Viscountess Bolingbroke.
5. Henry Ellis (*c*.1721–1806, explorer and colonial governor. On retirement he frequently wintered abroad.
6. John Ingamells gives Green as probably Nathaniel Green who appears in several other sources.
7. Livorno, but Leghorn in English – port of Tuscany much associated with trade with England.

303

This Apartment had very lately been Occupied by M[r]. Drake[1] And was Esteemed the best in the House tho 74 Steps from the Ground Floor, And the Stairs being divided into different Landing Places made it appear Seven Stories High –[2]

We made a Visit to M[rs]. Barry[3] who resided at M[r]. Partridges[4] And afterwards walked about the Town, The principal Street with Flag Stones, and Crouded with People of all Nations mixed with Jews in great numbers – The Cabriolets which Stood to be Hired at the End of this Street were of a very Singular Construction and had a Small Well under the Foot Board in which was kept Provender

304

For the Horse, and likewise Serves for the Manger as we Observed Several of the Horses Feeding – The Town is fortified on the Land Side with good Bastions and wide Ditches,[5] it is Said to be Two Miles in Circumference, but has only One Large Square at the upper End of which is the Cathedral[6] Recd Letters from Cha[s] dated Feb 25th.

Tuesday March 25th
We walked upon the Mole & Amused Ourselves with Seeing the Shipping & the Felucca[s] which go & Come from Genoa. Wrote Letters to Miss Knight at Rome & others to England –

Wed. March 26th.
M[r]. & Miss Gascoyne Arrived & took an Apartment in the Same Hotel with us & we Din'd together

---

1. Francis Drake (1764–1821), diplomat. He was known to have been economical so presumably the apartment was good value.
2. Corri's Hotel – not traced.
3. Mrs Barry was a writer and author of *Memoirs of Maria, a Persian Slave*, 1790.
4. Probably not an hotel but James Partridge (c.1738–1813), a well-established merchant in Livorno who possibly took in paying guests.
5. The town has now greatly expanded beyond these original limits but the ditches (fossi) still exist.
6. The Duomo in Piazza Grande – it was badly damaged in WWII.

305

Thursday March 27th
Before Breakfast we Walked on the Mole,[1] M[r]. Udney the English Consul at Leghorn Called And Engaged us to Dinner to morrow,[2] At Noon walked about the Town with M[r]. & Miss Gascoyne, And afterw[ds] Dined with them, and met M[r]. Birt whose Brother (the Minister of Twickenham) had married a Daughter of M[r]. Gascoyne[3]

Friday March 28th.
M[rs]. Barry with her Daughter Came in the morning to go with me a Shopping to Buy a Carpet for the Bed-Side which in Travelling we never found at an Inn, And I fortunately met here with Some from England which I gladly Purchased & found very Comfortable – At Two o Clock took M[r]. & Miss Gascoyne in Our Carriage to Dine with M[r]. Udney where we met Cap[t] Lutwick,[4]

306

Cap[t]. Sutherland, Cap[t]. Eyre[5] & M[r]. Green the late Consul at Nice, but M[r]. Udney being very Suddenly taken Ill could not Receive his Company; but desired We would make use of his Box At the Theatre in the Evening which we did Paying only Two Paoli[s] Each Person, which is the Price of the parterre and which Every Person Pays at a Foreign Theatre, tho' he has a Box for the year – The Play-house was Extremely Neat of an Oval Form with Boxes to the Top, being Five Ranges And Every Box has a Screen to draw up in the Front which Incloses it when not used – The Governors Box was in the Center of the First Range of Boxes above the Parterre, The Consuls Box (in which we were) was upon the Same Level & the Third from

---

1. Presumably the Molo Mediceo – it was damaged in WWII.
2. John Udny (d.1802). He was British vice-consul at Leghorn according to Ingamells' *Dictionary* . . .
3. According to Ingamells this was almost certainly John Heyliger Burt (d.1817) whose brother Robert Burt had married Sarah Gascoyne in 1786.
4. Not listed in Inhamells' *Dictionary* . . .
5. Ingamells gives no futher details for Captains Sutherland and Eyre beyond listing their existence.

307

the Stage,[1] The Dinner at M[r]. Udney appeared to me So Singular
that I Shall describe it –

Soup

Pigeon Pye   Sweet Bread Cut[s] (?)

Center
A Plateau

Beef Bouille   of Glass   Salt Beef Boild

Nothing

Anchovies   upon it   Artichoke Bottoms

One Grey Mullet
Second Course
Three Pigeons

Lobster   Potatoes

Plateau
As
Before

Pease   Spinage

Leg of mutton

Apple Pye   Cream

[NB. There are two blank leaves at the end of this volume]

---

1. Not the Teatro Goldoni which dates to the nineteenth century but either the Teatro
   delle Commedie or degli Avvalorati.

Volume 2

Tour to Italy in 1793

Continued[1]

308

Saturday March 29th –
Wrote Letters to England, M[r]. & Miss Gascoyne left Leghorn
Early this morning intending to go by Sienna to Rome, and at
Noon we went through Pisa to Lucca – At the Gate of the Entrance
into this Town we Observed in Large Letters Inscribed <u>Libertas</u>[2]
the Guard House adjoins & round the Ramparts are Several Small
Barracks for Soldiers with Centinels before them – We went to the
Cross of Malta intending to Stay the Night, but they wanted Two
Sequins for an Apartment, therefore we [left] the House And went
to the Panther where we found Apartments as well Furnished for
One Sequin, and to give Eight Paoli[s] Each for our Dinner & the
House in Every respect very Clean & Comfortable[3]

309

Sunday March 30th.
This morning I went with my dear Farr in a cabriolet from Lucca to
See the Baths[4] Sixteen miles distant Leaving Our Female Servant
Phillips at the Inn, till we Returned, but took Our Courier Du
Ponts with us – As we passed the Fields near Lucca we observed
the wheat very forward, The Rye in full Ear, The Pease in Bloom

---

1. Mrs Bentham's journal continues on the sixth leaf of the second volume with this
   title and with page 308 on the seventh leaf.
2. The Porta San Pietro – it is surmounted by a pediment which contains a tablet with
   the inscription "LIBERTAS" and was built between 1565–6.
3. The Albergo della Pantera, a well-known inn at the time. The panther was also the
   symbol of the city.
4. The much frequented Bagni di Lucca, the site of numerous curative and hot
   springs.

& Almond & Pear Trees in full Blossom. The Vines in Leaf but
our Road Soon took us Amidst the Mountains & often Close to the
Side of a Small River running through the Stony Bed of a Torrent
– The Mountains tho' very High were Covered to the Top with
Chesnut Trees & at the Bottom were Vineyards, the whole form-
ing most beautiful Scenery. Sometimes we were on the Edge of the
River, with

310

a Bridge of a Single Arch Crossing the Bed of a Torrent – but
So Steep the Ascent and So Narrow that only foot Passengers or
Mules following Each other could go over them. Before we came
to the Baths we were obliged to Quit our Carriage and walk near a
mile as we were not provided with Mules to Ascend the Mountains
We found the Baths in detached Buildings, Six or Seven together,
& Others a Quarter of a mile distant On the whole more than
Thirty Baths, but that to which we gave the preference was Called
Saint Johannes[1] and had a Covered Walk in Front with a Colonade
before it, and within were Four Separate Baths, and Three others
behind being in all Seven, Each Extremely Neat Either Marble or
Polished Stone & the water of

311

Different Heat, Some only Lukewarm And others too warm to
Continue long in it; but all were Clean and Transparent, And
we were told that the Baths could be Emptied and filled in Two
Hours.

We Saw the Apartments Inhabited last year by Lady Spencer[2]
and her Daughter Lady Duncannon.[3] It consisted of a Number of
very Small Bed Rooms with One Sitting Room and was the upper
Floor of a House that was Situated about the Middle Height of
the Mountain And by descending a very few Steps communicated
with a Walk leading to the Baths of Saint Johannes – this Walk was

---

1. Bagno San Giovanni.
2. Margaret Georgiana, Viscountess Spencer (1737–1814).
3. Henrietta Frances, Viscountess Duncannon (1761–1821). She was in Italy for the
   sake of her health.

Inclosed by a Hedge of Box resembling Myrtle & the View from it was between High Mountains that were Covered to

312

the Top with Trees & Vineyards At the Bottom with a Small River rolling over a Torrent Bed full of Large Stones. The whole Scenery Romantic beyond Description And the Residence Seclusion from the World as there very only [*sic*] a few Cottages Scattered around for the purpose of being near these Baths – We were told that Lady Spencer gave Fifty Sequins A month, tho' at the Village in the Bottom Called Ponte a Serraglio[1] we were asked Only Twelve Sequins a month for an Apartment consisting of Two good Family Bed Rooms & Two Servants but certainly the Situation not So Convenient for Bathing as those upon the Mountains –

After Staying a Considerable time in this Romantic Country We Returned to a Late Dinner at the Panther at Lucca –

313

Monday March 31st
Left Lucca this morning and Crossed the Valley in which this City is Situated, The Fields were Planted with Corn, between Rows of Trees that had Vines hanging in Festoons upon them, women were digging the Ground with Spades which they use instead of the Plough

About Six miles before we Arrived at Pistoia[2] the Road leaving the Valley on the Right hand turned towards the Mountains And we Ascended and descended Continually Small Hills till we Came to the Town which is Situated at the End of a Valley And is at the Bottom of a very High Mountain. The Town is Paved with Broad Flag Stones looked Clean and the Shops gave the Appearance of Trade going on In less than a mile from the Town we began to Ascend and

---

1. Ponte a Serraglio – village close to Bagni di Lucca.
2. Pistoia – town midway between Lucca and Florence.

314

Continued for Two Hours one Steep Ascent winding round the Mountain, which I think is the Highest part of the Apenines, [*sic*] as we had Six Horses to Our Carriage, part of this Mountain was Cultivated with Vines and Olive Trees near to the Top & at the Summit a Grove of Fir Trees, The whole Country looked Luxuriant in Vegetation

The Second Post from Pistoia the Road Descended & we came amidst Barren Mountains Covered with Stone, Rock and Slate – with Torrent Beds between Over One of which was a Bridge of Nine Arches[1] – It was Seven o Clock before we arrived at Marcella[2] tho' we had never Stopt longer than to Change Horses – Since we left Lucca distant Five Posts & Half about 40 Miles.

315

Tuesday April 1st

We left Marcella at Seven this morning, having passed the Night at the Post House, not a good Inn but tolerably Clean for an Italian One – for the Two first Posts We found it necessary to have Six Horses to Our Coach as the Road was generally upon the Ascent Winding round very High mountains And bringing us nearer & nearer to the Apenines which were now Covered at the Top with Snow, and the Highest Point Called L'al Popino appeared frequently to be close to us[3] – and Separated only by a very narrow Valley through which was a Torrent Bed – but the mountains through which we gradually Ascended were Covered allmost to the Top with Beech Wood and we Sometimes Saw a few Cottages made with

316

Large Sticks Standing upright And the Interstices filled with dry Leaves, And were Inhabited by the Poor Wood Cutters with their Families – And we often heard in these Solitary Regions the distant

1. Not traced.
2. Presumably San Marcello Pistoiese.
3. The highest peak in the locality is Monte Cimone at 2165 metres.

Sound of the Axe Cutting down the wood – At the Bottom of these Mountains were Only very narrow Torrent Beds which Separated them from other Mountains of Equal Height –

The Third Post we Descended for Seven Miles – at the Fourth Post we again Ascended but it was Amidst Barren Rocks Between the Second & Third Post we had Passed Two Low Pyrademical Pillars which were to denote the Separation of the Tuscan Dominions from the Modenescs[1] and the mile Stones marked 51 from Florence & 61 from

317

Modena – At the Fifth Post we turned Short to the Left leaving the Snowy Apennines behind us, and we began to Descend towards a Cultivated Country, tho' continuing for Some time between High Hills with Small Inclosures of Grass at the bottom in which Sheep were Feeding – At the Sixth Post we rejoiced to find Ourselves once more in a fertile Country where the Purple Crocus And the yellow Cowslip were growing in the meadows, and We Stopt at Paulo,[2] Intending to Stay the Night – but the Beds were So Dirty, that we Only Satisfied Our Hunger (having had no Refreshment the whole Day) And went Six Posts more to Modena[3] where we Arrived at Midnight – And went to the Aquila Nera got Some Boiling water for our Tea

318

And Retired to Rest –[4]

Wednesday April 2ᵈ
The Road we passed yesterday Over the High mountains from Pistoia to Modena is remarkably good, having been lately made at a great Expence by the Duke through his Territories;[5] He being very

---

1. Territory of the province of Modena.
2. Pavullo nel Frignano.
3. Modena – town on the via Emilia now in the province of Emilia-Romagna.
4. Osteria L'Aquila Nera – inn once existing in Modena.
5. Grand-duke Ferdinand III of Habsburg-Lorraine. Initially he was an enlightened ruler, his outlook being changed by the invasion of the French and his consequent flight to Vienna.

desirous of having Travellers pass through his Dominions, and to Engage them, He has Settled the Postage not to Exceed that Road which goes through Bologna tho' his Road is much longer

At Modena the Inn keeper Pays a Tax to the Duke for Every Person that Comes by Post to his House, which makes the Price for Apartments High, Ours Consisted of Three Bed Rooms a Sitting Room, a Large Anti [sic] Room for Servants to Dine in they were all well Furnished but Very Dirty –

319

After Breakfast we went to See the Duke[s] Palace =[1] The Front Handsome with a Clock Tower in the Center, Eleven Windows On Each Side with a Tower at Each End – At the Top of the Great Staircase is an Open Arcade leading to the Three Sides of the Square of which the Front Building made the Fourth – The State Apartments Only are Shewn, the Room of Entrance is Lofty and Handsome with Several Chandeliers hanging from a Cove Ceiling, this Room being Occasionally used for Balls And Concerts – On the Right is a Large Handsome Chapel[2] And on the Left a Suite of Rooms Hung with Crimson Velvet And many good Pictures – Two of the Rooms are Rooms of Audience – Another has a State

320

Bed in it, And at the End of the last Room the Doors are of Looking Glass which Extends the View and has a good Effect and when opened communicates with a very pretty Theatre – the Side Scenes of which Represent a Continuation of the Boxes filled with Company in Masks and the Effect is good.[3]

Adjoining the Apartments is a very Handsome Library, and a Museum with Cabinets of Amber Coral &c &c –

---

1. The Palazzo Ducale – one of the largest of such structures in Italy. It was erected from 1629 on the site of the old castle. It now houses a military academy but the ducal apartments are open to the public.
2. Now the Tempio della Gloria?
3. The court theatre was in existence by 1669 but that seen by Mrs Bentham was probably the building as renovated and enlarged between 1749–50 by Antonio Matteo Cugini (1697–1765)

The Gardens adjoining have neither Taste nor Situation to make them tolerable – at a little distance is an Elegant little Building Called the Rotunda, from whence are Nine Points of View formed by Opening a Paltry Canvass with Perspective Painting; but the whole Seems to be without a meaning

321

Thursday April 3[d]-

We went to Several of the Churches. The Pantheon appeared the Best[1] = The Town is kept Clean and many of the Streets have Arcades in front of the Houses under which is the Shops

This City is Situated in an Extensive Valley Bounded on One Side by the Apennines – the Fields are well Cultivated with Corn & divided by Rows of Trees with Vines hanging between them.

The Women in this Country and almost throughout Italy Carry the Linnen to be washed to the nearest Brook or River. We frequently Saw Twenty together throwing Linnen into the River, taking out again & Beat it upon a Board – In the Town the women Spin & Knit as they walk in the Streets –

322

Upon Leaving Modena we went Two Posts to Reggio,[2] a Small Town but full of People and has the appearance of Trade

From hence Two Posts more to Parma[3] where we had an Apartment at the Post House the Albergo Reale and found it a most Comfortable Clean House[4] Our Apartments both here and at Modena were Charged a Sequin Each Night – and Eight Paoli[s]

---

1. At the time the pantheon of the Este family was the church of Sant'Agostino which was enlarged for this function between 1669–70 on the initiative of the duchess Laura Martinozzi, wife of Alfonso IV, but was transferred to San Vincenzo in the early nineteenth century.
2. Reggio Emilia
3. Parma – town on the via Emilia midway between Modena and Piacenza.
4. Albergo Reale – a notable inn at the time.

Each Person for Dinner, besides a Charge for Fire, and likewise for Breakfast though we had our own Tea & Coffee

Friday April 4th
The principal Street of Parma is Broad and has a Large Square at the upper End; which is Used as a Market Place for all kind of things. –[1] We went

323

To the Cathedral a Heavy Gothic Building, which at this time was Repairing, & Mass was performing in the Chapel underneath the Choir –[2] we likewise went to See Several Other Churches but after having Seen those at Rome these did not Engage much of Our Attention –

We went to the Academy[3] And were Shewn Some very fine Engravings, and painting & Sculpture which had gained the Prize Annually bestowed on the best Specimens produced in Each Art. In the Gallery were Some good Copies of the best Sculpture in the Florence Gallery – and we Saw a Painter Copying the Virgin and Child with Magdalen & Saint Jerome done by Corregio [sic] in the year 1518 – the Colours now looked as Bright as if just finished[4] – We went from

324

hence to the Royal Library consisting of Two Long Galleries and Several Small Rooms adjoining, in which Several Gentlemen were Reading and writing =[5] The Librarian Shew[d] us Several Bibles in different Languages – And Several Books Printed by Our English

---

1. Presumably the Strada Mazzini and Strada della Repubblica which meet at what is now the Piazza Garibaldi.
2. The Duomo of Parma – a Lombard Romanesque building with early Gothic additions.
3. Now the Galleria Nazionale but still contained within the Palazzo della Pilotta.
4. The Madonna & Child with St. Jerome, or, Il Giorno, commissioned from Correggio in 1523 for a private chapel in Sant'Antonio Abate but now in the Galleria Nazionale di Parma.
5. Presumably the Biblioteca Palatina founded in 1761. It is part of the Palazzo della Pilotta complex.

Baskerville[1] And Others by Bodoni who now Lives at Parma, and from whom we Purchased Gray[s] Elegy And Several other Books of his Printing =[2]

We Went afterw[ds.] to See an Antient Theatre Built Entirely of Wood & upon a Singular construction – neither Logements or Boxes, but Seats ranged on Each Side forming an Oblong – but no Parterre[3] & Adjoining to this Theatre was Another for Concerts, in form

325

resembling another Theatre [in] The Pit were Chairs for the Company to Sit during the Performance And where the Stage is usually were Elevated Seats for the Common People & likewise round the House with a Façade in Front to give the Appearance of Boxes. The Musick was at the upper End of the Pit under what in England is Called Front Boxes –[4]

We went from hence to the Gardens Reale adjoining to a House belonging to the Duke[5] but He never Resides in it, being Cheifly at his Palace in the Country,[6] and when he comes to Parma he is in a Small Old House near the Library. We likewise Walked in the Publick Walk adjoining to the Botanic Garden[7] and upon the Ramparts but the View from both was only Over a Flat Tract of Country –[8]

---

1. John Baskerville (1706–75), printer and typographer.
2. Giambattista Bodoni (1740–1813), typographer. Bodoni trained in Rome but settled in Parma to manage the ducal press. Thomas Gray's *Elegy written in a country church-yard* was first published in 1751.
3. The Teatro Farnese built for Ranuccio I in 1618 by Giovan Battista Aleotti. It was badly damaged by bombing in 1944 but restored by 1956 to something like its original appearance.
4. Possibly the Teatro Ducale dating to 1688. It was demolished in 1829.
5. The Palazzo del Giardino built for Ottavio Farnese from 1561. It has a large park attached. The palace is now given over to an official function.
6. The Ducal Palace, or Reggia at Colorno.
7. The present Orto Botanico was created in 1770 by Giambattista Guatteri for Ferdinand I and the conservatory dates to 1793 thus being a recent addition at the time of Mrs Bentham's visit. It is now run by the university.
8. The city was surrounded by walls until the late nineteenth century. As in many such cases they have been replaced by wide circulatory streets.

326

Saturday Apr^l. 5th.

Walked before Breakfast in the large Square at the upper End of the Principal Street – which was filled with little Booths resembling an English Fair. It was market Day And in the Street were a great number of carts drawn by Red Oxen, the Carts had been filled with Corn which was now deposited in Sacks within an open Colonade over which was a Build^g like a Town Hall in a County Town The People Seemed Busy and Every Appearance indicated Trade

The Farnese Palace, which we had visited yesterday, had many fine proportioned Rooms, but they were Paved with Squares of Red & white marble, and all the Furniture even the Hangings had been sent to Naples, & nothing left but Brick Walls[1] – The Po which runs Close to the Garden

327

Renders the Situation capable of great Improvement had the Duke Chose to reside there

We left Parma at Ten this morning and upon our Road to Plaisance,[2] we Saw mountains on Each Side with their Summits Covered with Snow – I Supposed One Range to be The Alps the Other The Apennines = Our Road was Excellent and went through the middle of a Valley Cultivated with Corn divided by Trees with Vines hanging between We Staid the Night at Plaisance Our Inn the Post House & very indifferent – We Walked about the Town and in the Large Square is an Old Gothic Hotel de Ville[3]

---

1. The Farnese dynasty of Parma became extinct in the male line in 1731, the duke at the time of Mrs Bentham's visit being Ferdinand of Bourbon-Parma (1751–1802). When Charles of Bourbon, the Farnese heir, also succeeded to the throne of Naples he transferred the collections in Rome and Parma to that city and these are largely shared between the Museo di Capodimonte and the Museo Archeologico Nazionale.
2. Piacenza.
3. The Palazzo Comunale – a Lombard Gothic structure on an arcaded base dating to the late thirteenth century. It still serves as the town hall.

with Two very fine Equestrian Statues in Bronze de Ranuce And de Alexandre Farnese[1]

The Ramparts are Planted and form a pleasant Ride or Walk –

328

We Visited the Convent of Saint Augustin where there is a very Elegant Chapel =[2] The Streets are Narrow, but in One I observed a Handsome House with Twenty One Windows in Length It belonged to the Marquis Mandenni[3]

Sunday April 6[th.]
Left Plaisance at Seven this morning and arrived at Novi by Five, where we Staid the Night, Our Inn the Croce de Malta tolerably good –[4] On the Road, we had passed Several Small Streams running through Large and wide Stony Beds for the Torrents = The Country till within the last Two Posts was Beautiful – a great number of Fruit Trees in Bloom & may in the Hedges on Each Side of the Road. The Towns we had

329

Passed were Shabby & poor in Appearance, Some were in the the [sic] Dutchy of Parma & others in Savoy; but Novi the first in the Genoese Territory, the Streets here were Narrow and none of the Houses good & the last Two Posts were through a Marshy Country –[5]

Monday April 7th.
We Left Novi this morning at Eight – and took Six Horses, as the Road to Genoa was one continued Ascent or Descent Amidst High

1. Two equestrian monuments by Francesco Mochi (1580–1654). That to Ranuccio Farnese dates to 1620 and that to Alexander to 1625.
2. Sant'Agostino – the convent dates to the late sixteenth century but the church was only completed in 1608. The monastery was suppressed during the Napoleonic period and subsequently purchased by the city in 1828. It was used for various purposes, latterly for staging exhibitions and other cultural events.
3. Mandenni – not traced.
4. Albergo Croce di Malta – it survived into the nineteenth century.
5. Novi Ligure – town between Tortona and Genova.

Mountains; but the whole Way was Interesting. The first part from Novi Either Vineyards or Trees were Upon the very Summit of these Mountains – afterwards the Road went between Barren Rocks, And we passed Gavi, a Fortress upon an Insulated Rock,[1] in the

330

middle of these mountains, which have an Undelated appearance on all Sides, and are washed at the bottom by a Torrent.[2] We Soon after Passed the <u>Bocchetta</u> the Summit of the Appennines [*sic*];[3] and tho it was Twelve at Noon, yet the Fog was So thick, with a mistley Rain, that we could not perceive the Valley Below, nor the Rocks Above, And Scarcely the Road we were upon = Immediately on Descending from this great Height, the Fog began to Clear, And we could perceive the Hills beneath us had many Houses Scatter'd about – And from hence the whole Way to Genoa was most Beautifully Picturesque, often we Seemed in the midst of Gardens, The Fruit Trees were

331

in full Bloom and in Every Place appeared Luxuriant Vegetation

We Arrived at Genoa about Three of Clock – And for Some Miles before had a Beautiful View of the Sea, with the City in Front of it, Sheltered in the back Ground by a Hill And forming together A most Picturesque Scene –[4]

We went directly to the Santa Marca, near the Le Place de L Annunciate and took a very Comfortable Apartm^t consisting of a very good Sitting Room, Two Bed Rooms And Dressing Room for which we were to pay at the rate of Half a Guinea per Night

---

1. Gavi – town south of Novi Ligure – it is west of the modern motorway between Alessandria and Genova.
2. Presumably the Fiume Lemme.
3. Passo di Bocchetta.
4. Genoa or Genova – city and port on the eponymous gulf.

& One Crown each person for Dinner; but the Table was better Served than any we had found Either at Rome or Naples.[1]

332

The City of Genoa is Built On the Side of a mountain in the Form of a Semi Circle Round the Harbour. And in respect to magnificent Buildings And Beauty of Situation is I think Superior to Any City in Italy, but as the Palaces in Strada Balbi, and Strada Nuova[2] are Painted On the Outside with Variety of Colours they rather resemble Scenery in a Play-House than Habitable Houses; & the more So, as the Streets are narrow & Paved with Flag Stones, And more fit for Sedan Chairs than Carriages, And is the Vehicle most used, as there is but few places in the City to which a Carriage can go, for there are no Squares, nor more than Three Streets wide Enough for Coaches; the other parts of the Town, are Alleys & only of Sufficient width

333

to Admit Chairs and tho' the Hired Ones are but Indifferent, we made use of them to Convey us to the different parts of the City.[3] And went first to See the Palace belonging to Marcellino Durazzo which has an Extensive Front with Superb Apartments, and from the Great Stair case, the Steps Of which are marble, is a Gallery Communicating with a Terrace Paved likewise with marble, and Commanding a most delightful View of the Harbour –[4] from hence we went to the Palace Brignole Rosso, which had in the upper Story a Compleat Suite of Seven Rooms fitted up with great Taste & Elegance. The First Room is an Anti Chamber, the

1. The Albergo di Santa Marta close to the Piazza della Nunziata. It was a notable inn for three or more centuries. N.B. There is a slight problem with transcription here. Mrs Bentham has written Marca or Maria not Marta – ed.
2. Strada Balbi and Strada Nuova – two of the streets in Genoa notable for their palaces. They are now called Via Balbi and Via Giuseppe Garibaldi, the latter name being changed in honour of the general in 1882.
3. Mrs Bentham is referring to the old town towards the port. It was at one time most disreputable but in recent years has been favoured by the younger middle classes making it an attractive locale.
4. Palazzo Durazzo-Pallavicini begun by Bartolomeo Balbi but ceded to Marcello Durazzo in 1710. It has a hanging garden to one side (giardino pensile) and was briefly the royal palace before becoming a museum in the nineteenth century.

Second a Drawing Room which communicated with Two Others Each opening into Bed Rooms, which likewise communicated with a Bath a Dressing Room & Closets – All Elegantly Furnished & highly Ornamented With Gilding, Sculpture & Embroidery –[1]

334

We Went likewise to the Dominico Serra which is Furnished in a most Superb Style, And the Saloon Exceeded in Gilding and Glass, any Palace we had Ever Seen –[2]

And from hence to the Francesco Balbi –[3] In the Afternoon we went to the Palace belonging to the Doge, and to See the Celebrated Statue of Saint Sebastian[4] at the Church of Carignon = from the Top of the Tower, to which we Ascended by 320 Steps, we had a very fine View of the City and the Harbour –[5]

We went to the Jesuits and S. P Neri where we Saw the Oratory, in which Concerti[s] [sic] Spirituali are Occasionally Performed –[6] and we likewise went to the Church of the Annonciata, which is Rich in Marble & Gilding, tho' the Outside is Shabby old Brick –[7]

---

1. Palazzo Brignole Sale or Palazzo Rosso in what is now via Garibaldi. It was erected in 1675, bequeathed to the state in 1874, and is now one of Genoa's notable picture galleries.
2. These decorations were recent, the palace having been acquired by the Serra family in 1780 and the work commissioned by Giacomo Serra. The palace is now part of the University of Genoa.
3. Palazzo Gio Francesco Balbi – it became part of the University of Genoa in 2001.
4. The four crossing piers of the church contain figures of saints. That of St Sebastian dates to 1663–8 and is by Pierre Puget (1620–94) who worked for a period in Genoa.
5. Santa Maria di Carignano in the eponymous piazza to the south of the old town. It was designed by Galeazzo Alessi in 1522 but work continued for more than a century. It has twin towers to either side of the façade.
6. The Chiesa del Gesù begun in 1552 probably to the design of Giuseppe Valeriano, and the Chiesa ed Oratorio di San Filippo Neri. The latter was completed about 1676 in an elaborate Baroque style and the adjacent Rococco oratory was added in 1749. It is still used for concerts.
7. The Basilica della Santissima Annunziata del Vastato – the church was largely built and decorated in the seventeenth century. A Neo-classical façade was added in the early nineteenth century and it was badly damaged in WWII, both events making it a very different building from that seen by Mrs Bentham.

335

The Shops in Genoa appeared to be well furnished with a Variety
of Articles, and a great display of Gold fillagree work – The Cheif
Trade carried on is in the Manufactories of Velvet – Rich Silks,
Stockings – Gloves & Artificial Flowers Wine – Oyl, dried Fruits
& Anchovies

The Bread is remarkably white And good, and likewise the Veal.
The Beef is brought from Piedmont – And the Parmesan Cheese
is Excellent –

There being very few Coaches used, as Sedan Chairs is much more
convenient, and the only Vehicle that can go in many parts of this
City; therefore the Town is very Quiet and in an Evening no Noise
is heard

We Walked in the Evening upon the Ramparts which is a narrow Paved Walk between Two very Low Walls & goes round the
Harbour[1] – One Part has a

336

Range of Warehouses, Painted On the Outside With a Variety of
Colours, and all merchandise at Coming into Port is put there

Wed[y] April 9th
We Rode this morning to See a Villa at Poggio, belonging to Del
Marchesa Lomellino, near Four mile distant – on the Sea Shore
=[2] The Front of the House was open to the Sea, and on Each Side
of the Approach to it, were Gardens for Vegetables, with Orange
Tree[s] intermixed, and the whole Inclosed with Hedges of Myrtle

In the Back Front of the House was a Beautiful Lawn, upon a

1. Although much of the "old" town behind the harbour survives, huge damage was
   done to the port in WWII. Now, an unfortunate elevated motorway separates the
   town from the waterfront.
2. Villa Lomellini Rostan at Multedo (Pegli). The villa, built for Angelo Lomellini
   between 1564 and 68, still exists but the notable garden has over time been destroyed
   by the gradual advance of the Genoese suburbs along the coast.

Level with the First Floor, and this Lawn was Surrounded by a Circular Walk

337

Planted with Ever Green Oaks some Standing in Clumps – others Single. And Various Walks leading from them on all Sides, Some upon the Level, Others Ascending and Descending, the whole Ground laid out in the very best Style of an English Garden, The Trees tho' cheifly Ever green Oaks, yet were intermixed with Large Myrtles And Lauristinus – And the Back Ground of this Garden was formed by Nature with the most beautiful Picturesque Hills in Various Shapes Rising gradually One above the Other = Several Small Buildings were judiciously placed in different parts – One was a Hermitage in which was a Chinese Hermit Bowing his Head upon your Entering. Another was a Thatched Circular Building, with a Round marble Table in the Center, & in the Corners

338

Were Tea Cups of the Staffordshire manufactory made in England. The Windows were of One very Large Square of Glass, And the tout Ensemble formed One of the most desirable Situations that Fancy could form –

Upon our Return we Stopt to See the Villa of Marcellana Durazzo at Cornigliano,[1] and afterwards upon Entering the Town we went to the Palace of Prince Doria And walked upon the Terrace in Front of the Garden, which Commands a very fine View of the City & Harbour – The Orange Trees were now bearing both Fruit And Flower in the Open Air –[2]

We went from hence to the Albergo, which is a large Building for

---

1. Villa Durazzo Bombrini at Cornigliano Ligure to the west of Genoa proper. It was begun in 1752 for Giacomo Filippo Durazzo and still survives, being used for events, etc. The park is open to the public.
2. The Palazzo Doria-Pamphilj or del Principe built for the admiral Andrea Doria in the 1520s. The notable villa still exists but is near to the sea and now surrounded by roads and other buildings. It still has a small garden towards the sea but hemmed in by the coastal motorway. It is open to the public.

the Reception of the Poor and likewise for ^{the} Educating [of] Poor Children[1]

339

Thursday April 10th
We Left Genoa this morning at Six, the first Seven miles after Quitting the City is most beautifully Picturesque, the Road winding at the bottom of Mountains by the Side of a Torrent Bed, & these mountains were Cultivated with Pease, Beans, and Vegetables of Every Sort, intermixed with Corn, Vines, & Fruit Tree^s of all kinds, with a great number of Houses Scattered upon the Sides and Painted in great Variety of Colours; From the Bed of the Torrent we were Two Hours continually Ascending to the Bochetta,[2] from whence we Went to Ottagio [sic][3] a miserable Poor Little Town, where we found Lord Bristol[4] who had been detained there by Illness Some Days; Mr Lovell his Chaplain[5] was with him And both must have been distressed for many things had not the Owner of a Hotel at Genoa with whom

340

his Lordship had frequently Lodged Come Every Day to Supply them with many Articles necessary to their Comfort – After Some Conversation with Mr Lovell we went on And passing through Novi where we had Stopt in going to Genoa We went forward to Alessandria[6] where we Staid the Night – at a dirty Inn – The Town Old Ill Built, Streets Narrow and Only One Large Open Square

1. The Albergo dei Poveri, located in Piazza Emanuele Brignole was instigated by the latter in 1652. Part of the building is now the Faculty of Political Science of the University of Genoa. A part is also included in a view of Genoa by James Hakewill – see T. Cubberley & L. Herrmann – *Twilight of the Grand Tour: a catalogue of the drawings by James Hakewill in the British School at Rome Library*, Rome, 1992, No. 2.22.
2. The Passo della Bocchetta – a mountain pass on the old road between Genoa and Alessandria to the north.
3. Voltaggio – small town on the old road between Genoa and Alessandria.
4. Of course, the famous Frederick Augustus Hervey, 4th Earl of Bristol (1730–1803) after whom so many hotels on the Continent are named.
5. Rev. Trefusis Lovell, archdeacon of Derry.
6. Alessandria – town north of Genoa and between Turin and Piacenza.

which is used as a Market Place And a dirty Old Gothic Cathedral is Situated at the End =[1] The Only thing worth notice is the Long Covered Bridge Over the Po –[2]

Friday April 11th.
We Left Allessandria [*sic*] Early in the morning [the] Road to Asti[3] we found to be a deep Sand, and narrow, but from Asti, was a wide Spacious

341

Road to Turin, The Country Flat but well Cultivated with Corn – In the Fields were Women digging Others driving the Plough, and doing all kind of Husbandry work About Twenty Miles from Turin we came in full View of the Alps at this time Covered with Snow And forming a long Chain of dreary Mountains; but within Five miles of the City, the great number of white Buildings upon Small Hills was Picturesque = And we passed Moncalieri a Palace belonging to his Sardinian Majesty,[4] upon Entering Turin[5] we drove to the Albergo Reale,[6] kept by Mr Trevor'. Maitre D'Hôtel, but finding the best Apartments Engaged by Lady Maynard[7] And Coll. Bradyll,[8] we went to the Hotel D'Angleterre, and got a very good Apartment – And were Soon Supplied with Food which we much wanted having had no refreshment Since six in the morning And it was now past Seven in ye Eveng[9]

---

1. The old Gothic Duomo was commandeered by Napoleonic forces and eventually rebuilt in the early nineteenth century.
2. This bridge was replaced by another in the Napoleonic period which was itself replaced by that designed by Richard Meier and completed in 2017. It actually crosses the river Tanaro not the Po which is slightly further north.
3. Asti – town midway between Alessandria and Turin.
4. Castello di Moncalieri – the palace was originally built as a fortress but was transformed into a royal residence of the House of Savoy in the fifteenth century. It is now occupied by the Carabinieri but the state rooms are open to the public.
5. Turin – city in northwestern Italy, once the capital of the Kingdom of Sardinia.
6. Albergo Reale – not traced.
7. Nancy Parsons, wife of the second Viscount Maynard. She had previously been the mistress of the Dukes of Grafton and Dorset.
8. Colonel Braddyll – he is listed in Ingamells' *Dictionary* but nothing else is known of this individual.
9. Hôtel d'Angleterre – a notable inn in the eighteenth century. Thomas Jefferson also stayed there.

342

Saturday April 12^{th1}
After Breakfast we Called upon Mr. Trevor the English Minister,
who Received us in the kindest manner; Returned Our Visit in the
Evening, and Engaged us to Dinner next Monday –

At Noon Mr Hay the Son of a Gentleman who Lives about Sixty
Miles from Dublin,² and with whom We were Acquainted at Rome
Came to Visit us, and we Engaged him to Dinner, and likewise to
go with us to See Les Vignes de la Reine a Small Palace about a
Mile from the Town Situated on an Eminence and Commanding a
Very good View of the City –³

It is Furnished very Neatly and the Floors of wood were Parqué;
a Hall of an Octagonal Form was the Center, with Four Rooms on
Each Side In the Back Front the Ground Rises very Soon and is
Covered with Trees and Vineyards intermixed, and

343

Walks winding in different directions. Upon Our Return to the
City we drove to the University⁴ in the Strada di Po – And Saw
the Royal Library, in which were Several Gentlemen Reading,
it being Open for certain Hours Every Morning and again in the
Afternoon

The Librarian very politely Shewed us Several very Curious And
Scarce Books – from hence we went to the Riding House & The

---

1. Palazzo Ducale – it was begun in 1634 and is now the home of the Italain Military
   Academy.
2. Mr Hay is listed in Ingamells' *Dictionary* but no other facts are known about this
   individual.
3. The Villa della Regina – the complex was built for the Prince Cardinal Maurice of
   Savoy in the early seventeenth century and was a retreat for the royal family until the
   mid–nineteenth century. It has recently been restored and is now open to the public.
4. The building opened in 1720.

Kings Stables[1] – afterwards to See the Opera House which has not been made use of the Past Two Years –[2]

Sunday April 13th.
M[r]. Hay Came to Breakfast and Stay [to] Dinner – He went with us first to the Cathedral in which the Royal Family were Sitting in a Tribune near the Altar;[3] upon

344

their Return to the Palace, we Saw the Prince & Princess of Piedmont,[4] The Duke de Chablais[5] And the Duke D'Aoste[6] who Passed very near us – we then went to See the Royal Apartments in which are a good Collection of Pictures and a very Handsome Library – All the Floors Parqué & very Neat – The Hangings of Crimson Velvet. With Gold Lace and much Gilding The Comte de Provence (Brother to the unfortunate King of France)[7] Passed through the Room we were in, which communicated with his own Apartments in the Pallazzo [sic] Castello Reale

We Rode afterw[ds]. to Valentino a Small palace of the Kings a little way out of the Town On the Banks of the Po – and walked in the Gardens[8] – Returned to Dinner & in the Evening Rode in the

1. The old Royal Stables were built in 1670 to the design of Johann Gregor Memhardt (1607–78). By the late nineteenth century they were proving inadequate and incorporated into a new building.
2. Mrs Bentham is referring to the old Teatro Regio which had been closed by royal order in 1792. The theatre had opened in 1740 but was destroyed by fire in 1936. A new building by Carlo Mollino was opened in 1973.
3. The Duomo of Turin was begun in the late fifteenth century but much of the building dates to the seventeenth century when works were carried out in connection with the Holy Shroud which is housed here. Surprisingly, Mrs Bentham does not mention the latter.
4. Carlo Emanuele di Savoia (1751–1819), later King of Sardinia. He married Marie Clothilde of France (1759–1802), sister of Louis XVI.
5. Duke de Chablais- a subsidiary title of the House of Savoy – at the time Prince Benedetto di Savoia (1741–1808), son of Carlo Emanuele III di Savoia.
6. Duke of Aosta – title traditionally given to the second son of the Kings of Sardinia, the holder at the time being Vittorio Emanuele di Savoia (1759–1802).
7. Louis Stanislas Xavier de Bourbon (1755–1824), younger brother of Louis XVI. He reigned as King of France from 1815 until his death.
8. The Castello del Valentino – palace built for the wife of Vittorio Amedeus I in the mid seventeenth century. It is now the home of the faculty of Architecture of the University of Turin but is still surrounded by a botanic garden.

345

Corso[1] from Porta Nuova to the Citadel[2] – There were a great
Number of Coaches and We Saw Amongst others the Comte de
Provence, The Duke de Chablais And The Duke D'Aoust

Monday April 14th
After Breakfast we Rode to the Veneria Reale a Palace of the Kings
Ten miles from the City, it used to be a favorite Hunting Seat – as it
abounds with Game – The Grounds are Extensive but formed into
Long and Broad Avenues with Hedges on Each Side And Rows of
Trees – In one part there is a Sylvan Theatre and Labyrinth – near
the House is a very fine Orangerie 540 feet in Length and 96 Feet
wide and near it a very Elegant Chapel[3]

The Rooms in the Palace were

346

Furnished with Rich Figured Silk the Manufacture of Piedment –
And in the Apartment belonging to the Prince of Piedmont were
Several Rooms of fine Japan. The Floors Parqué and Fire Places
in Every Room –

The Stables very Spacious And a great number of Horses from different Countries were there – Upon our Return to Turin we Dined
with M[r]. Trevor who had very kindly Invited Coll de Salugé[4] to
meet me, in Consequence of the Enquiries I had made about Him
and his wife Madame; who was a Daughter of M[r]. Pattle[s5] And

1. Presumably what is now Via Roma. The street was laid out by Ascanio Vittozzi for
   Duke Carlo Emanuele I of Savoy in the late sixteenth century and leads from what is
   now the Porta Nuova railway station to the Piazza di Castello.
2. The Citadel of Turin was built for Duke Emanuele Filiberto (1528–80) by Francesco
   Paciotto and begun in 1564. It was finally demolished as obsolescent in 1856 leaving
   only the gatehouse which survives as a museum.
3. Veneria Reale – a former royal residence in what is now a suburb of the city. It was
   built for Carlo Emanuele II from 1675 but later abandoned in favour of Stupinigi.
   After long usage for military purposes, restoration finally began in the 1970s and the
   palace reopened to the public in 2007. Some of the interiors are by Filippo Juvarra.
   The chapel, also by the latter, is dedicated to St Hubert.
4. Colonel de Salugé – not traced.
5. Almost certainly Thomas Pattle (1742–1818), sometime director of the Est India
   Company. He is known to have been acquainted with the Benthams.

[*sic*] English Gentleman, at whose House in Paris, I Resided in the year 1775; when both the Coll and herself were upon a Visit to her Father – The Coll was now Commandant of Ivrea[1] = we likewise met at M^r. Trevors

347

Several Other Gentlemen at Dinner And One Lady the Comtesse Montigny[2] The Dishes were all Silver, the Plates of Beautiful China – In the Afternoon walked on the Ramparts with M^r. Trevor and in the Even'g Rode to the Corso –

Tuesday April 15th
We Went after Breakfast to See the Superga,[3] which is a Handsome Church & Monastery on the Top of a Mountain Five Miles from Turin; Built in Consequence of a Vow made by Victor Amadeus[4] in the year 1706 when Turin was Beseiged by the French

The King and Royal Family go Every year on the 8th. of Sep^br to Commemorate the Delivery of the City –[5] Under the Chapel is the Mausoleum or Burying Place for the Royal Family in which

348

Are the Remains of the Grandfather And Father of the present King with Recesses for future Kings & Queens, all Extremely neat & finished with Expensive Marble – The Choir And the Library are likewise very Handsome and the Cloister or Convent adjoining very Spacious – The View from this Place is very Extensive commanding the Vast Plain of Lombardy with the Alps Covered with Snow in the Back Ground – We were Two Hours in going from Turin to this Place, and Staid there as long, Amusing ourselves with the View of the different Towns And Villages, as well as the

---

1. Ivrea – town north of Turin on the road to Aosta and the Alps.
2. Possibly Catherine de Macé, wife of Charles Paul Léonard, Comte de Montigny (1760–1808).
3. La Superga – basilica overlooking the city designed by Filippo Juvarra for Victor Amadeus II and built between 1717–31. The crypt houses the tombs of many members of the House of Savoy.
4. Victor Amadeus II (1666–1732), Duke of Savoy.
5. The day the siege of the city by French forces was lifted in 1706.

City of Turin which is Situated at the Bottom of this Mountain –
upon Our Return Coll. De Saluge Dined with us
Turin the Capital of Piedmont is the Residence of the King of
Sardinia, It is Situated in an Extensive

349

Valley, Watered by the Po – and at the Confluence of this River
with the Dora – The Air is moist and Thick Fogs very frequent
– The Four Gates to the City are Handsome, and the Streets are
Wide, & kept Clean by means of a Kennel[1] with running water
being in the middle – The Strada di Po has a Colonade on Each
Side but the best Shops are in Strada Nuova – The Piazza di San
Carlo is Large and has Portico[s] on Each Side

NB This was the first Day we found the Heat great – we having
for the last Fortnight had frequent Rain

Wednesday April 16th.
We Went this morning to the Convent of Capuchins, which is
Situated upon a Small Circular Hill, Half a Mile from the City,
on the

350

Banks of the Po; The Convent And Chapel Entirely Covers the the
[sic] Summit of the Hill and there is only Some under wood with
a few Trees that Surround the Building The Effect of the whole is
Singular And very pleasing as an Object – And from the Terrace is
the best View of Turin[2]

In the Afternoon we went to the University[3] in the Strada di Po
to See the Museum and Collection of Medals with the Celebrated

1. Kennel – a gutter.
2. Sta Maria al Monte dei Cappuccini. The church was designed by Ascanio Vitozzi in
the late sixteenth century but not completed until 1656.
3. The University building in via Po was erected for Vittorio Amedeo II in the early
seventeenth century. The faculties of the present university are now spread throughout the city.

Isiac Table[1] – from hence we Rode to the Valentino[2] And the Citadel

In the Evening the Chevalier de Saluge Called & told us that the King had this morn'g Signified his Intentions of giving him a Regiment of Chasseurs now Quartered at Nice –[3]

351

Thursday April 17th
We Left Turin this morning and Observed that the Only Pleasant Situation near the Town was the Range of Small Hills Called Les Collines, on which the Palace, Les Vignes de la Reine, and the Couvent des Capuchins, and Several Pretty white Houses are Scattered about. Every Other Part is Low And backed by the Alps which on this Side is like a Perpendicular High Wall (Higher than the Eye can reach with pleasure) and the Top Covered with Snow – The Atmosphere is Thick, Heavy & moist – The Roads even near the Town are Rough, Stony & Bad – Money in Circulation So Scarce, that paper is made use of even for Three Livres –

The Land near the City

352

Appears to be well Cultivated. And Animal Food, particularly Beef, Extremely good – and likewise the Bread & the Butter – but the People are Poor and Disconted [sic] – In the Shops we saw the English Casimere[4] and Other Woolen Cloths –

1. The Bembine Tablet or Mensa isiaca – a bronze tablet, probably Roman, but imitating Egyptian hieroglyphics. It was used before the modern development of Egyptology to try and decipher the ancient Egyptian sign language but to little avail. Stolen by Napoleonic forces, it was returned to Turin after the wars and is now displayed in the Museo Egizio. The latter now shares the Palazzo dell'Accademia delle Scienze with the picture gallery, the Galleria Sabauda
2. The Castello del Valentino on the bank of the river Po. It was built for Christine Marie of France, wife of Victor Amadeus I in the early seventeenth century. It is now houses the Faculty of Architecture of the Polytechnic of Turin.
3. At this time Nice was still a part of the Duchy of Savoy. It was annexed by Napoleon and returned to Savoy until finally being ceded to France in 1860.
4. Murray gives similar spellings as an alternative to cashmere.

As we went towards Milan we met 300 Cavalry and many Bagage Waggons – In the Evening we Stopt at Vercelli[1] And found a tolerable Inn

Friday April 18<u>th</u>
Continued Our Route towards Milan, and between Turin and that City we Crossed 24 Rivers – Two of them by Long Bridges Seven by Flying Bridges composed of Boats – Ten by Short Bridges And Five Streams by D<u>o</u>

353

The Country Improves much near Milan, Rich Pasture Grounds And Hedges with Honey Suckles & Wild Roses – many Fields with Rice[2] – Cows of Every Colour were Feeding, And the Grass in many Places was begun to be mowed upon the Road we passed a Poor man with a Cloak made of Reeds Strung together with a Cord, & tyed round his Neck; which Seemed effectualy to keep him from the Rain –

At Milan[3] we went to the Albergo Reale and found a very good Apartment tho' Dull as the windows Opened only towards the Court yard of the Inn –[4]

Saturday April 19th
Walked about the Town, went to the Cathedral[5] and Saw Every thing worth the Attention of a Stranger

354

And afterwards went to many of the Principal Churches and from thence to the Ramparts And Publick Walks: The Town is Large,

---

1. Vercelli – town north east of Turin on the road to Milan. It is now bypassed by the motorway.
2. Rice – the crop is still grown between Turin and Milan and is notably used today to make risotto.
3. Milan – the capital and principal city of Lombardy. For most of the eighteenth century the duchy was controlled by the Austrian Habsburgs.
4. Albergo Reale – a notable inn at the time.
5. The famous Duomo. It was begun in 1386 but not actually completed until the twentieth century.

but the Buildings are not good, The Streets Narrow And the Pavement Bad – The Publick Garden is a Flat piece of Ground and the Walks in Strait Lines – but the Communication with the Ramparts renders them Pleasant – as the part of the Ramparts to which they adjoin is Planted on Each Side with a double Row of Chesnut Tree[s] forming Two good walks and a Carriage Road between which is the Corso where the Company meet Every fine Evening

We Spent Our Evening in Answering Letters from England, and Receiving Visits from M[r]. Leeson the Brother of Lord Miltown and M[r.] Burton Brother to Lord Conyngham[1] & M[r]. Hay,

355

Sunday April 20th
In the morning we went to Casa Simonetta, about Two miles from Milan, where there is a most Surprising <u>Echo</u>, which Repeats the Human Voice Forty times[2] – upon our Return, M[r] Leeson, M[r] Burton, M[r] Hay and D[r] Cicery[3] Dined with us, and We took them in our Carriage to the Ramparts[4] in the Evening where the Number of Coaches was astonishing, and many of them were Stationed Two deep On Each Side of the Road to See the other Coaches pass, in which Every One was Dressed in full gala[5] – tho' no Publick Amusements were at this time permitted, It being <u>Easter Day</u>, nor was any to Commence till Eight Days after –

---

1. Probably the Hon. Francis Nathaniel Burton (1766–1832), second son of the second Baron Conyngham – see Ingamells' *Dictionary* . . .
2. Villa La Simonetta – formerly a country seat outside the walls of the city proper, a number of early travellers mention the echo. It is the sole surviving suburban villa from the period and has recently been restored, and now houses the Civica Scuola di Musica Claudio Abbado.
3. Dr Cicery – this is the only known note of this character according to Ingamells' *Dictionary* . . .
4. These were the Mura Spagnole built in the sixteenth century. They remained until the nineteenth century but served little military purpose and had been transformed into a promenade by the time of Mrs Bentham's visit. The city's road system still reflects their existence.
5. Gala – in this context, fine or showy dress.

356

Monday April 21ˢᵗ
We went this morning to See the Ambrosian Library,[1] Founded
by Cardinal Frederic Borromeo, Arch Bishop of Milan[2] – from
hence we went to the Arch Dukeˢ Palace[3] & were Shown the State
Apartments, which were Furnished with Rich Crimson Silk made
at Milan, and Tapestry from the Gobelins – The Floors were
Parquée in Variety of Forms and kept Extremely Neat – The Ball
Room magnificent and well Propor^tioned Seven Windows on Each
Side & between Each Window a Large Mirror, and Two Mirrors
at each End of the Room with a Door of Entrance between = the
Room when full contained Eighteen Hundred Persons and was
usually Lighted by wax in Fifty Lustres = Round the Room, at a
great Height, was a Gallery, where Persons were

357

Admitted to See the Dancing – Near this Apartment was a Riding
House, And likewise the Rooms Inhabited by the Family.[4]

From hence we went to the Cathedral and descended to the
Subterranean Chapel in which is placed the Corpse of Saint Carlo
Borromeo in a Case of Chrystal Set in Silver Gilt – The Face
looked very Dark, but perfect The Body was richly Cloathed in
Crimson Silk with Gold Trimming The Right Hand laid upon
the Bosom, and upon One of the Fingers was a Fine Ring – and
a Brilliant Cross was Suspended Over the Bosom – The Chrystal
Case formed an Altar, and upon it was the usual Ornaments of
Silver Candlesticks &c &c – This Small Chapel was very Rich in

1. The Biblioteca Ambrosiana – founded by Cardinal Federico Borromeo in 1609. It
   contains Leonardo's Codex Atlanticus amongst many other precious items.
2. Federico Borromeo (1564–1631) – cousin of San Carlo Borromeo and like him,
   Archbishop of Milan. He was created cardinal by Sixtus V in 1587 at the age of 23.
3. The Palazzo Reale to the right of the Duomo. A palace has existed on the site since
   the Middle Ages but the palace was transformed in the 1770s for the Archduke
   Ferdinand of Austria. A large part of the building is now used as a museum and exhibition space.
4. The royal stables were razed as late as 1925 but the chief damage to the palace was
   caused by incendiary bombs falling nearby in 1943.

Silver –[1] We went afterw[ds]. to the Top of the Tower 512 Steps – from whence we had a very

358

Extensive View of the Vast Plain of Lombardy, and the Alps = The City of Milan is Supposed to be near Six Miles in Circumference, but many Vacant Pieces of Ground are within the Walls – and in general the Buildings are very indifferent – not any Squares – and only One large Open Place which is near the Cathedral[2]

In the Evening we went to the Corso, The Coaches were more than Three Hundred in number And many kept Stationary, that the Family in them might See Others pass = The Arch Duke and Dutchess were in their Carriage passing up and down between the Others –[3] The Croud of People walking Innumerable, And in the Streets at Every House were People Sitting in the Balcony[s] or looking out at their windows = The women with their heads Dressed with Feathers And Flowers as if going to an Opera.

359

Yet the Rooms in which They were Sitting appeared to have Only walls white washed – and to be miserably Furnished –

D[r]. Cicery Visited us in the Evening and advised us to go to See the Lake of Como before we went over Mount S[t] Gothard –[4]

---

1. The Scurolo di San Carlo – the crypt of Saint Charles Borromeo. It was designed by Francesco Richini in 1606 and decorated with scenes from the life of the saint in silver-plated relief. The rock crystal urn was donated by King Phillip IV of Spain.
2. The ascent to the roof of the cathedral is still a popular tourist attraction though the view is not so extensive due to the addition of taller surrounding buildings. A few years after Mrs Bentham's visit, James Hakewill drew two views of the city from the roof – see T. Cubberley and L. Herrmann – *Twilight of the Grand Tour: a catalogue of the drawings by James Hakewill in the British School at Rome Library*, Rome, 1992, Plates 22 & 22A.
3. At the time Francis II of Habsburg-Lorraine (1768–1835), reigned 1792–6, and Maria Theresa of Naples (1772–1807).
4. Como and the eponymous lake – directly north of Milan and on the route to the Saint Gotthard Pass.

Tuesday April 22[d]

Went to S[t] Maria della Gratia to See the Picture of S[t] Paul, Painted by Gaudentio di Ferrara – and Christ Crownd with Thorns by Titian – We likewise went into the Refectory of the Convent to See the Last Supper Painted in Fresco by Leonardi de Vinci[1] and Esteemed to be One of his most famous works – from hence we went to Observe the Shops, which certainly are more Showy and much Larger than Any at Turin, or I think in any Town in Italy

In the Evening went to

360

the Corso on the Ramparts And at Our Return to Our Hotel was most agreeably Surprised to find M[r] Trevor, who had just Arrived from Turin = His Servant told Our Courier that M[r] Trevor had not more than one Hours Notice to Pack up, And we afterw[ds.] learnt that the French had Entered Piedmont.[2]

Wed[y] April 23[d]

Walked in the principal Streets And went into many of the Shops – Observed most of the different Articles of Wedgwood[s] Ware[3] was Imported here from Leghorn – And from Bohemia they have every Article in Glass, and Cut as well as it is done in England – and the Shape of English Decanters they have Manufactured in Bohemian Glass[4]

---

1. Sta Maria delle Grazie – church built in the late fifteenth century and most famous for Leonardo's last Supper in the refectory. Gaudenzio Ferrari's St Paul in his studio, dating to 1543, was removed to France shortly after Mrs Bentham's visit and is now in the collection of the Musée des Beaux Arts, Lyons. Likewise, Titian's Christ crowned with thorns of 1542/3 commissioned for the Confraternity of Santa Maria delle Grazie is now in the Musée du Louvre, Paris.
2. Mrs Bentham is probably referring to the Saorgio Offensive of April, 1794 which had been planned by the then General Napoleon Bonaparte, though the war with France had begun in 1792.
3. Of course, the wares produced by the manufactory founded by Josiah Wedgwood in 1759.
4. Bohemia, now part of the Czech Republic has been for centuries famous for its glassware production.

361

Manchester Goods of all Sorts from England are Sold here, and likewise all Sorts of Cutlery from Birmingham –[1]

In the Markets I observed they Sold Pease, Beans, Asparagus and Even Strawberries by Weight – Frogs in abundance, the Head and And upper part was Cut off, leaving Only the Two Legs united by a little piece of the Back, which was Skinned, yet the animal was Sufficiently Alive for the Legs to move – These were likewise Sold by Weight –

In the Evening M[r.] Trevor who had Dined with the Arch Duke Came to us in Consequence of a Note we had Sent to Request his Advice in respect to which Mountain would be most Eligible for us to go over into Switzerland – at first he advised S[t]. Bernard – but in that Case

362

We must Leave Our Carriage at Aouste,[2] and Return to it And Pass through the Tyrol as it would be impracticable for Any Carriage to Cross the Mountain for Some weeks = but during our Conversation He altered his Opinion, And Said, "that as there was a Report of the French being near the other Side of Saint Bernard, we had better go to Bellanzoni,[3] And Should we find the Passage for the Carriage Over Mount Saint Gothard difficult – or the Charge very Exorbitant, we could from thence Enter the Tyrol – before He left us He gave us Some very Interesting Intelligence respecting Robestspierre [sic] =[4]

---

1. Presumably indicative of the influence of the English Industrial Revolution on European trade.
2. Aosta – the first large settlement in Italy after crossing the St Bernard Pass.
3. Bellinzona – town in Switzerland on the Ticino river at the point where roads diverge to cross the Alps. It is still the location of the divergence of two motorways going north (or meeting coming south!).
4. Maximilien Robespierre (1758–94), the French revolutionary politician. He was executed on 28th July for his role in the "Terror" but Mrs Bentham may be referring to his role in the execution of his fellow revolutionary Georges Danton who was executed on 5th April that year.

Messrs Leeson & Burton And Dr Ciciri came to take Leave of us as we proposed to go in the morning –

363

Thusday April 24th

Left Milan this morning Early. We had found Our Apartment at the Albergo Reale much Cleaner than any Other in Italy And the Beds very Comfortable. The Floors (tho' Brick) were Entirely Covered with Tapestry, and we only regretted not having a View into the Street; but we Looked only into a Court yard – at Milan there are neither Squares, nor Large open Places Except One Spacious Open Place where the Cathedral is[1] – We Saw at Milan a Small Chapel On the Sides of which were placed Human Sculls, Said to be those of Persons who were Killed in Battle by the Founder of this Chapel –[2]

We Arrived at Como, Twenty Five miles distant from Milan at Noon. It is a Small Town at the Head of a Beautiful Lake, about a Mile in Breadth[3]

364

And Fifty in Length, It is frequently to appearance Land Locked, and Some of the Bays Expand Five miles in Breadth with Elegant Villa^s on Each Side belonging to Milanese Families who Reside here in the Summer Months = On Each Side of the Lake the Mountains frequently Rise very High, and Steep to the Edge of the water leaving only Terraces one above the other for Garden – many of these Mountains are Covered with Olive and mulberry Tree^s mixed towards the Bottom with Vines – Others are Covered to the Summit with Chesnut Tree^s. & Others are only Bare Rock –

We went about Twenty miles up this most Beautiful Lake to

1. Piazza del Duomo.
2. San Bernardino alle Ossa – when a neighbouring cemetery ran out of space a chapel was added to contain the bones of the deceased. The church was destroyed by fire in 1712 and replaced by a larger edifice.
3. Como – town at the foot of the eponymous lake. It is almost directly north of Milan and still popular as a summer retreat for wealthy Milanese.

Cadenabbia were [*sic*] we Dined and Staid the Night in a most Comfortable House, The Rooms very neat and the View from them most delightfully Picturesque —[1]

365

Friday April 25th
Left Cadenabbia very Early in the morning, and in going down the Lake Stopt to See the House Described by Pliny, where there is the Fountain which Ebbs and Flows like a Tide —[2] The Water throughout this Lake is So Extremely Transparent that it Reflects the Mountains On each Side as if They were divided Half on Land & Half in Water — The Sound of Bells Ringing in the different Villages On the Sides of the Lake, added to the Luxury of the Scene we passed; And I do not think a more desirable Place for Retirem[t] can be throughout Italy —

We Staid but a Short time at Como, during which we took Some refreshment at the Inn which is Situated at the Head of the Lake, The Apartments appeared Comfortable, but we went Sixteen Miles in the Afternoon to Varese A Poor miserable Town, where

366

We Staid the Night[3] — The Road from Como hither Extremly Bad, but a very good One at this time is making, which added to Our difficulties, for Sometimes we were Obliged to go upon this New Road and the Ascent to it from the old was So Steep that more than Twenty Men who were at Work upon this Road were necessary to Assist us in getting Our Coach Over the different Places we had to pass = At Varese the Arch Duke has a Palace, but it is a very indifferent Building[4]

---

1. Cadenabbia – village on the western shore of the lake of Como at the point where the two lower arms of the lake meet.
2. The actual villa seen by Mrs Bentham is the Villa Pliniana built in 1570. It was later drawn by James Hakewill and is now a hotel. The adjacent waterfall flows intermittently and is described by both Pliny the Elder and Younger.
3. Varese – town north of Milan between Como and Lago Maggiore.
4. Presumably the eighteenth-century Palazzo Estense now housing the town's library, etc.

Saturday April 26.

Left Varese and our Bad Inn Very Early and went Fourteen Miles to Laveno,[1] where we immediately got into a Boat And was Rowed round the Borromean Islands – Upon Isola Bella is a Large and

367

Handsome Palace, but in a Ruinous Condition[2] – The Garden which adjoins is Composed of many Terraces One Above the Other, each full of Orange Trees and Figures of Men Horses &c &c –[3] At the Back of this Island are a number of wretched Hovels, Inhabited by very Poor People

Another Island was Covered with Houses Inhabited by Poor Fishermen[4]

But my favorite Island was Isola Madre, upon which were many Trees of different Sorts and all appeared flourishing – Several Small Cows were feeding upon Excellent pasture, and many Pea Fowls and Pheasants were Running about, The House upon this Island appeared to be a Comfortable Residence, but there was only One[5] – from hence we passed Palanza[6] and Crossed over to Laveno, where Our Coach was put on Board a Large Barge with Five Oars, and Seating Ourselves in the Coach

368

We went down the Lake Maggiore; On each Side of which were High Rocks & Mountains much more Stupendous than those of Como, and not so Pleasing tho' some were Covered with Trees Others Barren Rock =[7] Many Small Towns were Situated at the Bottom of these Mountains tho the Ground was Steep to the Edges

---

1. Laveno – town on the eastern shore of Lago Maggiore. It is still a crossing point having today a modern car ferry.
2. The large palace was not finally completed until the mid twentieth century.
3. The famous garden with its notable "teatro" dates to the seventeenth century.
4. Isola dei Pescatori.
5. Isola Madre – still largely devoted to horticulture with a more naturalistic style of garden than that on Isola Bella.
6. Pallanza on the western side of the lake opposite Laveno.
7. We would probably say that Mrs Bentham was going "up" the lake as she was travelling northwards. The mountains do crowd in more closely at this point.

of the Lake = about Half the Length of the Lake it takes a Bend to the Left And in the Center of this Bend is a Fort Surrounded by the Water –[1]

In the Evening we Stopt at a Small Town on the Edge of this Lake called Cadenabbia And Staid the Night at a most miserable Inn – which we thought more advisable than trusting Ourselves to the Barge men & Continuing upon the water –[2]

369

Sunday April 27

Left Our wretched Inn Early in the morning and again Embarked, Seating ourselves as before in the Coach – but the wind Still continuing against us it was Noon before we reached Magadine at the End of the Lake,[3] where there is a few miserable Houses, from One of which we got Horses to take us to Bellinzona Nine miles distant but the Road Bad And full of Stones[4] – We Dined and Staid the Night at a Comfortable Inn kept by M^sr Andrezzi – The Town consists Only of Two narrow Streets, but being Situated at the Foot of High Mountains, with Forts and Battlements, looks very Picturesque tho' the Forts are merely Ornamental And could be of no use –

370

This morning was Engaged in Aranging the manner of Our Passing Over St Gothard, and Our Coach was Cleared of Every Article of Baggage as it was to be Carried over the mountain Upon a Sledge, for which purpose Four Oxen and Seven Men were to attend it – We Ourselves had Five Saddle Horses Or Mules. One for my dear Son, Another for myself with a man to Lead it the whole way –

---

1. Castelli di Cannero – remains of the Rocca Vitaliana built for Ludovico Borromeo between 1519 and '21.
2. Presumably this is an error and Mrs Bentham is referring to Cannobio – the last town on the western shore of Lago Maggiore before the Swiss border.
3. Magadino – on the eastern side of the lake opposite to Locarno, and now like the latter across the border in Switzerland.
4. Bellinzona – town at the junction of the roads to the St Gothard and St Bernard passes.

The three others for maid Servant, Courier, and Andriazzi who was to Superintend the whole. Each man, Each Horse and Each oxen were to be paid for at the rate of Five Shilling per Day Allowing Four Days to go over the Mountain And Two to Return This upon Calculation was £24. but we were to Pay Forty Louis

371

the additions being allowed for Expence in taking the Coach up the Mountain, tho' we heard afterwards that Andriazzi agreed with People to take it from Ariola[1] the Last Town On the Side of Italy to Ursera[2] the First Town on the Side of Switzerland for Six Pounds

At Noon we quitted Bellinzone And went in Four Hours to Pollegio[3] about twelve Miles distant, where we Staid the Night and found decent Accomodations with Clean Beds

Tuesday April 29<u>th</u>

During Our very Short Stay at Bellinzone we had met with Le Chevalier Bueler de Buel, who had the Rank of Brigadier in the King of Sardinia[s] Army[4] – He appeared to be a Sensible man near Seventy years of Age and was Returning to his native Town Schwitz in Switzerland –[5]

372

And Expressed a great desire to be of Our party, which to us was a pleasing Circumstance as He had frequently Passed Over Saint Gothard = The Road we had travelled yesterday to Pollegio Was at the Bottom & winding round the Base of High Mountains to Day we Ascended and the Road was a considerable Height upon the Mountains with Torrents at the Bottom Rolling over Large Stones and forming Beautiful Cascades – The Rocks frequently hung Over the Road which was So Narrow that it was with difficulty

---

1. Airolo.
2. Ursera – the Romansh name for Andermatt.
3. Pollegio – village on the Ticino north of Bellinzona.
4. Chevalier Bueler de Buel – not traced. The Royal Sardinian Army – the army of the Duchy of Savoy – it became the Royal Italian Army in 1861. The ruler at the time was Victor Amadeus III of Savoy (1726–96).
5. Schwyz – capital of the eponymous Canton in Switzerland.

the Coach was kept from falling Over, many men being necessary to Support it on One Side – And in many Places it was Stuck fast by the Projecting Rock, from whence it was with great difficulty Separated – But the Scenery was Beautiful beyond Description.

373

In the Coach thus Supported by men I continued this morning for Five Hours, and was told that I was the first person that had Ever Ventured to be carried in that manner – as the Extreme Narrowness of the Road upon So great a Height made it appear Tremenduous[1]

From Pollegio we were Five Hours to Dazio[2] where we Dined at a very Comfortable Inn and Afterw^{ds} Three Hours in going to Ariola[3] where we Staid the Night at a very indifferent House –

At Some little distance from Ariola before we arrived there the Scenery of the Country became very Picturesque – The Mountains Closed together and appeared to have been Cleft as under at the Bottom just wide enough to admit a Small Torrent of Water with a very narrow Road on the Side of it –

374

Left Ariola very Early in the morning to have the advantage of Passing St Gothard before the Sun had melted the Snow – The Road immediately began to Ascend very Steep, and in a Short time we were in the midst of Snow And Our Mules frequently Plunged into Holes which had been made in the Snow by former Travellers We therefore thought it more Safe to depend on Our own feet and immediately dismounted and ^{Each} were Supported by the Arm of a Strong Man, And a High Pole tipped with Iron at the End – In Three Hours we Arrived at the Convent at the Highest Point of Saint Gothard that it is practicable to Reach – here the Monks of the Order of Capuchins Opened their Door and Received us in a most

---

1. Murray gives this spelling.
2. Probably Deggio, south-east of Airolo.
3. Airolo – town in the canton of Ticino. It is now close to the entrance to the St Gothard Tunnel and pass.

375

Hospitable manner[1] – giving us Bread, wine and Chocolate, and I thought it the best made and the best tasted Chocolate I Ever drank – After Staying with these good men and a very good Old woman Half an Hour, it was thought advisable Once more to mount Our Mules, and by a gradual Descent we arrived in Two Hours at Ursera where we found a most Comfortable Inn – with Clean Beds and Boarded Floors – And tho' it was but Eleven o Clock in the morning we determined to Stay the Night. Our Feet had been wet with the Snow and we felt Ourselves fatigued – In the Afternoon we walked about this pretty Village Situated amidst mountains with Beautiful meadows & a running Stream amidst them –

376

The Weather was Uncommonly Fine, not the least Wind, and the Monks at the Convent told us they had few Days in a year So delightful, for tho' we were in the Regions of Snow, yet we found it at times So warm as Inclined us to pull off our Great Coats –[2]

Thursday May 1st.

We quitted Ursera Early this morning, and in a Short time Came where the Mountains actually Closed together, And the Road was Cut through & under a high Rock – The passage was narrow And rather Dark tho' not of any great length, but at the End Appeared a most Tremenduous Scene Called Le Pont de Diable A very narrow bridge Crossing Over a Stupenduous[3] Fall of Water[4] The Spray of which mounted up

377

to a great Height and Covered Astonishing High Rocks – The Road very narrow with a Torrent Rolling most boisterously at the

1. The St Gotthard Hospice, a refuge for travellers, has been rebuilt several times over the centuries, latterly after having been destroyed by a fire in the early twentieth century.
2. Possibly monks from the nearby abbey of Disentis.
3. Murray gives this spelling.
4. The Devil's bridge or Teufels-Brücke over the river Reuss – it has been swept away by floods and replaced on a number of occasions.

Bottom making a Tremenduous Noise And this Awful Scenery Continued for near Two miles when it Changed to mountains Covered with Fir Trees, And soon After we perceived a mixture of Other Tree^s with the Firs and the whole Face of the Country was Beautiful – The Road frequently going through Groves of Fir & winding round the middle of High mountains with innumerable Cascades Descending from the Top And Torrents Rolling over Immense Rocks at the Bottom = From Ursera to Steg we were Five Hours going Amidst the most Picturesque Scenery of Various Sorts Equally So whether Tremenduous

378

Or Beautiful – The Inn at Steg[1] appeared but Indifferent – but the Beds looked Clean – We did not Stay long but went on to Altorff[2] – where we arrived in Three Hours the Road going through Orchards & meadow Grounds The Town Small – Our Inn the Lion Noir, very Dirty, but we were obliged to Stay here the Night.[3]

Friday May 2ᵈ.
Being told that there would be a Diet[4] of the Canton held on Sunday to Elect Magistrates for the next Two Years we determined to Stay and See the manner of this Democratic Election – and as the Inn at Altorff would be Crouded with People on this Occasion, we walked this morning to Endeavour to get Rooms at Fluellen[5] a Small Village at the beginning of the lake of Lucerne where Our Coach & Ourselves were

379

To Embark – At this Village we found a very neat Apartment at a

---

1. Steg – now Steg-Hohtenn – town in the Canton of Valais in the southwest of Switzerland.
2. Altdorf or Altorf, the capital of Canton Uri.
3. Hôtel du Lion Noir – it existed into the late nineteenth century.
4. Before the French Revolution brought changes to Switzerland each canton had its own "diet" or governing body.
5. Flüelen – the "port" of Uri on Lake Lucerne. It played an important role as a place for the comings and goings of travellers between Lucerne and the St Gotthard Pass before the advent of the railway and the motorway.

Small Inn, kept by a M^r. Arnold who was Father to Our Landlord
at Altorff – And we Agreed to take Possesion of it in The Evening

In the Afternoon we looked at the Arsenal at Altorff which con-
tained Arms for 2000 Men[1] We likewise went to See the Council
Chamber in which were Some Prints Representing the Building
And Procession of the Marquis de Vergennes when He Signed the
Treaty in 1777 at Soleure[2] – And likewise a Print Representing the
Five Works Exhibited in Consequence –

In the Evening Our Coach Arrived having been much longer than
Ourselves in Crossing Saint Gothard – We immediately got into it
and went to Fluellen –

380

Saturday May 3^d
The morning was passed in writing Letters to England to be put
into the Post at Lucerne, We afterwards Sauntered upon the Bank
of the Lake, of which from Our Apartment at the Inn, we had a
good View – The Mountains around us were of a great height, And
the Summit of many, were allways Covered with Snow – most of
them were barren Rock – but the Town of Altorff is immediately
under One, that is Covered with wood to the Top And Appears
very Picturesque – The Chief Business of the Town consisted in
its being the Place where all Goods must Pass that are going into
the North of Italy – Or Coming from thence into Switzerland –

381

Sunday May 4th
We went after Breakfast to Altorff to See the Magistrates proceed
to the Diet – They were Seven in Number, all Dressed in Black,

1. The arsenal or Zeughaus at Altdorf still exists.
2. Jean Gravier de Vergennes, French Ambassador, signed a treaty of alliance with the
   Swiss Cantons at Soleure in 1777.

with their Hair in Bag, & had Swords, tho' they were on Horsback.[1] The Saddles were highly Ornamented. The Militia attended and marched before Them, with the Flag or Colours flying, the Painting was a white Cross in the middle, and the Quarters Yellow & Black – The Field where the Diet was held was about a mile distant from the Town, and after the Procession had passed us, we followed – A large Circle was formed under a Hill, And in this Circle the Candidates Harangued the Peasants who were Standing in great numbers upon Benches round – And the Choice of Each was determined by Show of Hands, or rather Fingers, for the

382

manner of Opening and Shaking the Fingers was very Singular –

Upon the Hill Seats were placed for the Women to See what passed in the Circle below, – And Four men were likewise there to determine upon Oath the Majority = The Magistrate of the Police, who was likewise Dressed in a Black Silk Coat had a yellow Silk Cloak thrown Over One Side, So that his Dress was Half Yellow and Half Black

The Drummers belonging to the Militia had likewise party Colour'd Cloaths – and one of their Stockings Yellow Seamed with Black, and the Other Stocking Black Seamed with yellow – with a Coat divided in the Same manner by different Colours – The Weather was Extremely Fine, and we Returned to Fluellen much pleased with the Sight –

383

An Extract from Mallet du Pan's Account of Switzerland[2]

Vallies Enclosed among the Alps And Peopled with Shepards preserves the Simplest System as the most Suitable to their Condition –

---

1. The spelling does exist but is very antiquated. It seems likely that this example is merely a spelling mistake – ed.
2. Jacques Mallet du Pan (1749–1800), French journalist of royalist persuasion. The extract is possibly from his *Mémoires historiques*, 1783.

At a Bernese peasants Every thing was found in its Place, nothing neglected, nothing Omitted, nothing put off – His Roomy House, His Farm, His Lofts, His Cattle, were Models of Arrangement and Neatness, and Skill – His Apparent Slowness never Stopped the round of his Labors, invariably marked out –

If He were Seldom found Expeditious, He was as Seldom Idle – This Love of Order, This deep Sense of the Rights of Property, appeared in the minutest Particular – A Gap in a Hedge would have passed for an Outrage. No One Ever Trod out of the Footpath that led through a

384

Field – The Grounds and Tillage protected by Inclosures were Still more So by the National Character.

Monday May 5th
We quitted Fluellen at Eight o Clock this morning, and Embarked on Board a Large Boat which we had Hired with Nine men to Row – The Coach was placed in the middle in which we occasionally Sat –

M[r]. Douglass who had Travelled to Fluellen in a Small Cabriolet being much distressed to get to Lucerne, we offered to give both himself & his Carriage a place in Our Boat – And being like-wise much Sollicited[1] by a very pretty Girl About Thirteen, the Daughter of the principal Inn Keeper at Lucerne who had been Visiting her Relations at Altorff, to give her And her Uncle L'Abbé Krench[2] permission to go with us, we Obliged Them, and by So doing, gained many

385

Anecdotes relative to the present Situation of Switzerland – The Lake Commenced at the Little Village of Fluellen and the Rocks on Each Side were a great Height and very Steep to the Edge of the Lake for the first Five Miles – Soon after we Came to A Small

1. Murray gives this spelling.
2. L'Abbé Krench – not traced.

Chapel Called William Tells where we Stopt to See the Paintings which Represented the Various Circumstances of his Life,[1] from Hence the Lake Extended more in a direct Line And we Saw the Little Town of Bruner Situated on the Shore[2] with Schwitz the Capital of the Canton[3] above it a little more Inland – but the Mountains Soon Rise above Schwitz –

The Lake Here takes a Bend And the Mountains become more Covered with Wood – And Another Small Republick was at the Foot of these Mountains[4] – when we had gone about Three Fourths

386

of the Length of the Lake the Scene Changed from High Mountains to Little Hills, with many Beautiful Woods, And many white Houses Situated in Meadows and this Scenery continued to Lucerne[5] which made a fine Appearance at the End of this Lake Twenty Seven Mile in Length from Altorff – The Day had been Beautifully Fine and immediately on our Landing we went to M[r] Bielmann[s] L'Aigle D'or a most Excellent Inn, with Boarded Floors white and Clean, and very Comfortable Beds, with great Attention and Civility.[6] In the Evening we had Rain for the first time during many Weeks

Tuesday May 6th.
Wrote Letters to England – and afterw[ds] walked with Monsieur L'Abbé Kock[7] And Mad[lle] Bielmann to See the Convent of Urselines,[8] where Two of the Religeuse Showed us their

---

1. Tell's Chapel – it was rebuilt in 1881.
2. Brunnen – town on lake Lucerne.
3. Schwyz – the town is the capital of the Canton of Schwyz.
4. Presumably Mrs Bentham is referring to another canton bordering the lake of Lucerne such as Nidwalden.
5. Lucerne – at the western end of the eponymous lake.
6. L'Aigle d'Or – a well-known inn at the time.
7. Kaspar Joseph Koch (1742–1805), enlightened priest and Swiss patriot.
8. Ursuline Convent

387

Bed Rooms, we likewise Saw the Cathedral, in which there was
an Organ Said to be the largest in Europe[1] – we afterw^ds walked
upon Several Covered Bridges,[2] which afford a most pleasant and
Convenient Walk Either in Summer or Winter, As the Covering
guards Equally from the Heat and Cold, and the Openings on
Each Side gives a View of the Country which here is beautifully Contrasted, having On One Side a Fertile and Picturesque
Country; On the Other, Snowy Mountains Rising one above the
Other in the most Terrific Forms – And these Bridges Are of a
great Length – from hence we walked to a Farm House to See
the Dairy, in which the Shallow Wooden Trays for milk were
Extremely white & Neat.

At Two o Clock we went by appointment to General Pfiffer^s

388

who very Politely Shewed us himself the model he had made of the
Mountains and the Lakes in Switzerland[3] – taking the Center from
Lucerne – we then made a Visit to Monsr Balthasar Secretaire du
Conseil,[4] He has Published Several Books in different Languages
and has a very good Library in his House which is fitted up in the
Neatest manner. And he likewise Shewed us a very fine Collection
of Prints &c &c upon the whole we were So much pleased with the
Situation of Lucerne And the adjoining Country that we thought
it a most desirable Residence – And here the Late Lord Montague
with his Friend M^r. Burdett Resided many months before they
made the fatal Experiment of Passing the Rhine at Lauffenberg –[5]
Bread, Butter Fish and meat Excellent at Lucerne –

---

1. The organ of the Hofkircke – the original Baroque organ was later altered and
   enlarged on several occasions.
2. The Spreuer-Brücke and the Mühlen-Brücke
3. Francis Louis de Pfiffer, lieutenant-general in the French army. On retirement to his
   native Lucerne he created a large-scale model of the Swiss Cantons.
4. Josef Anton Xaver Balthazar (1761–1837). Politician and librarian. His private library
   became the basis of the Cantonal Library in 1832.
5. George Samuel Browne, 8th Viscount Montagu (1769–1793) and his friend Charles
   Sedley Burdett determined to go down the Rhine falls in a fishing boat and died in
   the attempt.

389

Wed^y May 7th

We Quitted Lucerne this morning Having Hired Four Horses to take us to Berne; but we left this Place with Regret for the adjoining Country is most delightful The Small Hills Covered with Clumps of Trees and Varied by Rich Meadows intermixed, forms a most Picturesque Scene – The Lake in Front of the Town is bounded by Immense Mountains whose Tops rising in Various Forms are Covered with Snow And look Tremenduous, yet Contrasted with the Rich Pastures & Small Hills and the Beautiful Little River meandering amidst them makes Lucerne a desirable Residence

This Beautiful Scenery continued about Three Miles and afterw^{ds} we passed through a Rich Country much resembling the best parts of Devonshire the Road continually Ascending and Descending Small

390

Hills, with Meadows, Orchards & Corn Fields, on Each Side of the Road, and at a very little Distance were Small Hills Covered with Beech – The Farm Houses resembled Long Barns. They were Built of Wood with deep Pent House Roofs – on the Ground Floor are Rooms for the Family, and Stables for the Horses. The Corn and the Hay Loft is over.

We Stopt to Bait the Horses at Roida,[1] a Small Village And from thence went to Morgenthall[2] which was Eleven Leagues from Lucerne, & there Staid the Night The Inn was Clean & Neat, the Country Beautiful and Watered by Several Clear Streams – We Saw many Women at Work in the Fields Some digging – others Ploughing and many Planting Potatoes – all appeared Stout & Strong made = And many were Washing of Linnen in Tubs as is done in England –

---

1. Roida – not traced.
2. Morgenthal – village between Lucerne and Berne.

391

Thursday May 8ᵗʰ
Left Morgenthall Early in the morning And went Nine Leagues
to Berne The Road continued to lead through a Country highly
Cultivated, and frequently through fine Woods of Oak and Beech
with Hedges of Weymouth Pines –[1] And many Cherry and Other
Fruit Trees were often intermixed = The Dress of the Women in
the Country, continued to be a Bodice and Petticoat of Woolen
Cloth Sewed together, but of different Colours – with their Hair
turned up to the Crown of the Head, and then Plaited in Two
Braids hanging down below the Waist – upon their Heads were
Either Straw Hats Ornamented with Four Knots of Red & Green
Ribband – or Black Silk Caps with Black Gawse or Lace Border but
the married Women have their Hair tyed up Close to the Crown of
the Head – The Women

392

in general Wear Red Stockings

We Arrived at Berne about Three o Clock and went to the Falcon
where we found very good Apartments and in Every respect good
Accomodations –[2]

The City of Berne appeared to be the best Built Town we had
Seen during our Tour[3] – The Houses are Built of white Stone
resembling those of Bath in England –[4] The principal Street has
an Arcade on Each Side under which are the Shops, and the First
Floor of the House stretches over this Arcade –[5] The Windows are
Sashed and Open like Folding Doors The Houses in general are

---

1. Weymouth pine – Pinus strobus. The tree was a native of north America and had
   been brought to England by Captain George Weymouth of the Royal Navy in 1605.
   The timber was used in the construction of ships for the navy.
2. The Falcon – a long-standing hostelry at the time.
3. Bern – on the river Aare and the capital of the eponymous canton. Since 1848 it has
   also been the seat of the federal government.
4. The city of Bath is of course built of Bath stone, an oolitic limestone found in the
   locality of the city, though it is of a honeyed colour.
5. The city was noted for these arcades or Lauben.

Three Stories in Height – with Garrets in the Roof, but between the Third story and the Garret is a Pent house Roof which is Tiled – The Streets are Wide, and are formed in a

393

Curve but So gradually as not to Appear Crooked, tho they are not in Strait lines – a Running Stream goes through the middle of many of the Streets, but it neither offends the Eye, nor adds to the Beauty = There are Several Fountains, and a great number of Publick Walks in different parts of the Town[1] – The Ramparts & the Platform are Planted with Trees, and ornamented with Benches Painted Green – and Some of the Walks at the different Ends of the Town extend to a Considerable distance with Trees on Each Side and Benches – The River Aar Runs in a Semi Circle and forms a natural Rampart to the Town as the Ground on which the Town is Built Rises immediately from the River –

The Shops are well Supplied

394

with Various Articles, I Saw Blankets, Casimeres, And Callicoes from England – The Ladies dress being much like the English, The Bonnet – Hat, or large Cap for morning and walking – Provisions here are very good, Bread, Butter & Milk Excellent –

At Noon Mad[lle] Turrelini made us a Visit, in Consequence of letters She had received from M[r] Wickham And we Engaged her to Dine with us –[2] before which, She went with us to the Cathedral[3] & to walk on the Platform – And to See the Council Chamber –[4] It being the Time of the Fair I went with her a Shopping – And

---

1. Many of the fountains date from the sixteenth century.
2. Mademoiselle Turrelini and Madame Turrelini are mentioned on several occasions. The name is very unusual. However an Italian Protestant family called Turrettini from Lucca settled in Geneva in the late sixteenth century and prospered. It seems likely that this is the origin of the name.
3. The Minster – a late Gothic building.
4. The Rathaus – the original building was erected between 1406–16 in the late Gothic style and this is the edifice seen by Mrs Bentham. Alterations occurred in the nineteenth century and again in the 1940s.

Purchased A morning Dress of the manufacture of Nismes near Lyons[1] – We likewise made a Visit to Lord Robert Fitzgerald who had a House about Two miles from the Town –[2]

395

In the Afternoon we went to See the Arsenal in which there was a great number of Cannon with Small Arms &c And a Figure of William Tell with his Son & the Apple upon the Head of the Child –[3] We went afterw^{ds} to the Wood which forms a Circle of Some Miles round the Town & many delightful Walks are Cut through this wood which is upon the Edge of the Hill just above the River and gives most Beautiful Views of the adjacent Country = The Walks are kept very Neat at the Expence of the Town and are more Extensive than any I ever Saw belonging to Any City, and are calculated for Either Riding or Walking – Upon our Return to our Inn Mad^{lle}. Turrelini took Leave as we were to quit Berne the next Morning –

396

Saturday May 10th
After breakfast we went to Thun,[4] a Small Town very pleasantly Situated upon the River Aar – Four Hours distance from Berne – The Church is upon the Hill which rises above the Houses in the Town and the Ascent to it is near 254 Steps – From the Church yard the View of the Lake and the Environs of the Town is very Picturesque[5]

The Country from Berne hither is very pleasant tho' the Rich Woods to [sic] do not Extend far; on this Side of Berne we passed in View of the House Inhabited at this time by Lord Robert

---

1. Presumably Nîmes, but not close to Lyons.
2. Lord Robert Stephen Fitzgerald (1765–1833), diplomat. He was minister plenipotentiary to Switzerland, 1792–5.
3. The old Armoury or Zeughaus was demolished in 1876 and the collection transferred to the Bernisches Historisches Museum.
4. Thun – town south-east of Berne on the Thuner See.
5. The Stadtkirche.

Fitzgerald which appeared to be little more than a Farm House in a pretty Situation = The Inn near the Bridge at Thun, we found very Comfortable, Our Apartments looked upon the River – and our Provisions of Fish, Bread Butter, Milk and Tea

397

good, And Wine Excellent, with M^r· Offenhauser Our Landlord very Attentive and Obliging

Sunday May 11th
and Close to the Mouth of the River is a very good Old Family House Inhabited during the Summer months by a Gentleman from Berne And very near it is a Small but neat House with a little Garden belonging to a Man whose Name was Zibach,[1] He had Lived Some time in England with M^r· Thompson of Rohampton [sic] in Surry, [sic][2] and now Offered himself to be Our Guide to the Mountains = He frequently Let his House during the Summer And an English Lady & her Daughter M^rs. & Miss Cruttenden of Lausanne had Given Him Two Guineas a Month for it –[3] There was a good

398

Sitting Room, One very large Bed Room with Two Beds in it, Two Servants Bed Rooms, a Kitchen and Pantry^s &c and for Two Crowns more, they were allowed to have whatever the Garden produced = This man had the Fishing upon the River for a considerable Length, and Sold the Trout and Perch at 4 Basche and Half per Pound, about 7^d· pence English money =[4] On the Banks of this River were many Stacks of Beech Wood Cut in pieces of proper Lengths for Fire, which Sold for 7^s. & 6^d Six foot in Length And Breadth = At the Church[5] we found a numerous Congregation Assembled, attending to a Sermon Preached in the German Language, The

1. Zibach – the surname exists but this individual is not listed in the *Historisch-Biographisches Lexikon der Schweiz*.
2. Probably Andrew Thomson of Roehampton, died 1796.
3. Mrs Cruttenden – not traced.
4. Batzen – coins of a small denomination produced in Bern before the advent of the Swiss franc.
5. The parish church was built in 1738.

Seats in the Church consisted of Forms in the middle, Three deep on Each Side, and all had Backs to them – but no Pews – The Men[s] Heads were uncovered and

399

Very few of the Women had any Hat or Bonnet upon their Heads.

At Noon we went in a Small Open Chaise with One Horse upon the Side of the Lake to See a very pretty Villa With a Garden and a Wood adjoining it, belonging to Mon[r] Le Conseiller Frisching of Berne,[1] from it was a fine View of the Alps, particularly The Blumlis The Eiger, and Scheckaun[2] [sic] which are Some of the Highest and are allways Covered with Snow with the Village of Overhausen[3] at the bottom of a Hill On One Side of the Lake – upon Our Return to Thun we passed through Quart[4] another Small Village – afterw[ds.] we walked to the Castle[5] where the Chief Magistrate of Thun Resides, he is Called the Bailiff[6] – from the Castle the View of the Lake

Page 400

And the Mountain Alps with the Rich adjoining Meadows form a fine Contrast of the Sublime and Beautiful. The Pont de Cander near the Village of Quart is of a very Singular Construction Uniting Two High Rocks, between which Runs a Considerable Breadth of water –[7]

Monday May 12[th.]
We Experienced this morning a very great Change of Weather, Yesterday the Heat was So great we Sought for Shade – To

1. Franz Rudolf Frisching (1733–1807). He belonged to a dynasty of Berne notables. His villa, Lorraine Gut, no longer exists but is recalled by Lorrainestrasse close to the river Aare, the area now being a suburb of greater Berne.
2. The Blümlisalp at 3669m, the Eiger at 3975m and the Schreckhorn at 4078m.
3. Oberhofen on the northern shore of the lake.
4. Possibly Gwatt on the southern shore of the lake.
5. Schloss Thun – the castle was begun in the twelfth century and now houses a museum and other functions.
6. Schloss Oberhofen was the administrative centre for the district until the French Revolution and overlooks the lake of Thun.
7. Probably the Pont de la Kander, originally a covered wooden bridge of a single span.

Day Extreme Cold with Rain And Snow, M<u>r</u> Offenhausen Our Landlord brought us in his Hand a Large Snow Ball – and told us a great Quantity was upon the Mountains – The Rain continued from Twelve last Night till Three this Afternoon After which we Walked upon the Covered Bridge and Observed the People bringing Home their Milk

Page 401

In very white, & very Shallow flat wooden Tubs; made to hang Close to their Backs, wide between the Shoulders, and gradually contracted towards the Waist, with Three Broad Hoops to Bind & Strengthen this Tub –

Tuesday May 13th.

We Left Thun at Seven in the morning & went in a Boat with Three Men to Row us, up the Lake, Thermometer at 45. The Mountains Called Scheckaun and the Eiger with a Long Chain of Others were Covered with Snow. In Four Hours we Arrived at the Head of the Lake and Landed at Newiss a Single House,[1] where we got a Cart and putting the Trunk which contained Our Night Linnen into it, we walked by the Side near a Mile to Underseven,[2] and through that Village About Half A Mile further to Inter-Lachen[3] Where we Stopt Half an Hour to

Page 402

Take some Refreshment, and afterw^{ds} We Embarked in Another Boat and Went in Three Hours to the top of the Lake of Brientz[4] and Landed at the Town,[5] where we got into a Char a ban and was conveyed in Two Hours more to Meyringen[6] a Village most Beautifully Situated Amidst Pasture Grounds in a Valley Under the Scheideck[7] a very High Mountain adjoining to many others from which there falls numerous Cascades from an Astonishing

1. Neuhaus?
2. Presumably Unterseen close to Interlaken.
3. Interlaken – between the Thuner and Brienzer See.
4. Brienzer See.
5. Brienz.
6. Meiringen – town on the river Aare east of the Brienzer See.
7. The Scheidegg.

Height. From One of these Cascades I counted Twelve different Falls of water The Village of Meyringen consists of Wooden Houses, which are likewise Covered with wood cut into the Shape of Tiles, and large Stones are placed upon the Roof in different parts to prevent the Wind un roofing the whole – The Houses are chiefly Inhabited by Peasants who have Large Dairy's – [*sic*] but neither Houses nor Boats in Switzerland are Ever

Page 403

Painted on the Outside or Inside The Only Fence from the Weather is a Deep Pent-House Roof which projects much forwarder than the Ground Floor, and Shelters a great Quantity of Billet Wood for Firing which is Cut in proper Lengths for Burning And Piled under the Windows all round the House to be ready for use and likewise to keep the House warm

The Peasants Live mostly upon Barley Bread made like a thin Cake – Potatoes, & milk with whey for their constant drink –

Few Families in the Swiss Villages have more than One Cow And One Pig killed for their Subsistence in a year – These are Cut up and Smoak Dried, and upon a Sunday Or Holiday a Piece of this meat is a Feast, for Milk is their usual Diet, and it is Supposed to Give the Health and Strength which is So Universal to the Natives of this Country

Page 404

For the Women in these parts do all kind of Laborious Husbandry

We found the Small Inn at Meyringen very Comfortable, and the Beds very Clean – and we Spent our Evening in walking to See the Various Cascades, from this place it is practicable to go over the Scheideck Mountains, but the Late fall of Snow rendered Riding Over it impossible and it would take at least Seven Hours to walk, there fore we determined to Return in the manner we came

Wednesday May 14th.

We Left the delightful Village of Meyringen Soon after Six this
morning And in Two Hours Arrived at Brientz where we again
Embarked upon the Lake, which is Smaller And not So Picturesque
as that of Thun; but the Mountains on Each Side are Steeper &
many Covered with Trees. upon Some

Page 405

were Small Pasture Grounds where we Saw the Peasants at this
time making Hay and Several Little Sheds of Wood Scattered
about in which they keep the Hay during Winter

The Lake of Thun has Some Houses near the Borders of it
Inhabited by Families from Berne who come there during the
Summer as the Milanese go to the Lake of Como,[1] And there are
Some Orchards And Vineyards Close to the Edge of the Lake, but
not So at Brientz; at the End of which, we Arrived again at Inter
Laken, but Staid only to take Some Refreshm^{ts} – And then got into
a Char a ban And went to Grindelwald[2] – The Road from Inter
Laken for the first Hour went through Extensive Pasture Grounds,
Planted with Apple Trees Pears and Wallnuts;[3] and a prodigious
Number of Cherry Trees, which appears to be the principal Fruit
Tree throughout this Country – They are Planted so

Page 406

Thick on the Side of the Road, that they frequently Hang quite
over, and as we passed we gathered them

After we had Rode one Hour the Road went a Considerable Height
up a Mountain through a Wood of Fir Trees with a Torrent of
Water at the Bottom and as the Road was very Narrow and full
of Stones & frequently at the Edge of a precipice it was really
Tremenduous

---

1. The Milanese bourgeoisie still of course maintain homes on Lago di Como or Lago
   Maggiore.
2. Grindelwald – town south east of Interlaken.
3. Murray gives this spelling.

We met many of the Peasants who were Soldiers Returning from their Annual Review, which is always Three days in Every year; besides which They are Exercised Every Sunday after Divine Service in their respective Parishes And Every Man from Sixteen years of Age to Sixty is Obliged to have his Name Enrolled, And whenever He Receives the Commission, or is at a Marriage, or Baptism He must appear in Regimentals – but as He never Wears them but on the above mentioned Occasions, One

Page 407

One Suit generally is Sufficient for Life

At Five in the Afternoon we Arrived at <u>Grindelwald</u> which is a Large Village with Several Houses about in different Pasture Grounds having large Dairy's [*sic*] belonging to them – The Mountains which are behind these Houses have Grass upon them almost to the top, while those in the Front are Covered Snow = Between Two very High Mountains are Two Extensive <u>Glacieres</u> which were full in View from the Windows of Our Inn – They appeared to me like Heaps of Snow which had fallen from the adjoining Mountain, and by being thrown in rugged Heaps, had been long congealed and Frozen, now appearing like Waves of Ice –

Thursday May 15[th.]
In the morning after fully Satisfying my Curiosity by Viewing the Glacieres[1] I walked to the Church which was filled with benches Except Two Pews

Page 408

One of which was for the Bailiff Of the canton, the Other for the Family of the Curate of the Parish who Inhabit a very Neat Parsonage House near the Church, and often Accommodate Strangers when the Inn is too full to Admit more –

I went into One of the Dairy[s] And tho' the good Woman belonging

---

1. The Upper and Lower Grindelwald glaciers.

to it did not understand the Language I Spoke, yet by Signs She entreated me to take Some Refreshment –

After Breakfast we Entered again Our Char á ban and went to the Beautiful Valley of Lauterbrun[1] where we Saw the Celebrated Falls of the <u>Staubach</u> which makes One Single Fall of 336 Feet perpendicular[2] – The Valley is Narrow And highly Picturesque, the Mountains being of a prodigious Height and in general Covered with Wood to the Summit – Whenever the Wood is Cut down Either in the Spring Or Summer months, it is left on

Page 409

The Mountains till Winter, and after the Snow has fallen it is brought away by Traineaus[3] while the Men are thus Employed in the Winter – The Women Knit and likewise make their Husband⁵ Cloaths as well as their own – for during the Summer months their whole time is Employed in the Field –

From the Valley of Lauterbrun We Returned to Inter-Lachen & there Staid the Night – The Inn tolerable And the Beds very Clean = tho' only white washed walls – but Boarded Floors And the People very Attentive & Civil

Friday May 16th
We Left Inter-Lachen Early in the Morning – This Village is pleasantly Situated in the middle of a Valley Encircled by Mountains; but the Valley appears like One very large Orchard full of Cherry, Pears and Wallnut Tree⁵ with Rich Grass at the Bottom = It is within Half a Mile of Unterseven and is joined

Page 410

By a Bridge, which we Crossed in going again to the Lake of Thun, & there We Embarked, and in Four Hours, we were Landed again

1. Lauterbrunnen south of Interlaken.
2. The Staubbach Falls – of 980 feet according to Baedeker.
3. Traineau – sledge. The word is used in English, the plural, of course, being traineaux.

at Thun, and Staid there the Remainder of the Day, walk'g upon the Banks of the River and in Beautiful Pasture Grounds –

Saturday May 17th.
Left Thun at Eleven in the morning having been Obliged to Send to Berne for Horses = The Road to Berne went through a Rich Cultivated Country finely Wooded and High Hills at a Considerable Distance – We Arrived at Three, but found the Falcon Inn[1] So full that we could not have Beds but by going to an Apartment belonging to the Inn on the Opposite Side of the Street – In the Evening we walked upon the Ramparts[2]

Sunday May 18[th.]
Left Berne Early in the morning & for Six Miles went through a very

Page 411

Beautiful Country to Gumen,[3] and in Ten Miles farther came to the Lake of Morat,[4] on the Banks of which there appeared to be Some Villages, but the Shores are Flat & consequently not [so] Picturesque as most of the Other lakes we had Seen – From Morat we went to Avanches & Stopt to See the Mosaic Pavement, Supposed to be in former Times a bath but now it is the Floor of a barn belonging to the Bailiff – we likewise went to See the Ruins of an Amphitheatre now in the middle of a Kitchen Garden[5] – Near the Gates of the Town but on the Outside the Earl of Northampton with his Daughter Lady Frances has for Some Time Resided in a very Indifferent House Situated in a Country that has no peculiar Beauty to Recommend it[6]

---

1. The Falcon Hotel remained popular with English travellers into the nineteenth century.
2. The city is bounded on three sides by the river Aare. The ramparts and fortifications at the eastern side of the old town were demolished in the nineteenth century.
3. Gümmenen.
4. The Murten See or lake of Morat.
5. The town of Avenches, south of the Murten See and the ancient capital of the Helvetii (the Roman Aventicum). The Roman amphitheatre at the edge of the town still survives.
6. Spencer Compton, 8th Earl of Northampton (1738–1790 (96?)). He had been MP for the eponymous town until he succeeded to the title in 1763. He is buried in Berne. Lady Frances Compton (1758–1832).

From Avenches we went to Payern[1] distant only 28 Miles from Berne And Staid the Night –

NB – There is no page 412 – ed.

Page 413

Monday May 19[th.]
Left Payern at Five in the morng And went Eleven Miles to Breakfast at Mondon[2] a very Ugly Town and a very Dirty Inn – The Road from Hence begins to Ascend and continues in that manner for Some Miles through and near many Fine Woods, and after Crossing the Hills Descends to Lausanne[3] a mean Ill Built Town in a Beautiful Country, near the Lake of Geneva It was near Six o Clock when we Arrived, tho' we had only Travelled Twenty Five Miles = The Town we found full of French Emigrants And could not get a Bed at the Golden Lyon to which we had been Recommended as the Best Inn,[4] and therefore went immediately to Our Banker, who Requested Mons[r] Des Miseri[5] who Lived opposite to the Inn, to Give us an Apartment in his House – as he was going to his

Page 414

Villa in the Country this Evening. The Apartment was well Furnished And the owner was very desirous of Letting it; but it being in the middle of the Town we declined taking it for more than the Night –

Tuesday May 20th
This Morning was Engaged in writing Letters to England, at Noon we made a Visit to Madame Cerjat[6] to whom we had brought

1. Payerne – town east of the lake of Neuchâtel.
2. Moudon – between Payerne and Lausanne.
3. Lausanne – town on the northern shore of the lake of Geneva.
4. A Rue du Lion d'Or still exists but not the inn.
5. Monsieur des Miseri – not traced.
6. Marguerite Madeleine Stemple (1736–1812). She was actually born in London and married Jean-François Maximilien de Cerjat (1729–1802) in 1754.

Letters And by her advice, went to M$^{rs.}$ Cruttenden an English Lady who Shewed us an Apartment in her House which we agreed to Hire. It consisted of a Dining Room upon the Ground Floor, A Sitting Room and Bed Room upon the First Floor, & upon the Second a Room with Two Beds, & over it a Garret – The use of a Kitchen, and a good Servants Hall The House was very pleasantly Situated at the End of the Town.

Page 415

And tho' the Road was at the Front of the House, yet there was a very pretty Garden paralel to it and Exactly opposite to our Window And from the Drawing Room which was at the Back part of the House we commanded a fine View of the Beautiful Lake of Geneva there being only Gardens And Meadow Grounds between the Lake and the House we Resided in, And from the Garden belonging to the House we had a Door that Communicated with the Fields – We Agreed to Give Five Guineas for a Fortnight And to Continue on the Same Terms as long as we pleased unless any Family Came that would take it for a Length of Time = Linnen we were to Hire And Firing we were to Buy = and we Agreed with a Traiteur at a Crown Each to provide our Dinners –

Page 416

The Bread, Milk and Tea for our breakfast we could Purchase as wanted, And we found Ourselves very Comfortably Settled in a New House very neatly Furnished, for tho' M^{r}. & Mrs Cruttenden had Resided Twelve years at Lausanne yet they had Built this House not many months when He Died last winter Leaving his wife and one Daughter Here; and Another Daughter married in the East Indies to a Son of Mr Pott^{s} a Celebrated Surgeon in England[1]

Wed^{y}. May 21st

Walked before Breakfast in the Fields towards the Lake – afterw^{ds} Mrs Weston made us a Visit, and at Noon we went (in a very Neat Chariot which we Hired to Attend us during Our Stay at Lausanne) to Visit Madame Cerjet [sic] & took her with us to Visit M^{rs}.

---

1. Percival Pott (1714–88), surgeon. He married Sara Cruttendon in 1740.

Page 417

Trevor the Wife of the English Minister at Turin[1] – We found her Residence to be part of a House Close to the Lake near a mile from Lausanne. She Bathes frequently, and in Riding, Walking, and Reading, passes many many months without having any Companion with her – Upon our Return we went to See the House where Voltaire Lived Some years ago[2] – and likewise to See the House in the Town where Gibbon the Historian Resided[3]

In this Country are a great Number of Wallnut Tree[s]. The Green outer coat is used for Dying And from the Nut is Extracted Oyl. The first Drawn is used for Eating with Sallad &c – The Second Drawn is used for Burning in Lamps – Cherry Tree[s] are likewise Planted in abundance and they not

Page 418

Only Preserve the Fruit, but They make a Liqueur much Esteemed in this Country –

In the Evening we took Miss Cruttenden and were drove through the Town to the Publick Walks where we Staid Some time & were much Amused by Seeing Some Gentlemen in the adjoining Walks Shooting with Bow & Arrow at a Target.

Thursday May 22[d]
Monsieur Cerjat,[4] and M[rs]. Trevor Came this morning, and the Weather being Showry & M[rs]. Trevor on Horsback we took her in Our Carriage Home, and by her Advice Sent cards to the English & Irish Families who were Resident Here – In the Evening we walked about the Environs of the Town –

---

1. Harriet Trevor (née Burton) (d. 1829). The couple had no children.
2. François-Marie Arouet, known as Voltaire (1694–1778), French philosopher. He frequented Lausanne between 1755 and '59, latterly at a house called le Grand Chêne.
3. Edward Gibbon (1737–94), historian. Gibbon converted to Catholicism in 1753 as a youth, and was sent in consequence to Lausanne in the care of a Protestant pastor.
4. Probably Jean François Maximilien de Cerjat (1729–1802).

Page 419

Friday May 23ᵈ

After breakfast we Rode by the Side of the Lake to Vevay about Ten miles distant from Lausanne¹ – We Stopt at the Crown a tolerable good Inn And Ordered a Dinner,² then Sent a Note to Monʳ. Martin Bertrand who had married a Sister of Mʳˢ· Wickhamˢ.³ He immediately Came to us and was desirous of Engaging us to Dine with Him but that we declined and only Requested his Company to Shew us the Town which He did by Walking with us near Three Hours, during which time we went to his House and Saw his Wife and Children – The House was allmost at the End of the Town in a Broad Street but the Back part of the House was very near the Beautiful Lake of Geneva which run Close to the Garden Wall.

Page 420

The Town of Vevay [sic] is upon the Edge of the Lake of Geneva And the Hills Rise gradually from the Back of the Town which being Situated very near the Head of the Lake where the Mountains On Each Side Seem allmost to join together It forms a very Picturesque Scene – but the Environs are not So pleasant Either for Rides or Walks as those at Lausanne to which Place we Returned in the Evening –

Saturday May 24ᵗʰ

Wrote Letters to England and at Noon went in the Carriage a few miles & then walked, upon our Return we Dined with Mʳ. Leeson Brother to Lord Milltown and met Lord Carmarthen Eldest Son to the Duke of Leeds⁴ and Seven other English Gentlemen – In the Evening I took Miss Cruttenden to Ecu Blanc⁵

---

1. Vevey- town on the lake of Geneva close to Montreux.
2. There is a Hôtel des Trois Couronnes at Vevey but this was only establishment in 1842.
3. A Martin Bertrand of Geneva is listed as a member of the Academy of Geneva for 1802.
4. George William Frederick Osborne, Marquess of Carmarthen (1775–1838), son of Francis Godolphin Osborne, 5ᵗʰ Duke of Leeds (1751–99).
5. Ecu Blanc – a hamlet outside Lausanne?

Page 421

Sunday May 25th
Walked in the Fields before Breakfast – at Noon Madame Cerjet
Came & went with us to Visit Lady Mary Blair at the Bois de Vand,[1]
a most Charming Spot about Two miles distance from Lausanne,
Commanding a fine View of the Lake and Surrounded with Wood
& Rich Pasture Ground, from thence we Rode about Two Miles on
the other Side of Lausanne and Called on M^{rs}. Weston And at Our
Return went to the Cathedral and Heard a Sermon.[2] Returned to
Dinner and passed the Evening in Writing Letters to England –

During Our Ride this morning we Observed the House now
Inhabited by Monsr. Neckar [*sic*][3] – a fine Situation and very near
the upper Town –

Monday May 26th.
Walked in the adjoining Fields before Breakfast and afterw^{ds} made
a Visit to M^{rs}. Trevor and took her to the

Page 422

Bois de Vand to Visit Lady Mary Blair,[4] who we found at Home and
we Walked with her in the Gardens And the Environs of the House
&c Afterwards we took M^{rs}. Trevor Home again & we Returned to
Dine at Lausanne – In the Afternoon I went again to M^{rs}. Trevor
and Brought her in Our Carriage to take Tea with us & to meet M^r.
And M^{rs}. Cerjat, She Staid with us till Nine in the Evening and
then a Sedan Chair conveyed her Home to the[5]

Tuesday May 27–
In walking before Breakfast this morning I met a Woman with a
basket on her Head Carrying her Daily Food to a Vineyard where

1. Bois-de-Vaux? – now a cemetery.
2. Cathedral of Nôtre Dame – it was probably begun in the late twelfth century and completed in 1275. Restorations were carried out by Viollet-le-Duc from 1873.
3. Jacques Necker (1732–1804), Swiss banker and finance minister to Louis XVI of France.
4. Lady Mary Blair (née Fane) (*c*.1739–1809), married Charles Blair.
5. A blank space is left here – ed.

She was Employed in Tying the Vines; upon my Enquiring what Pay She Received, I was told, that In this Country, The <u>owner</u> of the

Page 423

Land has H<u>alf</u> the Produce, And The Peasant who Cultivates the Ground, has the other Half for the Labour and Expences in raising the Produce

At Noon Monsr & Madame Turrelini with their Two Sons, Came to Visit us, She was the Daughter of Madame Villette with whom my Dear Son went from England to Geneva in the Year 1778 –[1] but On account of the present disturbances She with her Husband and Family have been Obliged to Quit that City And now Reside Three Hours distance from Lausanne where they Requested us to Come and Spend a day with Them and meet their Mother and Sister from Berne – Mad^{lle}. Turrelini from whom we had received So much Attention when we Stopt there in Our way to this Place – To Day They were going to Dinner at M^r. Cerjats.

Page 424

In the Evening we went to M^r. Floyers, An English Gentleman who had Resided here with his Sister And Daughter Some time / I believe a Dorsetshire Family[2] / we met there near Thirty Gentlemen and Ladies many of whom were English, Miss Floyer Played Country Dances upon the Harpsichord and Monsr Seigneux (Lord Carmarthens Tutor)[3] accompanied her upon the Flute – English Country Dances and the Swiss Walsh[4] were Danced Alternately. In Both Lord Camarthen Danced admirably & Seemed to Tread as Light as Air, yet his Countenance not Animated – Tea Coffee, Orgeat[5] & Lemonade were frequently offered and we Staid till Ten when the Company begun to Part –

1. Madame Villette – not traced.
2. The Floyers were indeed a Dorsetshire family.
3. Captain Seigneux according to Ingamells' *Dictionary*.
4. Murray gives "walse".
5. Orgeat – a cooling drink made from barley and orange-flower water.

Wed^y May 28th
Went immediately after Breakfast to M^rs. Trevor and took her to
See

Page 425

The Troops Reviewed, It being the Annual Review at which a
prodigious number of people were Assembled, but not a Carriage
Except the Chariot we were in & the Coach belonging to the Bailiff
Of the Canton, which was Drawn by Four Horses, and the Livery
of the Coachman & Two Footmen were Crimson Cloth with
handsome worsted Lace – After taking M^rs. Trevor to her own
Residence, I Returned to Lausanne, & walked to the Lake where I
amused myself with attending to the dashing of the Waves – It was
not more than a mile from the House we Inhabited at Lausanne to
Ouchi a Little Village upon the Edge of the Lake having a Small
Stone Pier Extending Some Distance into the Lake to form a
Harbour, from whence Boats frequently Carried different Articles
to the adjacent Towns upon the Lake –[1]

Page 426

I went to See a very pretty House near Ouchi which is Let often
in the Summer Season to English Families. It had a Covered
Colonade in Front towards the Lake, And this Expanse of Water
^was Bounded by Mountains, whose Tops were at this Time Covered
with Snow, but had a most Beautiful Verdure at the Bottom, with
many Little Villages Scattered about, and Behind the House the
Rich Pasture Grounds intermixed with Wood, made it a most
delightful Summer Residence –

In the Afternoon we took a Circular Route of Two Hours in the
Environs of Lausanne between Corn Fields, and Rich Pasture
Grounds And many very Beautiful Lanes, & had frequently many
Picturesque Views of the Lake –

---

1. Ouchy.

Page 427

Thursday May 29
At Noon I took M^{rs}. & Miss Cruttenden with me in the Carriage to
Beaulieu[1] where Monsr. Neckar now Resides and where his Wife
Died Last week –[2] It is only Half a Mile distant from the Upper
Town of Lausanne Situated on a Rising Ground and Commanding
a Fine View of the Lake

Macnamara who married miss Jones of Kensington Resided here
Last year –[3] From Hence we went to Chalais[4] Two Miles farther
Another delightful Situation upon a greater Eminence with a
Wood at the Back of the Grounds, and Here Sir Willoughby &
Lady Aston Resided one Summer[5] – we then Descended a little and
Rode one mile farther to Rennen Another Delightful Habitation
nearer the Lake and Amidst Meadows and pasture Grounds only
Three Miles

Page 428

Distance from Lausanne which appears on a Rising Ground –[6]

These Houses are frequently Inhabited by English Families during the Summer months and no Country can be more delightful
the Roads being Excellent and through Grounds that give the
Appearance of a Park –

Dined with M^r. Cullum and his Nephew M^r. Vernon[7] and in
the Evening went to Visit M^{rs}. Odell a lady from Ireland who

1. Beaulieu – locality close to Lausanne, it now houses a cultural centre.
2. Jacques Necker (1732–1804), Swiss banker and finance minister to Louis XVI of France. He married Suzanne Curchod (1737–94), salon hostess. She died on the 6th May. The Chateau of Beaulieu now houses a collection of Art Brut
3. Ingamells' Dictionary lists a Mr & Mrs Macnamara as travelling on the Continent at this time but no other details are known.
4. Chailly – village close to Montreux.
5. Sir Willoughby Aston, 6th Baronet (1748–1815). He married Jane Henley (died c.1823).
6. Probably Renens to the north of Lausanne and now a suburb of that town.
7. Ingamells' *Dictionary* gives a James Cullum (1754–1835) of Hardwick, Suffolk as travelling with his nephew.

Resides Here with her Eldest Son And One Daughter,[1] She is a Widow And has a Sister Miss Musgrave who Lives with Lady Gertrude Villiers, Daughter to the Earl Grandison We met Lord Carmarthen, & Mons[r]. de Seigneux with others, and Two Card Tables made the Evening Amusement –

Page 429

Received Letters from England dated the 16th Instant – and Employed Our Selves in Answering – afterw[ds] went to a Circulating Library & from thence took a Walk to the Lake not more than Half an Hour in going to it – In the Fields was Hay making – Dined with Lord Carmarthen and afterw[ds] took M[rs]. Trevor to the Bois de Vand where we took Tea with lady Mary Blair – & took M[rs]. Trevor Home in the Evening –

Saturday May 31st
Wrote Letters to M[r]. Fagen at Rome and M[r]. Partridge at Leghorn – M[rs]. Tucker Widow of the Late Member for Weymouth And Sister in Law to M[r]. Floyer with whom She has Resided Here Since her Husbands Death,[2] (M[rs]. Floyer having Died about the Same

Page 430

time Leaving One Daughter who is now Here with her Father And Aunt, both of whom are Engaged in her Education) – Came to Visit me – At Noon I took M[rs] and Miss Cruttenden to See a remarkable Fine Lime Tree which measured in the middle 19 f[t] 3 Inches round – and towards the Bottom it Extended to an Amazing width

In the Evening I went to bring M[rs]. Trevor to take Tea at Madame Cerjats where we met a very Large Party – Madame Cerjat has Three Sons in the British Army, one of them in the Blues – one in the Inskillings and the Third in [3] and Two Daughters at Home –

---

1. A Mr. Odell is listed in Ingamells' *Dictionary* as being in northern Italy in 1796 with his mother and sister.
2. John Tucker (1701–79), MP for Weymouth. He married Martha Gollop.
3. A blank space is left here – ed.

Sunday June 1ˢᵗ.
In Consequence of a Note received from Mʳˢ. Trevor this morning

Page 431

We went to her House And took her in Our carriage to the Cathedral[1] where we saw a Marble Tablet with an Inscription to the Memory of Mʳ. Legge A Son of Lord Dartmouth,[2] and Another Tablet to the Memory of Mʳ. Ellison Erected at the Expence of Mʳˢ. Crespigny –[3] there was likewise a Tablet Erected at the Expence of Mʳ· & Mʳˢ. Trevor to the Memory of Mʳˢ. Burton the Mother of Mʳˢ. Trevor, who Died while on a Visit to Them –[4]

In the Evening we Read a Poem Entitled The Poor Soldier – an American Tale and a Play Called the Widow of Malabar both written by Miss Mariana Starke who we Visited at Pisa The Dedication to Mʳˢ. Crespigny dated Epsom 1791 –

Page 432

Monday June 2ᵈ–
Engaged all the morning in Packing And preparing to Leave Lausanne but we Engaged the Marquis of Carmarthen, (with Monsʳ. de Seigneux his Tutor) Mʳ. Hore (a Relation of Lord Courtonns,)[5] Mʳ. Tomkinson a Cheshire Gentleman[6] – Mʳ. George Dawkins of Portman Square London And Mʳ. Vernon to Dine with us.

In the Evening Mʳ. Floyer And his Sister in Law Mʳˢ Tucker both of Dorsetshire – Mʳˢ· Odell & her daughter from Ireland, Mʳˢ. Clementson and Mʳˢ. Trevor Came to tea and we had Two Card Tables.[7]

---

1. The cathedral of Notre Dame dating to the thirteenth century. It was subsequently restored by Viollet-le-Duc.
2. William Legge, died 1784.
3. Robert Ellison, died 1783.
4. Henrietta Burton (1720–89), widow of Dr. Daniel Burton and daughter of John Roper.
5. A Mr. Hore is listed in Ingamells' *Dictionary* as being in Italy with Lord Carmarthen, 1794–5.
6. Possibly Henry Tomkinson (c.1741–1822) of Dorfold, Cheshire.
7. Mr Trevor frequently took leave from his duties and holidayed in Switzerland.

Tuesday June 3ᵈ.

After breakfast took Leave of Mrs· Cruttenden, with a Promise to recommend her House to all our Friends who Should Come to Lausanne and at Ten o Clock got into our Travelling Coach and went through Morges &

Page 433

Rolle to Nyon Twenty One mile from Lausanne,[1] The Road good And within Veiw of the Lake the whole way, The Country well Cultivated, Hedges on Each Side the Road & the Fields Varied by Vineyards Corn and Pasture Some wheat – but Cheifly Rye Grass & Clover –

At Nyon we walked by the Side of the Lake, and likewise upon the Hill by the Castle from whence we had a very fine View of Geneva[2] – And the Situation of Mont Blanc which at this time was wrapt in a Cloud.[3]

At Nyon the Form of the Lake of Geneva is best Seen as it takes the bend Here, and almost the whole Lake appears at One View – The Town is Small And very indifferently Built but the Environs are delightful & the Croix Blanc a good Inn[4] – before Dinner we went to See the China manufactory which is really Beautiful[5]

Page 434

We Dined for the first time during Our Journey at a Table D'Hote – & there met a young married Couple who passed for Americans but neither could Speak English and they Owned having been lately at Paris and their Travelling Chaise was uncommonly Handsome

Wednesday June 4ᵗʰ

Left Nyon Early in the morning And throughout the Country we Observed the People Mowing the Grass which in general was Rye

1. Morges, Rolle and Nyon – all on the shore of Lake Geneva to the west of Lausanne.
2. The castle now contains the local museum of antiquities.
3. Mont Blanc – the highest peak in the Alps at 4,810 metres.
4. Properly, La Croix Blanche but not traced.
5. The Nyon Porcelain Factory founded in 1781 by Jacques Dortu and Ferdinand Muller. It closed in 1813.

Grass mixed with Clover and looked Rich – We Returned through Rolle and from thence by the Chateau D'Aubonne[1] from whence is a very Extensive Prospect of the Lake & the Adjacent Mountains tho' I think G<u>enev</u>a is Seen better from the Terrace adjoining to the Chateau at Nyon

The Country through which we Passed was well Cultivated

Page 435

Rye Grass & Clover Mixed, Some wheat, and Some Rye and a great many Vineyards, The Trees were in general Wallnuts & Cherries and Some Pears – We passed through Cassonay a mean Dirty Town[2] and went to Yverdon[3] & Staid the Night at L'Aigle Royale a good Inn[4] – In the Evening we walked to See the Baths about Q^r. of a mile from the Town we Tasted the water & found it Strongly Impregnated with Sulphur,[5] but being Milk warm at the Spring it is not So Nauseous as the Harrowgate in Yorkshire –[6] The Lodgings at the Baths are Neat. The Price Half a Crown Each Night. The Rooms Open into a Gallery into which all must Communicate – There is likewise a table D'Hôte at 18 Basche per Head – Viz 2^s. & 3^{d7} – The Water for bathing is Heated in a Copper & from thence conveyed

Page 436

by Pipes into Wooden Troughs which form a Bathing Tub in Seperate Rooms –

At the End of the Town Close to the Lake is a Large Piece of Ground Planted with Trees and formed into a very pleasant Publick Walk – The Town consists of Three Small Streets and the Shops have no appearance of Trade & very meanely Built.

---

1. Château d'Aubonne – fortress in the Canton de Vaud begun in the eleventh century.
2. Cassonay – town north of Lausanne.
3. Yverdon – town at the southern tip of the Lake of Neuchâtel, the Roman Eburodunum.
4. Logis de l'Aigle royal – the actual building still exists.
5. The thermal baths still exist.
6. Harrogate – the spa town in Yorkshire famous for its water.
7. Two shillings and three pence in pre-decimal currency.

Thursday June 5th.
We Left Yverdon Early in the Morning & went upon a Rough Stony Road by the Side of the Lake Twenty One Miles to NeufChatel,[1] Stopping in the way to Breakfast at a very Dirty Inn – On the Side of the Road were Vineyards and Pasture Land

NeufChatel is Situated Close to the Lake, and Some of the

Page 437

Streets Ascend very Steep up a Hill – Others lie Level with the water – In the Publick walk which was near the Lake there was a prodigious Quantity of Wet Linnen Hanging from Tree to Tree, and a great Number of Dirty Children Playing –

We Staid the Night at the Falcon Inn which we found very Dirty[2] – at the Maison de Ville[3] in the Great Council Chamber we Saw Portraits of the Late & Present King of Prussia at full Length[4]

No Post Horses being allowed in Switzerland we were obliged to Pay Five Crowns per Day for Four Horses to go in Our Coach And to allow the Same for as many Days after our using them as was necessary for their Return Home from the Place we left them

Page 438

Friday June 6th.
Left Neuchatel Early in the Morning, and went Nine miles to Breakfast, at a House Close to the Lake of Bienne;[5] from whence we went in a Boat to the Island of S[t]_Pierre, Celebrated by Rousseau. It is Situated nearly in the Center of the Lake, And is

1. Neuchâtel – town at the northern end of the eponymous lake.
2. Falcon Inn – it no longer exists.
3. Maison de Ville – a recent building at the time having been erected 1784–90 to designs by Pierre-Adrien Pâris, a French architect. The handsome Great Hall is occasionally used for temporary exhibitions.
4. Frederick the Great (1712–86), reigned from 1740, and Frederick William II (1744–97), reigned from 1786.
5. The Bieler See.

truly Delightful.[1] A Stone Wall about 3 feet High is Built Round
it, and the Circumference is about Three mile – within the Wall,
is a Level Road, very good for Either Walking or Riding – On One
Side of the Island the Ground gradually Declines towards the
Lake, and is both pasture & Corn intermixed, above is a Vineyard,
And upon the Top, are many very Large Oaks and Beech Trees,
& Underwood with Walks Cut through; On the Other Side of the
Island towards Neuville, the Ground Rises

Page 439

immediately from the Wall, and is thickly Wooded, So as to afford
a Constant Shade = There is Only One House upon this Island,
which is a Large Farm House, with a Court yard Inclosing Stables,
& Cow Houses – And Every Domestic Office, we Visited the
Chamber in which Rousseau himself Slept – And was told, that we
might have a Dinner upon the Same Terms as at an Inn, but after
Satisfying Our Curiosity, We Returned to Our Boat & Afterw[ds]
to Our carriage, and Continued our Journey through a Delightful
Country to Nidau,[2] a Small but very Clean Town, and from thence to
Bienne,[3] where we Staid the Night at the Crown Inn –[4] the Best
& Cleanest in Switzerland, and Equal in Neatness to any Inn in
England – We went before Dinner to the Publick Walk which is at
the upper End of the Lake and Planted on Each Side

Page 440

with Trees. The Town is Small And very Still, Quiet, & no appearance of Trade – The Landlord of the Inn Shewed us a List of the
English who had been at his House, and Among Others we found
Sir John Dyer, with his Son M[r]. Dyer had been there in October
1788.[5] And the Landlord told us that M[r]. Beckford had been with

1. The Island of St. Peter is now connected to the shore by a causeway. Jean-Jacques
   Rousseau (1712–78) spent two months here in 1765.
2. Nidau – town at the northern tip of the lake of Neuchâtel and close to Bienne.
3. Biel/Bienne – sister town to Nidau at the head of the lake and the boundary of the
   French and German- speaking parts of Switzerland.
4. La Couronne – Goethe also stayed here. The building still exists but dedicated to
   other purposes.
5. Sir John Swinnerton Dyer, 6th Baronet (1738–1801) and Thomas Richard Swinnerton
   Dyer (1768–1838), later 7th Baronet.

twenty Servants at his House many weeks for which he had Paid him £300 Louis –[1] In this Town the Goats Come Every morning to be milked, & (I beleive) it is the general Custom on the Continent for the Cattle to be Drove into the Town to be milked, And the Linnen to be carried to the Rivers to be washed –

Saturday. June 7th.
Left Bienne Early in the morning And immediately Entered a valley where more Wheat was growing than we had yet Seen in Switzerland – The

Page 441

Range of Mountains Called Mont Jura now appeared Close to us[2] – and the Foot of these Mountains was the town of Soleure,[3] remarkable for the Treaty Signed in 1777 – by Vergennes;[4] The Engraving of which we had frequently Seen during the time we had been in Switzerland

The Town of Soleure is Small but very Clean and the Church at the upper End of the Principal Street is very Handsome –[5]

We Dined at the Table D'Hote at the Crown which appeared to be A very good Inn[6] – after Dinner we walked to the Hermitage about a mile distant – The Foot Path led through a Deep Recess in a Narrow Valley that was like a Cleft between Two Hills And admitted only a Narrow path And a Torrent – The Foot Path Continuall passing from Side to Side Over Planks of wood or Little Stone

Page 442

Bridges across the Torrent of which there were near Twenty in

---

1. The notorious William Beckford (1760–1844), writer and socialite. He travelled on the Continent in self-imposed exile in 1782 due to a homosexual scandal.
2. Jura Mountains – a sub-alpine mountain range north of the Western Alps and following the France-Switzerland border.
3. Soleure or Solothurn – town on the river Aare east of Bienne.
4. Charles Gravier, comte de Vergennes (1719–87), minister to Louis XVI of France.
5. The Cathedral of St. Ursus. It was designed by Gaetano Matteo Pisoni and his nephew Paolo Antonio and dedicated in 1773. Though the building still exists its was badly damaged by an earthquake in 1853 and again by an arson attack in 2011.
6. Hotel Krone – it was founded in 1418 and still exists.

Number. And on Each Side, the Rocks were So thickly Covered with Wood that the path was frequently quite Embowerd, & the continual Windings rendered it very Picturesque At the End of this Romantic Cleft in the Rocks, They Seemed to unite, & underneath was a Small Boarded Cottage, where the Hermit Lived, & directly Opposite A Mount Calvary with the Figure of the Bon Dieu, And a Figure in the Attitude of Weeping on Each Side, and An Altar at a Distance –[1]

Upon Our Return, we Entered the Carriage, And Observed many Chateau' delightfully Situated in the Environs of Soleure, where there are many fine Woods –

Page 443

The Road for Nine Miles was Close to the Chain of Mountains Called Mont Jura, where it Turned Short to the Left, and Entered between the Rocks which form the Lowest Ridge of Mont Jura. The Valley between These Rocks was Narrow and Picturesque, and Continually Winding So much So that the Road appeared frequently Inclosed, And the little Space of Ground which occasionally was between the Mountain and the Road was generally Occupied by Linnen that was Bleaching there.

At Cluse[2] the Mountains United again, Leaving only a Carriage Way, which could be Inclosed by Gates, & at this Spot, was an Ancient Castle –[3] The next Valley was Wider and we found in it a very Clean Inn Situated in a

Page 444

Small Village where we Staid the Night – Throughout this part of the Country we perceived a great Blight – In many parts whole Orchards were destroyed

---

1. The Verena Gorge hermitage – it dates from the seventeenth century and still exists.
2. The Klus valley.
3. Probably Alt-Falkenstein – it is now a museum.

We were told that the French[1] who were at this time On the other Side of Mont Jura committed the greatest Cruelties And very lately Guillotined Two Women, One of Them Standing at the Door of the House belonging to her Mistress Said " J'espere que cet Guillotine Finirons, upon which They Seized the Girl, whose Cries alarming her Mistress She Looked out of the window, & Said "Je Crois que vous etes Enragée de Prendre une Fille, Elle est mon Domestique – immediately They Entered the House dragged her Away and Guillotined Them Both –

Page 445

       Sunday June 8ᵗʰ
We left Our Inn (the White Horse at Boristal)[2] Early in the morning, having found in it One very good Sitting Room And Two very Neat Bed Rooms adjoining –. The Road continued through a Narrow & delightful Valley, with the Rocks often Close to the Road, and very Lofty in a Variety of Shapes; Now we perceived that the Chain of Mountains Called Mont Jura, which appeared at a Distance like One continued Mountain, was really Four in Depth; being Four Chain of Hills one above the Other – with Such Narrow Vallies between Each, as to be imperceptible to the Eye, till you are Close to them –

Page 446

After having passed through Two of these Beautiful Romantic Vallies, which were at Each End Inclosed by the Mountains allmost Joining, Leaving only the Space of the Road, And that Secured by Gates – we advanced into a Wider Plain with pasture Grounds on Each Side – and Soon after Arrived at a Little Village where we Breakfasted & found Excellent Bread, Butter and Milk for which we were Charged One Shilling each, tho' we found Our own Tea and Sugar.

From hence the Country became more Open and the Road was

1. At this early stage in the history of revolutionary France, Swiss democrats were assisted by French forces against their own "Ancien Régime" rulers.
2. Presumably Balsthal but Cheval Blanc not traced.

between Corn Fields, & Pasture Grounds Planted with Cherry Trees Wallnuts and Pears &c &c –

Page 447

The Corn was Wheat, Rye, and Barley intermixed with Pease, Beans, Potatoes, and Vineyards without any Separation by Hedge Or Wall –

From Soleure it is 36 Miles to Basle[1] where we Arrived at Four o Clock, And finding the Three Kings Inn full of Company,[2] we went to the Cicogne where we Staid the Night –[3]

In the Evening we went to the Cathedral a large Old Church in which is the Tomb of Erasmus[4] – and under the Same Roof is the Council Chamber &c –

Monday June 9th
Went to See the <u>Dance of Death by Holbein</u>[5] and afterwards to the Publick Library, walked about the Town which is Old & very few good Houses in it – The Streets narrow, and in general Steep in

Page 448

Ascents and Descents, which as the Pavement is very Rough renders walking very disagreeable The best part of the Town is the Close near the Cathedral, near which, there is a Terrace Walk Planted with Trees, and from it a good View of the Rhine, which Divides the Town from the Fauxbourgs – This Town being the principal Communication between Germany, Switzerland and Italy, must necessarily have considerable Trade, yet the Shops have no appearance of any Consequence but look Shabby Except Mons[r].

---

1. Basle – city on the Rhine in German-speaking Switzerland.
2. The Three Kings is still listed in Baedeker for 1911.
3. The Cigogne is also still listed in Baedeker for 1911.
4. The twelfth century cathedral contains the tomb of Erasmus of Rotterdam (1466–1536) who died in the city.
5. A mural depicting the Dance of Death dating from the mid fifteenth century existed here until 1805 and it is probably this to which Mrs Bentham refers. The painter and printmaker Hans Holbein (1497/8–1543) lived in Basle in the 1520s and produced his own series of prints of the subject.

de Michell^s Magazine for Prints which is one of the Best Houses in the Town[1] In the Afternoon we left Basle with an Intention to Stay the Night

Page 449

At Rhinfeldt,[2] but found the Inn there So full of Company were Obliged to go farther, and at the Distance of Three Miles found a Comfortable Clean House were [sic] we Staid the Night – Our Road from Basle had been through Fine Corn Fields, Planted with Cherry Tree^s and the Fruit being now gathering it looked very Cheerful –

After Quitting Basle we Soon Came to a barrier where Austrian Soldiers obliged us Twice to produce Our passport which we had taken at Basle. At Rhinfeldt The Soldier at the Gate obliged us to wait a Considerable time while he went to find his Commanding Officer – during which Lord Wickham

Page 450

Came and Entered into Conversation with us, Saying he had not left England more than Ten Days, & was now going by Innspruck into Italy[3]

Tuesday June 10th
Having passed the Night much to Our Satisfaction finding Our Beds &c Clean, We went to Breakfast at Lauffenburgh,[4] a Small Old Town having the Ruins of a Castle Situated on a Hill Commanding the Fall of the Rhine; That Fall So Fatal to Lord Montague[5] and his Friend Mr Burdett – These Two young Men, had Lived Some

1. Almost certainly that of Christian von Mechel (1737–1817), notable engraver, publisher and dealer.
2. Rheinfelden – town on the Rhine 15 kilometres east of Basle.
3. It seems most likely that this is William Wickham (1761–1840), civil servant and diplomat. He was married to a Swiss and knew the country well. Later that same year he was sent on a secret mission to Switzerland to negotiate with French nationals against Napoleon. However, he was never made a peer. Presumably he was also going via the Brenner Pass into Italy.
4. Laufenburg.- town straddling the Rhine which subsequently became two towns, one in Germany, the other in Switzerland.
5. See page 388.

months together upon the Shore of the Lake de Lucerne, and both understanding the managment of a Boat – and both being Excellent Swimmers; They

Page 451

Determined to Come from Lucerne by water, and go down this Fall – Vainly beleiving that if Any Accident happened They could Save themselves by Swimming. When They Arrived at the Place where Every Boat that makes this Passage is Unloaded, And many Persons are Stationed upon the Rocks on each Side the fall, with Strong Ropes that are fastened to the Empty Boat, for them to Guide her Safe, & if Successful She is then to go Some Distance before the former loading is put again on Board – These Gentlemen only put their Servant on Shore, regardless of Every Remonstrance He made, and Went on determined to Pass the

Page 452

Fall in their Boat – The Servant allmost Distracted Run to the Town, And before Lord Montague had Passed through the Bridge Hundreds of People were upon it, and amongst Them was the Person who attended us this morning; He told us that at the First fall the Boat was more than Half full of water – and at the Second Fall which immediately follows the First, The Boat Sunk and neither Boat nor Men were Seen again – nor after Every possible Search has Either of them been found = After minutely Examining this Interesting Place We Endeavoured to dissipate Our melancholy Idea[s] by observing the Variety of Dress in the

Page 453

Swiss Peasants who were Assembled at a Fair in this Town, And Such a Groupe of whimsical Figures could no where but in Switzerland be Seen – from Hence we pursued Our Journey through a Beautiful Valley with the Rhine frequently very near us, And the Road often through Fields of Corn without Any Hedge; but Planted on Each Side with Cherry and Wallnut Tree[s] and Bounded by Small Hills at a Distance Covered with Wood – The wheat looked very Fine and the Clover Higher & the Flower of a much brighter Red than Ours in England –

We Dined and Staid the Night at a Little Village where we Observed the Women to

Page 454

To have the Goitiers:[1] in general; The men of the Lower Class had Caps instead of hats upon their Heads, which they pulled off as a Token of Respect when we Passed them –

Wednesday June 11th
The Country which we passed through this morning was full of Peasants, Some Mowing the Grass, others making Hay, I counted more than Two Hundred by the Side of the Road, who appeared as if they were in One Field, no division being made by Hedges.

About a mile from Schaffhausen we left the Road and went to Lauffen[2] to See the Great Falls of the Rhine, So well Described by Coxe[3] – at this Place we Stood for Some time on the Opposite Shore and had a most Compleat View of the

Page 455

Rocks And the Stupenduous Fall of Water – We then Entered a Boat and Crossed the water to Ascend the Hill on the Opposite Side where we went into a Pleasure House belonging to the Chateau of the Baillif of Basle and from which we had a full View of the Winding of the River, and the Amazing Rocks it Passes over before it Falls down the Precipice After Staying a Considerable time to Contemplate this most Extraordinary Scene we Returned highly Delighted to Our Carriage. Soon after we met M[r] Hay who had frequently been Our Visitor at Turin and Milan – being like Ourselves determined to Stay Some time upon the Continent.

---

1. Goiter – swelling of the thyroid gland. It was common in alpine regions due to the lack of iodine in the diet.
2. Schloss Laufen from where there is an excellent view of the Falls of the Rhine.
3. *Travels in Switzerland . . .*, by William Coxe (1748–1828), published in 1789.

Page 456

His Father Residing within Six Miles of Wexford in Ireland –[1]

At Schaffhausen[2] we Dined and Staid the Night at the Crowns Inn
– a good House but very Extravagant –[3] We Walked to See the
Bridge So Celebrated for its Architecture And the Mechanick who
formed it –[4] The Town is Old but the Situation is far better than
Basle and more good Houses in it – The Rhine more Picturesque
And the Country Around very Fine –

Thursday June 12th.
Left Schaffhausen Early in the Morning and passed again in View
of the Fall of the Rhine, and from thence through a Country full of
Corn and Vineyards to Eglisau[5] a Small Poor Town

Page 457

in a Narrow Valley on the Banks of the Rhine, where we found a
very Clean an [sic] Neat Little Inn and made a most Comfortable
Breakfast – From Hence the Road immediately Ascended into
a Fine Corn Country which continued to Zurich a Large Town
Situated between Hills on the Banks of the Lima, and at the Head
of a Lake the Sides of which were Covered with a great Number
of White Houses on Beautiful Small Hills with Mountains Behind
and in the Back Ground are the Snowy Alps –[6] The Scenery at this
Place is more Beautiful than at Lucerne, but not So magnificently
Awful –. The Town by being Divided by the River Running Out
of the Lake may be more

Page 458

Chearful to Reside at than Lucerne, And having Two Publick

1. Wexford – county town of County Wexford in south-east Ireland.
2. Schaffhausen – town on the north bank of the Rhine close to Lake Constance.
3. The Crowns (Kronen) – not traced.
4. The celebrated covered wooden bridge built by the Grubermann family in the mid
   eighteenth century. Unfortunately, it was burnt down by the retreating French army
   in 1799.
5. Eglisau – town on the Rhine south of Schaffhausen.
6. Zürich – city at the head of the eponymous lake and on the river Limmat.

Walks which are very delightful It may be Classed as One of the best Towns in Switzerland –

We Dined and Staid the Night at the Epée a good Inn –[1]. In the Afternoon we Walked to See the Tombeau de Gesner –. It was at the End of the Publick Walk that is on the Banks of the River Lima – Planted with a double Row of Trees and Ending with a Circular & Gloomy Grove[2] –

Friday June 13th
Took an Early Breakfast and afterwards went with a Valet de Place to the Publick Walk that Commands the Head of the Lake – this is not So Shaded by Trees as the Other On the Banks of the River

Page 459

But the View is Extensive and the Walk delightful – From Hence we went to the Publick Library which is in a Neat Oval Room with Three Galleries Round it And at the End a Bow Window Commanding a very pleasing View of the Lake And the River –[3] There was in this Room Several Portraits of different Burgo Masters with Each a Broad Ruff round the Neck, Similar to that which is worn at this present time by Every Burgo master in his Official Capacity And They likewise wear a Sword as part of their Official Dress. But the Physicians and the Clergy wear only the Ruff – We likewise went to See The Town Hall and the Great and

Page 460

And Little Council Chamber –[4]

In Passing through the Streets we Observed many Houses were Six Stories above the Ground Floor, and yet appeared to be not Inhabited by more than One Family, Having Only One Door And Two Windows in a Line –

---

1. The Hôtel de l'Epée is listed in Baedeker's Switzerland for 1911.
2. The monument to the poet Salomon Gessner (d.1788) in the Platz Promenade
3. Now the Zentralbibliothek.
4. The Rathaus – built 1694–8.

The Shops were Small And the Best Goods were of English Manufactory – For a Twelve Inch Ivory Ruler the Price was a Crown as it was made in England –

We Dined a [*sic*] the Tâble D'Hôte where we had Pease Boiled in the Shell

At Three o Clock we quitted Zurich going through a Hilly but very Pleasant Country to Winterther[1] a Small Old Town in a Valley, And Staid the Night at the Soleil a Clean Inn –[2]

Page 461

Saturday June 14th
Extremely Hot, the Thermometer in Our Carriage Stood at 88 – We quitted Winterther at Six in the morning and went to Franbeld to Breakfast a Small Town the Inn tolerable –[3] from thence the Road Continued through a Fertile Country and Crossing Small Hills and going through a Wood of Fir Trees we descended to Constance a large and very Old Town, Situated at the Junction of Two Lakes in a Flat marshy Country –[4] In the Smaller lake were Several Islands, one of which appeared to have a Town upon it – And the Larger Lake Opens very wide and from the Quay resembled an Arm of the Sea –

Page 462

We Dined and Staid the Night at L'Aigle a Comfortable Inn,[5] and from Hence we were to take Post Horses, and therefore discharged the man who had brought us with Four Horses through Switzerland A Country in which there is no going Post – but the Traveller is Obliged to Hire Horses for the whole Journey and is in general Charged Six Shillings and Three Pence for Each Horse

1. Winterthur – town between Zürich and Konstanz.
2. The Gasthaus Sonne – the inn existed in the mediaeval period but was rebuilt in 1557. The building still exists but it is no longer an hotel.
3. Fraunfeld.
4. Constance or Kostanz on the eponymous lake.
5. The Hôtel de l'Aigle – the building still exists but it now houses a bank and offices. Goethe stayed there amongst other notable guests.

a day – and we paid for each day One Louis and a Crown, allowing the Same for as many Days as was necessary to take them back to the Place from whence they begun the Journey besides Paying One Shilling and Six pence Each day to the Postillion, and as we never went more than Three miles an Hour And was allways Obliged to Stop in the middle of the Day to bait We found Travelling in Switzerland much Dearer than Elsewhere –

Page 463

Sunday June 15th

We Left Constance this morning at Four o Clock. The Sun Rose as we Crossed the Bridge Over the River which Unites the Two Lakes – The Road Continued along the Side of the Lake a Considerable way, then Turned Short through Fields well Cultivated with Corn and bounded by Woods We went two Stages to Stochach[1] where we Breakfasted while the Horses were Changing – then went Two Stages more to Mengen but only Stopt while Horses were Changing And eat Some of Our Provisions from Our Basket – then went Two more Stages [to] Ehingen[2] which we did not Arrive at, till One o Clock in the morning, and found the Inn So bad, that we took Horses again to go one to Ulm which we did [not] get to, till Six o Clock in the morning, having been Twenty Six Hours

Page 464

in going 104 Miles; with Four Horses and never Staying at any Place longer than while the Horses were Changing –

At Ulm we went to the Golden Wheel, where Our Friend M[r] Hay (whose father Resides within Six Miles of Wexford in Ireland) had Ordered An Apartment for us – And to Bed I went immediately being Extremely Fatigued –[3]

---

1. Stockach – town at the head of the Uberlinger See.
2. Mengen and Ehingen – towns in Germany on the road to Ulm.
3. Ulm – city on the Danube in southern Germany. The Goldenes Rad still exists.

Monday June 16<u>th</u>
The Weather very Hot, and having had One Hours Sleep I Arose
And Dressed, and after Breakfast went to See the Boat which was
making to Carry us down the Danube to Vienna – the remainder of
the day was Occupied in Writing Letters to England –

Tuesday June 17th.
Walked about the Town of Ulm

Page 465

before Breakfast – and at Noon went on Board the Little Vessel
which had been Built the Day before to Carry us down the Danube
– This Boat was Covered in the Middle and divided into Two
Cabbins – The Largest of which was 7 feet & Half in Length And
Opened at the Head of the Boat by a Door – It was 8 feet wide,
Including a bench on Each Side of a Foot & Half in width on which
we sat during the Day and ^{it} was to Serve if wanted for Our bed at
Night –. The height of this Cabbin was 6 Feet 3 Inches and had a
Window on Each Side 17 Inches by 11 –. The Doors were in the
Center only 18 Inches wide And as One opened at the head of the
Boat, the Other being Exactly Opposite Opened into the Smaller
Cabbin of 4 feet 7 Inches in Length

Page 466

which the Servants Occupied and from which there was another
Door Opening to the Back part of the Boat where Our Coach was
placed –. The Length of the whole Vessel being 39 Feet –

By Two o Clock we had Passed under Three Wooden bridges – The
Shores on Each Side the River were Flat – Soon after we Passed by
Gunnersburgh which appeared a good Town & under Two more
wooden Bridges of Fifteen Arches each – near these were Several
large Boats with Three Cabbins in the middle Covered over for
Merchandise and a great Number of Horses Drawing these Boats
against the Stream –

At Nine o Clock we Went on Shore at Lantingen[1]

---

1. Günzburg and Lauingen – towns on the river Danube north-east of Ulm.

Page 467

And Staid the Night at a Very Comfortable House. The Distance ten Leagues from Ulm

Wed^y June 18th

This morning we were Called at Three o Clock and at Four Entered Our Vessel again – At Seven we Breakfasted upon the Bread Butter & Tea we had on Board & Our Tea kettle Boiling on a Chafing Dish of Charcoal – We passed Several Wooden Bridges this day and the Country on Each Side the River appeared Flat & uninteresting The Town of Donavert[1] Close to the Shore was the First in Bavaria which we passed about One o Clock. – at Three we Dined upon Cold Chicken &c and at Eight went on Shore at Neuberg where we Staid the Night.[2]

Page 468

Thursday.. June 19th

This morning we were again Called at Three o Clock and went on Board Our Vessel at Four – Soon after we had a Thunder Storm which Obliged us to keep Our Cabbin Door Shut but did not find any material Inconvenience at Six we breakfasted and at Eight Stopt at Ingolstadt[3] while the Boatman went to have his Passport Signed –. Both yesterday And to day, we passed Several very Long barges with Three Cabbins in the middle, all filled with Sacks and Tubs Carrying Provisions to the Army, and the Carved eagle upon the mast Shewed they belonged to the Emperor[4] Hitherto the Country on Each Side had Continued Flat, Except about Neuberg, where the Shore for near Two Miles was Covered with

Page 469

High Rocks and Trees Growing upon them from the Top to the

1. Donauwörth – city in Bavaria at the confluence of the Danube with the river Wörnitz.
2. Neuburg an der Donau in Bavaria.
3. Ingolstadt – city in Bavaria on the river Danube.
4. The Emperor – Francis II, Holy Roman Emperor, 1792–1806. He dissolved the Empire after a decisive defeat at the hands of Napoleon in 1806 and assumed the title of Emperor of Austria until his death in 1835.

Edge of the River; but the Shore afterwards became again Flat – and at Eight in the Even'g we Landed at Ratisbon –[1]

Friday June 20th
Having Staid the Night at the White Lamb[2] which we found to be a very Good Inn we determined to Continue there And after Breakfast went to See The Maison de Ville – The Room where the Diet[3] is held had Only white washed walls, and Benches Covered with Green Cloth, Another Room was Covered both Sides and Ceiling with a Brown wood highly Polished and in it was a Circular Table that there might be no Place of Precedency Among the Electors = In another Room was a Model of the

Page 470

Great Clock at Strasbourg, but what was more remarkable The heads of Two Men Over the Door, and One holding a large Stone & in the Attitude of Throwing it, The Other a Battle Axe [4]–

From hence We went to the Monastry [sic] of S[t.] Emeran Where we saw a Mont Calvery & Some Bad Pictures –[5] afterw[ds] went to Nôtre Dame, which is not worth Seeing –[6] and from thence to the Bridge which had Fifteen Arches Built of Stone –[7]

The Houses in Ratisbon are Only Lath & Plaister, The Pavement of the Streets Bad – and Even Where the Ambassadors Reside Narrow; Each of the Ministers have the Arms of their Country Over the Door of their House –

---

1. Regensburg – city in Bavaria at the confluence of the Danube, Naab and Regen rivers. It was known as Ratisbon in English well into the twentieth century.
2. Gasthaus Weisses Lamm – the building still exists and Haydn, Mozart and Goethe amongst others are known to have stayed there.
3. From 1663–1806 Regensburg was the seat of the perpetual Diet of the Holy Roman Empire.
4. The Old Town Hall at Regensburg, the home of the Imperial Diet, is now a museum dedicated to the history of the Holy Roman Empire.
5. The Abbey of St Emmeram was founded about 739 but the monastery was granted to the Prince of Thurn und Taxis in 1812 and the buildings are now generally called Schloss Thurn und Taxis.
6. The cathedral or Dom is dedicated to St.Peter.
7. The Stone Bridge dates to the twelfth century and is actually of 16 arches but that at the southern end was incorporated into the salt store.

Page 471

With One Lamp on Each Side We particularly Noticed that belonging to the Electorate of Hanover –[1]

The Publick walk Round the Town Commands a View of an Open Cultivated Country – Close to the Town Walls are Two Islands upon the Danube, and one has Thirteen Mills upon it Grinding Corn Night and Day –[2]

At Two o Clock we Dined at the Table D'Hôte, where only One Dish at a time was brought into the Room and that was Carved at a Side Table and Slices handed round to Each Person And Beer given instead of Wine –

In the Afternoon we found Our Courier Du Ponts So much Intoxicated with Liquor that He was totally Insensible where He was; And we dismissed Him this Evening –

Page 472

Saturday June 21st

This Morning at Four o Clock We Left Ratisbon taking Provisions On Board, we Breakfasted at Eight And Dined at Three – went Eighteen Leagues to Deckenden[3] where we got Good beds – but a Violent Thunder Storm coming just before we Landed had made the Ground Extremely Wet, and we hastened to bed after Washing Our Feet with a Strong Liqueur –

Sunday June 22[d]

The Boatman Carried me on his Back this morning at Five o Clock into the Boat – Our Inn being near the River and the Ground quite a Slough from the Rain which had fallen –

---

1. The prince of Brunswick-Lüneberg (Hannover) became the ninth prince-elector in 1692.
2. Some of the old Roman walls of the town still remain.
3. i.e. Deggendorf.

The Danube at this Place is very wide and the Wooden bridge which Crossed it

Page 473

had Sixteen Arches[1] = but not far from Hence We Saw The <u>Iser</u> mix its Stream with the Danube And the Country near the Shores became more beautiful[2] The Rising Grounds were Covered with Wood – at Eight o Clock We breakfasted, and at twelve We Stopt for a few minutes at Vilshoven where we saw a fair for Cattle – and many Booths in the Street, (tho it was Sunday) near a Fortnight before many Houses on the Side of the River had been on Fire and Only the Walls now remained Standing –[3]

After Leaving Vilshoven we Soon found Woods Sloping down to the Edge of the River and the Scenery Beautiful = but the Bridge at Vilshoven tho' of great Length consisted only of Fir Tree[s] laid at Length & without any Rail[4]

Page 474

on the Side = From Hence The River became more Agitated And frequently we saw Large Rocks at the Bottom = at Three o Clock we Stopt at Passau[5] & Went on Shore to See the Cathedral which is a Fine Gothic Building –[6] Mass was Performing as We Entered and The Priests at the Altar were in Rich Vestments The Canons Sitting in the Choir were in Light Blue mantles – before we Returned to Our Vessel We Purchased Bread for Our Dinner on Board, and was much pleased with having Seen the Town the Situation of which is Extremely Picturesque – upon the River towards Vienna it appears like an Island having One Side the D<u>anub</u>e and on the other Side

---

1. The bridge no longer exists but a new footbridge was completed in 2014.
2. The Isar joins the Danube between Deggendorf and Hengersberg.
3. Vilshofen – a conflagration on the 12th May 1794 destroyed a large part of the old town.
4. The first bridge over the Danube was constructed in 1591 but that seen by Mrs Bentham was probably that at the Salzstadel built in 1711.
5. Passau – city at the confluence of the Danube with the rivers Inn and Ilz. Though on the border with Austria it is in Germany.
6. The Cathedral of St. Stephen was built in an elaborate Baroque style from 1668 after a fire in 1662. Only the Gothic choir remained which is presumably the part Mrs Bentham mentions.

The <u>Inn</u> and the Buildings at the End of the Town appear from the River handsome = On the

Page 475

Opposite Shore of the Danube the Rocks are Steep and High And Covered with Wood, and upon the Summit are many Buildings Some of which resemble Fortifications

After the Junction of the River <u>Inn</u> with the <u>Danube</u> the water becomes more Rapid and of a Mud Colour & very Deep –

The Shore on Each Side now Continued to be High Rocks Covered with Trees to the Edge of the River till we Came to <u>Ingelhartz-iel</u>[1] where the Custom House Officers Came on Board and Examined very Minutely all Our Bagage, It being the First Town in the Emperors Dominions – tho' it appeared to us little more than a Village but we Staid the Night and found Our Lodgings tolerable –

Page 476

Monday.. June 23[d]
At Five o Clock we went on Board Our Vessel and Soon After it began to Rain, but Seating my Self in the Coach I had a Compleat View of the Beautiful Windings of the River with the Rocks on Each Side, much resembling those at the Hot Wells at Bristol –[2]

The Continual Windings formed Small Bays in which the River appeared land Locked – And the Shores on Each Side had Seldom more level Ground than formed a Road, or on which Some Scattered Houses were Built. And upon the Top of these Rocks were frequently Seen Castles or Ruins, and this beautiful Scenery Continued to <u>Asha</u> which we Passed about Nine o Clock –[3]

---

1. Engelhartszell – town on the Danube in Upper Austria.
2. There were two wells on the river Avon close to Bristol. Though the water was not as hot as that at Bath they were popular in the eighteenth century and the location in the Avon gorge was attractive in the "picturesque" sense.
3. i.e. Aschach an der Donau.

Page 477

Here the Shore immediately became Flat and Uninteresting, The Hills at a great Distance, And the many Little Streams with Shoals of sand gave the appearance of a Large Tract of Country Overflowed –

At Twelve we Came to <u>Lintz</u>[1] The Appearance of the Town from the River is beautiful The High Bare Rocks on One Side had Cottages on the very Summit, and Only Level Ground at the Bottom Sufficient for a Single Row of Houses with a Road in the Front – The opposite Side Equally Perpendicular but Covered with Trees and had a Road at the Bottom Close to the River – Houses & Convents appeared at a Distance upon High

Page 478

Mountains – The Bridge over The Danube at this Town has Twenty large Arches, but it is Built of Fir Tree[s] and has A mean Appearance being very Slight and without any Rails on the Side, merely Tree[s] Laid at Length –[2]

We Went on Shore The principal part of the Town was One Large Oblong Place[3] in which were Two Fountains And an Obelisk Surrounded by good Stone Built Houses with Shops and a Custom House office where we went to Shew our Passports – we went afterwards to the Cathedral a Handsome Church in which mass was Celebrating And at Our Return on Board went to Dinner –[4]

After Leaving Lintz the Beautiful Scenery was Succeeded

Page 479

By a Wide Expanse of Water with Sand Banks & Small Islands like

1. Linz – the capital of Upper Austria and the country's third largest city.
2. Probably the bridge linking Mautern and Stern. It was destroyed in the Austro-Prussian War of 1866 and replaced by a steel structure in 1895.
3. The Hauptplatz – it was originally laid out about 1230 AD. The Trinity Column dates to 1723.
4. At this time the Alte Domkirche built in the late seventeenth century. A new cathedral in the neo-Gothic style was built in the nineteenth century.

a Country over flowed – and thus continued Some distance when the River Entered again between High Mountains Covered with Trees to the Edge of the water and the Views were as Picturesque as any part of the Rhine –

In One part Called Strudel[1] at the Entrance of One of these Romantic bays were Two Ruins of Castles Standing in the River Surrounded by large Rocks and as they were nearby Opposite to Each Other the River formed a <u>Whirlpool</u> which Required Some Skill in the Boatmen to Pass in Safety –[2] and which we had no Sooner done that a Boat with a Woman in it Came from the Shore with a Little

Page 480

Little Box, in which was the Portrait of le Bon Dieu – She Came to Request we would Give a Tribute of Gratitude for our having passed this Whirlpool Safely.

This Romantic Scenery of Wood and water continued till we Landed at a Little Village Called Marbach where we Staid the Night and found Clean Beds.[3]

Tuesday.. June. 24th

Went on Board this morning at half past Three and as the Country was Flat and Uninteresting I got into the Coach where I Slept Two Hours – at Seven o Clock we breakfasted, and Soon after the Scenery Changed again, and the River Entered between very High Hills which produced a most Picturesque Scene of Broken Rocks with Sharp Pikes Rising to the Top of a Mountain like <u>Mont Serrat</u>[4]

Page 481

Soon after we passed a Small Town And a Bridge of Twenty

1. Strudengau – a narrow meandering section of the river. At the time navigation was hazardous due to whirlpools caused by the currents.. This was only mitigated in the twentieth century by major hydraulic work on the river.
2. A whirlpool or eddy known as the Strudel.
3. Marbach an der Donau – town on the river west of Melk.
4. Montserrat – many-peaked mountain range near Barcelona, Spain.

Arches Over the Danube –[1] The Shores again very Flat and a Wide
Epanse [sic] of Water –. But Towns and Villages in View – and at
a Distance Small Hills Cultivated with Vineyards which were the
First we had Seen Since we Left Constance in Switzerland –

The Only Traffick upon the Danube appeared to be Carrying
Salt in Small Tubs, & they were put in Long Flat Bottom Boats,
the middle part of which was Entirely Covered over with Fir and
formed into Three Cabbins – Forty and often Fifty Horses were
Employed with a man upon Each to Draw the Boats against the
Stream – and at this Time Provisions for the

Page 482

Army were Conveyed in the Same manner – But the Awkard [sic]
Construction of the Boats, and want of Attention to make them
Convenient prevents any Family Using them as Passage Boats to
Vienna, whereas with Boats like those upon the Rhine it would be
a pleasant way of Travelling

Within Three Miles of Vienna, at the Little Village of Nusdorff[2]
we were Obliged to wait Two Hours while the man belonging to
Our Boat Sent to Vienna for a Permit to go up the River which
here divides The lesser Channel going to the City, and the Large
to [3]

This Delay made it Eight o Clock before we Arrived at Vienna[4]
but the day was Fine, And the

Page 483

City appeared to Advantage for tho' the Surrounding Country was
Flat, yet it Seemed Covered with Wood – But a miserable Wooden
Bridge, Built very Slight and having Only Fir Trees laid at length to

1. Possibly the wooden bridge over the river at Krems. This was burnt down in the
   mid–nineteenth century and replaced by a steel structure.
2. Nussdorf – once a village on the Danube, it is now a suburb of Vienna itself.
3. A space has been left here for the place-name – ed.
4. Vienna – the capital of the Austro–Hungarian Empire at this time.

Serve as a Fence on Each Side, was a great Contrast to the Bridges Crossing the Thames at the Metropolis of England –[1]

Not during the Time that we had been on the Danube from Ulm to Vienna had we Seen Any better Vessel than these Composed of Rafts of Fir put together –

During Our Voyage we had found the Portable Soup which we had brought from England of great use[2] – with that

Page 484

And Cold Tongue & Chicken we had made delicious meals on Board our Vessel, and Our Tea & Coffee added not a little to Our Comfort And we had the good Fortune to find Every Night Clean Beds tho' the Houses were Shabby –

As Soon as Our Vessel approached Vienna my Dear Son went on Shore with M^r. Hay in Search of Lodgings And Soon Returned with a Coach which took us to le Boeuf Blanc where He had Engaged Three Large Rooms Hansomely Furnished with Beautiful Lustres, and the Squares of Glass in the Windows measured 25 Inches by 20, which were the manufacture of Bohemia.[3]

Wed^y June 25th
This morning Our Baggage was brought from the Boat, where

Page 485

It had remained during the Night opposite to the Custom House – After Unpacking &c we went to the Post House and had the Comfort of Receiving Several letters from my Dear Charles in England =. In the Evening we were drove to the Prætor a beautiful

---

1. The first stable bridge over the Danube was not erected until 1870. Previously to this a wooden bridge served as the crossing. This was frequently repaired or replaced due to flood and ice damage on the river. The reluctance to build a stone bridge may have been due to the perennial threat of invasion by the Turks.
2. Portable soup – an early form of dehydrated food to which water and salt could be added when required. It was first used in the mid–eighteenth century especially for sea voyages.
3. Le Bœuf Blanc – a notable inn at the time near to the custom house.

park where the principal Families in Vienna are to be Seen Every Day –[1].. We got out of Our Carriage and walked Some time with M[r.] Bootle[2] who was Spending Some time at Vienna, and another English gentleman whose name was Parkinson[3] – and afterwards went to the Ramparts as is Customary with the inhabitants of this City –[4]

Page 486

Thursday June 26th.
This morning we went to See a Courier who had brought Dispatches from the Army with an Account that Charleroi had been Releived by the Austrians and the French Defeated, & made his Publick Entry into Vienna –[5]

The procession Commenced with Soldiers Three & Three Abreast Then Two Soldiers with an Officer between Them –. Then Thirty Postilions Two and Two Continually Smacking their whips. –. Then Four Postilions Sounding a Horn with a Young Man in the Center who was the Courier & He was Continually Bowing to the People as He Passed through the Streets, This Ridiculous Procession was Attended by Crouds of People, and

Page 487

We Saw it from Coll Bradyll[s] Lodgings –[6] from which we went to See The Manége where Several Gentlemen were Riding[7] And from thence we went to the Salle des Ridotte which is made use of

1. The Prater – originally an imperial hunting ground, the park was opened to the public by Joseph II in 1766.
2. Probably Edward Bootle.
3. Probably Dr John Parkinson of Magdalen College, Oxford.
4. The ramparts were demolished in the 1880s to make way for the celebrated Ringstrasse.
5. In fact, that day the Prince of Coburg leading the Allied Army had failed to dislodge the army of the French Republic from Charleroi leaving the Low Countries open to French dominance.
6. Ingamells' *Dictionary* lists a Colonel Braddyll as being in Venice in 1794 but no further details are given.
7. Presumably the Spanish Riding School in the Hofburg. The present building was commissioned by Charles VI in 1729.

Only during the Carnival = The Largest Room Furnished with Pink & Silver Gawse And Silver Fringe hanging in Drapery over the Windows – Another Room for Dancing and Another for Cards with Open Galleries Round the Rooms and Communicating with Each Other –

From hence we went to the Ramparts and Returned to Our Lodgings to Receive M[r]. Muller[1] who Dined with us and offered Every Attention in his Power; but told us his Official Situation

Page 488

Required his constant Attendance Every Day from 9 to 12 and from 4 to 6 – After he left us we went in Our Carriage to the Præter; but not finding many Persons there we went to the Pavillion at the End of the wood Called the Lust House[2]

Friday June 27th
Violent Storms of Rain & Thunder all the Morning – However after breakfast we went to See the Bibliotheque de La Cour, which is the most Elegant Built Room for the purpose = In the Center is a Dome Supported by Eight Pillars, which Incloses Four winding Staircases Leading from each Corner of the Dome to the Upper Gallery, and in these Pillars Are Open Circles which contain A Bust and yet give Light –[3]

Page 489

The Other parts of this Elegant Room are described in Le Guide de Vienne –[4]

From the Library we went to the Museum where we Saw a very

---

1. Possibly Johannes von Müller (1752–1809), Swiss historian. He entered the service of the Emperor Francis II in 1793.
2. The Lusthaus – an eighteenth-century octagonal pavilion originally built as a hunting lodge but now used as a restaurant.
3. The Prunksaal – the central room of what is now the Austrian National Library in the Hofburg complex. It was built to designs by Johann Fischer von Erlach in the early eighteenth century.
4. Possibly the *Nouveau guide par Vienne pour les étrangers et les nationales de l'an 1792*, Vienna, 1792.

Fine Collection of Corals, Chrystals, Minerals &c &c in Five Rooms – all well Aranged [sic]¹

There was likewise Four Views of the harbour of Leghorn in marble And far Superior to any Mosaic work done at Rome. The Artist was Employed by the Emperor and the Expence having been Estimated it appeared that Each Picture Cost One Thousand Pound Sterling –²

A most magnificent and Brilliant Bouquet of Diamonds And Other gems was Given to the Late Emperor by His Mother Maria Theresia as an Addition

Page 490

To the Specimen of Gems that were Here in their natural State –³

The Gentleman who Attended us Seemed desirous to give us Every Species of Information on Account of Our being English –

From Hence we went to the Ecuries belonging to the Emperor in which were many English Horses – and Some from Hungary but the Stables were Entirely Wood, the Floor & The Stalls, where the Horses Stood –⁴ At One o Clock we had Permission to Visit the Arsenal –⁵ The Entrance under the Gate Way was Handsome and decorated with Arms placed in a Variety of Shape Four Figures in Compleat Armour Standing – The large Court yard within was full of Cannon & Four Rooms with Small Arms

1. The collection of minerals and gems, including the famous Bouquet originally given by Maria Theresa to her husband, are now in the Naturhistorisches Museum, Vienna.
2. These are Four views of the harbour at Livorno to designs by Giuseppe Zocchi (d.1767) and sent to Vienna from Florence – see A. Giusti – *L'arte delle pietre dure da Firenze all'Europa*, 2005, pp.170–5. Presumably they were commissioned by the Emperor Leopold II whilst Grand-duke of Tuscany.
3. Maria Theresa, Empress of Austria (1717–80) and Joseph II (1741–90), Holy Roman Emperor and Emperor of Austria (1780–90).
4. The Imperial Stables were built for Karl VI by Johann Fischer von Erlach. They have now been converted into an art complex.
5. The collection was transferred to a purpose-built museum in 1856 designed by Theophil Hansen, a Dane.

Page 491

Surrounded the Court Yard – The Armoury was well Aranged and the Various Devices Picturesque but what pleased me most was the Cap of Liberty[1] & Colours lately taken from the French by General Wurmser[2] – upon the Colours was Embroidered these words Par Les Amis, et Les Amis de la Liberté et de L'Egalité de Besancon – un Serre Battaillons Ducardo –

These Colours had formerly belonged to the King – and where the Fleur de Lys was They had Pasted a Piece of Striped Silk Over it – There was many Holes & Rents in the Silk

The Cap of Liberty was of a peculiar Form – made of Red Cloth Stiffened within Side by a Wood and fixed upon a Pole –[3]

Page 492

upon The cap were Letters Signifying The Year of Liberty And upon the Colours was a Tree Painted with a Red Cap

At the Return to Our Hôtel we met Mr Bootle who Came to tell us of Lord Howe having Beaten the Brest Fleet, and the Rejoicings at London on the Occasion –[4]

In the Evening we went through the Suburbs of Mariahof – Weider – Josephstadt, St Ulrich[5] &c going quite Round the City of Vienna

---

1. The Cap of Liberty or bonnet rouge was first seen in May 1790 and became a symbol of the Revolution in France. It was a Phrygian style cap and examples were said to have been knitted by the tricoteuses at the public executions in Paris.
2. Count Dagobert von Wurmser (1724–97), Austrian field marshal.
3. The origins of the symbol of the cap of liberty stems from the aftermath of the assassination of Julius Caesar but it was also used during the American Revolution before being adopted by the French Revolutionaries.
4. The largest naval action between France and Britiain during the French Revolutionary War took place on the 1st June of that year. It was a tactical victory for Admiral Lord Richard Howe (1726–99).
5. Mariahilf, Wieden, Josefstadt and Neubau (St. Ulrich's being in the latter district today)

Except towards the Prater[1] And we Passed the House & Gardens
of Prince Kaunitz just as his Death was Announced –[2]

Saturday June 28th.
Went to See the Belvedere[3] Situated in the Fauxbourg &

Page 493

Built by the Prince de Savoy but now belongs to the Emperor –
The Superieuse palace is a very handsome Building, containing
Twenty Five Rooms filled with The Paintings of Titian – Paul
Veronese – Raphael – Corregio – Leonardi de Vincis &c &c &c and
the most Eminent Painters of the Flemish School – From Hence
we went to a large Handsome Building at the Bottom of the Garden
Called Le Palais Inferieure[4] where was likewise a great Collection
of Family Portraits And Two whole lengths of the Late King and
Queen of France both very Strong Resemblances –

The Queen Dressed as I saw Her Majesty at Versailles Eighteen
Years ago – in white, with a Fringe

Page 494

of Gold, Large Hoop & the Petticoat in Drapery and Flounced –[5]

1. The Prater was originally an imperial hunting ground bounding the river Danube
but was opened to the public in 1766.
2. Wenzel Anton, Prince Kaunitz-Rietberg. He died on 27th June. A painting of the
palace and its surroundings by Bernardo Bellotto is in the collection of the Museum
of Fine Arts, Budapest.
3. The Belvedere – the summer palace of Prince Eugene of Savoy. It was built by
Johann Lukas von Hildebrandt and consists of an upper palace linked by a garden to
the lower palace below. It eventually became a Habsburg property and the gardens
were opened to the public in the mid eighteenth century. The palace now contains
the collections of twentieth-century art. The collection of old masters is now shown
at the Kunsthistorisches Museum.
4. The Lower Belvedere – the palace now contains the collection of Austrian Baroque
art.
5. Two full-length portraits now in the Kunsthistorisches Museum. Louis XVI in
coronation robes by Antoine François Callet, 1781, and Marie Antoinette, Queen of
France by Vigée-Lebrun, 1778.

In the Evening we went to a Comedie at Le Comtesse de Fries[1] – In which She and her Daughter Performed the Principal Characters – It was Melide, ou Le Navigateur – In Two Acts Between which Lemonade and Ice of Various Sorts were Offered to each person present –[2]

All the Beau Monde in Vienna were there, and we thought Ourselves much Obliged to M<u>r</u> Bootle for Three Tickets which he Sent us, one of which we gave to M<u>r.</u> Muller who Accompanied us – The Theatre consisted of a Pit only, and no more Tickets being distributed than the Room would contain – Each

Page 495

Each person at Entring took the Vacant Seat that He best Liked –

Sunday June 29<u>th</u>

Walked upon the Ramparts which Environ the City, and was much pleased with the compleat Idea it gave me of the Suburbs, which much Resemble S<u>t</u>. Georges Fields[3] But the Air, and the Small Ditches of Stagnated water must make it unhealthy, to which might be added a Continual Dust, that Arises from the Sand, and is So penetrating, that we observed most people holding Hankercheifs to their Mouth and Eyes –

The Common People of this Country if they are Females very frequently wear a cap of Entire Gold Lace, made in the Shape of a Scull Cap – having only a Cawl

Page 496

For these Caps They Give from Three to Five Guineas Each –

---

1. Grafin Maria Theresia Josefa von Fries (1779–1819), born Prinzessin von Hohenlohe-Waldenburg-Schellingsfürst. She was married to Moritz Christian Johann, Reichsgraf von Fries (1777–1826), an Austrian nobleman and patron of the arts. He was a friend of Beethoven.
2. Melide, ou Le Navigateur – French play dating to 1774.
3. St. George's Fields – area north of Hyde Park and west of the Edgware Road which was used as a cemetery from 1763 onwards but was sold for development in 1967, and is now a housing estate.

Others Wear Black Silk Caps with Black Lace Borders in the Same Shape – and the rest of their Dress is a jacket & Coat.

We Went to the Augarten[1] before Dinner; it is a large garden Planted with a great variety of Fine Tree[s] which form Shady walks, and a Broad Arm of the Danube washing the Banks makes this Place Extremely Pleasant – at the Entrance of these Gardens is a magnificent Pavillion in which are Several Rooms where Company may be Accomodated with Dinner or any Refreshment – And the Inhabitants of Vienna frequently Spend the Day there And often Dine under the Shade of

Page 497

these Beautiful Tree[s] – In the Evening we went to the Opera And during the Representation were Served with a Variety of Ice

The Logements are all Engaged by Families for the Year Our Seats therefore were in the Parterr Noble; which in fact is the best Place to See the Opera –[2]

		Stage		
Orchestra				*Orchestra*
3 Seats		*6 Seats with Backs*		*3 Seats*
D°		*D°*		*D°*
D°	*Open passage*	*D°*	*Open passage*	*D°*
D°		*D°*		*D°*
D°		*D°*		*D°*
D°		*D°*		*D°*
Passage		*Continued*		*Passage*
		Pit for Common People		

---

1. The Augarten Palace and park beyond the Danube. The park was opened to the public in 1775 by Joseph II.
2. Probably the Kaiserliches Hoftheater. It was originally built in 1709 but destroyed by fire in 1761 and re-opened two years later.

Page 498

We Went this Morning to See the Imperial Cabinet of Medals[1] which is Said to be Superior to Any Other in Europe for the Number and Scarcity of the Coins which Commence from the Time of Charlemagns[2] =

The Emperor Francis Expended great Sums of Money in forming this Collection And we Saw One Piece of Gold which was presented to the Emperor by a Private Gentleman Valued at Two Thousand and Fifty Pounds Sterling[3]

We likewise Saw a Piece of English Gold, Coined in the Reign of Charles the First, of the Value of Twenty Shillings[4] – His majesty being desirous to have the Pound Sterling in Circulation instead of Guineas – There were likewise

Page 499

Several Coins of Oliver Cromwell[5] And Some of the Pretenders by the Title of Charles the Third.[6]

In Another Room we were Shewn a fine Collection of Oryxes[7]

From Hence we went to See the Corpse of Prince Kaunitz which was this Day Exposed to View, Lying in State, and Dressed as if Living in a Suit of Black, With Silk Stockings &c The Countenance appeared that of un Homme Scavant,[8] and tho' Aged not like One of Fourscore and Four, which was his Age when He Died

---

1. The Cabinet of medals along with many other collections, was moved to the Kunsthistorisches Museum in 1891.
2. The Emperor Charlemagne (742–814).
3. Francis I (1708–65), Holy Roman Emperor and Grand Duke of Tuscany.
4. Coin known as the Unite which was first issued by James I to commemorate the Union of England and Scotland. The coin was reissued several times during the reign of Charles I.
5. Oliver Cromwell (1599–1658), Lord Protector.
6. Charles Edward Stuart (1720–88).
7. Murray's *Dictionary* gives the word as also meaning a "pickaxe". A collection of pickaxes seems unlikely. One must assume that this is a collection of oryx horns, specimens of which would have been of interest at this time.
8. This spelling is correct but presumably Mrs Bentham means "savant".

We went Afterw^{ds}. to the Garden of Prince Schwartzenberg Situated at the Bottom of the Belvedere and walked there an Hour – It is very Judiciously Planted

Page 500

to Conceal its Boundaries, and this Pleasant Garden is Open to the Publick –[1]

Upon Our Return We Went to the Lichtenstein Gallery – which contains a Valuable Collection of Pictures – but they were chiefly On Religious Subjects –[2]

In the Evening we were drove to the Prater which is an Extensive Wood of Oak and Beech On an Island upon the Danube And there are many Pavillions in different parts where Coffee, Lemonade Ice and Various Refreshments are Sold, even Dinners and Suppers are to be had, with Tables and Chairs put under the Tree^s, or Served in the Rooms of the Pavillion which are neatly Furnished and Communicate with a Variety of different Offices behind the Pavillion

From the Prater the Company

Page 501

Retire at the Close of day and go to the Ramparts, where Three pavilions are Erected on One of the Bastions to Supply Lemonade, Ice &c This Place being Small, and great Numbers of all Sorts of people going we thought it appeared more Calculated for Assignations than any good Purpose –

The City of Vienna is not very Large, The Ramparts which Surround it are not more than Three Mile in Circumference, and not any Houses adjoin, but a Circular Field Environs the City at the

---

1. The Schwarzenberg gardens behind the eponymous palace. The latter is now partly a hotel.
2. The collection of paintings belonging to the princely family of Liechtenstein. It was generally shown in the Garden Palace. The collection still exists but is now only shown to groups on a pre-booked basis.

Edge of which the Suburbs Commence – These are very Extensive but the Houses in general are Ill Built & the whole resembles a Number of Poor Straggling Towns crouded together –

Page 502

The Streets in Vienna are narrow, and there is One Square Or rather a Large Open Place And in that is an Obelisk And Two Fountains[1]

The principal Palaces are Situated in Such Narrow Streets that they make no Figure – but the Regulation made in passing Over the bridges which gives the Communication with the Suburb of Leopold is Excellent; the Two Outermost Passages are for Foot Passengers, One Used by those going from the City, The Other by those Returning; and the Two Innermost Passages for Carriages are Used in the Same manner –[2]

Page 503

Tuesday July 1[st.]

We went this morning to See the Imperial Palace[3] – Some of the Apartments were Hung with the Gobelin Tapestry Others with the Brussels – and many were wainscoted and Painted Stone Colour with Rich Gilding round – Not Any Window Curtains in the Apartments but double Windows The Panes of Glass were 34 Inches High, by 29 Broad – The Rooms were Floors Inlaid in Mosaic patterns and well Rubbed of a dark Brown Colour

The Emperors State Room of Audience fronted a Large Court

---

1. The only obelisk of the period is that at the foot of the Schönbrunn Hill which includes fountains, but the oldest open space is the Hohermarkt which has a monument with fountains designed by Johann Fischer von Erlach for Leopold I and erected 1729–32.
2. The Schlagbrücke?
3. The Hofburg. The palace was begun in the thirteenth century but over time developed into an enormous complex. There have also, of course, been changes since the time of Mrs Bentham's visit. Part of the palace is now the official residence of the President of Austria.

which was Surrounded by different Apartments belonging to the Palace –

Page 504

At the back of this Suite of Rooms, were the Private Apartm^{ts}. Which had a good View of the Ramparts, but were Smaller Rooms than the Other; The only Pictures in the Palace were the Portraits of the Empress of Russia and late King of Prussia in Half Length, and both were in the Room where the Emperor Joseph allways Dined with his Chair fronting the King of Prussia' Portrait –[1] In Two Rooms were musical Clocks, and a Piano Forte made in England.

There was another double Suite of Rooms Called the late Emperor Leopold^s Apartment,[2] And now used for Occasional Visitors And were occupied by the Pope when He was last at Vienna[3] The Furniture Rich Lyon^s Silk

Page 505

And in One Room an Elevated Circular Sofa in the Turkish Style to Receive Company –

On Each Side of the Late Emperor Leopolds Bed was a Door which Opened into a Circular Closet containing Four Doors which Opened to a Dressing Room A Study and Serv^{ts}. Bed Room

The Empress had the same on her Side the Bed =. In the Center of the Bed Room a Door Opened into a Small breakfast Room by which the Other Rooms Communicated with each Other –

From hence we went to the Convent of Capuchins to See the Masoleum [sic] where the Imperial family are Buried, and Descended to a Long Gallery, on Each Side of which were deposited the Remains of Several Emperors and Empresses

---

1. Possibly the half-length portrait of Catherine the Great by J.B. Lampi dating from the 1780s now in the Kunsthistorisches Museum, and, that of Frederick the Great (not traced).
2. Leopold II, died 1792.
3. Pius VI (Braschi), reigned 1775–99, visited Vienna in 1782 in an attempt to prevent the Emperor from interfering in ecclesiastical appointments.

Page 506

In Bronze and marble Coffins; We attended Cheifly to those of Leopold, Francis, Maria Theresia, and the late Emperor Joseph, who Strickly forbid Any Ornament to be put upon his Coffin, which remains a Plain Copper case, on which his Name &c is Inscribed = It Stands at the Entrance of a Little Chapel in this Gloomy Subterranean Place And in the middle is a Pompous One of Maria Theresia and her Husband Francis –[1]

We went from hence to See the Largest Branch of the Danube, Over which the Wooden bridge is 610 yards in Length[2]

In the Evening we went to the Prater and Examined the Place where the Fire-works are often Exhibited – The Scaffold Remains and likewise the Building in the Form of an Amphitheatre for the Company to Sit in –

Page 507

Wed^y July 2^d
Went this morning to Schonbrun[3] A Very magnificent Palace, It was Built for the Empress Maria Theresia = The Outside is Stucco with Green Jalousie or Blinds –

It is near Two miles from Vienna; The Situation Low and Marshy – but the Garden at a little distance is on Rising Ground from the Back Front of the Palace, and upon an Eminence the Late Emperor Joseph Built an Elegant Room with a Colonade on Each Side, and on this Spot The Palace ought to have been Erected –[4] The garden is in the Usual German Style the walks in Strait Lines, Some Covered And Some Open, with Statues in Abundance = Here is

---

1. The Imperial Mausoleum beneath the Capuchin church. Burials are ongoing in that the "heir" to the Austrian throne, Otto von Habsburg, was interred here in 2011.
2. Possibly the Augartenbrücke, a wooden bridge built in 1782 and then called the "New bridge", which was later burnt down by French forces.
3. The Schönbrunn Palace – the summer palace of the imperial family. It was begun in 1695 to designs by Johann Fischer von Erlach and was completed during the reign of Maria Theresa in the mid eighteenth century.
4. The Gloriette designed by Ferdinand von Hohenberg and erected in 1775.

a Grotto with a Fountain of Such pure water that The Emperor who Allways Drinks it, had Some

Page 508

Conveyed from Hence for his Beverage when He last Visited the Army in Flanders –[1] In One Corner of the Garden is a menagerie[2] with a great Number of Curious Birds, And likewise Animals, Each having a Plot of Ground with a Building upon it, and a Fountain with water, together forming a large Circle, with very High Iron barrs to keep them in their different Apartm[ts].

We Observed that particular care was taken of Two Large Eagles as being the Austrian Arms –

In One part of the Garden is a Ruin made to resemble a Roman Arch[3] – Upon Our Quitting the Garden we fortunately Saw the Emperor who was coming Out of his Carriage on his Return from Vienna = He

Page 509

Appeared Very Young, and in his Person Elegant, with an Animated And Expressive Countenance of Benevolence & Goodness of Heart –[4]

We Dined at a Traiteur[s] who is allowed to Accommodate Strangers in a Building adjoining to the Offices belonging to the Palace – and afterw[ds]. We walked Again in the Gardens and Saw the Orangerie[5] &c &c and in the Evening we Returned to Vienna. The Plan of the Palace of Schonbrun is in Le Guide de Vienne –

1. Flanders was ruled by the Holy Roman Emperor until the French Revolution and Francis II briefly commanded his forces in the campaign against the French in 1794 before handing over to his brother the Archduke Charles.
2. It was the world's first zoo having been built in 1752. The pavilion still exists.
3. Fake ruins created by Ferdinand von Hohenberg in 1778.
4. Emperor Francis II – he was 26 at the time.
5. The Orangerie dates to 1752. It is presently used for the giving of concerts.

Thursday July 3ᵈ.
Went to See the China manufactry[1] where we were told they
Employ 300 Persons = there was a Beautiful Table Service made
for the Queen of Naples,[2] And Some Plates Valued at Three
Guineas each – The

Page 510

The manufacture was Beautiful And Various, Some resembled
Japan So Exactly that it looked like Wood, and there was vases that
resembled exactly those Sir Wᵐ Hamilton had from Herculaneum[3]
A Breakfast Set, or Dejeuné [sic] in a Box for Two persons was
valued at Twenty Guineas,[4] but there was likewise very neat white
China Plates with Blue Borders at Nine Shillings a Dozen – – we
afterwᵈˢ. Went to make Visits to Lord Tyrone – Mʳ· Kruitner, [sic][5]
Mʳ· Angurstein,[6] Coll Bradyl &c &c – Mʳ. Muller Dined with us
And in the Evening we went to the Prater where we Walked –

Friday July 4ᵗʰ.
Went this morning to Kaltcberg about Four miles from the City It
is Situated upon a High Hill;[7] The Road to it through

Page 511

Vineyards, but at the Top is a Very Fine Wood and Here was formerly a Convent; but now Only Some Whimsical Buildings Erected
by Order of the Prince de Ligne,[8] who frequently Comes Here to
Enjoy the View of the whole City of Vienna which lies like a Map

1. The Augarten Palace Porcelain Manufactory. It was founded in 1718 but was taken
under imperial patronage in 1744 by the Empress Maria Theresa.
2. At the time, Maria Carolina of Austria (1752–1814). She was the sister of the Emperor
Joseph II.
3. The collection of Roman vases amassed by Sir William Hamilton (1730–1803) whilst
British Ambassador in Naples. He sold his first collection to the British Museum in
1771 but eventually assembled another.
4. Déjeuner – a breakfast set.
5. Mr Kruitner – previously given as Kuittner.
6. Possibly John Angerstein (1773–1858), son of the art collector John Julius Angerstein.
The former is noted in Ingamells' *Dictionary* as being in Venice in May of that year.
7. Probably Kalksburg in the hills south-west of the city.
8. Charles-Joseph, 7ᵗʰ Prince de Ligne (1735–1814), field marshal. He was born in the
Austrian Netherlands but after the loss of these territories to the French he served in
Vienna.

underneath Situated in an Extensive Flat Country as far as the Eye can reach – from Hence we drove through another Fine Wood to the adjoining Hill, from whence is a more Compleat View as it takes the Bend of the Danube as well as the whole City of Vienna = but the Innumerable Little Islands formed by the Danube gives the appearance of a Country Overflowed and were it not for the Plantations of Wood upon these Islands the whole

Page 512

Would appear a Morass; nor can it be a Healthy Country –

The Extensive Tract of a Flat Corn Country which has neither Tree nor Hedge within Sight is very Uninteresting, & the Hills we were now upon Extended but a little way – & We were obliged to descend by a Narrow Stony Steep Road to a Dirty miserable Inn where we paid a most Extravagant Price for a Bad Dinner – near this Place was a Convent[1] where we Saw a fine Suite of Rooms looking upon the Danube, and would have been a much better Situation for a Palace than Schonbrun; as the Road from Hence is Six miles to Vienna on the Banks of the Danube – And we Arrived at Our Hotel at 8 in the Evening –

Page 513

Saturday July 5th
My Dear Son went this morng at Eleven o Clock to Baron Mull the Hanoverian Minister,[2] where He met Lord Tyrone, M[r.] Kruitner M[r] Webb and M[r.] Prescot with whom He went to the Imperial Palace and was presented to the Emperor, who Received [Them] in his Uniform A white Coat, with Collar & Cuffs of a mulberry Colour; The waistcoat and Breaches of Buff – Colour, His Ribband under his Coat, and Two Stars on the Breast,. He had Boots on with Spurs –.. After the Ceremony was Over He Returned and went

---

1. Not traced.
2. Baron Mull – not traced.

with me to See a Large Hospital for the Sick & Lying In Women[1] It contained Several Courts which were Surrounded with Buildings & Seperated by Trees – and at the Extremity a detached Circular

Page 514

Building for Persons Insane –[2]

In the Evening we went to the Prater and walked till it was near Dark, we then were Drove to the Bastion where I Sat in the Carriage and Eat Ice, while my Son walked to Observe the mixture of Company Assembled –

Sunday July 6th

My Son went after breakfast to Leave Cards of Congé[3] with the Hanoverian Minister And the English who were Here – while I was Engaged in Writing Letters to England, and Packing to prepare for Our Departure – M[r]. Prescot, M[r]. Angerstein And M[r]. Hay Came to Engage us to prolong Our Stay but we had Engaged M[r]. Muller to Dine with us and bring Our Passports for to morrow – This Evening We Went to the Augarten garden And there walked near Two Hours

We

Page 515

We determined to take a Servant who was well Acquainted with the German Language to Travel with us as a Valet de Chambre And Courier, and therefore by M[r]. Muller[s]. Recommendation Engaged Joseph Esch a Bohemian, Born near Prague, to go with us to England, –

---

1. This was the old Allgemeines Krankenhaus now replaced by a modern hospital. The enormous site was developed during the eighteenth century and was originally a hospital for veterans. The site is now part of the University of Vienna.
2. This is the Narrenturm or Fool's Tower. The circular structure was erected in 1784 for housing the insane and still exists though part now houses the Museum of Pathological Anatomy. At the time it was the first such facility in continental Europe.
3. Congé – ceremonious leave taking.

Our passage from Ulm to Vienna down the Danube was

The First Day to Lantingen 10 Leagues

The Second day to Neuberg – 18 L

The Third Day to Ratisbon 18 L

The Fourth we Staid at Ratisbon

The Fifth Day to Deckenden 18 L

The Sixth to Ingeldartzil

The Seventh to Vienna –

The Boat to take us from Ulm to Vienna Cost us Twelve Louis

Monday July 7th –
At Eight o Clock we quitted Vienna And for the distance of Two Posts

Page 516

The Danube Run on Our left Under a range of Small Hills which Extend from Vienna; but Our Road (tho Parallel to the River) went Contrary to the Stream The Country Open Corn Fields but Flat and Uninteresting –

The Road after we passed the Second Post Soon Turned Short to the Right Crossing an extended Plain of Corn Country, which At the Third Post became mixed with Vineyards = The Wheat was now Reaping, and from Thirty to Sixty persons being together made the Scene Chearful but the Road was Rough and Stony, The materials being like the Northamptonshire Stone near Brackley –.[1] This Day we went Six Posts about 56 English miles – And Staid the Night at Znaim A tolerable good Inn & decent Beds,. The Town Considerable for

---

1. Brackley – town in the south of the county of Northants.

Page 517

the District of Moravia –. It is Situated on the Banks of the Banks of the [*sic*] Tegrens[1]

Tuesday.. July. 8th.
We Left Znaim and went Five Posts to Iglen,[2] a good Town And a clean Inn where we Staid the Night – The Country we had gone through was an Extended Tract of Corn without Hedge or Tree, in Every respect the Same as the day before – In the Town of Iglen we Observed both men and women to wear Long Woolen Cloaks which Extended to their Feet, tho' The Weather was very Hot –

Wed[y] July 9[th.]
We left Iglen at Seven, and went Six Posts to Kolin,[3] The Town was tolerably well Built, And had a large Square Opening in the Center,[4] with a Fountain but the Inn was Dirty and Bad.

Page 518

The Country we had gone through was more Varied than the Two former Days, and a great many Small Plantations of Fir Tree[s] upon gentle Elevations made it appear Pleasant –

Thursday.. July.. 10th.
We Left Kolin before Six, and Stopt to Breakfast at a Public House Six miles distant, in which The late King of Prussia Directed the Famous Battle between his Army and Marshall Daun who Commanded the Army belonging to the Emperor; The Cannon Balls which were Lodged in the Plaister without Side the House used to be Shewn to all Strangers; but the House having lately been Repaired, we were Obliged to be Satisfied with Eating Our Breakfast in the Room His Majesty was in during this

---

1. Znojmo – town in the south Moravian region of the Czech Republic on the river Thaya and close to the border with Austria.
2. Jihlava – capital of the Vyso⬚ina region of the Czech Republic.
3. Kolín – town 55 miles east of Prague.
4. Karl square.

Page 519

Memorable Battle –[1] From Hence the Country became again like
that we had passed through the Two First days from Vienna, Open
and Uninteresting but Fertile in Corn, and the few Trees which
were Occasionally by the Side of the Road were Mountain Ash –

The Post Houses Except One or Two, were Private Houses,
not Inns, which is a great Inconvenience to Travellers =. At the
End of Forty miles we Arrived at Prague[2] where we found good
Accomodations at les Nouveau Bains[3] and Dined for the First
time Since Leaving Vienna,. Having never been able to get far-
ther than Six Posts in Twelve Hours, during which we never got
Out of Our Carriage but while fresh Horses were put On, And the
Accomodations in this Country are So bad, that

Page 520

between Vienna and Prague the Distance of 203 miles many
Persons go without Stopping a Night upon the Road; – The
Houses throughout this Country are of Rough Stone, Plaistered
Over, And many in the Villages are Roofed with Wood Cut in the
Shapes of Tiles – and the Bedsteads at the Inns are only 2 feet 3
Inches wide –

In the Evening we walked to the Royal Castle,[4] where The Emperor
Resides when He is at Prague, And where his Sister The Arch
Dutchess allways Lives as being Lady Abbess of the Convent[5] – At
Our Return to Our Inn M[r.] Holme drank Tea with us, having lost
his Travelling Companion Mr Simpson in a very Sudden manner,
between Ratisbon and this Place, at a

---

1. Battle of Kolin, 1757 – a famous engagement where Field Marshal Leopold von Daun
   (1705–66) defeated Frederick the Great of Prussia.
2. Prague or Praha – now capital of the Czech Republic.
3. Hôtel Les Nouveau Bains – not traced.
4. The Burg, or Imperial palace. It was begun by the Emperor Charles IV and completed by Maria Theresia.
5. The Archduchess Maria Anna of Austria (1738–89) was appointed Abbess of the
   Frauenstift in Prague in 1766.

Page 521

miserable Village, where He was Only 18 Hours before he Expired. The Fever came on Suddenly and Increased So Rapidly, that no Assistance could be procured in time and from many Symptoms M[r]. Holmes thought that the <u>Bite</u> of a favorite Dog was the occasion of his Death –[1]

Friday.. July. 11[th.]
We found Prague a Large Town and the Situation very Picturesque being partly on a Plain and partly on a Hill, United by a Stone Bridge (Over the Moldau) of 700 Feet in Length, and Ornamented on Each Side with Statues in Stone[2] = From the Bridge, the Scenery of Houses Rising to a great Height in the form of an Amphitheatre with The Imperial Palace Situated On the Top is very Fine and the Breadth of the River, with

Page 522

The Two Little islands, Called Great and Little Venice adds much to the Beauty of the Prospect besides which the Battlements declining gradually from the Top of the Hill on the Left to the River at the Bottom makes The Scenery Compleat.[3]

We went after Breakfast to See The Palace – The Suite of Rooms Occupied by the Emperor when he is Here were partly New Furnished about Three years Since at His Coronation = [4] The Bed Hangings were Rich flowerd Crimson Sattin – but no window Curtains throughout

His Apartments neither Here nor at Vienna – but Green Jalousies on the Out Sides the windows,[5] and the Floors are all of Inlaid

---

1. Ingamells' *Dictionary* lists a Mr Hulme and a Mr Simpson as having been in Italy previous to this but no details of either man are known – ed. Mrs Bentham later gives the spelling as "Hulme" on several occasions.
2. The Karlsbrücke over the river Vltava erected between 1357 and 1507. It is adorned with 30 statues and groups of saints.
3. Islands – presumably Střelecký ostrov and Slovanský ostrov.
4. Leopold II was crowned King of Bohemia in Prague in 1791.
5. Jalousie – a type of shutter.

wood – In one of the Rooms was a Portrait of Maria Theresia in the Hungarian Dress –

Page 523

The Prospect from the Windows is beautiful. The City with the winding of the River, and the View of the Adjacent Country – but The Hills Rising very Steep prevents Any Publick Walk, and it is only in the middle of the Town, Where a Long Narrow Slip of Ground is Paved for that purpose, and Planted on Each Side with Trees Having Houses on One Side and a Road for Carriages on the Other –[1]

We Went to the Cathedral a Fine Light Gothic Building near the Palace,[2] – and afterwards went to the Jesuits Church, a very Handsome Building & highly Ornamented within, but what pleased me most, was a Large Window at the End of the Church Fronting The High Altar having an Organ on Each Side and join-ing the Window, with the Pipes gradually declining to the

Page 524

Gallery in Front, which had a Very Light and Elegant Effect –[3]

We went from Hence to the University[4] and the Maison de Ville[5] &c &c and in the Evening to the L'Isle de Venice,[6] a Very Small Island with Only One House upon it, where they Sold wine and where many Persons go to Dine under the Trees, for the Inhabitants of Prague being deprived by the Situation of the City (which is Under

1. Presumably meaning Wenceslaus Square, not a square but a narrow strip of open space. It is of mediæval origins but today the earliest buildings date from the eight-eenth century.
2. The Cathedral (originally dedicated to St. Vitus) was begun in 1344 but at the time of Mrs Bentham's visit had been seriously damaged by the Prussian bombardment of 1757 and was only restored in the late nineteenth century.
3. The church was dedicated to St Ignatius, the founder of the Order, and dates to the second half of the seventeenth century.
4. The Charles-Ferdinand University was created by the emperor Ferdinand III in 1654 by merging the old Carolinum and Clementinum institutions.
5. The Rathaus was rebuilt in the mid nineteenth century but keeping the chapel, tower and some other parts.
6. Strelecky Island – it was formed by the silting up of the river at this point and was in the past called Little Venice (Malé Benatky).

a High Hill with a River at the Bottom) from Having Any Meadow
or Even a Publick Walk to go to, frequent this Small Island, therefore tho' a Stranger is pleased with the Picturesque Scenery yet
Prague is not a desirable Place of Residence –.. The Jews have one
part of the Town Allotted for their Residence –[1]

Page 525

Saturday. July.. 12th.
Left Prague at Six in the Morning, and by Ascending a very
Steep Hill Arrived at the Outer Gate of the Ramparts, when [sic]
we Entered an Open Extended Country without Either Trees or
hedges, And the Roughest Stony Road that Ever any Coach passed
over, which continued for Five Posts, being Threescore Miles to
Aussig, where we Staid the Night: at a Very mean Shabby House,
but it being Midnight when we Arrived, And the Last Ten Miles
having been Jolted Over large Stones which Covered the Road, we
found Ourselves Incapable of proceeding further –[2]

Sunday July 13th
Left Our miserable Inn at Aussig at Seven this morning, and went

Page 526

Thirty Six miles to Dresden, The first Ten miles from Aussig We
found the Road continued to be So full of Large Stones that we
were continually Jolted from One Side of the Coach to the Other
Side, and had Every reason to fear we Should Sustain material
Injury – And the Country continued to be an Extended Plain of
Corn – at The Second Post from Aussig we Entered Saxony,[3] And
Two Posts more brought us to Dresden [4]-. We immediately Went

---

1. The Jewish Quarter or Josefov dates from the thirteenth century and amazingly
   largely survived the Nazi occupation of WWII because Hitler wished to make it a
   Museum of an Extinct Race!
2. Usta nad Labem (Aussig) – town on the river Labe (Elbe) close to the border with
   Germany.
3. Saxony was an electorate until 1806.
4. Dresden – city in south eastern Germany formerly the capital of Saxony

to the Hotel de Pologne,[1] where we Engaged an Apartment of Five Rooms, with Anti [sic] Rooms for which we were to Pay One Ducat per Night tho' it was the Third Floor – an English Gentleman, M[r]. Hulme of Braze Nose College Oxford, whose Family Reside in Cheshire, and who has

Page 527

Himself a Living upon the Banks of the Severn between Worcester And Bridgenorth, Called upon us And Staid the Evening –

Monday July 14th
M[r]. Hulme having an Apartment in the Hotel we were at, was Very desirous of being of Our party, for Since the melancholy Death of his Friend M[r] Simpson, He found being Alone in a Foreign Country very Uncomfortable. We therefore [we] [sic] went this morning together & Visited the Gallery of Pictures belonging to the Elector, Said to be the Best Collection in Europe [2] – and afterw[ds] went to See Some Engravings – and from thence to the Gardens belonging to Count Bruhl –[3] In the Evening took a Ride to the Dostra

Page 528

Dostra, which is a large meadow Ground On the Banks of the Elbe, and being Planted with a Double Row of Trees is frequented by the Inhabitants of Dresden both for Riding and Walking –[4]

Tuesday July 15th.
Mr Hulme went with us this morning to the Bibliotheque, which is a very Handsome Stone Building adjoining to a Publick Garden upon the Banks of the Elbe – The Library consists of Twelve

1. Hôtel de Pologne – a notable inn which existed until 1869. Mozart stayed there in 1787.
2. At the time of Mrs Bentham's visit the electoral collection was housed in the Stallgebäude. The collection had been built up by Augustus II and his son Frederick Augustus II. Famously, Raphael's Sistine Madonna was acquired in 1754. From 1855 the gallery has been housed in a building designed by Semper.
3. Brühl's Terrace – an architectural ensemble on the banks of the Elbe built from 1737 by Count Heinrich von Brühl. It was destroyed in WWII and largely rebuilt.
4. The Ostra-Allée – originally a tree-lined walk. It eventually succumbed to development.

Rooms besides One Large Saloon Supported by Eight Pillars of a Composition resembling marble

The Elector frequently Comes Here and Spends many Hours in Reading – It is Open Every Day from 9 to 12 and from 3 to 6, for Any Person to Read or write in the Rooms – we went afterw^{ds}.[1]

Page 529

into the Under Ground Apartments to See the Collection of China from the Beginning of Its being manufactured in this Country, and likewise Specimens of Every Sort both Useful and Ornamental from India

In the Afternoon M^r. Elliot (the English Minister)[2] And Mr. Gray[3] made us a Visit, And Mr. Elliot Staid to drink Tea with us – after which we Rode to the Grande Jardin Electoral,[4] And M^r. Elliot told us that the Weather Here was more variable tho' not So Damp as in England, for Heat and Cold, frequently Succeeded Each Other Several times in One Day – In the Winter, Traineaux are frequently made use of, as much Snow falls in this Country – The

Page 530

The German Stoves which are Used in this Country to warm the Rooms, frequently gives a Pain in the Head, Especially to those not Accustomed to that Heat

Wed^y July 16
We went this morning to See the Celebrated Green Vault or Private Treasury in the Electoral palace – The First Room contained a

---

1. The library was founded in 1556 but became much enlarged during the reigns of Augustus the Strong and Augustus II. The court library eventually became a state library and was opened to the public in 1788. In 1966 the state and university libraries were united becoming the Sächsische Landesbibliothek. At the time of Mrs Bentham's visit the library was house in the Japanisches Palais. The elector of that time was Frederick Augustus I (1750–1827).
2. Hugh Elliot (1752–1830), diplomat. He had been made ambassador to the Electorate of Saxony in 1792.
3. Possibly Robert Gray (1762–1834).
4. Now the Grosser Garten, it was commissioned by Johann Georg III in 1676 and the accompanying palace was built in 1683.

great Number of Models in Brass of the most Famous Statues, and Among Others, The Celebrated Toro Farnese –[1] The Second Room Clocks of Various Construction, The Third a Collection of Ivory Cut and Pierced in a most Curious manner, and in a Variety of Shapes, Viz all Sorts of Cups And Mugs. And a Ship most

Page 531

Completely Rigged with the Arms of Saxony on the Sails; The Fourth Room had Gold And Silver Goblets, and Cups in Various Shapes, Richly Ornamented with Precious Stones, The Fifth Room, contained a large Collection of Ostrich[s] Eggs formed into different Shaped Cups, and Ornamented with Jewels, In the Sixth Room was a Tea Service of Gold, Set with Diamonds, and a Table which measured in Length an Elle[2] and a Quarter; and One Elle in Breadth, on which was Represented the manner in which The Great Mogul Celebrates The Day of his Nativity – The monarch is Represented Sitting on his Throne, and The Grandees Are Prostrate before Him, and The Portico Crouded with Guards

Page 531a[3]

And Elephants, All richly Adorned with gems.[4] We were likewise Shewn the Order of the Golden Fleece[5] in Three different Setts of Jewels, with Swords, Epaulets, Hat Buttons & Loops, & Stars, all of them either Studded with Brilliants, Or Emeralds Or Ruby[s] And Two Sets of Diamond Buttons for the Electors Dress on Gala Days – likewise The Jewels belonging to the Electress – Viz a Necklace, Earings, Bouquet, and Head Dress; These Jewels are

---

1. The Farnese Bull – classical group excavated in the Baths of Caracalla in Rome in 1545 and removed to the Palazzo Farnese. Like the other Farnese "marbles" this was removed to Naples and is now shown in the Museo Nazionale.
2. Ell (elle is permitted) – a measurement of length – usually about 45 inches in England but varying elsewhere.
3. There are two pages numbered 531 – ed.
4. The royal household at Delhi on the occasion of the birthday of the Grand Mogul Aureng-Zeb – despite the title, a masterpiece of European goldsmiths art created by Johann Melchior Dinglinger in 1701–8. The work is covered with precious stones.
5. Order of the Golden Fleece – prestigious order of chivalry founded in Bruges in 1430.

said to be of Immense Value – As likewise were the Baubles which were Collected by Augustus the 2^d at a great Expence.[1]

From hence, we Entered The Palace. And were Shewn both The Publick and Private Apartments, which were Dirty and Old –[2] we then went to the

Page 532

Warehouse of China, and Saw a great Variety; but the Price much higher than that we give in England for the manufacture of India, and not so Good –

M^r. Gray Dined with us, and we Rode in the Evening to See a House Two Miles distant upon the Banks of the Elbe – which was the Summer Residence of Sir Morton Eden[3]

Thursday July 17$^{th.}$
Went this morning to See the Collection of natural History, which is kept in the Circular Building that Unites the Pavilion of the Zwinger, and was designed for an Orangerie – The Specimens of Marble and Ores of Saxony were great – and it is Said the Silver Mines in Saxony are Inexhaustible – In

Page 533

In One of the Apartments we Saw a most Extraordinary Length of Hair taken from a <u>Polish</u> Lady, It was said to be Owing to a Singular Malady that has been known more than Once to have been in Poland; where the Hair has grown for a length of Time to Such an Excess as to take away the Strength of the Person greatly, And if during the Malady, The hair of the Head is Cut short Every

---

1. The Grünes Gewölbe founded by Augustus the Strong, Elector of Saxony (1670–1733) in 1723 and named after the malachite green colour of the painted interiors. It was restored after WWII and still houses the treasures for which it is famous.
2. The Royal Palace had its origins in the sixteenth century but was largely rebuilt after a fire in 1701. This would have been the palace seen by Mrs Bentham. It was again extensively altered in the late nineteenth century before being, of course, destroyed in WWII.
3. Morton Frederick Eden, Ist Baron Henley (1752–1830), diplomat. At the time he was minister in Berlin but had been at Dresden from 1783 to 91.

part of the Body becomes Covered with Hair; but if it is Suffered to remain till the Cure is Effected by medecine, no Injury is done to the person by this Singular Malady –[1]

In Another Room we Saw Birds, & Beasts Stuffed, and a great Variety of Shells –

In

Page 534

In the Center Building of the Zwinger was a Model of the Temple of Solomon –[2]

From hence we went to the Gardens belonging to the Late Comte de Bruhl, and walked upon the Terrace which is on the Bank of The Elbe, And Commands a full View of The Bridge, which is in Length 540 Feet, and in Breadth 36 feet It is Built of Stone upon fifteen Arches, with a Slight Iron Railing on Each Side, and on the Middle of the Bridge are Centinels, who desire the Persons passing, to Walk on One Side as they go to La Ville Neuve, And the Centinels who are at the Other End of the Bridge, give Similar Orders, by which a Croud is prevented – And Regulations are made in this manner throughout Germany –[3] In

Page 535

In the Evening, we Rode to the Valley of Plauensche Ground, which Resembles many Little Valleys in Derbyshire, being very narrow, and having only the width of the Road and a Running Stream between very High Rocks – We Stopt at a Publick garden at

---

1. Probably an example of Hypertrichosis or Werewolf syndrome.
2. The Zwinger was dedicated to knowledge and housed the natural history collections, prints & drawings, and a library. At the time of Mrs Bentham's visit the displays included a model of the Temple of Solomon in Jerusalem. This had been commissioned by a Hamburg senator in 1680 but sold after his death to the King of Poland. The model was moved to Dresden but returned to Hamburg in 1910 and is now in the Museum für Hamburgische Geschichte. It is about 12 metres square.
3. The Augustus Bridge was rebuilt in 1907–10 and replaced that seen by Mrs Bentham which had been built between 1727 and '31, and itself replaced an earlier structure.

the Entrance of this Valley, & Saw many Ladies & Gentlemen who were Sitting under Tree^s – Drinking Beer and Eating Cakes –[1]

Friday July 18th

We went this morning with M^r. Hulme to See The Fortress of Kœnigstein, celebrated for the Strength of its Situation[2] – being upon a Perpendicular Rock of Very great height, and the Sides all round Equally Steep Except the Entrance which is formed by Art – At the Top of this Rock is a Level Plot of Ground, on

Page 536

On which is a Considerable Wood, And Some Meadow Ground, & There were Several Houses, Occupied by The Governor and Officers of the Garrison, and likewise a State Prison – The Well which Supplied them with Water was 1800 Feet in Depth, (whereas the Well at Dover is only 360 Feet deep)[3] The Well upon this Rock was made by Order of the Elector Augustus, at the Time that He Intended to have had a castle Built Here – but afterwards he was Satisfied with having Only a Pavillion Built; to which the Present Elector Comes often, This Fortress is Two Posts Viz Four Hours Drive from Dresden, And upon Our Return we Crossed The Elbe at the First Post, And went to Pillnitz The Electors Summer Residence, This

Page 537

This Place is Situated Close to The Elbe, with High Hills at the End of the Garden, at the back of the Chateau, which is Built upon

---

1. The Plauensche Grund – a picturesque and rocky part of the valley of the river Weisseritz. It has now been spoilt by developments and road building, but was at the time of Mrs Bentham's visit a tourist attraction and popular with artists. Johan Christian Dahl, amongst others, painted a view in the valley. Mrs Bentham is presumably comparing it with valleys in Derbyshire's Peak District.
2. Königstein – town on the Elbe close to Dresden dominated by its fortress. Most of the building dates to the sixteenth to eighteenth centuries. It was used as a prisoner-of-war camp in both World Wars.
3. The well at Königstein is about 500 feet in depth whereas that at Dover Castle approaches about 400 feet.

the Plan of a Chinese Palace – and tho' it is Small, it appears to be a very Comfortable Residence –[1]

We Saw the Elector And The Electress, with their Daughter a pretty Girl of Twelve years of Age Returning from their Private Chapel; to which They go Every day at Eleven in the morning, and again At Four in the Afternoon –[2]

We Returned to Dresden and Dined at Six o Clock –

Saturday July 19[th.]
We went this morning to Visit M[r]. Elliot The English Minister who Shewed us the different Apart[mts] in his House just New Furnished

Page 538

And Commanding a very pleasant View of the Bridge over The Elbe, and Comte de Bruhls House And Gardens on the Opposite Side, He likewise Shewed us Some Rose Trees Twelve feet High, in a Garden adjoining to the Publick Library; and while we were Walking with him, he advised us to Avoid going to Holland, as the French were at this time within 30 Miles of Helvoet, and therefore He advised us to Return to England by Hamburgh –[3]

After parting from M[r]. Elliot, we went to See the different Churches – Nôtre Dame[4] And Saint Croix,[5] both Lutheran, The First is of an Oval form within, and fitted up with Pews below, and Circular Galleries Above, And appeared more like a Theatre than a Church = we Observed Several

---

1. Schloss Pillnitz on the river Elbe. It consisted of three buildings, two of which were built with Chinese elements.
2. Frederick Augustus I (1750–1827). He married Amalie of Zweibrücken-Birkenfeld in 1769. Their one surviving child was Princess Maria Augusta (1782–1863).
3. Via Hamburg in Germany and from there presumably by ship to England.
4. The Frauenkirche – it was erected 1726–43 but was, like much of the city, destroyed in WWII. It has recently been rebuilt, 1994–2004, to mark the re-unification of Germany.
5. The Kreuzkirche – originally a Romanesque basilica, the church was damaged by fire and bombing on several occasions, lastly, of course, in WWII. It was rebuilt and reopened in 1955.

Page 539

Priests, with ladies Sitting Close to them who Seemed to be at Confession – LEglise Catholique is a very handsome Building Situated near the Bridge, and by a Short Inclosed Gallery has An Entrance into the Electoral Palace.[1]

In the Evening we went to the Gardens belonging to Prince Antoine,[2] The Electors Brother, which are Situated at One End of the City and Inclosed by very Low walls that are Open to Every Point of View, and are adjoining to Corn Fields; The House is Cheifly One Floor, and has in the Center Three windows, with a pediment Top – And Five Windows on Each Side – From hence we went to Count Bruhls, And walked upon the Terrace in his Garden, which Terrace is of a great Height above the

Page 540

River and Commands a Beautiful View of the Bridge Over the Elbe –

The Streets in Dresden Are Swept Every Saturday, and having in the middle many Places Open between the Pavement Covered over with Boards, The Common Sewer is kept Clear And Conveys away all kind of Dirt

Near Dresden is a Large manufactory of Table Linnen, Equal to Our best Irish –[3]

Sunday July 20th.
Mr. Gray Breakfasted and Dined with us – At Eleven He took us to L'Eglise Catholique, Where we Saw The Elector and Electress

---

1. The Cathedral of Dresden, formerly Katholische Hofkirche, was restored in the 1980s after bombing in WWII and again after reunification, including the bridge to the castle. The original church was designed by Gaetano Chiaveri and completed in 1751.
2. Prince Anton of Saxony (1755–1836). He succeeded his brother as King of Saxony in 1827. The Prinzenpalais became the home of the second son of the royal house from 1781 onwards. It was badly damaged in WWII and razed thereafter.
3. Saxony was one of the chief linen producing centres of Germany at the time.

with their Daughters in One Tribune – And in Another were The Electors Two Brothers And their Wives[1] – And in Another

Page 541

Tribune The Electors Sister[2] – after The Sermon there was a band of musicians who Played in the Organ Gallery and Several Vocal Performers – Afterwards we saw The Elector and Family go through the Gallery Leading to The Palace, The Electress and the Ladies were Dressed in S<u>acks</u> of Silk,[3] And the Trains of Each were holden by a Page – The Elector And likewise his Brother had on The Order of the Blue Ribband.[4]

In the Evening we Walked in the Little D'Ostræ, a Publick Walk, which is Planted with Tree[s] On each Side, and is nearly Opposite to the Publick Library. And divided by The Elbe[5] – We met Prince Antoine and his Wife, who is Daughter to the Duke of Parma –[6]

Near

Page 542

Near Dresden are The Mines of Cobolt, from which is made The Fine Saxon Blue, and much of it is Sent to England to make the Fine Blue China.[7]

The Bohemian Glass Lustres Are very Elegant, and are Sold at a very Low Price – The Panes of Glass in the Windows at Vienna frequently measured 34 Inches by 29

But The bedsteads in general measured only Two Feet Six Inches.

---

1. Anton married Maria Theresa, Archduchess of Austria (1767–1827) in 1787.
2. Theresia Maria Josepha of Saxony (known as Maria Anna) (1761–1820). She remained unmarried.
3. Sack – a woman's gown falling loosely at the back with a train from the shoulders.
4. Probably the Order of the White Eagle, Poland's highest order of chivalry.
5. The Ostra Allée – a former walk which led from the Zwinger across the river Elbe towards the village of Ostra.
6. Actually Princess Caroline of Savoy, daughter of Victor Amadeus III.
7. Probably meaning the Erzebirge mining district close to Dresden.

At Vienna and at Prague we paid for Breakfast Sugar One Florin Viz 2$^{s.}$ 4$^{d.}$ p Pound[1] And could not get good Tea for less than 14^{s} p pound[2]

The German Stoves are allowed to be very prejudicial to Health as they make no Circulation of Air in the Room –

Page 543

At Prague The late Emperor Joseph Ordered The Convent belonging to the Jesuits to be Converted into offices for Post Letters, and likewise for Post Horses,[3] And when we applied at the Chancery office for Passports The principal Officer in that Department Observed, what Advantages an English gentleman Enjoyed, who could Travel and yet leave His Property Secure, but not So with an Austrian, nor a Subject of any Despotic Power

We had found a great Thickness in the Air Ever Since we left Italy, very much like that we Experienced in England in the Summer of the year 1783[4]

Page 544

Monday July 21
We left Dresden this morning Early, having been much pleased with The City and its Environs, which are Bounded by a range of Hills about 20 Miles distant, All of them Covered with Vineyards Or Woods, The latter being the Chief Fuel used in the Country And the Vineyards producing a Vin de Pays like Small Rhenish A very pleasant Beverage –

The Elector is said to be a Very Sensible man, and Lives much in the Domestic Circle of his own Family, & With his Two Brothers

---

1. That is two shillings and four pence in pre-decimal currency.
2. Likewise, fourteen shillings in pre-decimal currency.
3. Presumably in part of the Clementinum, the ex-Jesuit complex now housing the national library.
4. The summer of 1783 in England was exceptionally hot and was known as the "sand summer" due to the fact that a volcanic eruption in Iceland caused there to be an exceptional amount of ash in the atmosphere.

who are both married, and his Unmarried Sister, all of them having Apartm[ts] at Pillnitz[1] – but at the Same time it is Said he has
much Hauteur – and Shews his Brothers as well as his Ministers,
that He will be Obeyed –

The

Page 545

The Elector and all his Family are Catholics, tho' his Subjects are
Protestants – It is Observable that there are a great many Deformed
Persons here, and in general the People are Low in Stature – The
Peasantry do not wear Either Shoe or Stocking and we met this
morning great numbers of them carrying Vegetables to Market –

We were Three Hours in going the First Post to Messein,[2] where
The China manufactory is – The Building is Spacious and Situated
Upon a Hill, with The River Elbe Running at the Bottom; but as
the Manufactory at Berlin[3] is thought to be much Superior to this
we only Stopt to Breakfast And went on 4 Posts to Leipsich being
about 70 miles[4] – The Country after the First Post begun to be
Open, for there we Crossed The Range of Hills that Encircles the
Plain on which Dresden is

Page 546

Situated – but tho' the Country continued fertile in Corn there was
not any Vineyards, yet it was very Pleasant till the Last Post before
Leipsich. When it was Stony, Sandy, and a marshy Level – It was
Ten at Night when we Arrived at The Hôtel de Saxe at Leipsich,
And not having had any thing to eat Since nine in the morning, we
were glad to find M[r.] Hulme (who left Dresden One Hour before

---

1. Pillnitz – suburb of Dresden to the east of the city on the river Elbe. The Wasserpalais
   and Bergpalais were designed by Matthäus Pöppelmann (1662–1736).
2. Meissen – town 25 km from Dresden on the Elbe. The production of porcelain began
   there in 1710.
3. Frederick II of Prussia occupied the town in 1756 and relocated some of the artists to
   Berlin to found the Königliche Porzellan Manufaktur.
4. Leipzig – city in Saxony notable as a centre of culture and learning.

we did in the morning) had Ordered Supper, which we partook of together And Retired at Midnight –[1]

Tuesday July 22[d].
We Went after Breakfast to See The Church of Saint Nicholas, which has been for the last Seven years under the hands of different Workmen,[2] Ornamenting it

Page 547

And fitting it up in the Elegant Style of a Musick Room – The Roof or Canopy Over The Pulpit is in the form of a Dome, and within it is Painted in a variety of beautiful Colours, and Supported by Four Gilded Columns, and on the Top a Gilded Bunch of Flowers like a Girandole – The Approach to the Altar is like An Oblong Vestibule, with Three Paintings (in Pannels) on Each Side, And Gilded Girandolas between. The Waggon Roof to this Approach is Rich in Carving = The Body of this Church is fitted up in a Circular Form, with a Covered Gallery Round it, like a Place of Publick Amusement – and Over it An Open Gallery = The Seats Below of a Corresponding form And at the Entrance of the Church A Small Vestibule Exactly opposite that which is the Approach to the

Page 548

Altar, and on each Side are Elegant Openings like Small Chapels, One with The Baptismal Font, The Other intended for the Burial Service = The whole has the Appearance of One of the most Elegant Concert Rooms in Europe. The Circular Roof being Supported by Pillars like Palm Trees – This Church has been Constantly used Every Sunday for Divine Service, tho' the Workmen are Employed in it Every Other day in the Week –

The Streets in Leipsic are most of them Spacious, and there are two Oblong Open Places for the Sale of Poultry and vegetables,

---

1. Hôtel de Saxe – the hostelry dates to about 1711 and existed until 1909. After WWII the building was demolished and a new hôtel built on the site.
2. The Nikolaikirche – begun in 1165 but remodelled into a Gothic hall church in the sixteenth century. At the time of Mrs Bentham's visit it was being given a neo-classical interior by Johann Dauthe.

Round the Town are Two or Three Paralel Walks, Planted with Trees And a Road on the Outside for Carriages – not that many of the Inhabitants keep Coaches, for Here

Page 549

Are not any Noblesse; but all are in Trade, and being of Equal Rank, They form Parties to meet Every Evening at a Publick Garden adjoining to the Walks, where there are Several Large Rooms in which They Play at Cards, & Drink Beer & Smoak the Pipe; Every Wednesday upwards of Two Hundred Dine Here, and Stay the Evening – In One of the Shops I observed a great Quantity of Wedgwoods Ware, which they Sell as Cheap as in London – Plates from Two Shillings a Dozen to Four – There was likewise Some very Elegant Sets of Dejeuné,[1] as High as Five Guineas for Two persons, It was Pale Green Ornamented with white and Gold –

There were many Houses in Leipsic that had Five Stories in the Roof, besides being Four Stories High from the Ground –

Page 550

The University of Leipsic is no more than a large Old School Room, and is a very miserable Shabby Building, near it, and under the Same Roof, are Apartments for the Professors –[2]

In the Evening we went with M![r] Hulme and drank Tea at the Great Room in the Publick Garden, where I Observed the Men Played High, at a Game resembling Loo –[3] And throughout Germany They are fond of Billiards –

Wed[y] July 23[d]
Left Leipsic early in the morning The Day proved So Extremely Hot that we were Six Hours in going The First Post to a miserable Town, where we Changed Horses, And was Eight Hours

---

1. Déjeuner – a breakfast set. It has not been possible to identify the actual set but it is likely to have been Queen's ware.
2. Mrs Bentham is possibly referring to the old Collegium Paulinum, an ex-monastery building. It has been replaced by a new building begun in 2007 but still retaining the old name.
3. Loo – a card game.

more in getting to Wittemberg,[1] Where we went directly to See the Portraits of

Page 551

Luther, and Melancthon, and underneath Each, a Small Piece of the pavement was made to Open, an [sic] upon a Brass Plate was Inscribed "Martin Luther Died 13th. Of the Callens of march Aged 63 in the year 1546, and Upon the Other was Inscribed Phillip Melancthon Died 13 of the Callans of May in the year 1560 Aged 63 = thus it appears that both these Men Lived to an Equal Age –[2]

The Country through which we had passed this day, was for the First Post Open Corn Country, but the land appeared to be very poor, The Two last Posts was in general Extensive Fir Woods – The Town of Wittemberg is One Long Street, Our Inn The Golden Star was On the Outside the Town, And very Clean –[3] but the Dinner So Singular, that it may be mentioned First The Soup was Cold and made of Beer and Raisins – next Red Herrings

Page 552

With Cucumbers Sliced – & next Boiled Beef made Red – next Fish (like Cod) Cut in Slices and afterw[ds] mutton Cutlets.

Thursday July 24th

Left Wittemberg at Six in the morning, And went through a Sandy Country for Two Posts – And the People who were Ploughing in the Fields had Three oxen a breast – The few Villages we passed through [had] Ovens in the Road, Standing at a distance from the Houses – We were Six Hours in going the First Two Posts, And then was Obliged to Stay One Hour for Horses = From Hence the The [sic] whole Country was a deep Sand, not a Blade of Grass, or Corn to be Seen for many miles – The Last Post we arrived at was a Small Town Called Beelitz,[4] where the mistress of the Post

---

1. Officially Lutherstadt Wittenberg.
2. Martin Luther (1483–1546), priest and church reformer, and Philip Melanchthon (1497–1560), theologian and reformer.
3. The Goldener Stern – it no longer exists.
4. Beelitz – historic town in Brandenburg.

House detained us Two Hours and would not permit us to go on with the Post Horses we Came with any further, but Obliged us to wait for Horses

Page 553

Coming, that belonged to her – This Circumstance made it Eleven at Night before we Arrived at Potsdam[1] & got to Our Inn L'Hermite[2] near the King of Prussia[s] Palace –[3]

Friday July 25th

Went immediately after Breakfast to See the Palace which was Inhabited by the Late King and in which He Died –[4] and where in his Last Illness He used to be Amused with Seeing from the Windows the Officers and Soldiers Exercise in the Court yard or garden = In One Room he could See Every Person that came Over The Bridge to Enter The Town which greatly Amused Him – This Palace is a Large handsome Building Situated very near the River,[5] and from The number of Boats that are continually Passing, is Pleasant; but it is very much Out of Repair, and the Furniture, which was formerly very

Page 554

magnificent is now very Old – In Some Rooms there appeared a great Profusion of Silver –

From hence we went to the Gallery at Sans Souci, It was Built during the Seven Years war, It is in Length 300 Feet, In breadth 36 Feet, And 42 Feet in Heigth; with a Waggon Roof at Each End, and in the Center a Dome – The whole Richly Ornamented with Gilding, and the Sides fitted with many of the best Pictures of The Flemish School = The Building is of Stone, and the Front decorated with Statues, The Floor was formed with Large Squares of Fine Marble; In the Front was a Continued Range of windows,

---

1. Potsdam – town near Berlin on the river Havel and seat of the Kings of Prussia and later Emperors of Germany.
2. L'Hermite – a notable inn in Potsdam for many years.
3. The Stadt-Schloss, Potsdam.
4. Frederick the Great – he died at Sanssouci on 17th August 1786.
5. River Havel.

and at the End were Stairs Leading to the Garden;[1] From this Gallery we

Page 555

We went to Sans Souci, which nearly adjoins it, and is an Elegant Stone Building, and has likewise Only One Floor, Situated upon a Fine Terrace commanding a full View of the Town of Potsdam, & the Winding of the River, with the Bank of Wood above it –[2]

The Center of this Building is a noble Circular Saloon with Three Windows, And on Each Side of this Room are Three other Rooms, which were at this time Inhabited by the Two Princesses who are married, One to The prince Royal, The Other to his Brother –[3] In One Room was their Harpsichord,. In Another The work Basket &c appeared as if it was the Room They constantly Occupied,. And In the Third were Two Small Tent Beds with Green Silk Curtains &c and beyond in a Small Bow window Room at the End was the Library

Page 556

Opening into a Cradle Walk – The Other Side of the Saloon in the Center was occupied by Les Dames D'Honneur, who were in Attendance on the Princesses – All The Windows in this Building were fronting The Terrace, Viz Three in the Center Bow, and Six on Each Side, with Three in a Bow at Each End – The Apartments were Furnished Elegantly but not magnificent – At a little Distance is a Building which Corresponded to The Gallery, and is devoted to the Reception of Company, as The King frequently gives Dinners to his Officers and Generals = This Apartment was Rich in Gilding – from Hence We Went to The Belvedere and had a

---

1. The Picture Gallery (Bildgalerie) at the palace of Sanssouci was built between 1755–64 to house the collections of Frederick II. The sculptures on the garden front are by Johann Gottlieb Heymüller and Johann Peter Benckert.
2. Sanssouci built for Frederick the Great (1712–86).
3. The future Frederick William III (1770–1840) married Louise of Mecklenburg-Strelitz in 1793 and his brother Louis Charles (1773–96) married Frederica of Mecklenburg-Strelitz in the same year.

good View from it of The Country And the Environs.[1] We next went to See The New Palace

Page 557

which was Built between the years 1763 and 1769[2] – The Building is of Plaister Coloured like Red Brick, with Pilasters of Stone, and Elegant Corinthian Pillars – The Back Front consists of a Center with Five Windows – then Ten windows on Each Side, and a wing of Eight Windows – The Center Room is very Singular, Resembling a Grotto filled with most Beautiful Shells, Chrystals, Ore[s] and Various Sorts of Marble; Three Arches on Each Side with Fountains, and the Doors on Each Side which Communicate with the Apartments in the Palace are Covered with Shells So as to appear part of the Grotto – The Suite of Rooms On Each Side and likewise the Apartments over, are most magnificently Furnished with Rich Silk, and the Chairs have

Page 558

have Silver and Gold Frames, A great Number of Fine Pictures And Beautiful Inlaid Floors; The Domestick Offices, are in Two Elegant Buildings, forming part of a Circle in the Front of the Palace – The Back Front is to the Garden, which is bounded by a Wood, in which are a great Variety of Walks that Communicates with Sans-Souci – And there are many Single Statues, and likewise Groupes, in the wood, and an Elegant Chinese Temple[3] – but The present King never Resides more than One month in a year in this magnificent Palace And that is only for the purpose of giving a Fête –

In the Afternoon we Went to See The Tomb of the Late

1. The Belvedere aus dem Klausberg. It was designed by Georg Christian Unger and erected 1770–2. The building was badly damaged in WWII but finally reconstructed 1990–3.
2. The New Palace was built between 1763 and '69 as Mrs Bentham informs us. It was erected to celebrate Prussia's success in the Seven Years' war. The palace escaped any damage in WWII. The Grotto Hall mentioned is attributed to Carl von Gontard.
3. The Chinese House was built by the garden architect Johann Gottfried Büring between 1755 and '64 in the Chinese Rococco style popular at the time.

Page 559

King, and his Father, in the Church of Le Garrison, and from thence we walked about the Town, and in the Gardens of the Old Palace –[1]

Tho' the Coffins of the Kings were placed in a Spacious Marble Masoleum, yet that of the Late King was Only Plain Black Tin – The Masoleum is under the Pulpit in the middle of the Church Where The King Receives the Sacrament with the people, nor is the Closet in which The Royal Family Sit, Ornamented in the least, but it is Opposite to The Pulpit –[2]

The Town of Potsdam appears like a deserted Town, The Grass grows in many of the Streets, which, tho' wide and well Built, have not any Foot Pavement – but most of

Page 560

the Houses have a flight of Steps at the Door, which leads to a Dirty kennel of Stagnated filth in the Front of the Houses, & is not Only very disagreeable, but must be Unhealthy, as there does not appear to be any Sewers to Carry it away –

The Facades to the Houses are Elegant in Architecture with Corinthian Pillars & Pilasters, but appear to be Inhabited by Very Poor People, Each Family having Four Soldiers to Live with Them, for whom they are Obliged to Cook what Food they Chuse to Have –

In the middle of the Town is Le Bassin, a Large Square Planted with Trees – forming different Walks, and in the Center is an

---

1. The Garrison Church was a Calvinist institution and the parish church of the royal family until 1918. It was designed by Philipp Gerlach and completed in 1732. Largely destroyed in 1945, a rebuilding programme has been controversial due to the fact that the Nazi Party used the building during its time in power.
2. The coffins of the kings were removed to safety during WWII and finally reburied at Sanssouci in 1991 after the reunification of Germany.

Island, on which, is a Brick Building to which the Late King frequently Came to Converse with a Favorite Minister –[1]

Page 561

The Church of Saint Nicolas has a Beautiful Façade.[2] It is Situated in a Large Open Place Opposite to the Palace,[3] And a fine Obelisk is in the Front of the Entrance to the Palace, but in this Open Place is a Market kept, where we Saw almost Every Woman who Came to Buy have a Bright Brass Kettle in her Hand –[4]

The Maison de Ville is in this market Place, but like the Palace, and Every Other Building, is falling into Decay –[5]

The Front of the Palace towards the Garden consists of a Center of Five windows with Columns Supporting a Pediment – The adjoining Range of Building which is set back consists of Nine windows on Each Side, And then a projecting wing of

Page 562

Five windows – The Side Fronts contain 32 windows divided into Six and Three – The Front to the Street is a Semi Circular Low Building, with a Portico Dome, Inclosing a Court yard –

The Present King never makes use of the Old Palace, And the New Palace is Only made use of during a Week Or Two in a year to Give Fêtes, To Sans Souci He goes Occasionally, but his Favorite

1. The Bassinplatz – originally a swampy area, it was drained in 1737–9 and a Dutch-style pavilion was built on an island at its centre. The latter was demolished 1945/6 to make way for a Soviet military cemetery.
2. St. Nicholas' Church – the present building was designed by Karl Friedrich Schinkel in the 1830s. Again, it was badly damaged in WWII. That seen by Mrs Bentham was erected by Philipp Gerlach in the 1720s, itself replacing a Gothic original.
3. The City Palace was built between 1744 and '52 but was burnt out in a bombing raid in 1945. It was reconstructed (2013) but not without a great deal of controversy. The building now houses the parliament of the State of Brandenburg.
4. The original obelisk in the Old Market was erected between 1753 and '55 to a design by Georg Wenzeslaus von Knobelsdorff (1699–1753) and was 25 metres high. It was badly damaged by bombing in 1945 and rebuilt 1978/9 using marbles from Russia and Yugoslavia.
5. The Old Town Hall (Alte Rathaus) was designed by Jan Bouman. It was badly damaged in WWII and subsequently rebuilt. It is now a museum.

Residence is a Small House of Five windows in Front, And Seven
on Each Side; and Three of the windows in Front Are Supported
by Columns, and left Open at the Ground Floor, forming an Open
Arcade, The Ornaments are painted white in the Center – and
Painted At Each End Red to resemble Brick

Page 563

The House Contains Only a Ground Floor and One Floor Over
it, with A Lanthorn or Gazebo On the Top;[1] It is Situated about
One Mile from Potsdam – And the Road leading to it, is from the
Bridge At the End of the Avenue from Potsdam towards Berlin,
which is Planted with a double Row of Trees, and Crosses at this
Place a River, So that Potsdam is in an Island –

At this House the Present King generally Resides during the
Summer months like a Private Gentleman

Saturday July 26th
Went this morning to Berlin[2] Twenty Two Miles – The Road
in general was Paved, The Country Sandy And Open – At the
Entrance Of Berlin The Streets appear Handsome being Wide and
well

Page 564

Built, but the Stench Arising from the Gutters of Stagnated Filth
is very Bad –

We were Obliged to Drive on Our Entering Berlin immediately
to the Custom House, where after Staying Some time, the Person
there told us the officer would Come to Our Inn and Inspect our
Bagage; we then went to L'Aigle D'Or[3] to Dinner And afterwards
to the Bankers –

---

1. The Marmorpalais designed by Carl von Gontard and Carl Gotthard Langhans as
   the private residence of the king. It was damaged in WWII and restoration work only
   began in 1990. It is now open to the public.
2. Berlin – at the time the capital of the kingdom of Prussia.
3. Der Goldene Adler – the inn survived into the nineteenth century.

Sunday July 27th
We went after Breakfast to See The Palace –[1] The Queen[s] Apartm[ts]
were richly Furnished with Velvet And Silk manufactured at
Berlin, The Chimnies were Open & made for Burning of wood
– The Rooms in general were Hung with the Same Silk as The
Furniture, The Floors were all Parquee, or Inlaid.

Page 565

Over The Queens Apartments were Rooms devoted to Foreign
Visitors, and Others in which The King Gives Dinners upon
particular Occasions – The Side Board of Silver, and the Gallery
where The Musicians Play during Dinner was of Massy[2] Silver;
So great a Profusion of Silver is probably not to be Equalled in any
Court in Europe

After Seeing this Palace, we called On M[r]. Paget the Third Son
of the Earl of Uxbridge who was now the English Minister at the
Prussian Court,[3] & afterw[ds] Called on D[r]. Browne,[4] having Letters
for Both – We then went to See Mont Bijou where the Queen
generally Resides in Summer, but at this time was gone to Some
Publick Baths –[5] The

Page 566

Apartments consisted of 72 Rooms all upon the Ground Floor, &
not Any Rooms Over. The Building is upon a Singular Plan, being
Two long Suites of Rooms parallel to Each Other, & United by
One Room at the End of Each Suite, which Communicated with
the Other, and both Range of Rooms Surrounded by a Shrubbery..

1. The Berliner Schloss – the palace seen by Mrs Bentham dated to the early years of
   the eighteenth century. Again, the building was badly damaged in WWII and was
   eventually demolished by the East German government in the 1950s. It is now being
   rebuilt as a museum.
2. Massy – weighty and solid.
3. Sir Arthur Paget (1771–1840), politician and diplomat. He was sent to Berlin as
   Envoy-extraordinary in 1794.
4. A Dr. M. Browne was made physician to the court at Berlin in 1789.
5. Montbijou Palace – a rococo palace in central Berlin. It was badly damaged in
   WWII and the ruins were razed by the East Germans in 1959. At the time of Mrs
   Bentham's visit it was the home of the queen, Frederika Louisa of Hesse-Darmstadt
   (1751–1805).

The Situation is at the End of One of the Principal Streets in the Town.

From Mont Bijou we went to the Catholic Church Built in the Form of the Pantheon at Rome[1] –. The Ceiling of which was beautiful, resembling The Rays of the Sun, from hence we went to LEglise Garnisa where we found the Congregation Consisted Cheifly of Officers[2] – In

Page 567

This Church we saw Five Emblematical Figures in Five Frames, Each with a Medallion Of Some General who had been Killed in Battle, and we saw Three Monuments of different Kings of Prussia – we then went to L'Eglise de Chateau[3]

In the Afternoon went to the Opera House which is of an Oval Form, but Only Open during Carnival or upon Some Great Festival, And no Person can at those times be Admitted but by Billets from the King, as is is allways Free of Expence – The House is Elegant, And the Royal Box in the Center Supported by 8 Pillars very Richly Gilt – The Pit is Lighted by a Large Lustre in the Center[4]

Page 568

Of the House, which contains 50 Wax Candles with a Reflector

In the Evening we went with M[r]. Hulme to le Comedie,[5] which

---

1. St Hedwig's Cathedral – it was the first Catholic church built in Berlin since the Reformation and was designed by Georg Wenzeslaus von Knobelsdorff but modelled on the Pantheon in Rome. It was completed in 1773 but again, badly damaged in WWII and reconstructed between 1952 and '63.
2. The Garnisonkirche – already noted.
3. The Schlosskirche at Buch? This church was begun in 1731 to the designs of Friedrich Wilhelm Diterich. It was destroyed in WWII but rebuilt in a simplified form in the early 1950s.
4. The Linden Opera – the original building was designed by von Knobelsdorff and opened in 1742. This building was burnt down in 1843 and replaced.
5. Possibly the Komödienhaus opened in 1776.

was The Deserter,[1] and we got a Logement in the First Range, The House tho' Small was Pretty & well Lighted. The Performance was Over before Eight o Clock, and it was full Day Light when we Returned to Our Inn –

Monday. July. 28th.

Went this morning to See the Kings Apartments, which were Divided by a very handsome Saloon opposite to The Parade.. In this Saloon The Officers wait before They are Received in the Presence Chamber –[2] On the Left of The Saloon is a fine Suite of Rooms, Furnished with the

Page 569

Richest flowered Silk manufactured in Prussia, which is the Same as the Lyons – The Chandeliers and The Lustres were magnificent, The Floors Parqué in a Variety of Shapes, The Ceilings Painted, and the Ceiling of the Concert Room Gilded Carved work, mixed with Looking Glass – And the Ornaments of the Room Correspondent – The Large Dining Room was from the Ceiling to the Floor Looking Glass On One Side in Pannels and the window Shutters between were the same, which at Night, had the Effect of One Continued Mirror through the Room – The Squares of Glass in the windows were 31 Inches by 28 – and many of the Looking Glasses in different Rooms were 112 Inches by 52 – The Library Tables and Others were made in a Variety of Shapes, & all of mahogany

Page 570

The Musical Clock Played like a Harpsichord Accompanied by a Flute –

On the Right hand of the Saloon of Entrance were a Suite of State Apartments most magnificently Furnished – The Presence Chamber was Crimson Velevet Richly ornamented with Gold

---

1. This is mostly likely *The Deserter* by Charles Dibdin published in 1773. It is known to have been given on the Continent. Another possibility is *Le Déserteur* by Louis-Sébastian Mercier.
2. Probably the Schweitzersaal and the Königszimmer, both of course now destroyed.

– and at the Bottom of the Room Exactly Opposite The Throne was a very Fine Marble Figure of Time, upon a Pedestal, with a Golden Globe at his Foot, and a Golden Scythe in his Hand. The Crown and Cushion at the Top of the Canopy and in the Center of the window Curtains

We did not See any carpets, but the Fire Place[s] were Large and Open, to Burn wood – There were many very Fine Pictures –

Page 571

particularly a Beautiful Magdalen Couchant, Copied from Corregio, [sic] Or from Bartoni[1] [sic] – from Hence We Went to See The China manufactory, which was Beautiful but very Dear –[2] Some of the Plates had landscapes in the Center, The Price of which was Four Guineas – a Plate – And a Tea Set of Eighteen Cups and Saucers was Fifty Guineas – The white Common Plates without any Flower Or Figure was One Shilling Each – This China when Imported into England is Taxed Cent per Cent – And the Prussian Government Prohibits Entirely Wedgwoods manufactory –

We likewise went to See the Military Academy, where 260 Boys Are Educated at the Kings Expence from the Age of 13 to 17 –[3]

Page 572

And Exercised Every day as Soldiers, And do Duty as Such in this Academy; From Hence, we went to Le Place Guillaume, where Five Statues are Erected to different Prussian Generals, at the Extent of a Square Piece of Ground, that is Planted all round with Trees –[4]

The Streets of Berlin appear wide and handsome, and Near the

1. Possibly a copy of the Penitent Magdalen by Pompeo Batoni in Dresden. It was destroyed in 1945.
2. The Berlin porcelain manufactory was first established in 1751 but in 1763 Frederick II adopted the firm as his own and it became the Royal Porcelain Manufactory Berlin.
3. The Académie des Nobles, or Académie Militaire founded by Frederick II in 1765.
4. The Wilhelmplatz in Friedrichstadt. It was decorated with statues of military heroes after the Seven Years' War in 1769.

Palace are Two Large Open Places, which have distinct Building at the upper End, that appear very Handsome, One of which, is the Dwelling of Prince Henry,[1] One [*sic*] One Side is the Publick Library,[2] and Opposite to it, is the Opera House – and at the Other End, is L'Eglise Catholique, and All are Fine Specimens of Architecture.

We Entered the Library which was a very Large Room Divided

Page 573

by Open Book Cases, from hence We went to a Statuary[s], and saw a Strong Likeness of the Late King – In the Afternoon we Drove to The Park which adjoins to One of the most Beautiful gates of the Town at the End of the Ville Neuf and the Publick Walk, It is a Wood of Considerable Extent divided into a great Number of Rides and Walks, which are United in the center, by a Circular Plantation;[3] Near the middle of the Park is Belle Vue, a Large House belonging to Prince Ferdinand,[4] And near the House is the River Spree – In the wood are Several detached Houses where People go to Drink Coffee &c And at one of these Houses we had Tea, and Saw Several Elegant Dressed Persons Playing at cards, and many Ladies Knitting under the Shade of the Tree[s], who appeared to be Persons of Fashion

1. Prince Friedrich Heinrich Ludwig of Prussia (1726–1802). He was generally known as Heinrich. The palace, built between 1748 and '66 became the main building of the Humboldt University in 1809 when Prince Henry's widow left.
2. The Royal Library had a long history but was granted considerable assets and autonomy in 1770 and a new building was erected on what is now the Bebelplatz between 1775 and '85. This building, restored since the war, is now the home of the Faculty of Law of Humboldt University and the library has new premises.
3. Of course, the notable Brandenburg gate designed by Carl Gotthard Langhans (1732–1808) and built between 1788 and '91. It replaced the old gate in the town wall. The thoroughfare, now Unter den Linden, leads to the Tiergarten, once a royal hunting ground but opened to the public by Frederick II in 1742.
4. Prince Augustus Ferdinand of Prussia (1730–1813), general and prince of the royal house of Hohenzollern. Bellevue palace was built in 1786 as a summer residence for the prince by Michael Philipp Boumann (1747–1803) and was the first Neoclassical building in Germany. It was damaged in WWII and is now the residence of the President of Germany.

Page 574

Tuesday July 29th.
We went this morning to Charlottenberg One Hours Drive from
Berlin, Situated at the Extremity of the park;[1] It is a Palace belong-
ing to The King, but it appeared to be neglected and Dirty, The
Building was of great extent, and the Gardens were large, and
Bounded On One Side, and at the Bottom, by The River Spree
– There was Several Elegant Buildings dispersed about the
Grounds, which were partly laid out in the English Style, and as
well as ground Could be, that was quite Flat: On One Side, Berlin
was the Object, and the Town of Spandau On the Other Side –[2]
after walking near Two Hours in these Gardens, we went to See
a very Elegant House with a pretty garden, belong[g] to Madame
Reitz, who is said to

Page 575

to be a Favorite of the Kings[3] – upon Our desiring Permission to
See the House, a young Gentleman Came, and in English, desired
us to Come into the Parlour, and after Some Conversation, he
Ordered a Servant to Shew us both House And garden, and we
were told He was Lord Templeton –[4]

Upon Our Return to Berlin we went to The Church of Saint
Nicholas, to See the Monument Erected to the Memory of
Puffendorf who was Buried there in 1642 –[5]

---

1. Charlottenburg – now a suburb of Berlin on its western side. The town was founded
   in 1705 and named after Sophia Charlotte of Hanover, consort of the future King
   Frederick I of Prussia. After his elevation the palace was greatly extended.
2. Spandau – now one of the "boroughs" of greater Berlin, the town lies to the west of
   the city at the confluence of the Spree and Havel rivers.
3. Mrs Bentham is being diplomatic. Madame Reitz was Wilhelmine Enke (1753–
   1820), mistress of Frederick William II. She married three times, lastly for convenience to Johann Rietz, a councillor to the king. She was later ennobled as Gräfin von
   Lichtenau.
4. John Henry Upton, 1st Viscount Templeton (1771–1846). The house was known as
   the Lichtenau palace. It no longer exists.
5. Samuel von Pufendorf (1632–94), German philosopher. He died in Berlin and his
   monument still exists. The Nikolaikirche was the oldest church in Berlin. It was
   badly damaged in WWII but restored in the 1980s.

In the Evening we went to The Gardens of Mont Bijou, &
Examined The Plan of the House, which was One Continued
range of Building projecting a little in the Center, & Contained 72
Rooms With 58 windows towards the Garden –

Page 576

Wed[y] July 30[th.]
This morning more than One Thousand men were exercised upon
the Parade before the Windows of Our Inn – The Men made a fine
Appearance, their Regimentals Blue Coat, with Red Collar & Red
Cuffs, and white waistcoat and Breeches – Black Stockings and
Large Hat.

After Breakfast we went to See The Kings Stables and the Manége,
in which, One of the Kings Servants was breaking the Horses, and
told us He had been Twelve times in England – we then Went to
See The Riding House, which was Ornamented on Each Side with
Looking Glass, and Afterw[ds] went to L'Ecole Veterinnaire, a Place
where the Horses are Electrified, & there we saw a Large Electrical
machine –[1] Near this

Page 577

was an Elegant Small Building where Anatomical Lectures upon
Horses are Read to Pupils –[2]

These Buildings are Situated in a Small garden which was
Purchased by The King for the purpose, as Every thing relative to
the Army Engages his Attention –

At Two o Clock we went to Dine with M[r]. Paget, The Chargé
d'Affaires, and at his House we met D[r]. Browne Physician to The
King, and M[r]. Ricards who is a Genevese[3] & Resides Here with
D[r]. Brown[s] Family, & has been at Berlin Some years – And like-

1. Possibly to test reaction to galvanism, the action of electricity on the muscles.
2. The Tieranatomisches Theater by Carl Gotthard Langhans built in 1790. The building still exists and is now used as an exhibition space.
3. Mr. Ricards – not traced. Possibly Ricard?

wise we met a M^r. Aylmer Nephew to Sir Chas. Whitworth.¹ At half past Five the Company Separated & we took a walk in The Park

Page 578

Thursday July 31st

This Morning being Showry, we Drove about the Town to See the different Streets, and when it Ceased to Rain, we walked Sous Les Arbres which is the Only Publick Walk in Berlin.² It is in the Neuve Ville (Called Fredericstadt) near the Palace, and where most of the Best Houses are Built – On each Side – In Front of the Houses a double Row of Tree^s forms Two Paralel Roads for Carriages, and the Center is Railed in for a Walk, & at the farther End is an Open Circular Place with a very Fine Stone Portal Supported by 8 Pillars And Called The Brandenburgh Gate –³

We Dined at D^r. Browne^s with M^rs. Browne and Three Daughters

Page 579

And Mr Paget, M^r. Ricard, & M^r. Aylmer = before Six the Company Separated, & we went to walk in the Park with Mr Hulme –

Friday August 1st.

This Morning M^r. Hulme left us And proceeded on his Journey to Hanover, as we thought it not advisable to Travel the Same Road on the Same Day, least we Should not be Supplied with Post Horses, as M^r. Hulme allways wanted Four Horses, And we wanted Five –

M^r. Paget Chargé d'Affaires de Son Majesté Britannique, and Le Docteur Browne Conseiller Privé Et Medicin du Roi, with another Gentleman, Came to Our Hôtel, and Dined with us – The

---

1. Sir Charles Whitworth (c.1721–78), politician. His daughter Catherine married Sir Henry Aylmer in 1774, hence the connection. Mr Aylmer – not traced.
2. Unter den Linden which, of course, still exists.
3. The famous Brandenburg Gate built by Carl Gotthard Langhans in a severely neo-classical style between 1788–91. It actually has 12 Doric columns, 6 each side and the whole is surmounted by a quadriga.

Day being very Showry, I did not go Out – but prepared for Our Departure which was fixed for To Morrow –

Page 580

Saturday Augst 2^d
Left Berlin at Four in the morning, and went through the Beautiful Brandenberg Gate to The Park, which we passed through to Charlottenberg, and from thence to Spandau, and Passed near the Fortress[1] in which Baron Trenck was Confined[2]

The whole Country a Deep Sand, but finely wooded to Charlottenberg, and afterwards Open And Cultivated, but the Crops of Barley to Brandenburgh[3] were Poor, We Arrived there at Five o Clock, And went to The Black Eagle a decent Inn, but Paid most Extravagantly for a miserable Supper[4] The Town is Small divided by a River, and Only One tolerable Street and that Badly Paved, The Country around Low & Marshy, The adjoining Fields had many

581

Trenches Cut in them, which were filled with Black Stagnated water And the Roads So Bad that the Postilions were frequently obliged to Cross the adjoining Fields –

Sunday Aug$^{st.}$ 3^d
Left Brandenberg at Three in the morning, The Road, within a Short distance from the Town, was through large Woods of Fir, & deep Sands for many Miles. And then the Soil was Black, And Muddy, from which, Six Horses with difficulty carried us on,

---

1. Spandau Citadel – a fortress built between 1559 and '94. It is on an island at the confluence of the Spree and Havel rivers and is now a museum.
2. Presumably Baron Franz von Trenck (1711–49), soldier. Trenck's father was also a soldier in the Austrian army and thus Franz was born in Italy though he was of Prussian nationality. After a somewhat colourful military career he died in a prison in Brno.
3. Brandenburg an der Havel – town, as its name suggests, on the river Havel west of Berlin.
4. The Schwarzer Adler is still listed in Baedeker's *Northern Germany* for 1913.

we Sometimes observed Poor Crops of Barley, & Potatoes, but frequently Only Heath; and tho' we only Stopt at the first Post House to Breakfast, yet it was Nine o Clock before we Arrived at Magdeburgh.[1] However we found a good Inn, Le Roi de Prusse,[2] which determined us to Continue there the next Day – We had Violent Rain & Thunder all this Day.

Page 582

Monday Aug[st] 4[th.]

This morning we walked about The Town, which is Large, tho' Only One Wide Street in it, but the Houses in it are well Built and Handsome, and there Appeared to be Some good Shops; Magdeberg is the Capital of the Dutchy of that Name in the Circle of Lower Saxony, and is Situated on The River Elbe, which is divided Here into many Branches, and the Streets united by Bridges –

We went to the Cathedral, which was formerly a magnificent Building, but now very Old, and the Back part blocked up by very Shabby old Buildings – The Choir is Dirty, tho' at the High Altar is a Table of Jasper Stone, Eighteen Feet in Length, And Eight Broad, & Two Thick, The Organ is reckoned very Fine, We Saw The Statues of the

Page 583

Five Wise Virgins with Countenances Smiling, And the Five Foolish Lamenting, Both done very Well, and The Marble Statue of S[t]. Maurice The patron of the Church, with Some very fine Carving in Bass Releivo about the Pulpit, and likewise The Emperor Otho Over The Altar of a Chapel –[3]

---

1. Magdeburg – town in central Germany on the river Elbe. It was heavily bombed in WWII.
2. Roi de Prusse – not traced.
3. The cathedral was begun in the early thirteenth century in the Gothic style but was badly damaged in WWII. The latter included the destruction of the organ. The grave of Otto I, Holy Roman Emperor, the sculptures of St Maurice and St Catherine, and the five wise and foolish virgins still exist.

Luther the Reformer,[1] was Educated in this City, which is Supposed
to be the Strongest Place in the King of Prussia' Dominions.. We
went hence to the Citadel,[2] And Saw the Place where The Marquis
de La Fayette was Confined –. It was a Low brick Building, with
Two windows very Strongly Barricaded with Iron, And a wooden
Fence at a little Distance in the Front of it, to prevent any Person
hearing him Speak – but the Building was Situated upon a large
Open

Page 584

Square in the Center of the Citadel[3]

Upon the River we observed a great Number of Mills for Grinding
Corn; and there is a Considerable Trade carried on by the
Reception of merchandise brought from Hamburgh On the Elbe,
and Sent from Hence by Land to Leipsic – The Vessels which
Come from Hamburgh are Flat Bottomed, like the West Country
Barges in England, and have like them, Dirty Cabbins at the End
– The Ramparts near The Cathedral form a Pleasant walk, being
on the Side of the Elbe,[4] but the whole Country Around is a Flat
dreary marsh And watery. –. Frederick The First Built a Palace in
this City, which was in a Large Handsome Square opposite The
Cathedral, And on One Side was the Arsenal.[5]

Page 585

And On the Other Side were Houses for the Duke of Brunswick[6]

1. Of course, Martin Luther (1483–1546).
2. The fortress was built on an island in the river Elbe from 1683 to 1702. It was razed in the 1920s.
3. The notable Gilbert de Motier, marquis de Lafayette (1757–1834), soldier. He famously fought in the American War of Independence and was a member of the Estates-General of France. Becoming persona non grata in France, he fled to the Netherlands and was captured and imprisoned by Austrian troops in 1792.
4. The ramparts were begun in the thirteenth century and expanded over the years. By the time of Mrs Bentham's visit they were the strongest fortifications in Prussia. Those behind the cathedral still exist.
5. The Princes' Palace in the Domplatz became the Museum of Natural History in the nineteenth century but was destroyed in WWII.
6. At the time Charles William Ferdinand, Duke of Brunswick-Wolfenbüttel (1735–1806).

And the Governor, – and a double Row of Tree[s] Planted in the Square –[1]

Tuesday Aug[st]. 5th

We left Magdeburgh at Five this morning, and went Over a Wide Extended Plain for Thirty Miles to Helmstadt – The first 20 Miles was One Continued Slough, for throughout The King of Prussia[s]. Dominions there is not any regular made Road, And the Postilions Drive as they can best pick the way, & The Ground being marshy, and in many Places Covered with Water, The carriages frequently went into Holes on One Side, or the Other, which made Our Journey not Only Unpleasant

Page 586

But really Dangerous; For the first two Hours after Leaving Magdeberg, we had it in full View, but afterw[ds] we Ascended a Rising Ground, and had on Each Side Cultivated Ground Viz Wheat, & Barley, with Potatoes, And Cabbages, intermixed, but the Road continued a Slough till within Ten Miles of Helmstad, It then became Sandy –

We Arrived at Helmstad[2] at Four in the Afternoon, and Staid the Night, tho' we found Our Inn The Prince of Prussia but Very Indifferent –[3] yet we thought it not Advisable to Travel in the Night – The Town is very Ancient, and Situated in the middle of an Open Extensive Corn Country – and Round the Outside of the Town Walls, is a walk Planted with Tree[s] –[4]

Page 587(a)

Wed[y] Aug[st] 6th–

We Left Helmstad at Five this morning, and immediately found a Regular made Road, which convinced us that we had Entered the

---

1. The Domplatz.
2. Helmstedt – formerly an historic Hanseatic town, it is 45 kilometres west of Magdeburg and in the post-war period was an important crossing between East and West Germany.
3. An inn called the Prinzen von Preussen once existed in the village of Ströbeck close by.
4. The town formerly had a circuit of walls.

Dutchy of Brunswick[1] for The King of Prussia has no made Road in any part of his Kingdom that we had Seen Except, from Berlin to Potsdam

The Country now became Rich in Corn, and the Rising Grounds Covered with Woods – at Twelve o Clock we Arrived at Brunswick,[2] & immediately went to The Hôtel D'Angleterre,[3] but could not be Received – It was The Great fair, and The Town full of Merchants from Hamburgh and Leipsic &c who displayed all kind of merchandize in the different Shops – However The People of the

Page 588(a)

Inn Recommended us to Private Lodgings Opposite, where we had an Elegant Apartment, and were Supplied from the Inn with whatever we wanted, but Paid Equal to One Guinea a Night for Our Lodging –

Before Dinner we went to See The Arsenal, which we found very Dirty, The Building had been a Church, and was now made use of for cannon, which were placed at the Bottom, and The Gallery[s] formed Two Rooms for Small Arms, all of which appeared Rusty –[4]

In the Evening went to The Play – and afterw[ds] Mr Douglass (The Son of Lord Douglass) who we were acquainted with at Rome, Came to Visit us, & with him

1. The Duchy of Brunswick-Lüneburg – the duchy became part of the greater Germany in the nineteenth century but was only officially dissolved in 1918 becoming a member state of the Weimar Republic.
2. Brunswick (Braunschweig in German) – historic town in Lower Saxony, a member of the Hanseatic League and at the time, capital of the Principality of Brunswick-Wolfenbüttel.
3. Hôtel d'Angleterre – the building became a hotel in 1745 and survived as such into the nineteenth century. It was badly damaged in WWII but rebuilt using the original entrance doorway.
4. The arsenal was housed in a former monastery, the Paulinerkloste, from the beginning of the eighteenth century until 1867. The building itself was demolished in 1903.

Page 587(b)[1]

M[r]. Mesurier, who was lately Come from England to Supply the
Place of M[r]. Ballard, who was with M[r]. Douglass in Italy, but being
Obliged to go to England, M[r] Mesurier Came to Supply his Place
as a Travelling Companion to M[r]. Douglass.[2] They had Both been
Dining with The Duke And Dutchess of Brunswick, who Dine at
Two o Clock, and expect their Visitors to Leave them Soon after
the Coffee is drank, which is allways before Four, And if there is
any Evening Party, The Company Return at Six, & the Interval is
generally devoted to making Calling Visits[3]

At Brunswick, and all the way from Dresden, we Observed The
Peasants to wear Caps with a Broad Furr Border round The Face –

Page 588(b)

Thursday Aug[st] 7th
This Morning we went to See The Palace belonging to The Duke
of Brunswick.[4] The Front was a Pediment in the Center of Five
Windows, Ornamented with Columns, and 4 windows On Each
Side – The Palace is then joined by Two Extensive [side] Ranges of
Buildings, formin [sic] on the whole 3 parts of a Square, And The
Fourth left Open for The Approach – The Center Building had
been lately New Furnished, And One large Room Contained The
5 windows under The Pediment – and the 4 windows was in Two
Rooms, on Each Side the Center – One, and at the Back of these Five
Rooms were Several Smaller, all in the modern Style, with Floors

---

1. There are two page numbered 587 and 588.
2. The Hon. Archibald Douglas (1773–1844). He had been travelling in Italy with his
   tutor Charles Ballard who was replaced by Mr Mesurier.
3. Duke Charles William Ferdinand of Brunswick-Bevern (1735–1806). He married the
   Princess Augusta of Great Britain, sister of George III, in 1764.
4. The palace was begun in 1718 by Hermann Korb but burnt down in 1830. Its replace-
   ment was badly damaged in WWII and itself replaced by a replica façade housing
   spaces for cultural activities and a shopping centre.

Page 589

Parqué, and Hung with Rich Silk. The German Stoves were placed in Recesses of a Beautiful Composition resembling Marble –

One of The Side Ranges of The Palace, is Occupied by the Hereditary Prince, and the Other by The Duke and Dutchess of Brunswick –. The New furnished Rooms in The Center being devoted to Gala Days and Visitors – adjoining to the Back part of the Palace is The Church, which The Family attend, and which has a Communication with The Apartments – while we were looking at The Church, The Duke passed us, and politely Bowed, He appeared to be a very Handsome man, and much like an Officer –[1]

From hence, we went to The Cathedral a very Old Building,[2] where we saw The

Page 590

Tombs of Prince Henri Coeur de Lion, and many Other Princes of The Family of Guelfes, The Tombs were in the Souterrain[3]

In the Evening we went to the Italian Opera, given by The Duke, it being the Birth Day of Some part of his Family; The Duke and Dutchess, and the Hereditary Prince and Princess were there, but did not Sit in their State Box, but in the Balcony Boxes on Each Side of the Stage, And their State Box, which is in the Center of the House, was Occupied by their Attendants in the Same manner as if They had been there. The House was intolerably Dirty and very Small –[4]

Friday.. Aug[st] 8th.
We left Brunswick this morn[g] at Five o Clock, and went through an Open Corn Country

---

1. The church was presumably destroyed along with the palace in the fire of 1830.
2. The cathedral of St Blasius – it was dedicated in 1226 but became a Lutheran church after the Reformation.
3. Henry the Lion, Duke of Saxony (c.1129/31–1195). He was a member of the Welf dynasty and is buried in the crypt.
4. Presumably the Opernhaus am Hagenmarkt opened in 1690.

Page 591

to Hanover,[1] but the Roads were very Bad till within the last Ten Miles, when we found a regular made Road tho' Sandy.. It was Planted on Each Side with Trees, and had Small Pyramidical Mile Stones; and at the Entrance of the City, was a Toll Gate, & Turnpike Tickets, Similar to those in England.[2] We went directly to L'Hotel de Londres.[3]

Saturday.. Aug.st 9th
This Morning we went to See Les Ecuries[4] belonging to the King of England, in which were near 300 Very fine Horses, many of Them milk white, and many of Cream Colour, from hence we went to the Palais de la Busche,[5] now belonging to the Duke of York, who had it Furnished in an Elegant Style when He

Page 592

Married the present Dutchess, whom He brought Here, & Staid Ten Days, before They proceeded to England —[6]

The Outward Front of The Palace is a Center of Three Windows, & Five on Each Side – The Suite of Rooms are 5 in Front, and as many looking to a Court yard Behind, where the Offices are for the Servants; The Situation being in a Street, there is no Garden but The Rooms and Doors &c Are Painted in a Peculiar Elegant Style by an Italian [Name Varona][7] who Resides at Berlin, and was Employed in

---

1. Hannover – capital of Lower Saxony on the river Leine. It was, of course, at the time still united to the British crown, George III being also Elector of Hanover.
2. In the eighteenth century tickets were given to travellers passing through a tollgate as a record of payment. The toll was levied on roads built and maintained by various parties.
3. The building dates to 1682 but became "Im Schilde von London" or simply "London-Schenke" in 1714. It was destroyed in WWII.
4. The palace was destroyed in WWII and presumably the stables also.
5. Known as the Altes Palais, it was destroyed in 1943. The palace was originally built for Johan Clamer von dem Bussche (died 1786), Minister of State, but was purchased by the Duke of York in 1786.
6. Prince Frederick, Duke of York and Albany. (1763–1827), second son of George III. He married Princess Frederica Charlotte of Prussia in 1791.
7. Varona – not traced.

doing the Same to the 8 New Rooms in the Palace at Brunswick;[1] – The Furniture is of Rich Lyon[s] Silk, of Various Colours, & The Rooms Pannelled with the Same – The

593

The Floors Parqué, The Entrance for the Carriages & The Great Staircase, Highly Ornamented with Painting, and the whole truly Elegant – On the Ground Floor was only Anti Room And Dining Room one [sic] One Side of the Gate Way, and On the Other Side Three Small Rooms for the use of the Duke, with a Private Staircase leading to the Apartment above Stairs – We went from hence to the Kings Palace On the Opposite Side of the Street, It is a Large Old House, The Rooms are round Three Sides of a Court yard.[2] The Furniture very Old & Dirty, but there were Some very Handsome Silver Chandeliers – about The year 1789 at the Time of The Kings Malady,[3] Several Models and Plans

Page 594

of Furniture & Bedding, was Sent from England, with Orders to make Every Article immediately; and the Hanoverians worked Nights as well as Days, for a Considerable Time, till The Bed, and many Other Articles were Completed; But as The King did not Come, They are now become very Dirty, tho' never have been used

A very neat Chapel has a Communication with the Palace, And likewise there is One to the Theatre, and the Opera House, but there is not the least garden belonging to it, the Situation being in a Street, It appears Confined –

In the Bed Room Occupied by George the Second, was a Private

---

1. The Braunschweiger Schloss seen by Mrs Bentham was begun in 1718 by Hermann Korb but burnt down in 1830. A second palace was badly damaged in WWII and replaced by a shopping centre with a replica façade.
2. The Leine palace – it was begun in 1676 but rebuilt between 1816 and '44.
3. Referring to the intermittent mental illness of George III of Great Britain (1738–1820).

Door leading to a Staircase which Communicatd with the Apartment Occupied by The Countess of Yarmouth –[1]

Page 595

We went from hence to Mont Brilliant, a Small House near a Mile from the City, in which The Countess of Yarmouth used to Reside during the Summer –. The Gardens were laid out in the English Style, and are now Open to the Inhabitants of the Town, but They are not Large –[2]

In the Afternoon we went to the Publick Library,[3] to which The Late King, George the Second, was a great Benefactor, Here we Saw One of the Three Bibles that were Printed at Oxford upon Vellum – The University of Oxford had One, and Cambridge had Another, and the Third was Sent to this Library by George The Second, who was Accustomed to Send Books Every year to the Value of 600 Crowns, and Often more, but never Less –[4]

Page 596

We Saw here a Model of Leibnitz, and Two of his Portraits,[5] The Building is Large, but without any ornaments, The Two Lower Floors are for the Archives, The Third is One Large Room, but the Walls are only white washed, and the Books On each Side, and One Row down the middle of the Room –

Near this Building is The Parade, which is Planted with Several Rows of Trees and is the Publick Walk, at the Upper End of which, is a Fine Bust of Leibnitz under a Cupulo Supported by Pillars –

---

1. Amalie Sophie Marianne von Wallmoden, Countess of Yarmouth (1704–65), mistress of George II of Great Britain.
2. Mont Brillant – a pleasure palace immediately beyond the town. It was demolished in the mid nineteenth century and replaced by the Welfenschloss – the summer residence of the royal family and now part of the Leibniz University.
3. Now the Gottfried Wilhelm Leibniz Library – National Library of Lower Saxony.
4. This was the celebrated "Vinegar" Bible printed by John Baskett at Oxford in 1713. Although fairly common, only three copies were printed on vellum. That at Hannover still exists and is kept in the Leibniz Bibliothek, Inv. Cim 1/34: 1,2.
5. Gottfried Wilhelm Leibniz (1646–1716), German philosopher. He died in Hannover.

and raised upon a Mount[1] – besides This walk, there are Several pretty detached Pieces of Ground Planted with Trees – near the Town, and afford Pleasant Walks

Page 597

We Saw Several Servants belonging to the King of England in the Scarlet & Gold Livery as is given at St James',[2] And in the Ecurie, The King^s Livery is the Same as at the Meuse Charing Cross,[3] from hence We went to the Arsenal,[4] but did not find any thing worth Our Attention, and afterw^{ds} we went through the different Streets to The Hôtel de Ville –[5]

The whole Length Portraits of The King & Queen of England were Sent to Hanover immediately after their Marriage –[6]

      Sunday August 10th.
Mr Douglass & M$^{r.}$ Le Mesurier having Arrived Last Night from Brunswic, went with us this morng to See the different Churches both Catholic & Lutheran, & after Dining together, we went to Herenhausen[7]

Page 598

about a Mile distant, The Road to it is Planted with Tree^s – in Four Rows, leaving the Center for Carriages – & The walks on Each Side – The House had a Hall of Entrance which went quite through, and on Each Side were Four Rooms, all New Furnished, & The

---

1. The Leibniztempel designed by Johann Daniel Ramberg (1732–1820). It is was moved to the Georgengarten, 1934/5 and still exists. The bust of Leibniz is by Johann Gottlieb Schmidt and is now housed in the entrance hall of the Technologie Centrum.
2. That is the Court of St. James's – the official court of the British monarchy.
3. That is the King's Mews which was formerly at Charing Cross in London.
4. The old arsenal is now part of the Historisches Museum.
5. The Rathaus or Old Town Hall. It dates to the early fifteenth century but was much restored in the nineteenth century.
6. The full-length portraits of George III and Queen Charlotte by Allan Ramsay (1713–84) now at Buckingham Palace. A number of copies were made. Those for Hannover are now in the Historisches Museum.
7. Schloss Herrenhausen – the seventeenth-century summer residence of the Hanoverian royal family. It was destroyed in WWII but rebuilt from 2009 – '13 and now houses a museum.

Ceilings as well as The Rooms were papered – Several of the Beds had Silk Furniture, – and likewise an Apartment upon the Ground Floor with bed Room &c adjoining to the Garden Intended for the King, and lately made ready for his use, as (it was supposed) he was Coming to Reside Here On account of His Malady –[1]

The Gardens were laid out in Strait walks, & Temples in diff.t Places, with Figures & vases &c and The Fountains were Playing in Several parts of the Garden, which

Page 599

they usually do Every Afternoon from Five o clock till Seven, for an Amusement to the Inhabitants of Hanover, who frequently go there. at Our Return, we visited the Publick Cimitere, & Saw the Tomb of Wessler[2] – – And In the Evening told M.rs Douglas & Le Mesurier Our Intention of leaving Hanover to Morrow Morning –

Monday Aug.st 11.th

This Morning at Five o Clock we left Hanover, & went Fifty One English Miles to Diepnau,[3] which Place we did not Arrive at till Nine at Night, tho' we never had Stopt longer than to Change Horses; as Our usual method was to get Some Milk & Boiling water, at the First Post House we Came to, which with Our own Tea & Sugar, & Bread, which we had with us, gave us a delicious breakfast; tho' it was frequently in a Barn, for In

600

In going through Westphalia, the peasants Houses in general are large barns, at the upper End of which is a Fire place, but no Chimney for the Smoak, And on Each Side are Stalls for the cattle, and The Poultry are in the Middle – Their Beds are placed near The Fire, divided by Small partitions on Each Side, Such a Barn we found the Post House at Diepnau, with a Room for Travellers

---

1. Of course, the so-called madness of George III.
2. Wessler – not traced. The surname is very unusual – ed.
3. Diepenau – town on the post road between Hanover and Osnabrück.

on Each Side of the Entrance, & Here We were obliged to Stay the Night.

The Country from Hanover to Diepnau, was Flat – but Cultivated, Except One or Two Extensive Heaths, & they were marshy, and frequently Covered with Muddy water – The Roads So Bad, that the Postillions Stopt to Bait Every German Mile, (which is Five English) tho' we had Six Horses – at the First Post

601

From Hanover, we met an English Courier, who had just Come from the Duke of York at Breda –[1] Between Hanover And Diepnaw, we Crossed the River Weser in a Boat –

Tuesday Augst 12th.
Left Our Barn at Diepnau this Morning at Five, and had found it more Comfortable than we Expected – we Arrived about Noon at Boomte,[2] which was going Twenty Six Miles in Seven Hours with Six Horses to Our Coach – Here we found a Decent Post House Built with Plaister, And like a Habitable House – with the Arms of England Over The Door, which proved we had Entered The Bishoprick of Osnaburg, The Road had been from Diepnaus

Over wide Extended Marshy Heaths, full of Black mudd and water, but from Hence to Osnaburgh, it

602

It was better, & The Country was Cultivated; The distance Fifteen Miles, And we Arrived at Four o Clock and went directly to the Kaiser a very comfortable Inn –[3]

Before we Dined, we went to See The Duke of Yorks Palace,[4]

1. The Duke of York was at the time leading Anglo-Hanoverian forces in the Allied campaign against the French in the Low Countries.
2. Bohmte – town on the river Hunte 20 kilometres north-east of Osnabrück.
3. A hotel called the Kaiserhof survived in Osnabrück until WWII.
4. The Prince-Bishop's Palace was built from 1667–75 but now houses the University of Osnabrück.

as Bishop of Osnaburgh[1] – It is a Handsome House, with 17 Windows in Length in the Front, & a Mezzanine Floor both Below & Above The Principal Floor – There is a Court yard in Front, And a Garden with a lawn & a Shrubbery Behind – The Hall of Entrance near a Hundred Feet, with a handsome Staircase in the Middle, opposite the Door of Entrance, The Staircase was a double flight of Steps uniting at the principal Floor Opposite The Door in the Center of the Musick Room, which was 84 by 42 – and Communicated at the End with a Spacious Dining Room, and at the Other End

603

With The Dutchess[s] Dressing Room, Bed Room, & Wardrobe; all these were in the Front of the House towards the Court yard, and the Dining Room had likewise a Communication with the Offices Below – The Back Front towards The Garden, consisted of Eight Rooms, all New and very Elegantly Furnished with Rich Lyons Silk in Some Rooms, & Thin Lutestring in Others; The Ceilings, Doors &c most Elegantly painted in the Italian Style by Varona, who has been many years in the Service of the King of Prussia, & the Man who Painted the Duke of Yorks Palace at Hanover – We were Shewn Two Sets of Chairs ornamented with the Work of the present Queen of England,[2] & Sent as a Present to The Duke of York, the Embroidery Of one Set was upon Cloth, the Other upon Nankeen, & both very Beautiful & the Flowers very Natural

604

Wednesday Aug[st] 13th.

The Country about OsnaBrugh is Pleasant, being Small Inclosed Fields, with Rising Ground at a Distance, Covered with Woods – The Town is not Large, nor the Streets wide, nor is there any Publick walk, nor any appearance of Trade – We left this Place at Five in the morning, and after the First Post, found the appearance of the Country much Changed, and saw again the miserable Effects

---

1. Ernest Augustus, Duke of York and Albany (1674–1728), the younger brother of the future King George I of England. He became Prince-Bishop of Osnabrück in 1715
2. Charlotte of Mecklenburg-Strelitz (1744–1818). She married George III in 1761.

of Prussian Governm^t for Here The King of Prussia' Dominions commenced again, and we saw nothing the whole Day but wide Extended marshy heath, frequently Covered with Mud & water –

At Nine o Clock we Arrived at the Village of Bentheim^1 40 Miles from Osnabrugh, Situated upon part of the Small Range of Hills which Separates the Extensive

605

Marshy heaths from those we had Crossed this Day – At the Top of the Hill, and adjoining to the Village, is the castle, formerly the Residence of the Count de Bentheim, but now Inhabited by an Officer with Twenty Hanoverian Soldiers; It being Mortgaged to the King of England. ^{2} The Ground about the Village is Cheifly Meadows in Small Inclosures

Thursday August 14th.

We left Bentheim this morning at Five o Clock, and after Driving round Small Inclosed Fields which are at the Bottom of this Small range of Hills, we Crossed Another Extensive Marshy Heath, and then Entered an Inclosed Cultivated Country, with a Number of Whiteters[?] Grounds,^{3} and Houses Painted in the Dutch Style, We Dined at Delden,^{4} a Small Town, & afterw^{ds} Went to Devenden, & Staid the Night –

606

Friday.. August.. 15th.

We left Devenden^5 this Morning at Five, The Town appeared large & like a Dutch Town very Neat – There was a Navigable River near the ramparts on the Out Side of the Town –. We breakfasted (as usual) at the First Post, & then went to Vourthuyson^6 where we

---

1. Bad Bentheim – town in Germany close to the Dutch border.
2. The castle, though suffering many vicissitudes is still owned by the Prince of Bentheim-Steinfurt.
3. Presumably whitening grounds.
4. Delden – town in the Dutch province of Overijssel.
5. Presumably Deventer – town in Holland.
6. Voorthuizen – village in the province of Gelderland.

found only a Single House, therefore we Drove on to Amersfort, a Considerable Town, but found no Inn that appeared Comfortable for a Night,[1] we therefore took Some refreshment and hastened on to Utrecht[2] where we Arrived just before the gates were Shut, & went directly to the Place Royale, which we found An Excellent Inn.[3]

Saturday Aug[st]. 16th
Walked before Breakfast about Utrecht, which appears to be a very desirable Town for families to Reside at,

607

Whose Fortunes will not Admit the Expence of Living at the Hague

The markets at Utrecht are are [sic] well Supplied, The Houses are Well Built, and in the Environs, The Walks are Pleasant –

At Ten this morning we left Utrecht, and passing through Several Small Towns and Villages, Arrived at The Hague at Five, And went directly to the Ouden Doelen,[4] a very good Inn, and the best Situated of any at the Hague – but Lord and Lady Kerry being there, with Fifteen Servants, rendered Our Accomodations not So good as they would Otherwise have been –[5] The Road from Utrecht to the Hague, we found Pleasant, being frequently by the Side of a Canal, and The Distance only 35 Miles –

---

1. Amersfoort – town in the province of Utrecht.
2. Utrecht – city in central Holland and capital of the eponymous province.
3. The Place Royale Inn – a notable hostelry at the time.
4. Logement De Oude Doelen – a notable hotel at the time. It survived into the nineteenth century.
5. Francis Thomas-Fitzmaurice, 3rd Earl of Kerry (1740–1818). He married Anastasia Daly (d.1799) in 1768. They were known to be extravagant.

608

Sunday Augst. 17th
We went this morning to the Dutch Church,[1] and afterwards we
walked in the wood, and met The Prince of Orange who paid great
Attention to us –[2]

In the Afternoon we went to The French Church,[3] and Heard a
most Excellent Sermon upon The Sixth Commandment "Thou
Shall not Kill".[4] The Preacher Alluded Strongly to the present
Times – The Service begun by The Clerk Singing part of a Psalm,
The Reading a Chapter from The new Testament – The Minister
then in the Pulpit Examined a Boy (who was Standing at the
Foot of the Pulpit) Some part of the catechism And afterw^{ds} He
Preached an Excellent Sermon and when

609

He had Ended, He continued in The Pulpit and Christened a
Child, Coming down Only to Sprinkle it with water when it was
Named, and Ascending again to The Pulpit to finish the Service

My Dear Son went to Dine with Lord St Helens,[5] who likewise
had Invited me, but as I heard there would not be any Other lady,
I declined going –

In the Evening we walked through The wood, intending to go
to The House belonging to The Prince of Orange, but before we
Arrived there, we saw The Prince, and all his Family, Sitting in
the wood & Drinking Tea –

1. Possibly the Grote of Sint-Jacobskerk, or the Nieuwe Kerk. The latter was built
between 1649 and '56 by Peter Noorwits. It is now a concert hall.
2. The prince had to retire to England in the following year due to the worsening political situation.
3. Probably meaning the Old Catholic Church. It has a baroque interior dating to 1722.
4. As given in Exodus, 20.13 and Deuteronomy, 5.17.
5. Alleyne Fitzherbert, Baron St Helens (1753–1839), diplomat. He held a number of
posts but was at this time ambassador at The Hague.

Monday. Augst 18th

We walked before Breakfast about The Hague, which is the most desirable Town in Holland to Reside at.. The great Number

610

of handsome well Built Houses adjoining Each Other,. The very Pleasant Wood for walking, And Excellent Fish and Fruit, with Every Sort of Provision Good, makes The Hague more Eligible than any other Dutch Town

After Breakfast we left The Hague, and in Three Hours Arrived at Rotterdam, the most Pleasant Commercial Town I ever Saw in any Country,. We got an Apartment at le Marechal de Turenne,[1] & Spent the remainder of the Day in walking about the Town by the Side of the Canals – The Houses were Built of Brick and Tiled or Slated, And the Foot paths Paved with Clinkers = On Our Road Here we had Observed many Large Wooden Buildings, in which the Tobacco Leaves were Drying – & a great deal of Tobacco Growing in the Fields –

611

Tuesday Augst. 19

Left Rotterdam this morning, & Went to Helvoet, where we found Letters from my Dear Son in England – We Dined & Staid the Night at Dobson^s Inn,[2] a tolerable good House, but before we Dined Our carriage was put On Board The Princess Royal a packet Commanded by Capt. Deane[3]

In the Even^g we wrote Letters to my Dear Son in England, and likewise to The Banker at Hanover for Letters which had been Directed for us And never Received –

---

1. Le Maréchal de Turenne – a popular hotel in the eighteenth and into the nineteenth century. Franz Liszt stayed there.
2. Dobson's Inn – not traced.
3. Presumably a regular service as both this packet and the captain are mentioned elsewhere as making the same crossing.

Wed^y Aug^st 20th
Staid this Day at Helvoet, The wind not permitting us to Sail.

Thursday Aug^st 21
We were Called this morning at Six o Clock, and Hurried On
Board The Princess Royal Capt Deane

612

Where We got Some Boiling water and breakfast upon Deck,
Expecting to Sail immediately, but The Wind Changed, and it was
Twelve o Clock before we left The Harbour – In Two Hours After,
a Boat followed us with a Signal that Dispatches must be put on
Board, and Our Ship was Obliged to wait for Colonel Hutchinson
of The Guards[1] to Come On Board with them. Our Other passengers were Sir Jeromie Fitz Patrick,[2] and an officer from the Duke
of York^s Army, and Another Officer who was Aid de Camp to the
Prince of Cobourg, And Colonel Woodford,[3] and a French Family
from St Domingo[4]

The Wind Continuing Contrary, The motion of the Ship Soon
made me Sick, & I was Obliged to go to my Cabbin, where I
Continued Extremly Ill all Night.

613

Friday Aug^st 22^d
Continued Extremely Ill –

Saturday Aug^st 23
At Four this morning The Capt Sent The mail on Shore, at Sole,[5]
on The Suffolk Coast, And tho' The Wind Blowed Violently, And

1. Colonel Hutchinson – not traced.
2. Presumably Sir Jeremiah (also Jerome) Fitzpatrick (c.1740–1810),physician and prison reformer. Another interest led to him being created inspector of health for land
   forces later that same year.
3. Lieutenant-Colonel John Woodford (d.1800)?
4. These were probably refugees from the Haitian Revolution in Santo Domingo.
5. Sole Bay has largely disappeared, the coastline here having been smoothed out by
   coastal erosion over the intervening two centuries.

it Rained, yet Colonel Hutchinson, Coll Woodford, and The Officer belonging to The Prince of Cobourg, and a King^s messenger, went with The mail on Shore

In the middle of the Day Some more of the Passengers went on Shore, near Dunwich on the Suffolk Coast,[1] and I went upon Deck & Staid there til Night – where we were within Sight of the Two Light Houses at Orford Ness;[2] but found it impossible to proceed, And as The weather grew very Tempestuous, The Anchor was dropt

614

And when the Rain Increased There appeared Sparks of Fire in The Sea, and we were Called from Our Cabbins to See So Wonderful a Sight – and The Captain Striking The Sea with a Stick, The Ocean looked like Vivid Fire –[3]

Tho' The Ship was at Anchor, yet it Rolled So much that I found my bed very Uncomfortable, but I heard Sir Jerome tell many Droll Storys to keep up the Spirits of Our Company, and after Midnight I got Some Sleep –

Sunday August 24th
This Morning, at Four o Clock, My Dear Son Came to my Cabbin, with the glad Tidings that The Ship would Soon be in Harwich Harbour, and I hastened upon Deck, where I had the Happiness to See Harwich,

615

And we got on Shore at Eight o Clock, and went directly to the White Hart Inn, kept by Mr. White;[4] I desired Sir Jerome to Breakfast with us, And to Prescribe for My Dear Son, whose Health appeared to be in a very precarious State –

1. Dunwich – town on the Suffolk coast. It was once a port but the sea has much eroded the shoreline in the past three centuries,
2. Orford Ness – a shingle spit 10 miles in length. The lighthouse remaining was erected by William Wilkins in 1792.
3. Possibly an occurrence of St Elmo's Fire.
4. The White Hart Inn was kept by George White at this time. It is now demolished.

After Breakfast, I went into a warm Bath, and Rejoiced that I could Change Diet for Cleanliness, and my Dear Son did the Same –

In the Afternoon went to Church,[1] where I thought I could not be Sufficiently Thankful to The Supreme Being for permitting me to be Once more in England –

In the Evening walked with my Dear Son to The adjoining Camp, where the North Lincoln, and Bedford Militia, were under Roll Call,[2] and we Retired afterw^ds to Comfortable & Clean Beds

616

Monday.. Aug^st.. 25th
The Coach having been Damaged by bringing it on Shore, we were Obliged to Continue at Harwich till Noon to have it Repaired –. But afterw^ds we took Post Horses & went Twelve Miles to Ipswich,[3] where we Dined and Staid the Night at The White Horse a Clean and Comfortable Inn –[4]

Tuesday Aug^st 26
Went this morning Twelve miles to Stow market,[5] and Fourteen more to Bury,[6] where we Breakfasted at The Angel Inn[7] – afterw^ds we went Fourteen Miles to New market,[8] & Changed Horses at The Ram Inn,[9] which appeared to be One of the Best Inns upon the Road – we Amused Ourselves by Seeing The Subscription Rooms[10] which are Elegantly fitted

---

1. Presumably St Nicholas but the church was rebuilt three decades later.
2. The two militias were probably raised under the Militia Act of 1759 and presumably were on duty due to the state of relations at this time with Revolutionary France.
3. Ipswich – town on the Suffolk coast at the estuary of the river Orwell.
4. The Great White Horse Hotel in Tavern Street. The building still exists though much altered.
5. Stowmarket – market town between Ipswich and Bury St Edmunds.
6. Bury St Edmunds – town between Stowmarket and Newmarket. It still preserves much of its old character.
7. The Angel Hotel. It was rebuilt 1774–6 and still exists. The building has a thirteenth-century undercroft however.
8. Newmarket – town in west Suffolk. It developed as a coaching town but later, of course, became synonymous with horse-racing.
9. The Ram Inn – it later changed its name to the Rutland Hotel and still exists.
10. It was rebuilt in 1844.

617

fitted up, and consisted of a Billiard Room, a card Room, & another for The Game of Hazard,[1] besides which, there was a large Dining Room And Coffee Room for breakfasting, fitted up in different Recesses for the Transaction of Business of the Turf – In a Front Court adjoining is a Colonade, where The Betts are made by those who cannot Enter the Subscription Room –

The Kings Palace is a very Old House Situated in the middle of the Street, It was Originallly an Inn, but Improved And Additions made to it, by King Charles[2] – The Duke of York Soon after his Marriage brought The Dutchess Here, upon which there was a new bed, but The Front of the House was not Even white washed, And Remained Dirty –. From Hence

618

We went Fourteen Miles to Cambridge and Staid the Night at the Rose Inn,[3] which has been lately New Furnished, but what made us more Happy than we had long Since been, was The Arrival of my Dear Charles to join his Brother, for which he Came from London –

Wed^y Augst 27
We went this morning to See Kings College Chapel,[4] Trinity College Library,[5] and the walks behind Clare Hall –[6] At Noon Mr Dancer who had Come with my Son from London, Returned with Our Travelling Coach; and we pursued Our Journey in my Son^s Chariot, and a Hired Chaise to Huntingdon[7] 16 Miles, & from

---

1. Hazard – a dice game.
2. Charles II rebuilt the palace but this building was mostly demolished in 1819.
3. The row of buildings known as the Little Rose Inn close to Peterhouse in Cambridge still exists.
4. The famous late Gothic chapel of the College begun in 1446.
5. The library of the College designed by Sir Christopher Wren and completed in 1695.
6. Presumably the famous "Backs" behind Clare College, formerly Clare Hall.
7. Huntingdon – market town now in Cambridgeshire important in former times as a crossing point of the river Ouse.

thence we went to Stamford,[1] And Staid the Night at the George Inn a very comfortable House[2]

619

Thursday Aug[st]. 28
Left Stamford this morning at Six, and went to Ferry Bridge[3] And Staid the Night at The Swan, a good Inn,[4] and the Situation Very Pleasant; here we found Two men servants belonging to my Sons waiting Our Arrival. They having Come from London hither in the Mail Coach

Friday Aug[st.] 29th
Left Ferry bridge after Breakfast, And went to Wetherby,[5] where we Stopt to See M[r] Beilby Thompson[s] House and park, Called The Grange[6] And from thence, went 8 Miles to Harrowgate,[7] where we found the Granby[8] So full of Company, that we were Obliged to have Private Lodgings, for which we were to Pay Three Guineas per week, till we could be accomodated at The Granby –

620

Saturday Aug[st] 30th.
Violent Rain Obliged us to Stay in Our Lodgings till the Hour of Dinner, when I went with my Eldest Son to The Granby, and My

---

1. Stamford in Lincolnshire. It was an important town on the Great North Road before the advent of the motorway.
2. The George Hotel on the corner of the High Street with what is now Station Street – it still exists.
3. Ferrybridge – village in West Yorkshire on the river Aire.
4. The White Swan at Ferrybridge, Yorkshire.
5. Wetherby – market town in West Yorkshire on the river Wharfe. It was a traditional stopping place on the Great North Road.
6. Beilby Thompson (1742–99), landowner and MP. Beilby or Micklethwaite Grange was built in the seventeenth century and expanded later, but demolished in 1962.
7. Harrogate – spa town in the West Riding.
8. The Granby Hotel, Harrogate. It still exists, though much altered, and is now a retirement home.

Youngest Son Dined by Invitation of M^{rs}. Biscoe[1] at the Dragon,[2] but we all were together In the Evening at The Granby

Sunday Augst 31st

We went in the morning to the Chapel upon the Common, made a Visit to M^{rs}. Biscoe at The Dragon, Dined at The Granby, & became Acquainted with M^{r}. & M^{rs}. Sales of Gower Street Bedford Square

Monday Sep^{br}. 1st.

Rode to The Well before Breakfast And drank Three Glasses of the Harrowgate water,[3] and at Noon Removed Our Apparel &c to the Granby, and took Possession of a Very Comfortable Apartment –

621

Tuesday Sep^{br}. 2^{d}

My Dear Son Bathed this Eveng in The Warm Bath,[4] And never was well after; On the 17th. we Removed to York,[5] & took Private Lodgings to be near D^{r}. Hunter,[6] but He gave us no Hope of Recovery, And We Lost Him for Ever on Monday the 22^{d}– And ^{He} was Buried in The Cathedral at York on Friday The 27th. of September 1794 Where a Marble Monument is Enacted to The Memory of John Farr Abbot –[7]

1. Mrs Biscoe – not traced.
2. The Dragon, a notable inn in Harrogate, dates from the seventeenth century but was demolished in 1901.
3. There was more than one well supplying the sulphurous water at Harrogate. Mrs Bentham is possibly referring to the Old sulphur well which is now covered by the Royal Pump Room but which was at the time in the open air.
4. Bathing in the hot spring water was considered beneficial to health though the facilities for doing so at Harrogate were not properly organized until the early decades of the nineteenth century. It appears that Mr Farr went to a facility to do so but the water was also brought to clients' hotels at this time.
5. The historic county town of Yorkshire.
6. Presumably Alexander Hunter (1729?–1809), physician. He practised in York from 1763 and was involved with the treatment of the mentally ill as well as having an interest in the practice of taking the local waters.
7. He is commemorated by a modest wall plaque.

The following three pages are not numbered – ed.

Observations[1]
At Naples, and in many Parts of Italy, we Observed Single Men Travelling in Carriages of a Shape resembling a Large Shell fixed upon a Pedestal, The Carriage had Two Wheels, and was Drawn with One Horse –

At Berlin, and throughout The King of Prussia[s] Dominions, The Roads are very Bad, The Soil being Either Deep Sand, or Deep Mud – No Vineyards, No Variety of Fruit, and what they have is Bad, and The Vegetables are very Indifferent – The Beer is Bad, and The Fuel very Dear, being Cheifly of wood; for which, a great Duty is Paid.

Yet Foreigners who Visit Berlin may be Amused during The Winter, As The Queen Gives Cards & Supper during the winter Every Sunday, And The Princess Royal Every Monday,[2] The Princess Henry on Tuesdays,[3] Prince Ferdinand[4] On Wednesdays, And the Foreign Minister Receives Company at their Houses on the Other Evening of the week –

At Brunswick, is a Pavement of Flag Stones on Each Side the different Streets for Foot Passengers, & The Town is Lighted – and The Parqué Floors for Common use, are made of Deal, formed into Squares by Bands of Oak –

In many Houses upon The Continent, we observed The window Curtains were drawn upon a Circular Rod, instead of a Straight One, across the window –

Ladies Dress
At Verona in Italy, The Ladies generally wear a Black Silk Petticoat Over their Dress when They walk, and a Black Silk Cloak, & both together Look well.

1. NB – these final three pages are not numbered and are followed by four blank leaves.
2. Not traced.
3. Princess Wilhelmina of Hesse-Kassel married Prince Henry in 1752.
4. Previously noted.

In Germany, They wear Long Black Silk Aprons, or Very Long Cloaks trimmed with the Same, & Plaited round the Bottom.

The Lower Rank of Females in Germany wear Coloured Callicoe Cloaks, made very Long, and Caps that Shine like Gold, with Broad Borders of Lawn, falling Back from the Face –

In Switzerland The Daughters of The Inn Keepers frequently Speak many Languages, At the Foot of Mont St Gothard, The Girl Spoke French, Italian, and German, very well –

INDEX of persons and places